Jacques E. Levy

CESAR CHAVEZ
Autobiography of La Causa

W · W · NORTON & COMPANY · INC ·

NEW YORK

Front endpapers: A picket line at Schenley's vineyards, January 1966. © PHOTO BY JON LEWIS.
Back endpapers: Members of La Causa on the long march to Sacramento, April 1966. © PHOTO BY JON LEWIS.
Title page: Nearing Sacramento, marchers are outlined against the sky, April 1966. © PHOTO BY JON LEWIS.

Published simultaneously in Canada
by George J. McLeod Limited, Toronto

Library of Congress Cataloging in Publication Data

Levy, Jacques E
    Cesar Chavez: autobiography of La Causa.

    1. Chavez, Cesar Estrada. 2. United Farm
Workers. 3. Migrant agricultural laborers—United
States. I. Chavez, Cesar Estrada.
HD6509.C48L48   1975   331.88′13′0924 [B]   75-15747
ISBN 0-393-07494-3
PRINTED IN THE UNITED STATES OF AMERICA

1 2 3 4 5 6 7 8 9

To the members of La Causa whose suffering, endurance, and courage are an inspiration.
And to Judy, Brian, and Jacqueline for their
patience and understanding.

Contents

Book VII TARGET FOR DESTRUCTION
1971–May 1975

List of Illustrations

Preface

When I first met Cesar Chavez, the farm labor leader, in February of 1969, he was flat on his back, disabled by a congenital back problem. Unknown to me, the union had just learned of a plot on his life.

I had come to Delano with the idea for a book, not knowing that he was adamantly opposed to any biography because he believed such a project immodest and presumptuous. My proposed outline, however, intrigued him, perhaps because so many previous attempts to form an agricultural union had gone unrecorded. If fate stopped him, others could not profit from his experience.

That February night, we met in his bedroom and talked for about an hour. It was a small room, barely large enough for two single beds and a chest of drawers. But then, the whole house was small, just two bedrooms, a living room, and a kitchen—cramped quarters, indeed, for a family with eight children.

I found Chavez unpretentious and candid as he discussed the union and the table-grape strike which had started three and a half years before. His speech was soft, sweetened by a Spanish accent, and his hands, unusually small, moved gracefully to illustrate his points. But his eyes were the focal point, dark brown and expressive, giving a sad countenance to his face until a smile flashed, transforming his features.

My first impressions were of his warmth and sincerity, and a gentleness which was disarming. I wondered how such gentleness could succeed in the brutal world of labor organizing. We hardly mentioned the book, whose outline he had read earlier in the day, but when I got up to leave, he asked in the plaintive schoolboy voice he sometimes uses, "Do I have to give you an answer tonight?"

"Of course not," I answered, fearing he would refuse. "Think it over."

Two weeks later I returned to Delano with another outline—this one omitting any mention of a biography. This would be a book about the union and its leadership, I wrote. The rest of the outline, however, remained the same, for in my mind the leadership was Cesar Chavez.

Jim Drake, who was Chavez's administrative assistant, smiled when he read it and asked me to attend the executive board meeting that afternoon. There, again in that tiny bedroom, I read the outline.

When I was done, Chavez asked everyone's opinion. He himself voiced none. When no objections were raised, I was told I could have access to information. No strings were attached.

And so the book was born. But instead of completing it in one year, as I had planned, nearly six years slipped by before the work was finished.

I quickly found Chavez's attitude reflected by others in the union. The atmosphere was informal, candid, open, and people were unusually frank in our interviews. Everyone, of course, was on a first-name basis, an atmosphere I have tried to recreate in the book.

At first, my interviews with Cesar came once or twice a week. Often union business would force a postponement or cancellation. As we discussed his parents and childhood experiences, Cesar became more expansive. Diana Lyons, who took over his scheduling and other chores, noticed that he seemed more relaxed and rested after our interviews. They became more frequent.

Then, as his back improved and he resumed his highly mobile activities, our interviews continued while I drove him from one rural area to another. It was our only opportunity for uninterrupted talks.

Once he suggested that I could get more accurate information about his early years if we could meet some weekend with his brothers and sisters, but he doubted he could spare the time.

When the weekend was finally arranged, it was a typical Chavez operation. We gathered on a Friday night at St. Anthony's Seminary in Santa Barbara—his parents, four brothers and sisters, and most of their children.

Although this was their first family reunion in years, Cesar insisted on taking advantage of the precious time to recall as much as possible.

The next morning, while he lay on a cot in one of the large dormitories, the children went out to play, and the family sat around his bed while I asked questions. There was a break for lunch and one for dinner, but otherwise the time was spent recalling the past. After dinner, the session continued until the early hours of the morning. The entire conversation, of course, was tape-recorded.

It was that weekend that Cesar Chavez told me he would like the book to be a biography.

As time went on, I was able to attend critical negotiations with the growers and to sit in on union planning sessions and discussions during the heat of battle. During the summer of 1970, I followed developments in Delano and Salinas on the spot, trying to be where the actions were planned and the decisions made. I repeated the same course during the bloody summer of 1973.

In exchange for this accessibility, I helped keep the press informed, since the union had no one to spare to handle the many calls that came in. I felt this was one task I could do that would not compromise my objectivity as a reporter. And it squared with my philosophy of the public's right to know.

Watching Cesar Chavez and his officers in action when the very existence of the union was at stake proved invaluable. Acting under extreme pressure, all their virtues and weaknesses were exposed. I have tried to faithfully record their words and deeds.

But the bulk of this book is written in the first person, by those directly involved in the action. That, too, is part of the story. For, while I taped every interview, Cesar adamantly opposed any autobiography. Several times, he said, he had turned down such requests.

This, then, is not Cesar Chavez's autobiography. It is the story of his life in his own words, but it lacks the key ingredient of an autobiography—the decision of what to include and what to emphasize.

Those decisions are mine, and mine alone. I remain responsible for what is left out as well as what is included. In some cases the narrative is as he told it to me. At other times, the narrative is recorded from his speeches or his reports or lectures to workers or members of the boycott.

Sometimes I blend his remarks from several sources to bring out his views. The technique has its drawbacks, for the style is bound to vary. But it is the only method possible to provide a well-rounded and accurate portrait of a man and a movement engaged in a struggle for social change.

Obviously, in such a broad-based movement, many have played key roles. Since it is not possible to include all that has happened, I have tried to select major events and typical actions that help paint an accurate picture of Cesar Chavez, La Causa, and their methods. For those who are left out—and they are legion—I apologize.

Also legion are those who helped me gather the information, submitted to interviews, or shared their homes and food during our travels. It would be impossible to list them all, but they share the spirit with which this book was written, a spirit best expressed by Cesar Chavez himself in two separate interviews.

After the executive board had given the book the green light, I had my first lengthy interview with Cesar. He told me how many thought of him as a devil with horns and a tail, while others embarrassed him by describing him as a saint.

He hoped, he said, that I would write a book that would picture him as he was—without distortion or embellishment.

Six years later, as I was pondering how to write this Preface, I thought of the unprecedented access given me to the innermost workings of the union. How could I explain it?

By this time, I felt I knew the answer, but I wanted to hear it from Cesar. "In effect, truth is your most powerful weapon," I summarized, after we discussed it.

"Yes," he answered. "And truth is nonviolence. So everything really comes from truth. Truth is the ultimate. Truth is God."

That was all I needed, but he had more to say.

"Truth is on our side, even more than justice, because truth can't be changed. It has a way of manifesting itself. It has to come out, so sooner or later we'll win."

And as he reflected on what he said, he concluded, "The amazing thing in the Movement is that we don't speak of these things. We don't sit down and analyze them and write about them. We don't have a little Red Book, but it's there, like English Common Law. Just experience. It's part of our tradition."

"And yet I can't conceive of any other leader letting a reporter attend meetings while a fight is going on," I said.

"That's the big argument we had in the beginning," he answered. "People were concerned that spies would come in, but I said, 'If there's nothing to hide, it's easier to work. It's easier than to spend all of our time trying to keep people from coming in because we're hiding things.'

"Of course, there are times when we try to hide our plans, but they get out. It may hurt us initially because the growers know ahead of time, but if it's a good plan, there's no way that they can guard against it. And openness works so well with workers, because we don't have to hide from them. We'll always fight their fight. If we can keep doing that, I think we'll be in good shape."

This, then, is the true story of Cesar Chavez and La Causa—the truth as perceived by those who lived it and witnessed it.

Acknowledgments

Seldom in nearly two decades as a reporter have I received such wholehearted cooperation in gathering facts as I have in covering La Causa. Time and again over the past six years I have been impressed by those most directly involved because of their candor and willingness to share confidential information.

The first to help was the Reverend James Drake, although he had never met me before. Then there was Lynn Anderson, Andy Asaldua, Susan Drake, Nancy Elliot, Mary Jean Friel, Jose Gomez, Larry Itliong, Diana and Mack Lyons, Marion Moses, Philip Vera Cruz, Richard Ybarra and all his assistants, and so many other members of the staff and volunteers who made the way easier.

For information in depth I am indebted to LeRoy Chatfield, Richard Chavez, Jerry Cohen, Marshall Ganz, Monsignor George Higgins, Dolores Huerta, William Kircher, Rita Chavez Medina, Gilbert Padilla, Fred Ross, and Paul Schrade.

I am thankful for the assistance of Dr. Philip Mason, director of the Labor History Archives at Wayne State University and to Senator Alan Cranston for opening doors in Washington. Of great help, too, was the editorial advice given by George Brockway, president of W. W. Norton & Company; Carolyn Lund, a gifted editor at the Press Democrat; Don Emblen at Santa Rosa Junior College; and Mrs. Dorothy Hansen, a good friend who also typed the final manuscript. Thanks, too, to Diane DiStefano who labored hard transcribing several hundred hours of taped interviews.

It goes without saying that without the enthusiastic cooperation of Cesar Chavez, this book could not have been written. I am deeply grateful for his help and his refusal to censor or influence the final contents of this manuscript.

Prologue

One hot summer night in 1962, Cesar Chavez pulled up in front of his house in Delano, checked the mileage, and brought to an end the first leg of the long organizing journey that was to be called La Causa. In 86 days he had covered 14,867 miles, picked peas, staked grapes, suckered vines, and carried the message to more than 2,000 farm workers in the fields, the dirt roads, and the family rooms of hundreds of tiny barrio houses.

I had been privileged to sit in on one such house meeting a few days before, along with four farm worker couples. Cesar opened with a few introductory remarks, and then, suddenly leaning forward as though about to confide some marvelous secret, asked softly if they had heard of the new organization he was building in the valley—the Farm Workers Association. None of them had, of course, nor was he all that familiar with it himself, having just that day decided on the name. But the words held magic, because heads came straining forward.

He sat in silence, letting the suspense mount before he went on. It was a movement, he said, in which farm workers could struggle to free themselves from the injustices of the job, the government, and life in general. There was no ready-made plan, he assured them. That was one of the reasons he was meeting with them and other workers—to gradually put together ideas based upon what they wanted, along with some of his own, such as the farm workers census. He then passed around some self-addressed three-by-five cards with lines on the back for the name and address of the worker, and for what the worker considered a just hourly wage.

The idea was an instant hit. Always before, one worker said, others had decided what he deserved. Now he, himself, was being consulted. "It's like letting us vote," he said, "on what we think."

When another asked what would be done with the census, Cesar explained that in the future the workers would use it in demanding their rights before appropriate government boards. But of equal importance, he said, the census would start a farm workers' file for future contacts. Many workers had already mailed the cards back, along with short notes urging him on, wishing him good luck. He had immediately rushed out and commissioned these workers to form committees to speed up the census and to spread the word of La Causa through the valley.

Cesar called for more questions, and other issues were raised— the use of Mexican braceros who took the jobs away from local people, the many times they had been cheated by labor contractors, the lack of toilets and clean, cold water in the fields.

They could have gone on all night, but Cesar cut in, explaining that when the workers had their own Association, many of these things would be changed. They would be able to stand up to the growers, he told them, and demand an end to the injustices they had been suffering for so many years.

"But all that," he said, "will only come after a long time, and all the hard work and suffering that goes into organizing and struggling with the growers for our contracts." He explained what that meant and again asked for questions. They all sat watching him in rapt attention until a soft-voiced woman near the wall spoke.

"When you're sick or there's no work, as in winter, we run up such big bills we have to spend the rest of the year paying them off. But I guess," she lowered her eyes, "there's no way the Association could . . ."

"Oh, yes," Cesar came in, "we could have what they call a credit union. It's like a workers' bank. During the season, each worker loans a little to the bank and learns to save that way, even if it's only a tiny amount. Then in winter, the bank makes loans to the worker at very low interest."

"Or when there's a death," another woman half-whispered, "and you have to go begging door to door for money to bury . . ."

"For that," Cesar cut in, "there could be group burial insurance. There is a law now where a lot of people all doing the same kind of work can all join a burial plan together through their own organization and pay a little each month to cover all the members of the family." At this the women exchanged quick looks. So many men who work in the fields die young.

"Or how about when you have to go to the welfare or the county hospital," asked the third woman, "and they turn you down? Or you get hurt on the job and the grower won't help you get your compensation? Would such things be the business of the Association, too?"

Cesar nodded. "The Association could set up service programs in different parts of the valley to give the workers the backing they need to fight the agencies. It wouldn't take long to set up such a program."

"How long?" asked one of the women.

Cesar spread his hands, palms up. "As long as it takes to find the people who are really interested. The best way to do this is in the homes, like here tonight." He paused, glancing at each of them. "Who would be willing to call a few people to your house, so I could come and talk to them?"

After a moment's silence, one man spoke. "It's a great idea, Mr. Chavez. The only trouble, it just won't work. The growers are too powerful." Most of the others began to nod solemnly, but over by the wall the soft-voiced woman and her husband had their heads together, whispering. Now and for the rest of the meeting, Cesar seemed to be speaking mainly to them.

"I think that's where we make our mistake," he began gently, "making ourselves believe the growers are more powerful than they really are. It's true, they're powerful all right, but if the Movement fails, it won't be because the growers are powerful enough to stop it, but because the workers refuse to use their power to make it go.

"Probably there is no one in this room who is willing to help." Cesar's eyes traveled from one of them to another. "Probably not even in this barrio," he went on. "But I know that somewhere in Tulare County I will find one who is willing. That's all I need— just one. Because that one will take me to others who feel the same, and they will make a Workers Committee for this county. When we have such committees in each important county in the state, we will call them all together in Fresno and map the future course of La Causa."

He rose now, putting his materials in order. The workers came up to shake his hand, some of them reaching for a few of the census cards as they filed out, until only the soft-voiced woman and her husband remained.

"I am one of few words," the man began, eyes shining, "but I like what you said tonight, Mr. Chavez. And there are some on my crew I think would like it, too. If I got them together over at my house one night soon, do you think you could take the time to come and tell them about it?"

"Hay más tiempo que vida," Cesar smiled, gripping the man's shoulder. It was an ancient Mexican dicho meaning there is more time than life.

That fall, about 150 workers meeting in Fresno approved a program of service based on the needs brought out at the house meetings, and that program was used in the next three years to draw more workers deeply into La Causa. When a worker received some desperately needed help, he could be expected to feel a certain amount of loyalty toward the group from which it came. And let that worker give a small amount each month to keep La Causa going and, on top of that, bring the organizers food from the field and have them over to dinner frequently—then that worker would move from mere routine loyalty to a sense of fierce possessiveness that only comes when one gives to another of that which he has so pitifully little himself.

In the mid-sixties, caught up in the longest continuous strike in farm labor history, La Causa partisans moved into levels of organization far deeper than most of them had ever known. They were "organized" in the agony of rolling out at 3:00 A.M. with only three hours sleep to go to a 4:00 A.M. meeting, to be dispatched to a dark picket line at 5:00 A.M., to see the sun sheer off the tip of Bear Mountain as a scab-crammed truck roared through the gate where the tractor dust rose up to meet the spray of pesticide, and to stand there all day long at the edge of the field calling unceasingly to the scabs to join them.

Then there was the dark, bitter organizing help that the weak can get from the strong. They got it when growers, cops, and Teamster goons beat and clubbed them and kicked them into La Causa; when grower-corrupted courts enjoined and jailed them into it; and when they were blasted into it by "unknown" gunmen hidden among the vines.

Finally, they got it when they were forced to create the most effective organizing tool in the history of La Causa—the boycott. They pulled the picket lines from the dusty valley roads and threw them around the big chain stores a thousand miles or more from the strike zone. People from labor, the churches, and the universities, often joining the lines merely to ease their consciences, were so well "organized" by abusive cops and store officials that they remained to convince a substantial segment of the American people first to boycott grapes, then head lettuce and Gallo wine. In giving these up, the people gave up some of themselves to the farm workers, and eventually increased ten-thousand-fold the field of organization of La Causa.

La Causa is a unique development, not only in the history of labor, but in the entire field of social action in this country. Conceived and launched by an organizational genius, powered by people who, day after day, for thirteen years have been pulled and torn by innumerable crises demanding instant attention, the Movement is now firing up a second generation of adherents. Its course is set, its foundations powerful and deep.

As La Causa expands, the tides of conflict ebb and flow; today a loss, tomorrow a gain, a bridge down today reappearing tomorrow in a pattern highly reminiscent of the inexhaustible vitality displayed by other freedom movements of our time. For, make no mistake, La Causa is a force for freedom; and, like all basic struggles of the poor and weak against the rich and powerful, it is geared for a long, long fight.

That large, initial corps—the raw recruits of the service program who became the veterans of one hundred strikes and boycott operations—will never again be slammed down into the dirt by the growers. Thousands more, under the contracts of the United Farm Workers, have had a taste of the way democracy can work for them in the fields. Out of such experience—out of the sacrifice and suffering that go into the never-ending organizing drive—flows their unconquerable will to hold together and fight for as long as it takes to win.

Book I

SEEDS IN
THE DESERT

Many had tried, but all had failed. This Cesar Chavez knew only too well when he took that fateful step to form a farm workers' union in 1962.

Few thought he could succeed. He was just a farm worker, one of thousands, easily lost in a crowd, small of stature, quiet, self-effacing, soft-spoken, poorly educated.

Some around him were moved by his sincerity and his vision, but they also were keenly aware of his handicaps—his poverty, his large family, his dark Chicano skin. Without help, how could he take on agribusiness, the most powerful industry in California?

And how could a man totally committed to nonviolence hope to battle an industry that had traditionally used all manner of violence to smash previous attempts to organize its workers?

The first clues to his success in building a union and becoming the leader of La Causa lie deep within the movement and the man himself. For the seeds of a movement take generations to mature, and its leaders have deep roots.

CHAPTER 1

A Step to Freedom

CESAR CHAVEZ RECALLS

It took me four years to think it through. I studied the problem, talked to many people, and thought about it constantly. And every time I analyzed it, I came right back to one basic thing. One set of strings had me so wrapped up I couldn't move. That was my financial security.

I realized that I couldn't do what I felt must be done without first giving up one of the best jobs I'd ever had.

As national director of CSO, the Community Service Organization, I lived in East Los Angeles and helped organize people in the barrios, our Mexican ghettos, all over California. The paycheck came regularly, about $150 a week that my family could count on week after week.

Yet security doesn't really come with a paycheck. You think you have security, but it's just momentary when you cash the check, I guess, or when you think of it. Actually it doesn't bring either security or peace of mind.

More than anything else, I wanted to help farm workers. I was a farm worker when I had joined CSO ten years before, and I thought the organization could help us. That's why I soon became a paid organizer on the staff. While CSO was doing some good for the poor in the communities, after a few years I began to realize that a farm workers' union was needed to end the exploitation of the workers in the fields, if we were to strike at the roots of their suffering and poverty.

I had done a lot of reading about farm labor unions, thought

3

about them, and questioned every farm worker I could find who had been involved in a strike. It was a sad history of defeat after defeat, strikes smashed with violence, the government in league with the growers, police helping to bring in scabs.

But the more I studied the mistakes that were made in the past, the more I believed growers were not invincible. If we fought them right, we could beat them. I had learned a lot in the CSO about organizing the barrios and the poor. I had learned about taking on the authorities to get help for the community, and I had learned tactics to curb injustice. I felt a union could succeed.

When I talked about starting a union, however, all I heard was that it had been tried many times before—never successfully—and it couldn't be done. One of my friends remarked, "Man, this Chavez is really nuts!" I couldn't convince the CSO directors to try it. I was tempted to strike out alone.

Only my financial security had me tied up and kept me from moving. There was my wife, Helen, and I knew it would be asking a lot of her to give up what we had. Here I was already thirty-five, with my first steady job in one location, after years of constantly drifting from one place to another, first as a migrant hunting for work and then as a CSO organizer. We had about twelve hundred dollars in the bank that wouldn't last six months if I left my job. And, more importantly, there were our eight children, the oldest thirteen and the two youngest only four and two and a half.

Helen and I had discussed the problem from many angles. There were the risks, the odds against success, and the desperate needs we saw daily all around us. Helen, naturally, was very worried about our children. If I quit, who knows what would happen? Where would the money come from for food and clothes and housing? I could only point to my own childhood where, despite our struggles and bitter experiences, ours was a very close and happy family. I was sure our own children could endure.

The more we talked about it, the more I organized her. I saw the trap most people get themselves into—tying themselves to a job for security. It was easier for us and our family to try to escape poverty than to change the conditions that keep so many workers poor. But we inherited the poverty from our fathers and our fathers from our grandfathers and our grandfathers from their fathers. We had to stop someplace!

Finally one day I said, "We can't organize farm workers like this. I could talk about how bad conditions are for them, how much I've done for them, and how much I'd like to do, and I can stay here and keep my job. Or we give up the paycheck, nobody tells us what to do, and we organize the way we want to do it."

"If we're afraid of that, then we might as well just forget it," I said. "You and I have got to liberate ourselves."

The ground already had been tilled, the seed planted. It wasn't hard to convince her.

"I'm willing to stick it out for ten years and really give it a trial," she said. "If it doesn't work, we can figure out something else."

So I resigned my job and set out to found a union. At first I was frightened, very frightened. But by the time I had missed the fourth paycheck and found things were still going, that the moon was still there and the sky and the flowers, I began to laugh. I really began to feel free. It was one of my biggest triumphs in terms of finding myself and of being able to discipline myself.

After all, if you're outraged at conditions, then you can't possibly be free or happy until you devote all your time to changing them and do nothing but that. The affluence in this country is our biggest trap, because we can't change anything if we want to hold on to a good job, a good way of life, and avoid sacrifice.

We began to do away with a lot of little things we thought we just had to have, things we really did not need. We began to get that commitment, that gut commitment—"all right, then, this sacrifice won't be for nothing. I made it for six months, nothing will stop me now." Then we began to build a community, we began to build what would become the Union.

Today I don't think our members are going to stop just at building a farm workers' union. In the course of that accomplishment other things are going to be revealed to them, not through me, but through the experience of living. I've heard them say, "We're not going to get paychecks. We're willing to put ourselves with our families on the line! Let's go!" You can't stop people like that. They can change the world.

The need for radical change is great and urgent, in the cities as well as in the fields, and if we don't succeed, violence will spread. Other movements will try to do it with violence.

But in seeking social change, I am positive nonviolence is the way, morally and tactically, especially in our society where those in power resort to clubs, tear gas, and guns. I have seen nonviolence work many times in many ways. When we organized California's vineyards, for example, it was the growers' violence, their manipulation of the police and the courts, that helped win support for our cause.

We can remain nonviolent because people outside the Movement by and large don't want violence. By remaining nonviolent in the face of violence, we win them to our side, and that's what makes the strength. And we organize that strength to fight for change.

My experiences in the Union had happened to me ten or fifteen times before in CSO. Every time I organized a little group on a smaller scale, the same thing happened. I organized from the ground up, helped people, got them together, and started fighting for what was needed. Pretty soon they were using their power effectively and trying to get things changed.

The Union is the same thing, just on a much bigger scale. What happens next may be even bigger. Out of each experience enough light is generated to illuminate another little stretch. Who knows where it will lead? And who can tell where it started?

CHAPTER 2

Carving a Homestead

CESAR CHAVEZ RECALLS

My grandfather escaped from the Hacienda del Carmen, one of the biggest haciendas in Chihuahua, Mexico, in the 1880s. His name was Cesario, but he was known as Papa Chayo, and he was just trying to flee injustice.

On the hacienda, they were slaves. The moment a baby was born, they would give him a tag and start keeping a book on him of all his expenses. By the time the child grew old enough to start working, he already was sold, he already owed a lot of money.

The Terrazes, the hacienda owners, had an arrangement with President Porfirio Diaz that the moment they saw a worker was a little rebellious, they could put him in the army. I guess the grower mentality is similar everywhere, and it hasn't changed. Here in the U.S., they just fire you for trying to organize and try to prevent you from getting another job.

When Papa Chayo took issue with one of the growers' sons on something that was clearly an injustice, they decided to draft him. Luckily the word got out right away, and he escaped alone in the middle of the night, crossing the border into El Paso, Texas. After he made enough money working on the railroad and in the fields, he sent for my grandmother and their fourteen children. My dad, Librado, was two when they crossed the border in about 1888.

My grandfather developed a hauling business around Yuma, Gila Bend, and the mining towns. As my dad got older, they worked together as long-line skinners, driving as many as twenty-two horses or mules hitched to one cart to haul their loads. Now

7

it's a lost art, but that's how my dad developed his skill with and knowledge of horses.

Eventually Papa Chayo and his family decided to settle down and chose the North Gila Valley along the Colorado River in the Arizona desert. I know that valley well, small and hot with very dry and rocky hills fencing it off to the east. In those days, without irrigation, that desert valley was forbidding.

Construction of a federal dam drew my grandfather and father there. They won a contract cutting firewood and hauling it to the site. Then five years later, when Laguna Dam was completed, they built a sturdy adobe house at the foot of the hills, dug some irrigation ditches, and homesteaded more than one hundred acres at the foot of those dry hills and along the valley floor. Our family farm was started three years before Arizona became a state. Yet, sometimes I get crank letters these days telling me to "go back" to Mexico!

My grandfather had fifteen children by the time he built his home, and most were living with him. One by one they married, built homes of their own, and settled in the valley or in Yuma, some twenty miles away. Only my father remained to work on the farm, staying there fifteen years until he, too, married on June 15, 1924.

My dad and mother married at a very mature age; he was thirty-eight and she was thirty-two. Her name was Juana Estrada, and she came from a different part of Chihuahua than my dad's family.

My mother was then a very tiny woman, little more than five feet tall, with a slender waist and delicate features framed by long black hair that fell over her shoulders. Her hands were small, and her fingers long and thin and agile. She talked a lot, her tongue skipping as fast as her mind from one thing to another, while my father was very quiet and never talked much. When he was younger, he was a large, powerful man nearly six feet tall and weighing more than two hundred pounds, with huge hands that were strong and clumsy. He was never afraid of work and often did too much.

One day, soon after their marriage, he was putting a tire on a truck when he collapsed. My mother had to get help to carry him into the shade. They got a doctor who warned him that unless he stopped working in the hot desert sun, he would get another sunstroke. The doctor even urged him to leave Arizona, but it was advice my father ignored. He felt responsible for his parents' ranch and, besides, his mother was ill at the time.

Shortly after my oldest sister Rita was born in 1925, Dad bought a business on the valley floor about a mile below his parents' ranch and just added that work to his field chores. There were three buildings, the grocery store where they lived, a garage, and a pool hall that had a little counter where sodas, cigarettes, and candy were sold.

The grocery store was small, but it had all the major items people needed, and my dad had a ready-made list of customers. Our family isn't tiny. My aunts and uncles each had a dozen or more children; there were at least 180 nieces and nephews then, many of those already married and with families of their own. So my dad did very well at first. Because people got their mail at the store, he was even made postmaster.

It was at our home in the store that I was born on March 31, 1927, and where Richard was born two years later. I was named Cesario after my grandfather, and Richard was named Ricardo. We have been nearly inseparable ever since.

Perhaps it was because business was so good and because of the growing family, that Dad decided to expand, to buy the rest of the forty-acre parcel around the store. How could he foresee what would happen? My dad often blindly trusted people, a trait that would get him and us into trouble many times later on. Since he had already bought the store from a man in the valley, he saw nothing wrong in making another deal with this neighbor. As Dad did not have money, he agreed to clear about eighty acres and stump it out. In exchange for that rough, strenuous work they agreed he would be able to keep about forty acres.

Because of the heat and his other responsibilities, progress was slow. Uprooting stumps was a strain on his horses, and the desert sun prevented work except in the early morning or late afternoon. Finally, though, the ground was cleared, and Dad requested his deed. The neighbor delayed him as long as he could. Then Dad learned of the double cross—the property already had been sold to a man named Justus Jackson.

My dad was never afraid to stand up for his rights. He was not cowed because the neighbor was an Anglo, a white man. He went straight to a lawyer, ready for a court battle. But the lawyer, who was also an Anglo, advised him to borrow money and just buy the land from Jackson. Later on, when my dad couldn't pay the interest on the loan, the lawyer bought the land from him and sold it back to the original owner. It was a rotten deal all around.

By this time, the country was in the depression, a word that meant nothing to me then, but a condition that would deeply scar our lives, despite my father's hard work. It wasn't until much later that I learned how others suffered, that I learned of the starvation, the deaths, and the terrible uprooting of families.

In the valley, when my relatives lost their jobs, my dad just took on more responsibilities and gave them credit. After all, they had to eat. But his generosity could only be stretched so far. There were too many relatives, too many mouths to feed, and what had once been an advantage now proved his undoing. It wasn't long before he had given all his store out in credit. Then the inevitable occurred. Two weeks before Franklin Roosevelt was elected president, Dad was forced to sell out.

The $2,750 he received barely paid off his creditors and nothing was left to pay the taxes that were owed and accumulating on his parents' ranch. Even then, however, we were luckier than most. We could still move in with my grandmother. I remember the ride over from the store in a horse-drawn wagon. It was about a year after Helena was born.

When I was small, that old adobe house which Papa Chayo had built seemed huge, but sizes are much smaller now than they seemed when we were children. The house had two wings divided by a covered breezeway about nine feet wide. It looked like it had been there forever; a long, low, solid structure that seemed to curve with the soil and be a part of it. There was an endless droning of flies around it, a sound that seemed to always be there and to have been there always. The house seemed indestructible, with walls eighteen inches thick supporting a foot-thick flat roof made of dirt piled on top of elm or cottonwood beams.

The roof was one of the big criticisms Dad had of this house. He had wanted to put on a gable roof, and Papa Chayo had said no. Actually it was good because it was so cool in there, but the roof was very, very heavy, and the beams had begun to sag a little. I remember two or three earthquakes while we lived there, and some of the earth dropping down on us.

Today the house in in ruins. The roof is gone, the wooden floor was removed and probably used for firewood. At one time our home was even used for cattle. It makes me shudder to think of it.

In 1932 when we moved into our adobe home, Papa Chayo was already dead and Mama Tella, my grandmother Dorotea, who was in her nineties and almost blind, lived in the south wing with Dad's sister, Josepha. We moved into the north wing, just a bare room used previously to store pumpkin, corn, and other crops. It was about sixteen feet wide and twice that distance from the front to the rear door. Two small rectangular windows on each side wall let in a little light. Inside it was dark and musty, and the wooden floor was well worn.

Of course, with the six of us in there, it was crowded. We had three beds packed in the back, an old battered bureau with a mirror, a chest of drawers, and a rickety table. A small area was screened with a cloth and turned into a closet. At the front of the room were a wood-burning stove and a big icebox which could hold three hundred pounds of ice. That was one of two items from the store that my dad had been unable to sell. The other, which sat in the middle of that room, was a worn pool table. Although we were poor, we had a pool table in the house!

Richard and I didn't want to sleep in our bed, so we just put a thin mattress on top of the pool table and slept there. The walls were covered with plaster which used to chip, and at night we would look at the walls and ceiling and make all kinds of discoveries. "Look, there's a face over there. And there's a dog," I would tell Richard. "And look in the corner, here's a rabbit. And a horse!"

The house, of course, had no electricity and no running water, but the canal was only about five feet from the front door, looking mean and deep to us then, its waters clay red with mud. We would put that water in big tanks, two fifty-gallon drums, and in a week's time, after two or three inches of dirt settled at the bottom, we could use it. Some years later, when we were in school, somebody spoke there from the health department and gave us a lecture about boiling the water. When we told my mother and dad, she wasn't impressed. "Aw, we won't boil the water. We've been drinking the water for years, and we haven't caught anything."

Despite what my mother said, though, it was not long after we moved into the adobe house that little Helena became ill. My mother had a reputation in the valley for her skill in healing, a skill she put to constant use, for she couldn't bear to see anyone in pain, and there were no doctors in the valley. She was especially knowledgeable in the use of herbs, choosing some to cool a fever, others to cure colic, and mixing brews for specific illnesses. Her faith in her skill was as strong as her belief in the saints and the Virgin of Guadalupe. But my sister did not respond. Diarrhea drained her of strength and dehydrated her body. In spite of all the remedies and all the prayers, Helena got worse.

It was a time when everything seemed wrong. The air turned heavy, the usually dry desert heat became muggy, and the clear skies filled with dark clouds. Though a storm is very unusual in

Arizona, there was lightning and thunder that shook the adobe walls. Rain came, big drops splashing on the dry soil and disappearing. As the rain grew more intense, Helena seemed to shrivel and shrink, her little body losing the last of its moisture. She died in my mother's arms.

And still the rain continued. Usually in the desert the storms are violent and brief, but this storm persisted. They couldn't bury her. It was several days before my dad and two or three of his brothers could put Helena in a horse-drawn wagon and drive up the hills to the lonely cemetery. But none of us went. I never knew why.

CHAPTER 3

Either Drought or Flood

CESAR CHAVEZ RECALLS

My father worked very hard, and he worked from sunup to sundown. Because his hands were too clumsy, he was very slow with cotton, but if it was anything that took strength, he was very good. I remember that later when he was sixty-five, he was swamping potatoes with men who were twenty, work I couldn't do. He was also a very good irrigator and knew a lot about both water and horses.

When we worked together as I got older, I would ask questions about all sorts of things. I was always very inquisitive, but he was patient, and he would answer me. I also learned a lot about crops by osmosis, just by watching him and imitating him. When I was very small I learned how to cut watermelons. Even when it was hard to find a ripe one, I would just go in, mostly on a hunch. Sometimes I looked at the leaves, which are supposed to be dry. Usually I just ran and touched one and had a feeling. I was the best watermelon cutter in the family.

As we got older, we helped my dad, first with little things and then bigger ones. We liked to harness the horses that were kept in the corral across the canal from our house. But putting on the collars was difficult. We were very small, and the horses were very tall. We would struggle with the awkward, heavy harness, heaving it up on the pole fence. Then I would balance myself straddling the top bar and fit the collar on the horse while Richard helped from the ground, pushing and tugging. My dad was very strict about putting the right collar on the right horse and making sure the straps wouldn't chafe. If they did, he would apply chewing tobacco to the bruised flesh and would get very upset because there was much work to do.

After a while Richard and I were put in charge of watering the animals and feeding them. Dad knew so much about animals that he could tell right away if the horses had not eaten or drunk.

I was too small to do the plowing, but we did other things that weren't as heavy. My dad needed all the help he could get. We worked around the plants with the hoe, and we'd weed and cultivate to keep the right amount of moisture in the ground. Unless the soil was worked hard, the water would quickly evaporate, and the land would bake and crack.

When my dad planted corn, squash, chili, or watermelon, he would plant enough for all the relatives, but we'd get very angry because we did all the work. "How come we have to do it? How come they don't do it" we would complain. "Never mind, just go ahead and do it," Dad would answer. Sometimes my uncle would come over with his sons and help with the cotton, and we would go over there and help him.

My mother raised chickens, and we gathered the eggs which she sold for five or six cents a dozen to people from Yuma. She also sold milk to them for something like three or five cents a quart. But then the depression got worse, and we couldn't sell anything. People didn't even have five cents.

Because there was simply no money around, everything was bartered. Mom would send us with a basket of eggs to someone, and we would return with bread or flour or something else in exchange. If somebody butchered an animal, all the relatives would get some of the meat. And when my sister Vicky was born in 1933, Dad paid the doctor by giving him several tons of watermelon.

But on the farm during the depression, we didn't suffer the way people in the city or migrants suffered. We had vegetables, eggs, milk, and chicken, and we had as much as we wanted. There were so many chickens, all we had to do was look under a tree or a bush to find a hen laying, and a few days later there would be seven, eight, twelve, or fourteen chicks. Yet, while we had plenty of chicken to eat, there were times we didn't have any salt.

In 1933, as if the depression was not hardship enough, everything in the valley slowly dried up, even the Colorado River, and we lost our precious supply of water. Our canal was an empty ditch. There hadn't been a drought in sixty-six years, but now, day after hot day passed without relief, and the lack of water prevented my dad from planting a crop. A drought any place is serious, but in the desert it can be catastrophic. The sun never relents, and there is nothing to cool it off.

The moisture in the ground vanished, and the soil became cracked clay. Even the trees seemed to wilt. Nothing could be done. While he didn't show it, I can imagine the despair my dad must have felt. It was another setback in his hopes to make enough money to pay off the taxes on the ranch. The ordeal lasted thirty-one days.

The canal was our life line, and it led to the first paying job I remember having. Our need for money was obvious, my parents didn't have to tell us. Richard and I started trapping gophers for the irrigation district. Today I wouldn't kill them any more than I would kill any other animal, but at that time it didn't upset me, probably because my father trapped them to protect the canal walls from being undermined.

As Richard and I checked our traps, three or four cats went around with us, the fattest cats in the world. I carried a small ax, a block of wood and an empty can of my mother's Tuxedo tobacco. When we found a dead gopher, we gave it to the cats after cutting off its tail on the block and putting the tail in the can to give to the gate master. For each tail we received a penny.

Another time I recall getting money was also the first time I saw a Filipino. My father had a little patch of lettuce which the buyers would buy before it was harvested. When I saw that crew of Filipinos, I asked my dad, "How come they're so small, and they can carry those big boxes?" I don't remember what he said, but I remember the Filipino foreman asked us for coffee, and we brought him a thermosful. He gave us twenty-five cents. To me that was a lot of money, the equivalent of a lot of gophers.

My father never talked to us about his debts, but I would guess now that he constantly faced a tax bill of several thousand dollars, an ever-growing bill that would finally become due in 1937 when the legal period of grace would run out.

As the strain increased, I remember once going to town with him to collect for the Bermuda grass seed he had sold. When he got his check from the seed house, he wasn't satisfied. "Let's go get drunk!" he said in disgust.

I looked at him astounded. I was about eight, I guess, and I remember it very well. Coming to Yuma was a big treat because we didn't come that often. And I knew about drunkenness, too, because, for some reason, all the brothers on my father's side didn't drink, but some of their sons drank heavily. So when he said, "Let's go get drunk," I was kind of frightened.

He set off quickly down the street, with me following. My dad loved ice cream and candy, but he didn't drink. While he didn't say as much, we could tell he had contempt for people who got drunk. This time we didn't end up in a bar either. In the old days they had those ice cream parlors that sold only ice cream. That's where he took me and ordered something very good, something so big I couldn't eat it all.

One morning, about a year after the month-long drought, we had another setback. We woke up to go to school, went to get water, and found the canal dry. It was a startling sight. Down the hill we saw water covering the fields, ruining the crops and flooding the watermelon. The break in the canal was easy to see, a big gash torn from the side of the bank not far from our house. All the water was escaping in a torrent, spreading as it went, and creating havoc. Then we noticed the pitiful bundles of feathers floating everywhere. Many of our chickens drowned.

I had a cute hen as a pet that we had found while hunting down some of the many rattlesnakes there were around. Because she had a misshapen wishbone, she left a trail similar to that of a snake. I had became very fond of that cute little hen, and when I found her body, I cried.

My dad was hired with his team of horses to help repair the break. I remember sitting there and watching as about eight teams were used in rotation doing what a bulldozer would do nowadays. They had a small scraper and would go in, get the dirt, and come to the bank of the canal. When one team needed a rest, the driver would just pull out of the way and the others would continue. The horses and men kept working until the canal was repaired.

It was also in 1934 that my youngest brother Lenny was born. When I woke up one morning, Rita told me a stork was going to bring us a little boy. Of course, I knew it wasn't the stork. I was very jealous. Richard and I were outside the house when a smaller cousin came and told us that my mother had had the baby. I was doubly resentful because he had to tell me.

The doctor was there, and a lot of water was being boiled. After the whole thing was over he came with his sleeves rolled up, sat in the kitchen, and began a big breakfast. My dad came out to get us, and we went through the kitchen to the back of the room where my mother was in bed with a tiny baby. I can still remember how small he looked. He was named Librado after my father.

CHAPTER 4

Dichos and Consejos

CESAR CHAVEZ RECALLS

I had more happy moments as a child than unhappy moments. Because my parents were middle-aged when they got married, they had a lot of understanding. They had passed that critical age when parents are very young and impatient with children. We didn't know what it was to be excluded. We were a very close family.

Now, in my case, my own family, I am always organizing, going to meetings, and coming home late. Sometimes I am not home for weeks at a time, and when I get home it's so late the children are asleep. Not long ago, it got so bad that my son Paul, who was twelve at the time, reacted. One night when I went to bed, I lay there looking up at the ceiling. I don't know how he reached up there, but right above my bed, where I could not miss it, he wrote "Paul." It's a strong message.

Back in those Arizona days, such reminders were unnecessary, as most of our activities were with the family. In fact, one of the three major influences in my life was my upbringing by my mother and dad and the kind of family we had. The other two were my years of training and experiences in CSO and the experiences in the Union.

I don't think we were babied, because my dad was strict about certain things. He was very stern about obeying him, but very lenient about many other things. If he asked us to do something, we had to do it, and he didn't want to tell us twice. He was affectionate, but in terms that were very different than my mother's.

17

She was affectionate and showed it by kissing and hugging, while my dad would just tug our ears or pat us on the head. He showed his affection differently. For instance, from the time we were very small, we never called my mother at night. If we wanted water or wanted to go to the bathroom, we called our dad. In those days the bathroom was an outhouse a long way from the house toward the hills, and he would carry us there.

My dad also used to build most of the little cars we played with. He taught us how to take a sardine can after it was open, cut the top off, and attach wooden wheels to it with wire or a nail. He also taught us how to make tractors out of wooden spools of thread.

But my dad was usually too busy to spend much time with us. My mom kept the family together. She was the sort of woman who had time for her children, who would talk with us. She used many dichos—proverbs—and they all had a real purpose. "What you do to others, others do to you" was one of them. "He who holds the cow, sins as much as he who kills her." "If you're in the honey, some of it will stick to you." Though she was illiterate, she had a tremendous memory. I think most illiterate persons do because they must rely on their memories.

She also gave us a lot of consejos—advice. She didn't wait until something went wrong, nor was she scolding when she was doing it. It was part of the training. At first I didn't understand, but she would make it easy for us. She would say, "He who never listens to consejos will never grow to be old."

I remember her story of the stone freezing in the boy's hand. It was a very disobedient son who came home drunk and got real mad at his mother. He picked up a rock and was about to throw it at her when it froze to his hand. Her stories were about obedience and honesty and some of the virtues. There were others that dealt with miracles. The range was very wide.

When I look back, I see her sermons had tremendous impact on me. I didn't know it was nonviolence then, but after reading Gandhi, St. Francis, and other exponents of nonviolence, I began to clarify that in my mind. Now that I'm older I see she is nonviolent, if anybody is, both by word and deed. She would always talk about not fighting. Despite a culture where you're not a man if you don't fight back, she would say, "No, it's best to turn the other cheek. God gave you senses like eyes and mind and tongue, and you can get out of anything." She would say, "It takes two to fight." That was her favorite. "It takes two to fight, and one can't do it alone." She had all kinds of proverbs for that. "It's better to say that he ran from here than to say he died here."

When I was young I didn't realize the wisdom in her words, but it has been proved to me so many times since. Today I appreciate the advice, and I use quite a few of the dichos, especially in Spanish.

I can't say that I always remained nonviolent in those days. I had a cousin about ten years older than I was. When my parents were away, he would hit us or grab my cat by the tail, spin her around, and throw her in the canal. One day when he did that I exploded. I got my dad's old shot gun and chased him away. He didn't know the gun wasn't loaded.

Just north of our adobe house was a little garden and a tree where we played, a little clearing bordered by thick mesquite bushes. This cousin started hiding there in the evenings when we had to get water or chop wood. Then he'd let out an eerie howl. I didn't know what it was, and I was terrified. Often my mother had told me, "If you don't mind me, you're going to see the devil!" That's what I thought of when I heard that howl.

One night, after he had scared us for about a year, Richard found out it was our cousin. "Get your BB gun," he urged. We sneaked out into the dark toward the bushes. When my cousin heard us and ran for his house, I aimed and fired at him twice. I hit him both times.

Although my mother opposed violence, I think the thing that she really cracked down on the most was being selfish. She made us share everything we had. If we had an apple or a tiny piece of candy, we had to cut it into five pieces.

As she was an excellent cook, she baked pies out of anything, even potatoes, sprinkling brown sugar on them. She would try to give us equal shares, but if one of us complained, "I got the smaller piece," she would take them away from everybody. Then the others would put the heat on the one who complained. Eventually we got to the point where we would say, "Well, I got the smallest piece, but it doesn't matter."

She also taught us never to lend money to our brothers or sisters. "If you were really brothers, you wouldn't let money come between you. You'd trust them." So instead of lending, we'd give them the money. Even today, none of us really cares much about money. We never make loans. If we have it, we give it.

My mother wouldn't let my brothers or me do women's work at home. She didn't want us to wash dishes or sew or iron a shirt. She said our sisters had to do it because they had to get trained. "If you do women's work, then you will expect them to do your work," she explained.

Although I didn't help my older sister Rita with the housework, sometimes I didn't do my work, and Rita would have to bring in the wood for the stove, which angered my mother. Rita was very conscientious about her work.

Rita was very smart. When she was about ten or eleven, for example, she learned how to use the Sears catalogue. Because we lived in the valley and Yuma was a small place, my dad bought everything by mail, from horses' harnesses to clothing. Rita became an expert, almost memorizing the pages, and made out the orders. Then she heard relatives complain about the catalogues. "Oh, they never send you what you want," they said. So she started making out their orders, and they would get exactly what they wanted.

Eventually there were so many orders, somebody in the Sears office in Chicago started writing letters to "Miss Rita Chavez." We were very impressed. We were even more in awe when Sears sent her a pen and pencil set after learning that Rita was only eleven or twelve.

At school, too, Rita was admired by the teachers. In fact, I was known only because of her. The teachers would say, "Oh, you're Rita's brother," and make all kinds of compliments about her.

Years later in CSO, she became a notary public and helped people with all kinds of complicated forms like immigration papers and applications for citizenship. Many still come to her now to make out their income taxes. What a tragedy that she was never able to go beyond the seventh grade. There is so much human potential wasted by poverty, so many children forced to quit school to go to work. Rita was one of thousands.

RITA CHAVEZ MEDINA RECALLS

Cesar was the right hand of my father's arm. My father knew he could count on him. All of us helped a bit with the crops, but Cesar did most of that work and chopped wood and took care of the animals. Actually he worked like a man, because that's the way father taught him.

Because my mother helped my father, by the time I was eight, I often cleaned the house and helped my mother out by cooking for the kids. Although I didn't know how to make tortillas, I tried anyway, and usually they were burned. Cesar got to like them that way. He'd look at my mother's tortillas and say, "No, they're still raw. I don't like them."

As we didn't have a washing machine, I did a lot of scrubbing on the washboard. Ironing, too. There was no electricity, so we had to do it the hard way, with old-fashioned irons and a wooden stove. We put the portable irons on the stove and used a portable handle to clip to the hot iron, switching from one to another when one got cold. To heat our water for washing we used a big tub outside, and we washed our clothes and bathed there.

And because we didn't have electricity, we used to do all of our homework with kerosene lamps. I used to hate those lamps because my dad insisted the glass parts had to sparkle. Of course, they often got black, and I had to clean them.

I remember the first year Cesar went to school. I guess he was seven then. Because we talked only Spanish at home, I used to tell him, "You're going to go to school, and you better learn your name." My father had taught me that the teacher would say, "What's your name, little girl?" and that I should answer, "My name is Rita Chavez," and other little things like this. So two years later, when Cesar was ready for school, it was my turn to teach him. We would play school, and he would sit by me.

But then, when it was time for school he said, "Oh, no. If they don't sit me by you, I'm not going to go to school. I don't want another teacher." We were very close.

The teachers were Anglos and school was in English, but I would say 95 percent of the people in the village of Gila were our relatives, and there were only a few families that were not Spanish-speaking. But the teacher thought nothing of changing our names the moment we were in class. She wouldn't pronounce his real name—which is Cesario—she cut it to Cesar right away.

"Cesar, how are you?" she asked, and he didn't know how to answer back. He was sitting there very quietly. Then all of a sudden he got up and sat by me. So the teacher said, "No, Cesar, you have to come over and sit at your own desk."

In Spanish he said, "Dile que no"—Tell her no—"I want to sit with you." And he started to cry. The teacher finally let him stay. He was very tough, very determined even then.

On the second day he was just as stubborn and insisted that he sit by me. Finally I threatened, "I'll tell my father what you did."

"Okay, don't tell him and tomorrow I promise I'll sit real quietly." And he kept his promise.

It was hard in those days. I used to get punished for speaking Spanish in the schoolyard, and then I would get mean. I'd say, "I'm going to speak and speak and speak," and I would speak Spanish a lot. But then the Anglo kids would tell on me. "Teacher, Rita is speaking Spanish and I don't understand." Boy, they would get me mad! I'm stubborn, really stubborn, as stubborn as Cesar. The more the teachers would tell me not to speak Spanish, the more I would.

Despite that, I loved school. It was only because I didn't have any shoes or any school clothes that I stopped going. Later when my father finally found a job and could get me shoes, I thought I was too old to go back. It's only afterward you realize you're never too old to learn.

CHAPTER 5

A Need for Faith

Getting to school was a big chore for me. Unlike Rita, I never liked school. They made me go, so I went, but they always had to push me to go. It wasn't the learning I hated, but the conflicts. The teachers were very mean. I also didn't like sitting in the classroom. I was bored to death. I'd just go to sleep. Once the teacher even sent a note home saying I was ill, that I had to be taken to the doctor because I was always falling asleep.

Every day it was the same routine. We got up pretty early, and I did several hours work getting water from the canal, taking care of the animals, gathering eggs, the usual hard work on a farm. Then I had to get ready, wash myself, and comb my hair. I didn't like to comb it, and I didn't like to wear shoes. Now I can't walk without them, my soles are too tender, but it didn't bother me then. I wore them only for school. The moment I got out of the schoolyard, I'd take my shoes off and put them over my shoulder, leave them someplace, and I couldn't remember in the morning where I dropped them. I would leave for school, forget something, and come back. Mother would say, "Come on, it's late!" and I'd go and come back again. I was late most of the time.

It was very cold, too, in winter, dropping below freezing at night. Those icy dry winds bit viciously, and going to school on those cold mornings was painful. We didn't have warm clothing, and the piercing winds sliced through us like a scythe through grass. We would go from our home to our aunt's house and try to warm up a bit. Then on to our uncle's house where we would try

23

to thaw out before dashing to our cousin's house and then to the school, which was down in the valley a good mile from our house. Every stop seemed to make the next lap colder, more cutting. In class our faces and hands would sting, then tingle for a while. Luckily the sun always routed the cold, and we would soon forget how we had shivered.

The school, which had three classrooms, was a tall, old wooden building in the shape of a T. Inside were old desks with initials carved all over, mostly those of my older cousins. When the bell rang, about two hundred students lined up on the walkway between the tamarack trees and marched in to the desks. That bell, mounted in a small belfry on top of the peaked roof, sounded like a church bell across the valley, and my favorite sound was the last toll. They'd say "Dismissed," and I'd just get up and start running.

In class one of my biggest problems was the language. Of course, we bitterly resented not being able to speak Spanish, but they insisted that we had to learn English. They said that if we were American, then we should speak the language, and if we wanted to speak Spanish, we should go back to Mexico.

When we spoke Spanish, the teacher swooped down on us. I remember the ruler whistling through the air as its edge came down sharply across my knuckles. It really hurt. Even out in the playground, speaking Spanish brought punishment. The principal had a special paddle that looked like a two by four with a handle on it. The wood was smooth from a lot of use. He would grab us, even the girls, put our head between his legs, and give it to us.

But I could take the spanking. What was worse was mispronouncing a word or making a grammatical mistake. With my Spanish accent and background, I couldn't avoid that. I'd get embarrassed and that hurt more than the paddling. Some teachers were really cruel, while a few—a very few—were understanding.

It's a terrible thing when you have your own language and customs, and those are shattered. I remember trying to find out who I was and not being able to understand. Once, for instance, I recall saying I was a Mexican. The teacher was quick to correct me. "Oh, no, don't say that!" she said. But what else could I say? In a nice way she said, "You are an American. All of us are Americans," and she gave me a long explanation I couldn't understand. I went home and told my mother, "Mama, they tell me I'm an American!" To me an American was a white man. My mother couldn't really give me a satisfactory answer either. She said I was a citizen, but I didn't know what a citizen meant. It was too complicated.

Yet, it was not something that I could dismiss or forget. There were too many reminders, too many times I would be called a Mexican in tones of ridicule or contempt.

Most of our relatives lived between our home and school, and our parents instructed us to stop by and say hello on our way back. Our relatives made us want to stop because of their kindness. All were very poor, but sometimes they'd have a cookie for us or, if nothing else, a glass of cold water. Maybe they had nothing, but the fact is they'd stop what they were doing to talk to us.

My uncle Ramon Arias was the one who taught me to read Spanish about the same time I learned to read English. I would go to his home after school so he could teach me. He was really racist, saying English is the language of dogs—lengua de perro— and would offer me fruit, candy, or a soda if I would sit on his lap so he could read to me. I found reading Spanish a lot easier than trying to learn English in school.

Arias was my aunt's husband on my father's side. Then there was Chico Salazar, my mother's uncle, who also used to hold us on his lap and read the Mexican newspapers to us. Probably they were the only two literate ones. Chico was an old shriveled-up man with a black patch over one eye, the result of an explosion or a mining accident. We had a lot of respect for him, and he, too, taught us a lot.

As we didn't have a church in the valley and it was very difficult to go to Yuma, it was my mother who taught us prayers. Throughout the Southwest and Mexico where there were no priests for a long time, the amazing thing was that people kept the faith. But they were oriented more toward relics and saints. My mother was very religious without being fanatic, and she believed in saints as advocates, as lobbyists, to pray to God for her. Her patron saint was St. Eduvigis.

St. Eduvigis was a Polish duchess who, in the early Christian era, gave up all of her worldly possessions, distributed them among the poor, and became a Christian. On the saint's birthday, October 16, my mom would find some needy person to help and, until recently, she would always invite people to the house, usually hobos. She would go out purposely to look for someone in need, give him something, and never take anything in return. If a man was selling pencils, she would give him some money but wouldn't take a pencil. She would look for people who were hungry to come to the house. Usually they would offer to do some work, like chop wood, in exchange for a meal, but she would refuse because, she said, the gift then was invalid. I think that is a very beautiful custom, and my dad must have felt pretty much the same way because he didn't object.

Mama Tella gave us our formal religious training. She was an orphan who was raised, I understand, in a convent, but she wasn't a nun. She was probably a servant. At the convent she had learned how to read and write in both Latin and Spanish. She was the only one of our four grandparents who was literate.

Mama Tella became blind in her old age. I think she could see a little light and shadows, but she progressively lost her sight. I remember she was very old, almost one hundred when she died in 1937, and she was in bed most of the time. She had a walking cane, and two of the older great-grandchildren or my dad or mother would take her for a walk. But mostly, as I remember her, she was always praying, just praying.

Every evening she would sit in bed, and we would gather in front of her. As we knelt by the doorway to her room, we would join her in the Rosary that seemed to drone on endlessly. We were required to kneel until the prayer was over, and if we started giggling, she would hit us with her cane. After the Rosary she would tell us about a particular saint and drill us in our catechism.

After Mama Tella had prepared us for our first Communion, my father brought my mother, Rita, and me to town one Saturday when he went to buy seed. He dropped us off at the Catholic church. Inside it was dark and silent as we faced toward the altar and crossed ourselves. The pews were empty, and we tiptoed in awe across the dim interior until we found ourselves standing before the priest, who seemed huge, standing in the shadows, his white skin appearing whiter in the dark.

My mother explained our purpose, but the priest shook his head. "They haven't had any religious training. They can't take Communion," he said looking down at us. "They must attend class here in Yuma first."

My mother argued, "They can't because we live out in the valley twenty miles away. We can't travel that far every week."

"Well, they can't make their first Communion unless they do. They have to know their catechism," the priest answered.

My mother was desperate. "Well, ask them something," she pleaded.

We were very nervous. The quiet of the church bore down on us, broken only by the argument between my mother and the priest, and we knew the importance of first Communion. But when the questions came, we knew the answers. Mama Tella's tutoring had been long, intense, and thorough.

Finally the priest was satisfied. He agreed we were ready to join the others for first Communion the next day. But first, he said, we must go to confession. Again I was very frightened. I had been told what confession was, but I didn't think I had anything to confess. I was led into a dark little room and somehow managed to go through with it.

After we left the church, my mother bought us special clothes. It was the first time I wore a tie, and Rita was dressed in white with a veil. I've since seen a picture of us. I couldn't have been over seven or eight. I guess we were frightened because our eyes were wide open, and our hands held the rosary. I had on brand new shoes, a brand new pair of pants, and a new shirt—everything, except my hair wasn't combed.

Since those days, my need for religion has deepened. Today I don't think that I could base my will to struggle on cold economics or on some political doctrine. I don't think there would be enough to sustain me. For me the base must be faith.

It's not necessary to have a religion to act selflessly. I know many agnostics who are more religious in their own way than most people who claim to be believers. While most people drawn toward liberalism or radicalism leave the church, I went the other way. I drew closer to the church the more I learned and understood.

To me, religion is a most beautiful thing. And over the years, I have come to realize that all religions are beautiful. Your religion just happens to depend a lot on your upbringing and your culture.

For me, Christianity happens to be a natural source of faith. I have read what Christ said when he was here. He was very clear in what he meant and knew exactly what he was after. He was extremely radical, and he was for social change.

CHAPTER 6

A Violent Death

CESAR CHAVEZ RECALLS

In 1931, a death occurred in the valley, a death that really increased racial tensions. People called it murder. They said Vicente Hernandez was killed by Justus Jackson, the same Justus Jackson who had sold the forty acres to my father.

Vicente was my double first cousin, the son of my mother's sister and my father's brother. He was working for Jackson as an irrigator. One night Jackson came and told Vicente the spillway was running over, and he had to go help him. That was the last time his pregnant wife Petra saw him alive.

A few hours later, there was a report Vicente had drowned. The story spread that Jackson had struck him over the head and dumped him in the water. But Jackson claimed Vicente slipped on a wet log and struck his head as he fell in. A coroner's jury later ruled that Vicente drowned.

Then the word went around that Jackson had gotten insurance for Vicente and put Vicente's mother as beneficiary. We were told Jackson kidnapped Vicente's mother and took her to Mexico to force her to sign the insurance over to him.

After a lot of pressure from the Mexican people, a grand jury began an investigation and indicted Jackson. I don't remember what happened, but the records show that Jackson was tried on a charge of larceny. He apparently was found guilty because he asked for a retrial. Then the district attorney dismissed the charge.

Racial tensions became worse at the start of 1936 when a long-anticipated project was begun at the north end of the Gila Valley.

The federal government started work on the Imperial Dam, which meant a lot of new jobs and a lot of new people, mostly from the South.

As money began to trickle back into the area, my father and a cousin rented the pool hall and service station he once had owned. Richard and I went there after school to handle the gasoline pumps and to help around the pool room. Although I had forgotten this story, Richard recalls that we started stealing cigarettes from the pool room. We would take home about four or five packs, put them in a can and bury them. The next day we would take them to school and give them away. When my father discovered what we were doing, we really got a beating. We never stole cigarettes again.

Because of the dam construction, school enrollment probably doubled, mostly white children from the South. Friction developed, and there were all kinds of clashes. As I recall, it was mostly name calling, but it bothered me because we hadn't experienced that before. We had been part of the community.

I was impressed at how well these new students spoke English, probably because I had such a hard time with it. It came so easily to them, I guess I became envious of their skill. One day after school I visited Uncle Arias, the one who taught me to read Spanish. Although his views about English were obvious—he would tell us, "Don't learn this gringo language, learn your own language!"—I thought he might be able to solve what was troubling me.

I asked him, "How come those little gringos can speak English so well and we can't?"

His feelings for the Southerners were so strong, he had a quick answer. "Oh," he said, "that's because they chew tobacco."

Richard and I looked at each other. We believed him. We figured it would help us, too, and we knew where my dad kept the chewing tobacco he used on the horses when they got chafed. As soon as we could, we got some of the pungent leaves, settled down by the corral, and started to chew. But the experiment didn't last long. Instead of our brains, the tobacco affected our stomachs. I remember we got very sick.

As tensions within the school increased, it was there that we first experienced discrimination and knew it. The first time it happened, it was a tiny incident, a chance remark, but one that I still remember. There were latrines in back of the school, and as I was returning from there, a couple of girls said something about "dirty Mexicans." I never forgot it. Words can be as painful as a switch, and many times those who say them are unaware how painful their words can be.

Nearly every noon now there were fights with the Anglos in school. I don't remember exchanging blows. My mother too often had told me, "It takes two to fight. One can't do it alone." But there were some heated arguments. It was after one of those, one day, that the principal intervened and paddled Richard, some cousins, and me. We were so angry at the injustice, his automatically taking the other side, that we just walked away.

"Come back!" he yelled, but we said we wouldn't and took off.

We ran toward the canal with him after us. When he saw the chase was futile, he ran back down the levee, over to the school to get his car. But we hid under a bridge, squeezed in the narrow space between the planks and the water, and he lost us. Then we went to my dad's garage to work.

Later that afternoon, Richard and I saw the principal's car coming down the road and quickly hid behind the pool room. To our horror the principal stopped for gas. We didn't dare come out. Dad was in the pool hall when the principal honked his horn.

"Where are those kids?" my dad asked, angry that we weren't there. The principal told him we had played hooky, and he couldn't catch us.

Later my dad spanked us. He knew why we had played hooky, but he didn't care about that injustice. If we were disrespectful, he told the teachers, they had authority to spank us.

Of course, life was not constant tensions. We had some good times too. Since my dad had the pool hall again, we learned how to play pool there. We were the pool sharks. I could beat anybody. After school Richard and I would race home, do the chores, and then run to the pool hall and stay until it closed around 11:00.

One day this stranger came from Los Angeles. "So you want to play?" he asked. I didn't know who he was, but there were some people there that knew him. They smiled. We played one or two games and I beat him. Then he said, "Well, let's play for a dollar."

I didn't have any money, but I went to my dad and said, "Give me a dollar to play. I beat him twice."

"You better watch out," my dad warned and refused to give me money. So I went to Richard. "I know I can beat him," I insisted. No luck.

"Well, we'll play for a dollar, and when you get the money, you pay me," the stranger said.

I said, "All right."

He cleaned the table. I didn't get a shot.

"What happened?" I asked bewildered.

Then he told me he had played as a professional for many years. "You play for pleasure. Don't play for money," he warned me. So he taught me a lot, taught me to be careful and taught me how to play pool. Now I only play for pleasure, but I haven't played in a long time.

CHAPTER 7

Tragic Summer

CESAR CHAVEZ RECALLS

We had barbecues every night in the summer, when the rhythm of our life was changed because of the intense heat. Our relatives would gather then and talk about the present and the past. To avoid the scorching midday sun, we'd get up at 4:00 when the North Star was at its brightest, way down on the horizon. My dad would wake us, and by the time we'd get breakfast, it would be just light enough to see. We would work for five hours or so before the sun drove us into the shade, and we'd only return to work in the late afternoon if we were very busy. On your own farm you can work such humane hours, but you can't when you work for somebody else, as we would find out only too soon, and as farm workers today know only too well.

After a sizzling day, we couldn't wait for the cooler summer evenings at home drinking lemonade or eating watermelon or corn. First my dad would put a lot of wood in the big fire hole between the back of the house and the old mesquite tree. Then, after the fire turned to glowing coals, we would toss in ears of freshly picked corn still in their husks and roast them. Nothing is more delicious.

Since our beds were outside during the summer, we sometimes huddled under their mosquito netting, even though we burned pans of manure to drive away the thousands of mosquitoes. From that safe haven, we listened to the lively conversations between my parents and their relatives.

It was then that we found out about our uncles, our grandfather, and some of our other relatives who had died. Because many of my relatives were miners, there were stories of miracles in the mines—accidents, mines caving in, and people not getting killed because of their strong beliefs. We had some good storytellers who kept us on the edge of our beds with adventure tales or spooky ghost stories. Others told stories from the Bible.

Then we heard about the Mexican revolution, the battles fought by farm workers, and how they won and lost. There were stories— a lot of them—about the haciendas, how the big landowners treated the people, about the injustices, the cruelties, the exploitation, the actual experiences our uncles had had.

Most of my uncles had left Mexico when they were a lot older than my dad and could remember what they had seen and gone through. They could recall, for example, the foreman who told the people not to eat salt because they would become dumb. They would examine that story and point out that the real reason this was done was not because salt would harm you, but because salt was expensive, and the foreman would pocket the money instead of buying salt for the people. Others then recalled they had been told the same thing about butter.

Stories were told over and over again of how Papa Chayo escaped from the hacienda, how no one could speak out for their rights, how they feared for their lives, how they were driven to flight. They never talked about revolution, but still it was there just under the surface. We learned that when you felt something was wrong, you stood up to it. Later, for example, when we were on a job, my father considered it dishonorable to be fired for being lazy; but if somebody was fired for standing up for a person's rights, it was quite honorable. I remember my dad would stand up for the rights of others, so we automatically did too.

We were told the story of how Papa Chayo was given five dollars to vote shortly after he came to Texas, and how a dozen years later that vote proved valuable when he applied for the title to his farm and was asked if he was a citizen. When he mentioned he had voted once in El Paso, they told him his vote made him an American citizen—even though he couldn't read or write. Years later, a law was passed that you couldn't vote if you were illiterate, a very bad law because it means that because you are poor, you lose every right, including the right to vote. My dad also thought he was a citizen since my grandfather was, and he voted too. It wasn't until citizenship requirements were tightened when the Walter-McCarran Immigration Act was passed in the 1950s that he learned he was not. That, of course, doesn't affect my citizenship, which wasn't given to me, but is my birthright.

Perhaps because of the five dollars my grandfather received and what it later meant, our relatives in Yuma took their political activity very seriously. Races were close, forcing the governor to campaign there. In the Gila Valley my dad was very influential, though I wouldn't call him a political chief. I doubt that he knew very much about politics. They would get together and decide who to support, then vote as a bloc, a potent political weapon. When the governor campaigned, he would come to a big political barbecue near the store, one of those deep-pit barbecues at which hundreds of people would turn out. I remember the ones in 1936, and I know they all voted for Roosevelt.

It was only natural then for my dad to think of the governor when he faced the loss of the ranch. The seven years of grace on the taxes were up in 1937, and he owed the state more than four thousand dollars. At the time, my dad didn't let us know of his worries, but I learned about them later.

Under the New Deal, Dad qualified for a loan, but that didn't take into account the local political and economic structure. The president of the local bank was Archibald J. Griffin, and Archie Griffin was the state. He was the wealthiest grower in the area, with land adjoining ours to the west and south. He wanted our land to sort of fill his out. My dad's application for a loan was blocked by the bank.

When my father went to Phoenix to see the governor, Dad couldn't get anything from him. The governor said, "We'll see what we can do." But a few days later we got a letter which said something like "I'm sorry."

It was a tragic summer. Everything was closing in on us, and misfortunes followed one after another. In July, Mama Tella died, a loss which my father must have felt keenly. Throughout his life he had been close to her, taken care of her and her needs, especially after Papa Chayo died.

Then less than a month after her death, Dad suffered another sunstroke. Yet how could he follow the doctor's advice to stay out of the sun, to ease up on the work? If anything, he would have to work harder than he had before. For despite his best efforts, all his work, and all his struggles, the state took legal possession of our ranch on August 29, 1937. Although our days on the ranch appeared to be numbered, my dad was not through fighting.

CHAPTER 8

No Longer Free

CESAR CHAVEZ RECALLS

Somehow another year passed and we were not evicted. I don't know why. I'm sure Dad did everything he could to find money, but he was unsuccessful. He could neither borrow any, nor make enough around Yuma.

In August of 1938, I think, he finally left home with several relatives to look for work in California. He must have been desperate to leave us behind, but he planned to have us follow him if he found anything. Then perhaps we could all help him make enough to save the farm.

The odds against him were enormous. California was experiencing one of the greatest invasions in its history. Thousands of people were streaming into California then, uprooted from the Dust Bowl or destitute because of the depression. Most of them thought California was the place where they could find work farming and make enough money to buy a little land. But their dreams were doomed. California was not what they imagined. To succeed in California agriculture, large holdings and irrigation were needed, and both were expensive, requiring huge sums to get started. Like my dad, the flood of poor entering the state had no idea that most of the land was owned by large corporations and wealthy growers who welcomed this torrent of labor only because it drove down wages.

Sometimes growers provided camps—without plumbing—and workers bathed and drank from irrigation ditches. Many families often lived on riverbanks or under bridges, in shacks built of linoleum scraps and cardboard cartons, or tents improvised from gunny sacks.

Though farm workers were harvesting vegetables and fruit, hunger was constant. The abundance of workers diminished the work load at the same time it drove down wages. There was little money for food. Some families survived on nothing but beans and fried dough, or perhaps just fried oatmeal, or dandelion greens and boiled potatoes.

Despite the odds, my dad was lucky. After he found a job in Oxnard threshing beans, and a place to live in a little shack in La Colonia, the Oxnard barrio, he wrote my mother telling her to come. Oxnard is a damp, foggy little town near the Pacific ocean about fifty-five miles north of Los Angeles. It was a place where later we would spend one of the worst winters in our lives, and where, many years later, I would get my first experience organizing farm workers.

To avoid the desert heat, we left late one night in my cousin's old Chevy jalopy which had a rumble seat. The car was eleven years old, the same age I was, and it was crowded. Besides my mother, my two sisters, and two brothers, we had two of our cousins along who did the driving, Ernesto Arias and Frank Quintero.

The old car chugged down the deserted highway, its headlights barely lighting the desert road. Although we were excited at the adventure of leaving for California, we slowly dozed off. It was about 2:00 in the morning when we stopped along the road to rest and change drivers. To conserve our battery, the headlights were turned off. The highway was quiet, and the sand stretched out into the night. Nothing could have been more peaceful.

Suddenly two cars bore down on us, their floodlights shattering the dark. Uniformed men piled out of the cars and surrounded ours. We were half-asleep, all scared, and crying. It was the border patrol, our first experience with any kind of law. Roughly they asked for identification, our birth certificates, proof of American citizenship. They harrassed my mother without mercy. She was terrified. She thought if she said the wrong thing, they would throw her into Mexico immediately. After all, even though she had lived here since she was six months old, she was born in Mexico. She couldn't speak English, and the only identification she had was the letter my father had sent her from Oxnard.

They started questioning Lenny and Vicky who couldn't speak English either, and then they grilled the rest of us in turn. Although our car was loaded, they were accusing us of somehow smuggling some Mexicans across the border and dropping them off in the desert. Nothing we said seemed to satisfy them, and the harrassment continued hour after hour. My mother must have died a hundred times that night. She was praying hard. Finally, after about five hours, they let us go.

The border patrol is just as bad today. The patrolmen are there to protect us, not harrass us, but they don't distinguish between Mexicans and Mexican-Americans. As far as they are concerned, we can't be a citizen even though we were born here. In their minds, "if he's Mexican, don't trust him."

A number of years ago I had my cousin Manuel draw the border patrolman as a member of the Gestapo with a Gestapo helmet and his boot on the neck of a farm worker. We distributed the cartoon throughout the Southwest. Did we get calls! A meeting was finally arranged in Washington with the top men of the border patrol. For about four hours I tore into them viciously, and we conducted no business. Because we had power behind us —a lot of heat from Senators Robert Kennedy and Harrison Williams—the border patrol officials tried to be nice, but you could see that hatred just oozing out. I just let them have it. Since then they've simmered down somewhat.

But that first time, they delayed us so long we ended up going through the desert in the heat of the day. We were exhausted, frightened, and angry. Because the car was old, we drove slowly trying to keep it from overheating. I think we slept by the side of the road near Banning the first night and arrived in Oxnard the next day.

When we found the little house in the barrio, we piled out of the car to explore our new surroundings. A weathered fence around the yard turned that shack into a fort. That's the way it was in La Colonia—many houses in one lot, very small houses, and lots of people in each house, unpaved streets, no lights, no sewers, just outhouses. And every house had a fence.

My dad was just bringing in some furniture with his brother Valeriano and his sister Carmen, Frank Quintero's mother. When we went inside, I saw a socket without a bulb hanging from the ceiling. I climbed on the bare bed springs to see how it worked, then called my brother.

"Hey, Rookie, look at that. Put your finger in there. It tickles you."

After Richard put his finger in the socket, I pulled the chain, and he let out a yell. The shock really scared him. When I was small, I was a travieso—a prankster. I didn't know I was mean, but Richard has told me that I was.

The first day we came to live in the Oxnard barrio, I suddenly realized what I had left. It hit me just like a ton of bricks. On the ranch in back of the house, we had a lot of trees where we played and built little bridges and little canals. But the first day we got to Oxnard, the landlady told us we couldn't play in front of the house. I thought, why not go back to the ranch. But my mother said we couldn't.

I was also shocked because, at home, we could leave our toys outside, but in Oxnard when we left them out the first night, they were gone. I just couldn't understand why people would take them.

Shortly after we arrived, my aunt sent me with a quarter to the store to get some chilis. A young clerk there took the money and gave me only two or three. As soon as I returned, my aunt knew I had been taken and told me to return them. Although I was reluctant, I had to do it. At the store, I told the owner my aunt wanted her money back. Quickly realizing what had happened, he chewed out the clerk.

That incident happened Friday night. The next Monday after school, the clerk was waiting for me. He pushed me against some rose bushes, knocked me down, and gave me a good beating. I was very small and didn't fight back, but I felt like I wanted to kill him. I remember I was afraid of him because he was bigger, but besides that there must have been something else that kept me from fighting. Maybe part of it was nonresistance. Probably I was afraid to fight also because of my mother. When I ran home crying, she remained calm, and we talked for some time. But when my dad arrived, he became so angry he was ready to go after the clerk. My mother, however, prevailed.

The days passed slowly, and I no longer felt free. I was like a wild duck with its wings clipped. I felt trapped. There were fences everywhere, too many people, and too much fighting. I couldn't understand how neighbors could live without knowing each other or talking to each other.

Being absorbed by that new environment was tough, and we resisted. But it was bigger than us, and we yielded and yielded and yielded. The only time we could escape was when Dad took us to the beach to gather driftwood for the stove. We had never seen so much water before. The beach stretched deserted for miles, and we could race along the shore with the same freedom we had had back in the Gila Valley.

We only stayed in Oxnard for two or three months, going to school for a half a day, then helping our parents the other half. We also helped them pick walnuts on Saturdays and Sundays.

Unlike the ranch, the work was drudgery. We knew it was work. There is such a difference between working for yourself and working for others.

The competition for jobs was too great, the wages too low, to make Dad's project successful. He decided to return to Yuma. Before we left, we bought an old Studebaker in Ventura, a 1930 President, dark brown with black trimming, a spare tire on each side of the hood, and a metal luggage rack on the back. I didn't know then how important that big ancient car would be to us. At the time, I especially admired its dashboard which was far more advanced than those we had on our old Chevy and Ford. This one actually had a mileage speedometer, an oil gauge, and a manually wound clock that kept good time. The Studebaker was big and very fast. My dad would cruise at sixty miles per hour and, unlike the other cars we had before, it could travel all day and part of the night without breaking down, even when completely loaded. It would pass everything—except gas stations. Gas then cost seventeen cents, and that old car went about eight miles to the gallon.

As we returned to the North Gila Valley in our Studebaker, we looked forward to going back to Laguna School. It would be Vicky's first time there and Rita had been preparing her for that for a long time. Because Vicky, my youngest sister, was quite fat, I would tease her. "Your real parents were gophers," I would say, "and one day when you fell in the canal, we picked you up." Vicky believed it, and the story made her cry.

For the past year Rita had been teaching Vicky to read the whole textbook. "See Jack, see Jack run. See Jane, see Jane run. See Baby, see Baby run." When the day came for school, Rita told the teacher Vicky knew English and could read. So after everyone was seated, the teacher asked Vicky to read the book. There Vicky sat, turning page after page, reading right through from front to back. She went like a tape recorder.

Then the teacher asked Vicky her name, and Vicky, who really didn't know English, couldn't answer.

CHAPTER 9

Losing the Ranch

CESAR CHAVEZ RECALLS

One day one of those legal ads in fine print appeared in the Yuma paper. I didn't see it, but it was one of many like it that was printed those years in the local paper. On February 6, 1939, the ad said, the Yuma County Board of Supervisors would sell at public auction 118.58 acres located in the North Gila Valley. It said nothing, of course, of Papa Chayo who plowed the land, irrigated it, and made it produce. Nor did it mention my dad who had continued the work and struggled there for the survival of his family. The ad made only one thing clear. The county now owned the land because the former owners failed to pay $4,080.80 due the county for taxes and seven years of interest on those taxes. Now the county wanted to turn the land to cash and return the property to the tax rolls.

Only two bidders appeared for the public auction. Who had money in those days? One was Archibald Griffin, that rich grower who needed our land to straighten out his property line. The other was my dad who needed his home and his land for his family. Only Griffin could afford to buy the land, but only my dad could not afford to lose it. Under those circumstances, the result was inevitable. My dad was the highest bidder. He had thirty days to come up with the cash for the $2,300 bid. But when he tried to get a loan in Calexico where his brother lived, he was unsuccessful. All too swiftly the thirty days ran out. Two weeks later the land was auctioned again. Since Dad could not bid a second time, he sent another man in his place. But Griffin got the ranch for $1,750.

Even then my dad didn't give up. For thirty years he had walked those fields, tilled that soil, tended those irrigation ditches, and worked unceasingly. His roots had grown and taken hold and nourished him in that soil. How can a tree survive uprooted? He could as easily give up his children as his land, and either was unthinkable.

Turning to a lawyer for help, he learned that under the Homestead Act he could get the land back for the amount Griffin paid for it. So when Griffin, knowing this, offered my dad $100 for his signature clearing the title, my dad refused to sign.

Shortly after that, a big red tractor came to the farm—at least it seemed big to me as my dad had always farmed his land with horses. Its motor blotted out the sound of crickets and bullfrogs and the buzzing of the flies. As the tractor moved along, it tore up the soil, leveling it, and destroyed the trees, pushing them over like they were nothing.

My dad would never let us carve our initials or do anything to those trees. "You shouldn't do that because it's bad," he'd say. He had taught us to respect nature. And each tree, of course, means quite a bit to you when you're young. They are a part of you. We grew up there, saw them every day, and they were alive, they were friends. When we saw the bulldozer just uprooting those trees, it was tearing at us too.

In the path of the tractor there was also a ditch going from the canal, a little ditch which we though was a big thing. Several of them criss-crossed the land for irrigation, and we took good care of them because if one broke, it meant a lot of shoveling, a lot of work to repair it. In those ditches were wooden gates we had made, checks really, to control the flow of water. But that caterpillar pulling a huge disc, drove over those arteries, filling them up and destroying them.

I remember the tractor heading for the corral. I shudder now to think of it. It was there that Richard and I had fun together riding the horses and the young calves bareback. Or at least we did until one calf bucked and threw Richard right through the pole fence. It was in that corral, too, that I first got on the big dapple gray stallion that nobody would ride because he was too spirited. One day I put a rope hitch around his muzzle and jumped on his back. He only bucked a little, and from then on I could ride him.

A few days before the tractor came, we had gotten the horses out and taken them to my uncle's place, a place which my uncle soon would lose, too. Although my dad had tried to sell the horses, he finally gave them away because there was nobody to buy them.

Now the tractor was at the corral, and the old sturdy fence posts gave way as easily as stalks of corn. It was a monstrous thing. Richard and I were watching on higher ground. We kept cussing the driver, but he didn't hear us, our words were lost in the sound of tearing timbers and growling motor. We didn't blame the grower, we blamed the poor tractor driver. We just thought he was mean. I wanted to go stop him but I couldn't. I felt helpless.

When we were pushed off our land, all we could take with us was what we could jam into the old Studebaker or pile on its roof and fenders, mostly clothes and bedding. As we were getting into the car, my mother was crying.

Rita wanted to stay back with one of our aunts and finish her last year of school, but mother wouldn't let her. "No, we all have to live together," she said, and we never separated.

I realized something was happening because my mother was crying, but I didn't really realize the import of it at the time. When we left the farm, our whole life was upset, turned upside down. We had been part of a very stable community, and we were about to become migratory workers. We had been uprooted.

Landownership is very important, and my dad had very strong feelings about the land. If we had stayed there, possibly I would have been a grower. God writes in exceedingly crooked lines.

Book II

UPROOTED AND ADRIFT

1939–1952

By the time the Chavez family crossed into California, close to three hundred thousand other hungry and destitute men, women, and children already had swarmed into the state, victims of the depression and years of drought that had turned their Southwestern farms into barren dust.

Urged on by agribusiness, the migrants chased the crops in a stream of poverty that moved from the Imperial Valley in the south during the winter, northward with the weather through the coastal and San Joaquin valleys.

California agribusiness thrived on the surplus labor that drove down wages. And the conditions the families experienced were no different than those endured by the waves of Chinese, Japanese, Mexican, and Filipino workers who preceded them, and the waves of other minorities that followed.

From those conditions and experiences that prevailed through the 1940s, on into the 1970s, came the fuel that fed La Causa and motivated its membership. The trials endured by the Chavez family and those they knew were branded in the mind of Cesar Chavez as a constant reminder of the need for change.

CHAPTER 1

Easy Prey

CESAR CHAVEZ RECALLS

We headed west; it was our only hope. I think the idea was that we would make enough money to redeem the property, because at first Dad often talked about going back to the ranch someday. He talked about that for a few years, but less and less. Finally he didn't talk about it anymore.

When we left Arizona, we only had about $40 which my mother had saved from the sale of our cow and some chickens. Soon even that little cash was gone. Then my dad's dream of regaining his land faded before the nightmare that he would not be able to provide even enough food for his children.

Our first stop was in Brawley, a little California town about twenty-five miles north of the Mexican border in the Imperial Valley. We had some relatives there who were going to join us— my father's brother Valeriano, his oldest daughter Narcisa, Vicente's widow Petra, and her son Ruben who was born soon after Vicente died at the spillway.

By the time we all were gathered, they were anxious to start. Everyone needed money. But my mother, who was very superstitious, wanted to wait a day. It was Tuesday, June 13, and she believed it was bad luck to start a journey on a Tuesday. There is a dicho, "On Tuesday neither get married nor embark," and she repeated it as she argued that we should wait. Besides, it was the thirteenth and Tuesday the thirteenth was especially bad. However her arguments didn't convince the others, so we left about 5:00 in the morning in two cars, our old Studebaker and my uncle Valeriano's, both heavily loaded with all we could carry.

We headed north along the deep blue waters of the Salton Sea, that huge salt water lake lying well below sea level in the middle of the California desert. After we had gone about seventy miles, Valeriano's car broke down. I think it had a flat tire. The sun was burning down, and the only shade was under a small tree where my mother took us while the car was repaired. Then she refused to leave.

"I told you, I don't want to leave on Tuesday the thirteenth. That's bad luck," she argued, using more dichos. "If a man is born on Tuesday, and he marries on Tuesday, his wife will leave him on a Tuesday." She said that doctors knew better than to operate on Tuesday unless they wanted their patients to die. Already one car had broken down, and she knew worse would follow if we kept going.

Nothing would move her. Although the desert was scorching, she wouldn't get back in the car. Instead she headed for a small bridge where there was a little more shade. We stayed there the rest of the day. That night we slept beside the road. Then on Wednesday morning we took off again. From then on, during our years on the road, we usually left on Mondays because she insisted it was bad luck to start either on Tuesdays or Fridays.

Someone had told my father there were peas to pick at Atascadero, just north of San Luis Obispo. We were just learning the ropes and were easy prey for such tales by labor contractors. My dad never learned how to guard against them. "This guy sounds good," he would say, and my mother would ask, "Are you sure he's telling you the truth?" "Well, he sounds very honest," my dad would answer.

So we drove through Los Angeles and headed up the coast past Oxnard, Ventura, and Santa Barbara. When we reached Atascadero, we learned the harvest had ended two or three weeks before. We drove around searching in vain for work. Then we were told there was some good picking in Gonzales another one hundred miles to the north where, they said, there was good money to be made, and children could work alongside the adults.

Some fifty miles up the road, just north of King City, my father stopped for gas, and my uncle decided to go to another gas station to save time. I was riding with him—I guess all children like to change cars—and when he stopped, I got out to go to the bathroom.

A short time later my uncle caught up to my dad's car on the highway. As he passed he shouted, "Is Cesario with you?"

"Yea, straight to Gonzales," my dad answered, and Valeriano's car sped on.

My mother sat up. "No, Librado, he's asking for Cesario."

They argued briefly, and my mother became anxious. Finally they caught up to Valeriano.

"What did you ask me?" my dad asked.

"Is Cesario in the car?"

"No," my dad said.

"Oh, we lost him!" my mother cried. "¡Mi hijo! ¡mi hijo!" And she became hysterical.

As the two cars turned around, some Filipino workers in the field heard her cries and saw her hands waving wildly. Not understanding Spanish, they waved back and shouted, " 'Bye, Lady. 'Bye." My brother Richard laughed as he looked back at them, but my mother was too upset to notice.

Back at the station I told the attendant my family had left without me. First he laughed, then he became worried because he thought they had left me on purpose.

"No, they forgot me!" I cried.

"They must not like you too much," he sneered.

"They like me a lot!" I answered. "They like me a lot!"

I remembered being told to call the highway patrol if we got lost. But before the police arrived, the cars were back at the gas station, and we were reunited.

That night in Gonzales, just south of Salinas, we found a room above a bar in an old two-story building. We hit the peak of the season, and there were cars and people everywhere, more people than I had ever seen. Although it was a small town, in those days it seemed big to me.

My dad went around asking about work. It was Friday night, and the jukebox was blaring downstairs. Petra met a cousin from Yuma who kept playing "Cuatro vidas" on the jukebox for her. The music was so loud we couldn't sleep.

The next day when we stopped for gas, another labor contractor came up to our car. We were obvious targets with so much piled in it. He said, "Where are you going? I know of a job. We've got a home, we've got pea-picking jobs over near Half Moon Bay. They pay good money, and it's good picking." We really went for it. So he said, "Look, here's my card. Take it to François Best over there."

We later found out he was getting paid for recruiting. He'd get twenty dollars a family. So we went and found peas there, and a lot of workers, but they were paying about half what he promised. And there was no housing. It was horrible!

We were told of a place where farm workers could stay in the mountains overlooking the ocean, but the only empty shack at the camp was an old broken-down shed propped up on the hillside. It was a painful contrast to our adobe home in Arizona. The doors were missing and so were many of the weathered, unpainted boards, which had probably been used for firewood. Two broken steps were in front of the entrance and, inside, on the dirt floor, there was garbage and other trash. As we didn't have a broom, we cut a branch to sweep the mess out, but the dust was so bad we had to sprinkle water on the floor first.

Other people lived in that camp, mostly old, single men. When my mother found out some kind of sickness was going around, and there was only one dirty outdoor toilet, she insisted we leave the first thing in the morning.

At the general store the next day, we met a Japanese lady who said she had a house we could rent for four dollars a week. It wasn't much of a place, but it had a huge wood-burning stove which pleased my mother.

Later we got our first work picking peas. It took about two hours to fill one hamper, walking along the rows bent double over the plants. Then we carried the full baskets to the end of the field and waited in a long line to have them sorted and weighed. The sorting was done in a trough with a chute. They would take only the peas they thought were good, and they only paid you for those. The pay was twenty cents a hamper, which had to weigh in at twenty-five pounds. So in about three hours, the whole family made only twenty cents.

After the weigh-in, we found there were no more hampers, no more work that day. There were so many unemployed people looking for jobs, they were like flocks of starlings.

Every day we went looking for work. As we drove around, my father was always admiring the land, noticing how fertile it was and noticing the equipment. He would get down and look at the ground, taking some dirt in his huge hands. "You could really raise things here!" he would say, or "Look at that plow! Look at that tractor!" Often he wouldn't agree with the methods being used. He would say this crop could have produced more if they had watered it on time. He was always noticing mistakes, looking for ways of improving things.

As for me, I was at that age where I didn't know what it meant to be without land to farm. I just felt restricted by all the No Trespassing signs. I felt caged. But I have a hunch my dad suffered more than anybody else, though he never showed it to us.

Well, every day we looked for work. At times we arrived too late, and there were no more hampers. On other days we could only find work for two hours or so. The house was costing us more than we were making, but our landlady helped out by giving us some fresh vegetables, eggplants, string beans, bell peppers, and corn.

After a week or so, when our money was nearly gone, we were again told there was good money to be made, this time picking cherries in San Jose. So we packed up and headed for San Jose.

CHAPTER 2

Get Out If You Can

CESAR CHAVEZ RECALLS

We arrived in San Jose on June 24, my mother's birthday, and stopped on Jackson Street by an isolated but crowded barrio where many farm workers lived. Again we had no place to stay.

The barrio wasn't large, just two unpaved dead-end streets running into Jackson and bordered on three sides by fields and pasture. It was no different than poor barrios are today—something like Earlymart or McFarland near Delano—shabby shacks and old houses with outside privies in the back. There were, of course, no sewers. Each lot was crowded with several houses and surrounded by tall, unpainted fences. In those two long blocks there were also maybe six Pentecostal churches. And there were lots of people.

This was the barrio called Sal Si Puedes—Get Out If You Can —and it is still prominent today, probably because it's dirtier and uglier than the others.

There are three versions of how Sal Si Puedes got its name, but I've never heard the third from the Chicanos. Only the first two were told by the old-timers.

Sal Si Puedes was a very rough barrio, and some of the fights were fatal. I don't mean there were that many killings, because a fight to the end didn't happen unless it was something serious. But the saying goes that if trouble developed, a neighbor would say, "If you think you can handle it, sal si puedes. Fight him in the street."

The second version developed because the streets were unpaved.

When the rainy season started, people who thought ahead parked their cars on Jackson Street. They would say to the ones stuck in the mud, "Sal si puedes, get out if you can."

Later a sociological reason was given—get out if you can financially—but I doubt that version. In those days, people were not going any place. They had deep roots there. If they did move out, they moved to some other barrio, but they were always coming back for visits.

When we first arrived in Sal Si Puedes, our problem was getting in, not out.

As people were just returning from the Mayfair Packing Company, my mother asked the ladies whether there was a house or a place or a room where we could stay that night. Our two cars, loaded with mattresses, baggage, and kids, told everyone a familiar story. But the answer was always the same. They were too crowded. There was no room.

Finally one lady told her of an old man who might have a room. "But he's crazy," she said.

"He's not very well, Don Pedro," someone else warned.

"Well, we'll chance it. See what happens. I have to put my children somewhere tonight," my mother said.

We were told nobody liked Pedro in the barrio. He was supposed to be a mean, tough guy who didn't like children and chased them out of his yard. He had fruit trees, and when they tried to steal the fruit, he would hit them.

But when my mother, who could make friends with anybody, talked to him, Don Pedro agreed to let us have a room which he had rented to a Chilean schoolteacher named Manuel. Although the Chilean got very angry at having to move, Don Pedro insisted.

"This family can't stay out in the street, Manuel. You move out of this room and use the little room. They're going to take this room," he said.

The room we got was about ten by twelve feet, and there were about eleven of us counting my uncle, aunt, and some cousins. The boys slept on one side, the girls on the other. We even kept our belongings there, but we didn't have a choice. At most we had five dollars left.

Behind the house there was an old broken-down garage which shook all over when you opened the door and walked in. We used it as a kitchen. It has an earthen floor, and in the middle was an old tub we used for a stove, burning wood in it and putting a makeshift grill on top. The smoke could get out through the cracks in the walls and through the open doorway.

Later that day, after we moved in, we walked to the little corner store, and the lady there asked, "Are you staying here?"

"Oh, yes, we live con Don Pedrito," my mother said.

"Oh, God! With Don Pedrito? Oh, no!" she cried, as if we should have nothing to do with that man. And she shook her head.

Early the next morning we went out to the cherry orchards, but it was the same story. Either they didn't have enough buckets, or they didn't have enough ladders, and always there were too many people.

Of course, the more people there were, the less they would pay. At first they had offered two cents a pound, then they cut it to one and a half cents. They could do anything they wanted to, because people just had to work.

For nearly two weeks we went out to the orchards, using the little money we made for beans, for gasoline, and for the six dollars a month rent we owed to Pedro Lopez. As it turned out Pedro was a good man, just a little eccentric. He thought we were well-mannered which, at first, surprised him. So he even got to like us.

We didn't get too much to eat. The work in the orchards was too erratic. But there was another Arizona couple living in that house who were on welfare. As they got more food than we did, they would sometimes give my mother some.

I remember once when Richard went out in the street yelling, "We don't have any food! We're poor!"

My mother got after him. "If you don't have any food, you keep your mouth shut. You don't say anything."

"Well, it's true," Richard insisted, his voice getting even louder, "We don't have any food. I'm hungry! I'm starving!"

My mother took him inside, and I can imagine how she felt.

After about two weeks the cherry harvest ended, and the apricots started. Everybody wanted to work at Mayfair Packing where they cut and pitted apricots for dry fruit. Since only about three families could work at each long wooden table, my dad would go there at 5:30 in the morning just to save us a place. As usual it was very crowded.

The fruit had to be cut all the way around, neatly, and pitted. The supervisor wouldn't let you cut it halfway around and then tear it apart. He was very fussy. Then the apricot halves had to be put neatly on long, six-foot wooden trays so they could all be sprinkled evenly with sulphur and dried.

Compared to the other families, we were inexperienced. We'd all cut as fast as we could, but we could only cut about three boxes a day. It wasn't that we were so slow, but we were so crowded together it made it hard to work. Because Lenny and Vicky were too small, they couldn't do any cutting, but they helped get rid of the pits.

Despite all our work, the family only made about thirty cents a day, so we ate a lot of apricots. To this day my dad hates them.

It was at that time that I first heard about the depression. I remember my mother told my cousin Petra that my father was very worried. She, too, was worried. As she told Petra, when we had the ranch, we at least had something to eat. So one day I asked my dad why we were getting so little money.

"Well, it's a crisis," he said. "A crisis. There's a depression." He said it resignedly, in a quiet, despairing way. Until then I didn't know what a depression was, but there were many others who had been living it and experiencing it for many years. And farm workers are living it still, though most other people today don't even realize it.

After the apricot harvest was over, there was no work until the prunes were ready. All my parents could do was wait, worry, and try to line up another job. One day a man who worked with us asked my dad, "Do you want to pick prunes?" He said he had this friend who was a labor contractor who would pay us $2.50 a ton in Gilroy about thirty miles south of San Jose.

"Yes, anything where we can make money. I need money for my children."

"You'll make a lot of money with your family there. You've got a big family, and they're all hard-working. Oh, yes, go to the prunes."

But after the arrangements were made, the man came back and told my dad, "I'm sorry. It's not $2.50. It's $2.25 a ton."

"No. I was going to go for $2.50, but I don't want to go for $2.25." There was something about the offer that made my dad suspicious. He continued looking for other jobs, but there were so many others in the same predicament, he was not having any luck.

Then the lady from Arizona in Pedro's house told him that she knew a nice Portuguese farmer on a hill east of San Jose. She suggested we try him. The orchards were on the sloping hillsides where there was less fruit, but the pay might be a little higher.

When she offered to take us there, my dad found the gas tank empty, and he didn't even have enough money for gas. He and Valeriano pooled their thirty-eight cents and spent it all for gas. Luckily it was only a dozen miles into the hills to Joe Medeiros' orchards.

Joe Medeiros was a wonderful man who was happy to hire us.

He also gave us a place in probably the best house we ever lived. It had hot water, butane, electricity, two bedrooms, and a clean toilet nearby. The house was a pleasant change from the cramped little room in Sal Si Puedes.

We were in the hills for about a month until the orchards were bare, working every day and making about twenty to thirty dollars a week. Medeiros liked us, and we promised to return next year. Before we left, Dad bought eight dollars' worth of groceries and got all kinds of things, including some meat that my mother dried and chopped up and fried with chili. She also went to a bargain basement in San Jose and bought Richard some school clothes for fifty cents.

We wanted to go see the San Francisco World's Fair which was only fifty miles away, but my dad said the traffic was too bad. Instead we headed south to Oxnard to work on the walnuts. We didn't know we were heading for one of the worst winters in our lives.

CHAPTER 3

Between the Dirt
and the Sky

CESAR CHAVEZ RECALLS

Picking walnuts was horrible work. Nowadays it's done mechanically. A caterpillar with a vibrator gets hold of the trunk and just shakes hell out of the tree. But in those days, long rough poles with metal hooks were used to shake the huge limbs. That was a man killer. While we were too small and too weak to do what a powerful machine does now, my dad was not. He'd wrestle the limbs and shake all the walnuts loose, using his whole weight and strength to strip one tree. When he got through, he'd have to sit down to take a break while we picked the walnuts off the ground.

Soon the walnut harvest was over, and we found ourselves again with no place to live. One of the ladies we met in the walnut orchards told my mother we could put up our little tent in a field behind her house. I don't remember her name, but I remember that she was involved in the big citrus strike people still talk about there. She would come in from the picket line, take off her shoes, and swear at the scabs, the strikebreakers.

Winter in Oxnard is wet and cold. When it isn't raining, the fog pours in thick from the Pacific leaving drops of water on everything it touches. It's no time to be living in a tent, because nothing ever quite dries out, and the cold damp air penetrates your clothes, your bedding, everything. But we had no choice. We were just fortunate enough to have permission to use that puddle-filled

55

lot. So we put up our tent—it was no more than eight feet long—and prepared for the long cold winter months.

To keep the rain water out that poured off the canvas, Dad dug a dike around the tent. Outside we had a fifty-gallon can we used for a stove, but unless we kept the wood dry inside the tent, we couldn't get a fire started.

Even without the wood inside, the tent was too small for all of us. There was room for Vicky, Rita, and my parents on fold-away cots, but Richard, Lenny, and I slept outside. We rigged up a bed with tall sticks at each corner, and a canvas slung over the top. There, in the middle of nothing, we slept in that field, just between the dirt and the sky.

Though we tried, we couldn't keep our shoes dry at night. We'd use a stick to push them way under the bed where there was a little dry spot, but they were always wet in the morning. Finally one day we solved the problem. We tied a stick horizontally between the two poles at the foot of the bed, wrapped our shoes and clothing, and used a little rope to hang the bundle from the stick under the canvas. In the morning we would get dressed on the bed and then jump off into the mud. Eventually my shoes fell apart, and I went barefoot.

Going to school without shoes was an ordeal. Kids can be devastating, and they would never let me forget it. We were going to Lady of Guadalupe School, one of two Catholic schools in Oxnard. One was for Mexicans while the other one, on the other side of town, was for Anglos.

This was the year Rita stopped going to school because she had no shoes or decent clothes. I guess Richard and I were not as sensitive, but I remember we had socks that didn't match, and my mother insisted we wear them.

"Oh, you've got to wear them, they're not that much different," she would say. Not that much different! One might be blue and another green. In school, of course, the kids look to see if there's a reason to make fun of you. When they did about our socks, Richard quickly had an answer.

"You're crazy. This is a new style. Everybody is starting to wear them like this." Soon many of the kids were wearing socks of different colors. I guess they had the same problems we did.

We also each had only one sweatshirt to wear, just that and no coat, a grey sweatshirt with a blue V-neck. How could I forget it? On weekends when we didn't go to school, my mother would take it off, and we'd stay shivering in the tent while she washed it.

One very mean kid, Fidel, the son of a labor contractor, constantly harassed us. "Why don't you change once in a while?" he would taunt us. He also made fun of us for not having a coat. Fidel was always well-dressed with a nice black leather jacket and gloves.

I felt pretty bad, and I felt mad, but I didn't know what to do. A kid can really be hurt that way. It was Richard who got back at him. "You're dumb," he said. "We have a lot of sweatshirts the same. My mother went and bought a lot, so we wear one every day."

Then Richard started to razz him. "You only have one leather jacket!"

"That's right," Fidel said.

"You only have one leather jacket. How come you don't bring different leather jackets? You only have one."

He had such a nice leather jacket and gloves we thought he was rich. His father, who was doing well as a labor contractor, ran a boarding house with lots of single beds. He not only made money charging people for their bed and board and their ride to work, but he also made money from his crew.

In fact my parents worked for him. Every morning about 5:00 they would leave with his crew looking for work picking peas. They had to pay him twenty-five cents for the ride. Sometimes they'd only make twenty-five cents a day which they had to give him. There were even days when they'd go out and couldn't find work, and they would still have to pay him the twenty-five cents. Usually my parents were gone about fourteen hours, but they only worked one or two. The rest of the time they were just waiting, waiting for work.

In 1958 when I was back in Oxnard with the CSO, I ran into Fidel's father again. At first I didn't know who he was. He was very old, broke, and just miserable. This lady, who was much younger than he was, came to see me for help. She turned out to be his wife. They were losing their house and were in bad shape.

We had to prove he was eligible for aid, so I went to his home to get his whole history. His name didn't ring a bell until I went over the record and saw he was a labor contractor. Then it hit me. I realized who he was, and I thought, should I help him?

Those earlier days came back vividly, and I thought again, should I help him? My first impulse was to drop it, thinking of all the things he had done to us. But then I saw him in the other room sitting in a chair, wrapped in a blanket and very thin. As I looked at him, I saw how helpless he was.

I didn't tell them I knew about him, I just said I knew how to help them. Eventually we settled the case, got him money for disability, got them some welfare payments, and got the real estate guy to wait for his payments—they were two payments behind.

So we helped them. Soon after that he died.

One day a lady told my mother, "If you get your car, I'll put some gas in it, and we'll get a few gunny sacks full of chili which we can dry out and do a lot of things with." We learned it was the custom when a crop ended to let the people pick the remains. After the beans were threshed, people would gather what was left. We could get five or six pounds of beans that way. The same with walnuts and green chilis.

The lady and my mother brought back seven or eight sacks full. We had a lot of chili to eat that year.

While there were still no jobs for my dad or uncle, Richard and I were always working. Actually I didn't look at it as work, it was a necessity. We would make jobs. At first we set up a little walnut shelling business. While people worked in the walnuts, they would steal some in a little bag or in their lunch pail. At the end of the season, buyers from Los Angeles would come, going down the streets shouting, "We buy nuts, we buy walnuts," in Spanish.

We learned they got more money if the walnuts were shelled into unbroken halves. So Richard and I set up a little business, and at night we'd crack walnuts which some lady brought to us.

On school days we would come home from school and do our homework quickly, roughly, to get it out of the way. I don't think I ever did mine, except once in a great while, but Richard did. Then we would go out to work. We weren't told to, we just knew we had to do it. We were really hustling to buy shoes or a sweater, but mostly we were hustling to buy food.

We did many things. We would chop wood for other people or go to the store for them. We would collect cigarette foil to sell to the junk man or walk along the railroad track and the packing sheds looking for empty bottles. We shined shoes and sold newspapers.

Every Sunday we would go to the Catholic church for the baptisms. It was the custom for the parents to throw money to the children outside. Richard and I worked as a team, one of us blocking so the other could get the coins. There was a lot of competition for those pennies.

On Saturday mornings we walked three miles to the old boxing and wrestling ring where they had matches on Friday nights. We helped clean the place up, making something like ten cents that way.

There was one thing we hated to miss—the Sunday movies with those Lone Ranger chapters. It was like the end of the world if we missed one of those, but it cost five cents to go to the show. That's how we finally got the idea of getting the job at the theater sweeping the floor every afternoon after school. For that work we got a nickel and a free pass.

When I compare my life at that time with my own boys at the same age, I have them beat. We were hustling all the time, working not for ourselves but for the family. But I could never get my wife Helen to do what my mother did, to have the children give her the money, to pool the money. If they earned a dollar, Helen wanted them to keep it. To me it meant a lot more, when I was a kid, to come and give my mother every cent. I felt proud to know that all of us did, and to know that there was some money for what we needed.

Even my father gave her his checks. It has only been recently that he started to rebel. Now that he is old, he gets his old-age pension check, and he keeps it. We find that so funny because he now has his own wallet with his own money, and he never did before.

It was about Christmastime in Oxnard when my mother met Natividad Rodriguez. She was also from Arizona. People in the neighborhood said she was a loudmouth, but after we met her we found out her heart was in the right place. She had some shacks that she rented, one right up against another, just like a Casbah.

It was raining dogs and cats one day when she saw us out in the tent.

"What in the hell are you doing out here?" she asked my mother. When she was told we didn't have any money to rent, she said, "Well, you better start packing up right now because you are going to move in with me!" Just like that.

"We don't have any money," my mother protested. "I really would like to move in, but we don't have any money. My husband isn't working."

"Who in hell is talking about money," she said. "Come with me. Let's go. Let's go see the house and see if you like it."

It was just a shack, just a roof, but there was a little heater inside, and it even had a wooden floor. We were excited. So my mother said it was fine, just beautiful.

"Okay, you move in right now. Just don't mention rent. Just forget it. If you have any money, you can pay me. If you don't have money, you don't have to pay me."

So we stayed there with a roof over our heads for the rest of the winter.

Because I was barefoot, Natividad gave me a pair of old shoes. Nobody threw things away then. Since these were two sizes too big, Richard said I looked like Mickey Mouse when I put them on, but I wore them to school.

Years later when I went back to Oxnard, Natividad was there still. She was crippled and really old. Later on she died. Her husband was younger than she was, and he became a very active member of CSO.

As the winter ended, my father finally got a good job in Conejo, about thirty miles from Oxnard. He worked for a labor contractor with about eleven other men, and I went with him. The job was cleaning those big wooden trays on which they put the apricots to dry.

This unlicensed labor contractor worked me and ordered me around while I worked right alongside the men doing as much work as they did, but he didn't pay me. My dad, who was paid between twenty-five and thirty cents an hour, made about thirty-two dollars in two weeks.

The worst winter of our lives so far was at an end, and we were ready to follow the crops. I don't know exactly how much money our family made our first year on the road, but it was probably about three hundred dollars. At this rate, there was no way we could get our land back.

CHAPTER 4

Labor Contractors

CESAR CHAVEZ RECALLS

There were many ways to find out where the jobs were. Sometimes we had friends who had been there before and, as the years went by, we would return to places where we had worked. But in most cases, we had to go through a labor contractor or a crew foreman.

When we first started, we'd hit a barrio with our car loaded down, and it was obvious we were looking for work. Sure enough, there'd be a labor contractor.

They had all kinds of tricks. When they offered a job, they would offer more money than they were paying, or they told us that we would make more money with the piece rate than we could possibly make. Housing was never what they said it was. "It's clean. It's got a garden. We've got a good camp," they would say. And always it was a pigpen. Always.

A contractor makes a little of his money from the employer, but he makes most of his money by cheating the workers. If he has fifteen laborers working by the hour, he steals fifteen minutes here, a half hour there. On payday he takes maybe an hour and a half out of their pay. When they argue, he says, "Well, it's a mistake. I'm sorry. I haven't got it here."

And it's not so much the money, it's the whole principle of being cheated out of something you had to sweat so hard to earn. It's not like somebody stealing fifteen cents from you, it's like somebody stealing fifteen cents worth of hard labor, which is an entirely different thing. It's a matter of destroying your manhood, taking away all your dignity.

Say we were picking potatoes. We'd have thirty sacks, but the contractor would only count twenty-seven. He waited until the truck was right behind him and started loading, so by the time he told us the total, the sacks were already on the truck. We knew how many there were, but we'd have to argue.

They were bad in all crops, but especially cotton. We picked cotton by hand then, and when a bag was full, we had to wait maybe a half hour to have it weighed because there were so many people waiting in line. As people were in a hurry—they wanted to go back to picking—the contractors were very tricky. They'd put the chain on the sack and call the weight before the picker could look.

One day Richard demanded to see the weight.

"Ah, there's so many people, get the hell out of here!"—except the contractor used worse words than that.

Richard knew he had over 100 pounds, but he was told something like 89. When my brother insisted on seeing the scale, the contractor tried to push him away. About that time, the contractor's son, who was a friend of Richard's, came up.

"You show this guy the weight if he wants to see it," he told his dad.

There were 112 pounds in the sack, and they were paying two and a half cents a pound. They were cheating everyone, but nobody questioned it.

The worst labor contractors sell cigarettes, beer, and candies for twice as much as they cost. Sometimes, when we had to borrow money to eat, they would lend five dollars, and we would pay them back double.

On payday we even had to argue with them for our pay. If payday was supposed to be Saturday, some of them didn't pay until Monday. We'd probably find him drunk in a bar, and he'd say, "Well, the boss didn't give me a check," even though we knew the grower had already paid him.

Many contractors make deductions on social security, then maybe report only half of what they take, or don't report any at all. Many times later in the CSO, I handled cases of retired workers where that had happened.

In many, many cases, workers have to buy their jobs, especially from unlicensed labor contractors who operate under the wing of the employer.

What happens with women is more disgusting. The labor contractor rides around in a truck or a brand new car with girls only sixteen, seventeen, eighteen years old. One day one girl is riding with him and gets a soft job doing nothing. Then he gets tired of her and lets her go, and he gets another one.

I've talked at meetings with women, and I say, "Never, never do that for a job!" But along the border, a lot of that corruption is going on, and they're young girls.

The tragedy is that those who have jobs have the lives of men and women in their hands. And those labor contractors have been exploiting our people for ages. I would say without hesitation that the most evil of all evils in the system is the farm labor contractor. Labor contracting is nothing more nor less than a remnant of the system of peonage.

The Chinese started this labor contracting, so goes the story. After the railroads were built, there were a lot of unemployed Chinese in cities such as San Francisco, Stockton, and Sacramento who began to go into agriculture. Some of the slicker ones, I imagine, would go to an employer, bring Chinese people from the city to work and back, and house them.

Then the tricks multiplied. The workers learn—they have only one way to go, to become a labor contractor. They do what others have done, plus other little tricks that they invent themselves. So it gets worse.

The system has become so vicious, our Union wants to eliminate labor contractors entirely. We want a Union hiring hall with the rules developed by the workers themselves to end all these pay-offs and other terrible actions that take place. Jobs in our hiring halls are given out on the basis of Union seniority, not favoritism or pay-offs, and the workers control the hiring hall to prevent abuses.

Our first year on the road, we really got taken by labor contractors. The second year we got a little bit better, and by the third year we knew more. We ended up being pretty sharp about defending ourselves. We could smell those guys and tried to avoid them whenever we could.

CHAPTER 5

Like Monkeys in a Cage

CESAR CHAVEZ RECALLS

Shortly after we left Oxnard, I got my first job paid by the hour. It was very difficult to get hired by the hour—most jobs were on a piece-rate basis—yet, although I was only twelve or thirteen and very small, I worked right alongside the men thinning cantaloupes in Brawley for a Japanese-American grower.

The Japanese-Americans were very difficult to work for, just slave drivers. Most people preferred to work for the big companies where supervision wasn't that strict, but after those jobs were filled, there was no place to go except the Japanese-Americans, who always paid a nickel less.

I remember some very unhappy episodes after Pearl Harbor, when the Japanese were relocated by the U.S. government. The Mexican farm workers rejoiced that the Japanese were put in internment camps just because the Japanese worked them so hard. In Brawley, people were celebrating. When I look back, I think it was an awful thing for the workers to have done, but to them it was like liberation.

Although the pay was twelve cents an hour, the grower paid me eight cents because I was small, but he expected me to do as much as the others. He didn't want us to put our knees on the ground because that slowed us down. He wanted us to move fast. But this was very difficult with a short-handle hoe, as our backs were bent double.

The rows of melons were from a half-mile to a mile long, with breaks for moving equipment or irrigation every eighth or sixteenth of a mile. Normally, when we reached a break, we would get up and stretch, look around, and take a drink of water. But this grower would be right there with a tin cup, so we could take a drink of water on the run and keep going. Sometimes he skipped a break; so we would move faster. It was torture.

On weekends we worked ten hours a day starting about 6:00 in the morning, while during the week I just would work after school.

The school in Brawley, also segregated, was worse than the one in Oxnard. They wouldn't let us speak Spanish. If we did, we were supposed to sit on a wooden bench in the back.

Out in the playground, our teacher, Mr. Hershey, would bring out baseballs, basketballs, or volleyballs, but we wouldn't play. We were more interested in the girls on the other side. By the time farm worker kids were fourteen, they were men of the world, like kids in the ghettos now. Some would have big hangovers, while others were probably on dope. Mr. Hershey would get angry because we wouldn't play and would line us up for the whole period. Then, at the end of forty-five minutes, he would march us back to class. He wanted us to line up like the infantry, but, of course, we wouldn't line up straight. Then he would yell, "You goddamn bastards, you remind me of the damn Mexican army."

And yet it was fortunate there was a lot of segregation then, because we got better treatment in segregated schools. We were not such oddballs. In integrated schools, where we were the only Mexicans, we were like monkeys in a cage. There were lots of racist remarks that still hurt my ears when I think of them. And we couldn't do anything except sit there and take it.

Because my mother was illiterate, she made us go to school. She would say, "I didn't learn, but you can learn, so you have to go." Even if we were in a place only one or two or three days, we'd go. Once Richard, Rita, and I counted the schools we each attended. The total was about thirty-seven, and I went to most of them. From the accumulation of all the things we had to go through, I can see now that we were really pushed back, beaten back, that education had nothing to do with our way of life.

School was just a nightmare. Probably the one I hated the most was in Fresno where Richard and I were the only two Mexicans in the whole school. When we went to the principal's office to register, we had to stand there almost all morning while he worked.

Later we listened to him on the phone saying, "Well, we've got these kids. I don't know what to do with them." Then he said, "Oh, yea, they're in the fourth grade, but they couldn't do that work." I thought to myself, how does he know I can't do that work?

And I heard him say things like, "What will we do with them?

You wouldn't want them in your class."—right in front of us! I don't think he really gave a damn. He didn't even realize what he was doing, which probably hurt more than if he did it calculatingly.

This happened many times. They would say, "the Mexicans," or "Yea, they're farm workers," or "these farm workers." Always their tone dripped with contempt.

Then when I came to class, I was frightened. I didn't know the lesson. I was given a seat, and the next morning I wasn't sure if that was really my seat. I was so frightened I was afraid to even ask the teacher for permission to go to the restroom. I didn't dare ask very often, as the kids laughed at my accent, the way I talked.

There were also a lot of challenges, mostly attempts at fights. I never fought back. I think Richard got into a fight once, but usually we talked ourselves out of it. I was probably too much of a politician to get into fights, and then there was my mother's influence. As I recall all her consejos, it becomes very clear that she built a strong foundation for me.

While life at school was very difficult, fortunately for us we were happy when we came home. We were right back into the womb, right back where we belonged.

Yet the houses we lived in, when we could afford one and get one, were dumps, shacks, or worse, places that had no water, often no electricity, and where we always were crowded. Even so, we would choose a house or even a garage that was in the community, the barrio, where we were free agents, rather than live in a labor camp.

When it was very hard to make a camp, Rita slept in the car. She was afraid of spiders, tarantulas, and snakes. If we came to an old house or an old barn, and she saw a spider while we were cleaning it up, she wouldn't sleep there. It would take her two or three days to move in. She'd sleep in the back seat of the car.

There were hundreds and hundreds of people in the camps, which were huge and all but bare of facilities. Everything was done outside, except sleeping, which was in tents. There were no washing facilities, just a spigot someplace or a stream where we went swimming to get clean during the summer.

The camps themselves were often very difficult to keep clean because of the numbers of people. Even if you did your part, you had to do more than your share, especially around the water faucet. There might be one faucet for fifty or a hundred families. And the toilets were always horrible, so miserable you couldn't go there.

Today camps are not quite as bad as they used to be, but they are bad. Not much has changed. The same labor camps which were used thirty years ago when we were on the road are still housing workers. And there is still the same exploitation of child labor and the same idea that farm workers are a different breed of people—humble, happy, built close to the ground.

We lived in one of those camps that second summer while we were picking raisins between Selma and Kingsburg in the San Joaquin Valley. One day I begged my dad all day to let me drive to town, but he said no. I knew how to drive. I would drive from the camp to work, inside the ranch, and back to the camp at noon for lunch. But I couldn't drive to town because I didn't have a license. I was only thirteen then.

So Rita and I went to town anyway without permission. As I was very small for my age, I had a pillow under me. Rita acted as spotter looking out for the police. We took the back streets because we didn't want to let the cops see us and succeeded in getting all the way into town undetected. Then, when I parked, I parked right in front of the police station. Luckily we didn't get caught.

We were going to a place in Kingsburg where they sold very good ice cream, but where they didn't let Mexicans eat. Actually that wasn't so uncommon. There were White Trade Only signs all over, though there were none at that place. But I knew. When Mexican kids went near the counter, one of the girls working there would come out from behind the counter and meet them, like my dog Boycott does now when a stranger walks into my home. "What do you want?" she would ask. "We want ice cream." "Okay, wait right here."

I never went inside; I'd go and send Rita and stay in the car. It's so shameful that this country would permit such things. To this day, when I go to a restaurant, even though I'm sure it's not going to happen, just before I get up to the door, I get this warning inside. Maybe, just maybe . . .

CHAPTER 6

Mired in Mendota

CESAR CHAVEZ RECALLS

We were nearing the end of our second summer when we got a job in a vineyard. Because it was in such bad shape, we were the only family working there, but we didn't know any better. The Johnson grass was way up and the vines were in such bad shape, it was hard to tell if they were vines or grass.

After a while we started complaining to my father, saying we should leave, but we were trapped. Each week, when my dad went to the contractor to get his pay, the guy just gave him a little money for food and promised him the rest later.

"I'd give you the money, but the winery hasn't paid me," he'd say.

We worked there every day of the week, even Saturdays and Sundays, for seven weeks. But my dad said we couldn't leave because we would not get any money out until the end of the season.

Very often labor contractors offer a "bonus." Actually it's not a a bonus. They withhold a certain percentage of your pay, and you have to stay to the end of the picking to collect it. It's to keep you there until all the fruit is harvested. Naturally, the more you pick, the less there is left, and the picking takes longer. Since you're paid by piecework, you make less and less. But then, you have that little extra money coming that keeps you there until the end of the harvest.

In this case, though, the contractor had all of our pay. At the end of the seventh week, when we went to get it, he had disappeared. After seven weeks of hard work, we were penniless.

My dad went to the labor commission, but they could do nothing. When they found the contractor, he had already spent all our money. Probably he drank it up.

But worse was to come. We had just enough gas to move maybe twenty-five miles to Mendota where there was a huge cotton camp packed with people. As all the cabins were full, we set up our tent.

We hoped to make enough money in the cotton to get to Brawley for the winter, but it was not to be. No sooner were we there than the rain started, and that was it. People couldn't even get into the fields to work. Although the rain would stop for a couple of days before starting again, the mud got so bad the cars were stuck in camp. Even a tractor came and got stuck. Luckily someone left one car on the road for emergencies.

Again my dad built a dike around our tent to keep the water out. For food, Richard and I walked along the irrigation canals cutting wild mustard greens, while on clear days my dad went fishing with a pitchfork somebody loaned him. Because of the rain, they had cut the water off in the irrigation canals, which had drained except by the gates. He would roll up his pants, take his shoes off, and just pitchfork big carp out of there.

I hate fish, I can't stand them, but those carp were really bad, all bones and full of mud. And poor Rita. She couldn't stand the smell of fish and would stay in the tent while they cooked outside. But we ate a lot of fish that winter.

Once in a while a group from Fresno would come up and distribute some food. There also were families on welfare who gave us a few things like surplus commodities, corn meal, and buckwheat they didn't like. My mother could bake excellent bread with it. Some gave us oatmeal we had to cook for about a half hour before we could eat it.

It was weeks before someone finally left the camp for the Imperial Valley, and we were able to move into a cabin. But even those shacks were damp. They had one window and no heat, no running water, and just one light bulb hanging down from the ceiling in the middle of the room. Those cabins were just empty shells surrounded by mud.

The central water faucet was all the way across camp from our cabin. We'd slosh through the mud to get there and bring back a bucketful. As for the outhouse, it was a quarter of a mile away.

The days stretched into weeks in this way until Christmas when the Migrant Ministry came from Fresno and brought us candy and presents. Considering everything, we thought we had a very good Christmas.

There was one incident in Mendota that I still remember, involving a farm worker who drank a lot. One day he had a big hangover, and his wife chased him out of the house. He was really shaking when he came over to our door and knocked.

My father refused to give him money. "He's just a wino," he said.

"Librado, I have to give to him," my mother insisted. "He might die of the hangover." And she gave him what she had.

All my dad said was "The next time a wino comes to the door, I'm not going to give him a penny."

It's amazing that Dad put up with it. That's what is really amazing. My mother was always like that. On the road, no matter how badly off we were, she would never let us pass a guy or a family in trouble. Never. During the Second World War, we began to travel in groups. We'd pick up families that were new, that had just been dumped into the migrant stream. After we sort of gave them an apprenticeship, they felt confident, and they'd take off.

My mother did a lot of this work. I didn't realize how important it was until years later. I didn't even understand what she was doing. In fact, I didn't particularly like the idea very much. The things she did, being unlettered, were really amazing, just dealing with the problems and trying to help people. And my dad gave her the backing that she needed.

We didn't get anybody to help us like that in the beginning. That's why we suffered so much, but my mother would tell us, "You always have to help the needy, and God will help you."

After I was married, I used to pick up families, too, until one day Helen said, "Look, I'm going to have a rule here. I want to be part of the decision making." I would pick them up when I was in CSO. We found this family once, stranded in a truck with about fifteen kids. We put them in the house, and they swiped everything we had. That just about killed me. That was the last time we had families in the house.

As for our stay in Mendota, we were stuck in that camp for forty days. Finally we made enough to get to Brawley where there was winter work picking cabbage, broccoli, and carrots. It was crowded there, too, but it was all there was.

RITA CHAVEZ MEDINA RECALLS

After being stuck in Mendota, we spent the rest of that winter in Brawley where Cesar, Richard, and my sister went to school. I didn't. My mother and I used to tie carrots in the field. We would leave about 3:00 in the morning in order to get a space to go to work. We would start work with headlights from cars and tractors.

It gets hot very early—well over a hundred degrees—and we couldn't work when it was hot, but we stayed in the fields in the shade until it got cool, and then we would start working again until we couldn't see at night.

In those days they had raffia, that grasslike string, to tie the carrots with, and we had to buy it by the pound. It was so expensive we'd soak it, then split it into four strands so that it would go much farther. Later they let that go, and we used wire.

We tied bunches by the dozen, and then we crated them; I think we got about five cents a dozen. My mother and I made about three dollars a day, and we had to pay three dollars a week to the person that gave us the ride there, plus our lunch. After we got home, about 6:00, we would cook, clean the house, and do all the chores.

On Saturdays and Sundays we would take the boys, Cesar and Richard, so they could help us. You needed the whole family in order to earn a little.

So I did carrots and hoeing for lettuce, watermelons, and cantaloupes. We used to cover cantaloupes in January with some kind of paper or plastic so the frost wouldn't hurt them. I did that a lot. And we did all the hoeing with the long hoe and the short hoe, trimming and thinning, everything.

Because in the field most of the work was piecework, we set a goal every day. It was Cesar who proposed it. He would say the amount, and we'd agree with him. Then we didn't quit until we reached it. My father'd say, "Let's go, it's late, and I am tired," and Cesar would say, "No, go sit in the car. We won't go until we make what we said." And we didn't. But Dad was old by then. By the time we were teen-agers he was reaching sixty.

We never went to work early, once jobs were easier to find. Other families would start at 5:00 in the morning, but our start would be 9:00 or 8:30. My dad never pushed us. He'd say, "Anything you can do is fine with me." He never said, "Well, you have to do so much today," or "Don't rest." We saw other families that did. "Don't sit down. Don't rest." Push, push. He never was that way. Maybe that's why we wanted to work. He taught us everything we knew, how to work, how to be honest with our work, and all of this.

My younger sister Vicky was the one who didn't care to work too much. Well, she was younger, too. But I remember Cesar would say, "Get up and work and help us," and she would say, "You help. You're dumb. I'm not going to help." So my father would say, "Oh, I'll work for her. Don't bother her. She's just little."

When we look back now to those days, Vicky just laughs. "I was lazy. I never did like to work." But Lenny, my younger brother, was just a little eager beaver. He'd get on there, and he didn't want anybody to beat him. He'd just go thrashing in.

I was the same. I'd rather go and work than stay at home. But I couldn't do a man's work. When we were picking tomatoes, I would just fill in the buckets, and Richard or Cesar would carry them for me. They wouldn't let me pick up heavy stuff. Same thing when we were picking peas or string beans. I never carried them out of the fields. They would.

Boy, it was hot out in the fields! And we had no water facilities and no toilets. We carried our own water in jugs, the type you get vinegar or apple cider in, and we'd wrap a gunny sack and wet it, real wet, and cool the water off. That's the only water we had. We kept it under shade, and it stayed cool. But then we'd run out of water, and we'd have to go all the way up to the farm to get some—maybe a mile away—and all the way back. You would spend about an hour going to get it, and all that was lost time. When you are working by piece rate, anything is lost time.

I remember Lenny would say, "I don't want to be the water man." But my father would always make him carry the water.

In 1942 my father got in a car accident. He was riding with a man, and his chest was injured. He wasn't in the hospital, but he did have to go to a doctor. The accident put him out of work for about a month or so.

That was also the year Cesar graduated from school, and he told my mother, "From now on, Mother, you're not going to step one foot out of the house to work anymore!"

So my mom said, "No, I want you to go to high school."

He said, "No, I'd rather not go to school. I'd rather see you home." She was pretty old, too. So she just stayed home and did the cleaning and the washing and the cooking, and we used to work.

CHAPTER 7

A Trail of Crops

All of us had the same reason why we didn't go to high school. After my dad was in an automobile accident, my mother had to go to the fields and so did Rita. No one had to tell me how bad off we were. I saw how hard they worked in the fields. It was an automatic thing for me to say, I'll go work, and I'll go to high school in two years.

But I never got there.

All of us had this decision—not only us, but most migrants. The only thing that has changed today is that migrants can at least go to a high school for a year or so before they must drop out. In those days, we couldn't even go into high school. But they drop out today for the same reason we didn't even enroll. It's an economic reason entirely.

I can't remember our other migrant years as well as the first two. As we moved around, they blurred. The crops changed and we kept moving. There was a time for planting, and a time for thinning, and an endless variety of harvests up and down the state, along the coast and in the interior valleys.

Some jobs were easy, and some were hard, but the worst—a man killer—was topping sugar beets. I was around sixteen or seventeen when I first topped beets in the Sacramento Valley. Those beets grew big, some of them weighing fifteen pounds. The soil, which was almost always clay, was wet and stuck to the beet as it was pulled out of the ground. My hand would split between the thumb and index finger as I pulled, and the stooping also was really painful.

73

After uprooting the beet, I topped the green off with a knife like a machete and tossed the beet on a pile between the rows. Then when the truck came, I loaded the beets by hand. Nowadays, all that work is done by machine.

Other hard jobs were thinning lettuce and sugar beets during the winter. Both were just like threads, the plants so small that when I looked at one, there might be ten plants there so close together all I could do was pull them out by hand.

I would chop out a space with the short-handle hoe in the right hand while I felt with my left to pull out all but one plant as I made the next chop. There was a rhythm, it went very fast. It had to, it was all piece rate, so much by acre, so much a row. It was really inhuman.

Every time I see lettuce, that's the first thing I think of, some human being had to thin it. And it's just like being nailed to a cross. You have to walk twisted, as you're stooped over, facing the row, and walking perpendicular to it. You are always trying to find the best position because you can't walk completely sideways, it's too difficult, and if you turn the other way, you can't thin.

Workers are still seen thinning by hand along Highway 101 past Salinas where the big ranches are. But it's a little different today, as they use pregerminated seeds planted in single lines instead of planting strips of seeds along a row. Even with that difference, though, thinning is still rough.

Another hard job was planting onions in January. First we had to take the seedlings, which were little bigger than a match stick, and clean, trim, and pack them in peat moss. We didn't get paid for that. It was done after working hours; so we could spend all day planting.

In the field we pulled the seedlings out of the patch and pushed them into the ground four inches apart, just like dealing cards— one, two, three, four—no rest, just walking fast, bent over, to push the plants in. We had to make the hole with one finger and stick the plant in there. Some farms had good land, which was lucky, but others had bullheads, little thorny things that punctured our fingers. It hurt, but we couldn't stop. We had to make that acre.

The rows were about six inches apart and a quarter-mile long, and the furrows, not more than eighteen inches wide, had rough clods that made it hard to walk. We could make about three dollars a day planting a half a mile. And our backs hurt all day long. Onions and carrots still are the worst paid crops, because they come during the winter when the work is very scarce.

Many things in farm labor are terrible, like going under the vines that are sprayed with sulphur and other pesticides. You have to touch those leaves and inhale that poison. Then there are the heat and the short-handle hoes and the stooping over. So many jobs require stooping. They should find a way of doing this work that will leave the human being whole.

I think it can be done, but it won't be until one of two things happen. Either the employers begin to see the workers as human beings, or the workers organize against the employers and demand changes.

I think this is where the employer shows the most contempt for his workers. For example, I think growers use short-handle hoes because they don't give a damn about human beings, they look at human beings as implements. If they had any consideration for the torture that people go through, they would give up the short-handle hoe. All that stooping is one reason farm workers die before they're fifty.

I remember when I was young, I'd come home, and I'd go to bed for a little while, and I'd be ready to go. But my dad couldn't do that. He'd stay there, and sometimes he couldn't get up to eat. That's true of a lot of men after they get past thirty-five. I remember my mom returning from work and going to bed. She didn't want to hear or see anything.

If the work can't be done with a long hoe, then it shouldn't be done. They can find a way. Growers talk of automation as a way of trying to scare people away from the Union. Others talk of automation in terms of throwing people out of work. But there are some jobs that should be automated, and we should help automate them, jobs that aren't fit for even a beast of burden, much less men.

The beet and cotton industries are now automated, and they should be. I remember young girls weighing 80 or 90 pounds carrying 110, 120 pound sacks of cotton. They carried those sacks not only to the scales but up ladders, way up, and then dumped them. I never understood how they could do it.

At some point in those years I began to take over, but not everything because my dad wouldn't permit it. He knew how much I could handle. The first thing I did was take over the driving, bit by bit, until I was doing it all. Because I had to work on the car and fix it, too, I didn't like that added responsibility. Mechanically I'm no good. But Richard was. He began to learn how to set spark plugs, and do the minor things like lubricate and oil the car.

Then I began to take on other responsibilities, and I liked it.

I began to set the quotas and choose the places. If it was a Saturday and there was going to be a dance, the quota would be a little lower so we could get out of there. While my dad never pushed us on the job, pretty soon I was talking about how to work better and faster.

There's a lot more skill in farm labor than most people realize. For example, grapes. Those without skill are going to cut a lot of green ones. Apricots are difficult, too. When the sun hits them early in the morning and late in the afternoon, they all look ripe. But once they're cut and dumped in the box, they look as green as lettuce. Prunes and wine grapes are different. All that's needed is a good strong back, a lot of stamina, a lot of strength. But apricots, table grapes, plums, and other fruit, where picking is done selectively, take skill.

I made a point of talking to the family about how to do a job better and faster to make more money. We were always finding ways of doing it more easily, telling each other little secrets we discovered.

We did not pick the same crops every year, but there was a pattern. Most winters we spent in Brawley where there were carrots, mustard, and peas. I did cabbage and lettuce in January, picking or working it, tying or loading it on a trailer. Then a little later we capped cantaloupe and watermelon, putting a wax paper over the plant to keep it from freezing and to keep the ground warm, just like an individual hothouse for every plant. When it got warmer, we came back, took the cap off, worked the ground around the plants, and thinned them, using a short-handle hoe.

Probably one of the worst jobs was the broccoli. We were in water and mud up to our necks and our hands got frozen. We had to cut it and throw it on a trailer, cut and throw, cut and throw. We slipped around in the mud, and we were wet. I didn't have any boots, just shoes on. Those crops were in December through March. In January to March there also were the cauliflower, mustard greens, onions, carrots, cabbage, and lettuce.

Then we worked in the watermelon, just picking up the vines which grew in the irrigation ditches and training them away from the ditches. The melons started in May, and I would work in the sheds for a labor contractor who was related to us.

In late May we had two or three options, Oxnard for beans, Beaumont for cherries, or the Hemet area for apricots, places that no longer have much or any of those crops. I think we did all at one time or other. Most of the time my dad would leave it up to us. "Do you think you'll like it?" he would ask.

We started making the apricots in Moorepark where they pick them up from the ground, just like prunes. In San Jose, on the other hand, we had to climb a ladder.

That would be the early part of summer. From there we had all kinds of options. We never did asparagus, and we only did figs once. The milk of the fig eats through your skin like acid. Some people put grease on their hands, but we couldn't do that. It was just awful.

We worked in lima beans, corn, and chili peppers, picked fresh lima beans for fifty cents a basket. Then in August we had grapes, prunes, cucumbers, and tomatoes. Those go into September and part of October. We would go before those crops started and wait in a camp until they were ready. For example there were raisin grapes about ten miles beyond Fresno. We had to be there at least a week in advance, or we couldn't get a job. That was a week of lost time, sometimes more, with no pay whatsoever.

Then we did cotton from October through Christmas. I just hated it. It was very hard work, but there was nothing else. After the cotton, just like ducks, we usually went back to Brawley to start with the crops in January.

So we traveled from the Imperial Valley in the south as far north as Sacramento and San Jose.

CHAPTER 8

Unions and My Father

CESAR CHAVEZ RECALLS

"You can't marry a job," my dad used to say. "You can marry a woman, but you can't marry a job."

I don't want to suggest we were that radical, but I know we were probably one of the strikingest families in California, the first ones to leave the fields if anybody shouted "Huelga!"—which is Spanish for "Strike!"

Once in Wasco we were picking cotton when another farm worker started arguing he was being shortchanged in weight. We argued for the worker, and when he quit, we quit, too. We quit many jobs over such arguments. We'd make a big issue of it.

If any family felt something was wrong and stopped working, we immediately joined them even if we didn't know them. And if the grower didn't correct what was wrong, then they would leave, and we'd leave.

We weren't afraid to strike, but those strikes weren't on the picket line. We would leave and try to take as many people as we could and go work elsewhere. When we felt something was wrong, we stood up against it. We did that many, many times.

We were constantly fighting against things that most people would probably accept because they didn't have that kind of life we had in the beginning, that strong family life and family ties which we would not let anyone break.

It made no difference whether Rita said it, or Richard or I, if one of us felt very strongly there was something wrong, my dad said, "Okay, let's go." There was no question. Our dignity meant

78

more than money. I remember times when it was a little hard to quit—we needed the money—but we didn't consider that. Our attitude was, we have to do it, and we accepted it.

But if you work and do your job, if you're not lazy, you always have them over a barrel, as you have something to bargain with —your own labor.

Our first direct experience with a union strike was in 1948, I think. We were picking cotton near Wasco in the southern San Joaquin Valley when a car caravan came by with flags, a bugle, and loud-speakers. They didn't stop. They just went slowly by, but you couldn't understand what they were saying, it was too loud. People stopped working, looked, and raised their ears like rabbits, and my dad said, "Let's go!"

We left right away. A sizable group left, but not the majority. Most of the people said, "Well, I won't come tomorrow."

We got in our cars and criss-crossed the whole valley driving by fields, tooting the horns, and asking others to join. We wound up in Corcoran in the evening and had a rally there.

As I recall, we struck for a few days, and then people began to leave the strike. Pretty soon there were just a handful of us, and the strike was over.

But those first few days we were really faced with a lot of people, big rallies. I think all of us were geared to getting large crowds out there. Somehow it was planted in our minds that if we didn't get a lot of people, we weren't going to win. So the moment the numbers dropped, people got frightened and began to leave. It's a very difficult thing to overcome. People are very poor, and they can't stay off work for long.

That strike was the one called by the National Farm Labor Union which involved several thousand cotton pickers in Kern, Tulare, King, and Fresno Counties. I lived in Delano then, but most of the activity was around Corcoran, because that's where the biggest acreage in cotton was. The growers had cut the wage, and the union struck to restore it to three dollars per one hundred pounds. Since I was just a worker, I didn't know what was happening up on top.

It was several years earlier, in 1941, that I had the first contact with a union when my dad and uncle were working at a dry fruit shed in San Jose. The CIO was organizing the shed workers, and Mexican and Anglo organizers came to our house to talk to my dad, uncle, and a couple of my cousins. My mother was very nervous, probably because she associated unions with violence. Her nervousness was similar to what we encounter now with some

of our members when we come around at the beginning of a strike
—they're wondering if they will lose their jobs. I wanted to hear
what was said, but they put me out. My dad thought I shouldn't
be there.

I remember my dad talking later one evening. He was very
impressed with the union, and that impressed me. He was saying
that the union representative had scolded him for having too
large a load on a hand dolly, although, he said, "It's not heavy. I
could handle even more than that." He was also impressed by the
ten-minute break. He was saying, "It's just fantastic. You get ten
minutes twice a day!"

My mom asked, "Well, what do the men do?" and he said,
"Oh, just go out and smoke."

"And what do you do?" my mom asked, as my dad didn't
smoke.

"Oh, I eat my candy," my dad answered.

We got the same reaction not so long ago at the Schenley workers yard, when we first got our contract. The workers wanted the
ten-minute break, but they were amazed by it, even these days,
when American workers in other industries just take it for granted.

My dad paid dues to several unions. In fact he was paying dues
to our rival union when I started this group. But I know Dad
didn't know that much about unions, except that they were good.
He joined the Tobacco Workers, the Cannery Workers, the National Farm Labor Union, the Packing House Workers, and the
Agricultural Workers Organizing Committee.

I must have gotten interested in unions through him. I'm sure
I didn't get it from my mother. For some reason I read more about
unions than I read about other things in the newspapers. I never
understood what a strike really was, but I knew when a strike was
going on, and I knew about the big fight that Walter Reuther
had to get elected in the United Auto Workers and the big campaign for the presidency of the CIO. I'd follow that in the paper
every day.

At one time I could name most of the international presidents.
I tended to look at unions like small governments in the country.
Actually, at the time, I didn't realize I was that interested, but my
first friend in Delano, Robert Jiminez, once told me, "Damn it,
all you do is read about those damn labor unions." I also remember he told somebody once, "Oh, Cesar, he knows all about the
labor unions."

I didn't really. I just knew the names. What I didn't know was
anything of the real guts of unions. And I never paid dues to any
union.

CHAPTER 9

Pachuco Days

CESAR CHAVEZ RECALLS

When I became a teen-ager I began to rebel about certain things. For example, I rebelled against the home remedies and herbs my mother used. I thought no one knew anything but doctors. And I rebelled against Mexican music. This was the age of the big bands, and I really went for Duke Ellington and Billy Eckstine. We would travel from Delano to Fresno to hear the bands, and in San Jose they had them every week.

I also rebelled against some of the religious customs, like the promesa or manda, where you ask the favor of a saint and promise to visit the chapel of the saint's church. It wasn't that I was strong in the church's more formal teachings by then, but just that I didn't approve of it.

There were other things, too. When I was younger, I really liked being with older people. But when I became a teen-ager, I got into that trap of thinking they were dull and uninteresting. Nowadays I again find older people very interesting when I have time to listen. They can tell you many important things.

And then I rebelled at the conventional way of dressing. I once said I was a pachuco, and I had a very difficult time explaining it. The pachucos wore their hair long, in a duck-tail cut; they wore pegged pants and long coats, long key chains, and a pegged, broad flat hat. Today what people remember are the pachuco riots in the forties in San Jose, Oakland, and Delano. But those riots were not the same as when the barrios and ghettos exploded in the sixties. The rioters were not Mexican. They were soldiers, marines, and sailors who raided the barrios attacking the pachucos.

I saw clippings of the Los Angeles papers with pictures of pachuco kids with pants torn to the thighs by police. If they had long hair, police clipped them, and if their coats were long, police cut them short. The pachucos would wear shoes with very thick soles, and police would take the soles off. Today police still act pretty much the same way toward nonconformists. They were pachucos then. Now they're hippies.

Not so long ago a Chicano came from Los Angeles to see me. He was full of tattoos. "I want to write something of when you were a pachuco," he said. "We want to make a movie. I want to show how a guy who used to be a pachuco in the streets rose to be a great leader of the barrios."

I looked at him surprised and started to protest.

"Don't worry," he interrupted, "I'm not going to write anything about dope."

He apparently assumed our pachuco days were like his. But all we did was wear some of the pachuco clothes, the pegged pants and the long coat. We didn't affect the key chain, or the hat, or the dope.

We needed a lot of guts to wear those pants, and we had to be rebellious to do it, because the police and a few of the older people would harass us. But then it was the style, and I wasn't going to be a square. All the guys I knew liked that style, and I would have felt pretty stupid walking around dressed differently. At Delano dances, for example, all the squares sat across the room from us, and we had a lot more fun than they did.

My mother wasn't violently opposed to our wearing those clothes, though she and my dad didn't like it much, but little old ladies would be afraid of us. And in Delano there was a whole group in the Mexican-American community who opposed pachuco clothes.

One day I went over to the driver's license department with my chukes on. As I went in, one of two ladies remarked, "I'd never let my son wear those! That monkey suit!"

They were having trouble with their license. So after I got mine, I went over to help them.

"Oh, what are you wearing those pants for?" one asked. "You're so well-mannered!"

" 'Cause I like to wear them," I said.

"Yea, but people say . . ."

"I don't care what people say," I said. "You said something about me. I don't care. I'm still helping you." It embarrassed them, but their reaction was typical.

The hard thing, though, was the police. We were so gun shy. For sure the cops would stop you anyplace, any time, and we were prepared for that. But when they stopped us at the theater in Merced, it was humiliating. We were thinking of going to the show, but we weren't sure. We were just looking around to see what was playing. A cop, who was just passing by, saw us and got on his radio. Soon two or three police cars arrived, and the officers lined us up against the wall. It was a bad scene. They made us take our shoes off, they just almost undressed us there. Then they gave us about ten minutes to get out of town.

We were a minority group of a minority group. So, in a way, we were challenging cops by being with two or three friends and dressing sharp. But in those days I was prepared for any sacrifice to be able to dress the way I wanted to dress. I thought it looked sharp and neat, and it was the style.

But our rebellion wasn't the kind of rebellion they have today —students and young people rebelling against society. That's a good thing. Today these kids have an idea. We didn't know exactly what was happening. We were a step behind them. It's all a matter of evolution.

And my children are not inhibited as we were. I saw my daughter Sylvia once seated next to a couple of white girls in high school. When she stood up, they made fun about her being Mexican. She just turned on them and answered back in strong terms. She didn't know I was there.

I remember I couldn't speak when something like that happened to me. I would cry or just walk away. But I remember my daughters Sylvia and Linda standing there with about ten white girls, taking them on for twenty minutes. Not an ounce of inhibition. Finally the other girls walked away. Sylvia was laughing, and she said something in Spanish, clearly making fun of them. We would have never done that. We just could never.

We had never experienced discrimination in Yuma when we lived there, but we encountered White Trade Only signs all over California. In Los Angeles we got off the highway and went to East Los Angeles, while in Delano we'd go to Mexican town. We didn't challenge it. Then in the forties we went back to visit Yuma, and there were those signs all over the place, White Trade Only.

My rebellion as a teen-ager wasn't against that, though. It was against Mexican music, my mother's herbs, and some of her religious ideas. But I didn't say I wasn't a Mexican. I didn't feel I wasn't. In fact I was pretty strong about being Mexican. Then after I got married, all of a sudden I began to appreciate mariachis and all those other things I was rebelling against. As I look back, I now understand what was happening. Everywhere we went, to school, to church, to the movies, there was this attack on our culture and our language, an attempt to make us conform to the "American way." What a sin!

I don't know why I joined the navy in 1944; I think mostly to get away from farm labor. I was doing sugar beet thinning, the worst kind of backbreaking job, and I remember telling my father, "Dad, I've had it!"

Neither my mother nor my dad wanted me to go, but I joined up anyway. It was wartime. I suppose my views were pretty much the views of most members of a minority group. They really don't want to serve, but they feel this awesome power above them that's forcing them to do it.

I had little choice, either get drafted or sign up. Since I wanted even less to go into the army, I enlisted in the navy when I was still seventeen.

Those two years were the worst of my life: this regimentation, this super authority that somehow somebody has the right to move you around like a piece of equipment. It's worse than being in prison. And there was lots of discrimination. Before the war, the navy had blacks and Filipinos who were given kitchen jobs, but no Mexicans. The only black man I ever saw who was better than a steward was a painter.

The Mexican-Americans were mostly deck hands. That's what I was. Most of my duty was in small boats, while part of it was land-based. I also was on a crew transport which went to the Mariana Islands, but I never was engaged in combat.

The food in the navy was terrible. I noticed that the Anglos would call the food all kinds of dirty names, and then eat it. On the other hand, if Mexicans didn't like the food, they just didn't eat it. I couldn't understand how Anglos could eat stuff they called by such names.

It was while I was in the navy that the theater incident happened in Delano, a story that's been twisted when it's been told before. I was home with a couple of navy guys from Texas on a seventy-two-hour pass, and we weren't in uniform.

For a long time, movie theaters throughout the San Joaquin Valley were segregated. It was just accepted by the Mexicans then. In Delano, the quarter-section on the right was reserved for Mexicans, blacks, and Filipinos, while Anglos and Japanese sat elsewhere. It had been like that since the theater was built, I guess.

This time something told me that I shouldn't accept such discrimination. It wasn't a question of sitting elsewhere because it was more comfortable. It was just a question that I wanted a free choice of where I wanted to be. I decided to challenge the rule, even though I was very frightened. Instead of sitting on the right, I sat down on the left.

When I was asked to move to the other section, I refused, and the police took me to jail. They didn't book me; they kept me there about an hour. The desk sergeant didn't know with what to charge me. He made a couple of calls. I would guess he called the chief of police and the judge because that's a natural thing to do.

The first call I think was to the chief. I don't know what was said, but the chief probably said, "What about drunk?" because the sergeant said, "Well, he's not drunk," and then he said, "Well, he wasn't really disturbing the peace." Then I suppose he called a judge or the city attorney. Finally the sergeant gave me a lecture and let me go. He tried to scare me about putting me in jail for life, the typical intimidation they use.

I was angry at what happened, but I didn't know then how to proceed. It was the first time I had challenged rules so brazenly, but in our own way my family had been challenging the growers for some time. That was part of life.

CHAPTER 10

Marriage

CESAR CHAVEZ RECALLS

I first met Helen when I was about fifteen. Our family had come to Delano for cotton during the fall, after stopping in Sacramento for tomatoes, and we were on the way back to Brawley in Imperial County. We couldn't find any housing in Delano, but there was a government camp, a tent city, in McFarland, and we stopped there.

The first couple of evenings I came to Delano to look around and went to this little malt shop, La Baratita, on Eleventh and Glenwood. There was a whole group of fellows and girls there. That's where I saw Helen the first time. I remember she had flowers in her hair.

After school she worked at the People's grocery store, and, of course, I became a very good customer. I started dating her. Since this was during the war, I often kid her that the only reason I went with her was that she saved cigarettes for me because they were very hard to get.

HELEN CHAVEZ RECALLS

I don't remember when I first met Cesar. That was a long time ago. I was going to Delano High School, and I must have been around fourteen or fifteen.

Both my parents were born in Mexico, and my father fought in the revolution. He would tell us about it, but we were very young. I was eleven when he died.

I was born in Brawley, but we were all raised in the Delano area, my two sisters, my four brothers, and I. For many years we lived on a ranch in McFarland where my mother and father both did field work. It was like horse stables that they fixed into housing, little one-room deals for a lot of families. My parents would chop cotton or do whatever work there was.

Cesar used to migrate and come by Delano every year. One day we were at a little sno-cone parlor eating sno-cones and listening to music when he came in with some other people. That's when I met him.

CESAR CHAVEZ RECALLS

Richard got married early in 1948, the first one of us to marry, and we were all surprised. Helen and I got married later that year in Reno, at the same time as my sister Rita, and then we had a church wedding in San Jose.

Just before getting married, I was in the cantaloupe harvest in Mettler near Bakersfield out in the desert. In those days every grower had a small shed to provide some shade. I worked there as a lidder putting lids on the boxes, working very fast using stripping and a hatchet. It's a highly skilled job and very demanding. I couldn't see Helen. In fact, for twenty-two days I never left the ranch. All I did was eat, sleep, and work about fourteen to eighteen hours each day. But I was lucky, because not long after that, the braceros took all those jobs, and we couldn't get them anymore.

After our wedding, Helen and I toured all the California missions from Sonoma to San Diego for about two weeks in the family car. I had saved a little money. The missions always have fascinated me. We also had hoped to see those in Mexico, but we didn't have the time or money. Instead, we came to Delano, where I worked in the grapes. Then, during the winter I picked cotton, a horrible experience.

We had a one-room shack without electricity or running water. It was bitterly cold, and we only had one of those little kerosene camping stoves, which we kept turned on day and night with water on it. But that stove didn't heat anything. We were miserable. When we stepped out of the shack, we stepped right into mud—thick, black clay. Since I was without a car, I had to ask for rides to jobs that were four, five, six, ten miles away from the camp.

I don't remember how long we stayed there, but we finally

borrowed money and went to San Jose where Richard was working on an apricot farm. He had a steady job and would fit me in
one or two days a week. The rest of the time I spent walking all
over town trying to find a job. I didn't even have money for the
streetcar. It was a terrible time, especially since Helen now had a
baby, our son Fernando.

What followed was even worse. We started sharecropping strawberries in Greenfield, in the foothills near San Jose. This family,
which had a seven-and-a-half acre farm, provided a small house for
my family and another small house for my parents, Lenny, and
Vicky. They also provided the fuel, electricity, and water and gave
us twenty-five dollars a week for groceries. That was it.

We planted the strawberries, picked them, and did all the work.
But it was a bad patch, really bad, and at the end of the season,
we had made no money.

For nearly two years we worked hard there without missing a
day, not even Christmas. Finally I left and made my dad break
the agreement. We were really being taken. We hadn't made a
dime.

By that time Helen and I had two children, Fernando and
Sylvia, born a year apart, and Helen was pregnant with Linda.
We rented a house from an aunt in San Jose and started looking
for a job. But we just couldn't find one anywhere. The best we
could do was pick string beans, making $1 or $1.50 a day and
working only a few hours because that was all the work there was.
Finally the employment office told us they wanted people up in
Crescent City, more than four hundred miles to the north.

We didn't even know where Crescent City was, and we had
never done any lumber work, but Richard, my cousin Manuel, two
other cousins, and I all got into a car and took off.

In the beginning it was very rough because we didn't know all
the tricks working in lumber. We worked so hard the first days
that when we came home, we couldn't eat or do anything. We
went right to bed. Even though we were young, the work on the
green lumber chain was just killing. Eventually we learned, and
it became easier.

After Richard built a little shack for us, we drove back to San
Jose to get our families. Linda was born in Crescent City and so
was Richard's son Freddy.

We stayed about a year and a half, then we got tired of the
winter weather. The constant rain was too much, so we returned
to San Jose where Richard became an apprentice carpenter, and I
got a job as a lumber handler in a mill.

CHAPTER 11

My Education Starts

CESAR CHAVEZ RECALLS

We thought the only way we could get out of the circle of poverty was to work our way up and send our kids to college. That's the trap most poor people get themselves into. It's easier for a person to just escape, to get out of poverty, than to change the situation.

We weren't saying then, we've got to organize a union. We weren't even asking why these conditions existed. We just felt they shouldn't be like they were. It was just a part of growing up, I guess. But, if later I hadn't encountered CSO, I wouldn't have known what was going on in the world. I got an education there.

Actually my education started when I met Father Donald McDonnell, who came to Sal Si Puedes because there was no Catholic church there, no priest, and hundreds of Mexican-Americans. We were some of the first members that joined his congregation for masses in a little Puerto Rican hall that was just a broken-down little shack.

Father McDonnell was about my age. We became great friends when I began to help him, doing a little carpentry work, cleaning up the place, getting some chairs, and painting some old benches. I also drove for him and helped him recite mass at the bracero camps and in the county jail.

One of the families that attended the masses was from Mexico, a lady and her daughter. As they were very poor, when her mother died, the girl came to see me to help with the burial. The first thing I thought was to have a collection and go to Father Mc-

89

Donnell to see if he could get the Catholic Charities to give some money.

There were a few others who had come in like that, and we'd helped them. This time, though, Father McDonnell said, "Why don't we do it ourselves?"

"Oh, Father, you're kidding," I said.

"No, we can do it. The law says . . . " And he reeled off what could be done. I didn't know anything about the law, so I said, "Well, if you're game, let's try it."

We borrowed an old litter, one of those army litters, took the daughter with us, and went to the county hospital to claim the body.

The lady at the hospital said, "You must be out of your minds. You can't do that! You got to go to an undertaker."

Father McDonnell said no, and he pulled out the health and welfare code and said, "Now look. The next of kin can claim the body." And that started an episode that lasted about three hours.

It was so ludicrous, I remember it very well. The lady said she'd call her supervisor in the hospital. The supervisor didn't know and called the hospital administrator. He didn't know and called the county counsel who said, "Well, yes, that's what it says, but I don't know." So he called the district attorney, who didn't know. He called the state attorney general.

In those days the attorney general was Pat Brown who later became governor, and he came back just like that, "Sure they have a right to claim the body."

We had to go into the cooler where the body was. The county hospital was not about to let us borrow their equipment, and they wouldn't let us get in the elevator with her.

That's where I hurt my back the first time, felt that sharp pain, when we were in the cooler and picked her up to put her on the stretcher. She was quite a heavy woman. We walked down two or three flights of stairs and out to the car, put her in the back of the station wagon, and took her home, a little shack near where I lived. The ladies came in, bathed the body, combed her, put on a new dress, put perfume on her and flowers and put her in the bed.

I think Richard made the coffin, and we placed the body in it and put the coffin on a couple of sawhorses. Father McDonnell celebrated the Rosary, and the next morning we had mass in that little shack. Then we got three three-quarter-inch water pipes. Four guys carried the casket and put it in the station wagon, using the pipes as rollers to roll it inside the car. The only money we spent was buying the land, $103 with tax and everything. The hole was dug, we lowered the body down by hand and covered the coffin ourselves.

Much later in CSO I did another burial in Brawley. Then after I started the Union, there was another case in Tulare. I threatened the funeral homes that, if they didn't provide a free funeral, I'd do it myself. So they gave us one free. I did that many times. I've never understood how people can spend so much money on funerals.

I began to spend more time with Father McDonnell. We had long talks about farm workers. I knew a lot about the work, but I didn't know anything about the economics, and I learned quite a bit from him.

He had a picture of a worker's shanty and a picture of a grower's mansion; a picture of a labor camp and a picture of a high-priced building in San Francisco owned by the same grower. When things were pointed out to me, I began to see, but I didn't learn everything the first time.

Everything he said was aimed at ways to solve the injustice. Later I went with him a couple of times to some strikes near Tracy and Stockton.

And then we did a lot of reading. That's when I started reading the Encyclicals, St. Francis, and Gandhi and having the case for attaining social justice explained. As Father McDonnell followed legislation very closely, he introduced me to the transcripts of the Senate LaFollette Committee hearings held in 1940 in Los Angeles. I remember three or four volumes on agriculture, describing the Associated Farmers, their terror and strikebreaking tactics, and their financing by banks, utilities, and big corporations. These things began to form a picture for me.

When I read the biography of St. Francis of Assissi, I was moved when he went before the Moslem prince and offered to walk through fire to end a bloody war. And I still remember how he talked and made friends with a wolf that had killed several men. St. Francis was a gentle and humble man.

In the St. Francis biography, there was a reference to Gandhi and others who practiced nonviolence. That was a theme that struck a very responsive chord, probably because of the foundation laid by my mother. So the next thing I read after St. Francis was the Louis Fischer biography of Gandhi.

Since then I've been greatly influenced by Gandhi's philosophy and have read a great deal about what he said and did. But in those days I knew very little about him except what I read in the papers and saw in newsreels. There was one scene I never forgot. Gandhi was going to a meeting with a high British official in India. There were throngs of people as he walked all but naked out of his little hut. Then he was filmed in his loincloth, sandals, and shawl walking up the steps of the palace.

Not too long ago I was speaking to a group of Indians including three who had worked with Gandhi. When I said I thought Gandhi was the most perfect man, not including Christ, they all laughed. When I asked them why they laughed, they asked, "What do you mean by perfect?"

I said I don't mean he was perfect like a saint in the sense that he didn't move. I said he was perfect in the sense that he wasn't afraid to move and make things happen. And he didn't ask people to do things he couldn't do himself.

I understand Gandhi more and more. To him duty was the first call. He had no compunction whatsoever about sending someone five hundred miles to take care of something, because he himself was willing to do it. I myself can't do all the things that I ask others to do, but then no one can try to imitate him, because it becomes false. You've got to take the whole philosophy and try to adapt it to your needs. I want to experiment with some of the things he did but not imitate him, because I don't think that can be done.

He had tremendous discipline, both personal and around him. He had all kinds of rules and insisted they be obeyed. So a group of thirty, forty, or a hundred men at the most was very effective, because they worked like a symphony. They were totally loyal to him. He wouldn't put up with anybody being half-loyal or 90 percent loyal. It was 100 percent loyal or nothing at all.

Then, of course, there were more personal things, the whole question of the spirit versus the body. He prepared himself for it by his diet, starving his body so that his spirit could overtake it, controlling the palate, then controlling the sex urge, then using all of his energies to do nothing but service. He was very tough with himself.

He believed that truth was vindicated, not by infliction of suffering on the opponent, but on oneself. That belief comes from Christ himself, the Sermon on the Mount, and further back from Jewish and Hindu traditions. There's no question that by setting such an example, you get others to do it. That is the real essence, but that is difficult. That's what separates ordinary men from great men. And we're all pretty ordinary men in those things.

I like the whole idea of sacrifice to do things. If they are done that way, they are more lasting. If they cost more, then we will value them more.

When we apply Gandhi's philosophy of nonviolence, it really forces us to think, really forces us to work hard. But it has power. It attracts the support of the people. I've learned that, if any movement is on the move, violence is the last thing wanted. Violence only seems necessary when people are desperate; frustration often leads to violence.

For example, a supermarket boycott is an effective nonviolent weapon. Fire is not. When a fire destroys a supermarket, the company collects the insurance and rebuilds the store bigger and better, and also marks off the loss on its income tax. But picket lines take away customers and reduce business, and there is no way for the store to compensate for that. It is driven by sheer economics to want to avoid picket lines.

Gandhi described his tactics as moral jujitsu—always hitting the opposition off-balance, but keeping his principles. His tactics of civil disobedience haven't hit this country on a massive scale, but they will. Anybody who comes out with the right way of doing it is going to throw the government into a real uproar. If they have a good issue, and they find a good vehicle for civil disobedience, they're going to be devastating.

Just imagine what would happen to this intricate government we have here. Look what happened with Gandhi's salt march and the civil disobedience that followed after it. He boycotted the salt so the government couldn't collect the tax, but then he showed the people how to make their own salt. He boycotted clothes coming in from England, but he turned around and showed the Indians how to make their own clothes.

I learned quite a bit from studying Gandhi, but the first practical steps I learned from the best organizer I know, Fred Ross. I first met him in Sal Si Puedes. He changed my life.

Book III

CRUSADERS IN THE BARRIOS

June 1952–March 1962

*"To carry on a hard-hitting program of civic action and militancy,"
Fred Ross once said, "you must have people who are of a certain tem-
perament, who just cannot live with themselves and see injustice in
front of them. They must go after it whenever they see it, no matter
how much time it takes and no matter how many sleepless nights of
worry."*

*Fred Ross was an organizer, a man of unusual skills, and a great
teacher looking for apt pupils as he moved across California organizing
in the barrios for the Industrial Areas Foundation. He discovered two
persons who fit his description—Cesar Chavez in San Jose in 1952
and Dolores Huerta in Stockton three years later.*

*Although twenty-five, Mrs. Huerta looked more like a teen-ager than a
mother of two toddlers. She was small, slender, with striking Indian
features and long, shiny black hair. Her tongue moved as swiftly as
her mind, and both left most other mortals in their wake.*

*Unlike Cesar Chavez, she had not followed the crops as a child, but
had lived most of her life in Stockton with her divorced mother who
ran a sixty-room hotel for farm workers. Her father worked in the
mines in New Mexico until he was black-listed for union activities.
Then he became a migrant farm worker and later served briefly in the
New Mexico State Assembly. Mrs. Huerta married at nineteen,
dropped out of college for a while and later got her teaching credentials. Her energies seemed limitless, and she became one of the driving
forces behind the Stockton Community Service Organization, despite
her constantly growing family.*

As for Cesar Chavez, at twenty-five he lacked the knowledge, the tools, and the power to change some of the conditions he experienced as a farm worker, and Ross, a tall, lanky Californian who looked the part of a hero in a cowboy Western—clean-cut, square of jaw, steady of gaze, soft of voice—appeared, as if from nowhere, to provide the knowledge and the tools.

Without skillful organizers, La Causa would have failed. And for both Chavez and Mrs. Huerta, CSO turned out to be a training ground that prepared them for major roles when the farm workers' union was formed.

CHAPTER 1

Fred Ross

Fred Ross never stopped working. He was very persistent, and it was lucky he was, because I never would have met him otherwise. I was trying to avoid him. It must have been in June 1952 when I came home from work one day, and Helen told me this gringo wanted to see me. That was enough to make me suspicious. We never heard anything from whites unless it was the police, or some sociologist from Stanford, San Jose State, or Berkeley coming to write about Sal Si Puedes. They'd ask all kinds of silly questions, like how did we eat our beans and tortillas. We felt it wasn't any of their business how we lived.

Helen was sure it was something good for us, maybe better jobs or more money, as this gringo had gotten our name from Alicia Hernandez, the public health nurse. Helen told me he had promised to be back that evening.

To avoid him I went across the street to Richard's house. Later I asked Helen what happened.

"He's coming back tomorrow," she said.

"Well, I'm not going to be here when he comes," I told her. And I wasn't. I just went to Richard's house again. "He must want something from us," I told Richard.

I watched him drive up, talk to Helen, and leave, then I went home. When Helen told me he was coming back again the next day, I said I wouldn't see him. Helen put her foot down. "Well, this time you tell him. I'm not going to lie to him any more."

When Fred arrived the next day, I was watching from the win-

97

dow in Richard's house. As he got out of his old car, he accident-
ally banged his knee, and it was obvious he hurt it. He was limping
as he walked to our house, a tall, thin man in old and worn clothes.
I saw Helen pointing out Richard's house. Fred limped across the
street and knocked on the door.

I just let him talk, partly listening to him and partly thinking
how I could teach him a lesson. He was about twenty years older
than I was, and I could see he was sincere, but I couldn't admit it
to myself. Somehow that bothered me.

He wanted to set up a meeting at our house as soon as possible.

"How many people do you want?" I asked.

"Oh, four or five."

"How about twenty?"

"Gee, that'd be great."

I already had a plan in mind. I invited some of the rougher guys
I knew and bought some beer. I thought we could show this
gringo a little bit of how we felt. We'd let him speak a while, and
when I gave them the signal, shifting my cigarette from my right
hand to the left, we'd tell him off and run him out of the house.
Then we'd be even. But somehow I knew that this gringo had
really impressed me, and that I was being dishonest.

When the meeting started, Fred spoke quietly, not rabble-
rousing, but saying the truth. He knew our problems as well as we
did. There was a creek behind Sal Si Puedes which carried the
waste from a packing house nearby. The kids downstream would
play in it, and they'd get sores. There were big holes in that creek
where the water would collect and stagnate, and where the mosquitoes would breed. He took on the politicians for not doing
something about it.

The more he talked, the more wide-eyed I became, and the less
inclined I was to give the signal. When a couple of guys who were
pretty drunk by that time still wanted to give the gringo the
business, we got rid of them. This fellow was making a lot of
sense, and I wanted to hear what he had to say.

He told us he was an organizer for CSO, the Community Service Organization, which was working with Mexican-Americans in
the cities. Later I would find out that it was Fred Ross who started
CSO. He talked about the CSO, and the famous bloody Christmas
case in Los Angeles a year earlier where drunken cops beat up
some Mexican prisoners. I didn't know what CSO was, or who
this guy Fred Ross was, but I knew about the bloody Christmas
case, and so did everybody in that room. Five cops actually had
been jailed for brutality. And that miracle was the result of CSO
efforts.

Fred did such a good job of explaining how poor people could build power that I could even taste it. I could really feel it. I thought, gee, it's like digging a hole. There's nothing complicated about it.

When he finished, I walked out to his car with him and thanked him for coming. I wondered what the next step was.

"I have another meeting now. I don't suppose you'd like to come?" Fred said.

"Oh, yes, I would!"

And that was it. My suspicions were erased. As time went on, Fred became sort of my hero. I saw him organize, and I wanted to learn. Right away I began to see that organizing was difficult. It wasn't a party. I began to see all of the things that he did, and I was amazed—how he could handle one situation and have a million things going in his mind at the same time.

I wanted to do it just as he did; so I began to learn. It was a beautiful part of my life. And eventually, like him, I became an organizer.

FRED ROSS RECALLS

I was born in San Francisco in 1910, so when I met Cesar I was barely forty-two, and I only had six years of organizing behind me. All that I had organized then was the Los Angleles CSO. That gives Cesar encouragement. He says, "Look what Fred Ross did after he was forty-two." By the time Cesar was forty-two, he had seventeen years of experience organizing.

I didn't start out to be an organizer, I graduated from Southern California with a general secondary teaching credential in 1936, but it was the depression, and I couldn't get a job. In 1937 I got a job with the state relief administration as a caseworker, in effect a social worker.

Then I quit and went to work for the Farm Security Adminis-tration, a federal job, in charge of their relief program in the Coachella Valley. They had a warehouse with commodities to give out, flour, beans, and such.

The next year I was put in charge of the federal farm labor camp at Arvin. That was the camp written up by John Steinbeck in Grapes of Wrath, the one the Joad family went to, but he finished his book before I got there. Later I was promoted to assistant chief of community services covering some twenty-five camps in California and Arizona.

When the war started in December 1941, my boss called and

told me that from now on, "We must work with the growers, and you don't have enough petty larceny in your heart to do that." So I went to work for the War Relocation Authority.

After the war I worked for the American Council of Race Relations, a Chicago-based organization, and went down to San Bernardino to help set up Councils for Civic Unity. Our goal was to create unity, and end the riots then going on between whites and minorities.

In Chicago, the well-known organizer, Saul Alinsky, used to play pinochle with Louis Wirth, the director of the American Council of Race Relations, who didn't like my work. He told Alinsky he had sent me down to make a survey, but that I was organizing people. "That's not why we sent him," he said.

Alinsky's ears pricked up. He was head of the Industrial Areas Foundation, which was doing community organizing in the Chicago slums, and he was looking for organizers. Alinsky hired me in September of 1947 to begin organizing Mexican-Americans in Los Angeles, as that was the hub of the whole Mexican-American population.

I'd been organizing for about six years in Southern California, five of those for the Industrial Areas Foundation, when I came north to San Jose, the largest Spanish center outside of Los Angeles.

It's been written many times that Saul Alinsky trained me and Cesar, but it's not true. I'd been at it over a year before I met him. I was the one who developed the house-meeting technique we used in CSO, and that developed in a kind of evolutionary way.

Of course, at the beginning, I didn't know anything as far as setting up a mass-based organization. I had never done it. But house meetings worked. Cesar later used the house-meeting technique to start the Union.

First I'd hold small house meetings for three weeks, building up to the big organizing meeting when we'd set up temporary officers. Then we'd organize through house meetings for several more weeks before the second organizing meeting. We then would have a working CSO chapter.

From the beginning in 1946, when I was working in the citrus belt, voter registration was the big thing we hit hard. That emphasis evolved, too. At first I couldn't figure out why there was no organization among Mexican-Americans, and why they were clear down at the bottom of the heap. Then about the second unity group I started, I got just a little hint of why.

They were fighting a segregated school case. The Mexican and black kids were going to one school, and the Anglo kids were picked up by bus and taken to another school. It was in Riverside County, a place called Belltown.

A bond election was coming up to fix up the good school, but there was not one cent for the horrible school. So the Chicanos didn't want those bonds to pass. Then they found out none were registered to vote.

As soon as a member of the NAACP started registering people and turned in a registration book, there was a difference. Since bond elections needed a two-thirds vote to pass, the school board saw they might have enough votes in the barrio to kill this bond if they joined with those people in the rest of the community who didn't want to pay any more taxes.

Later I went over to Riverside itself, the Casa Blanca barrio. An orange grower supposedly represented Casa Blanca on the city council, but always refused to come out there because the Casa Blanca people had gone on strike against him.

The Casa Blanca people were pretty anxious to dump him, and from the little I learned in Belltown, I got the idea of the balance of power. If the people all threw their weight one way, that's the way the election would go.

That was the first time I actually went down to the voter registrar and counted those registered with Spanish surnames. There were less than 10 percent in those particular precincts.

That was in 1946. It worked. I got the people registered in Casa Blanca, and they threw the orange grower out. They voted single shot—all voting for the opponent. If they had split their vote, the incumbent would have won. That was the first time I saw it work on a candidate.

As for Belltown, they gave in on the segregated school, integrated the schools, and the school bonds passed. So that set the pattern as far as my type of organization was concerned. I had all the proof I needed.

Later in CSO there were two broad-based programs we did wherever we went—voter registration and citizenship classes. We never left a place until we had put on both of those power-building programs.

I'd been working in San Jose over three weeks, and we'd already had the first organizing meeting before I met Cesar. I remember he was interested in what was in it for farm workers. That first house meeting on June 9 lasted about two hours. Just before I broke away I said I had another meeting at the Flores place. Cesar volunteered to show me the way.

Well, he was hooked. He wanted to move on and see how other

people reacted. Although he was still but a semiparticipant, at
least he saw the way people would open up at a house meeting,
especially when the meeting was relatively small so that they could
open up without being embarrassed to say what was on their minds
about their problems and the neighborhood.

The night after I met Cesar, we were going to start on the voter
registration drive, and he volunteered right away. That was another
proof of his interest. We only had one deputy registrar then, and
I'd already gotten fifteen to seventeen persons to act as bird dogs
going up and down the street pulling the people out to go down
to the corner and register. Cesar said he would be there the next
night, and he was.

At the very first meeting, I was very much impressed with Cesar.
I could tell he was intensely interested, a kind of burning interest
rather than one of those inflammatory things that lasts one night
and is then forgotten. He asked many questions, part of it to see if
I really knew, putting me to the test. But it was much more than
that.

He understood it almost immediately, as soon as I drew the
picture. He got the point—the whole question of power and the
development of power within the group. He made the connections
very quickly between the civic weakness of the group and the
social neglect in the barrio, and also conversely, what could be
done about that social neglect once the power was developed.

He also showed tremendous perseverance right from the very
beginning. Although Helen was quite sick at the time with a
kidney disorder, he was the only one in the whole organization
that came out every night for two months to push that voter
registration drive. For whatever reason, all of his actions were
invested with a tremendous amount of urgency.

He felt pretty hurt, I remember, when others started falling by
the wayside, people that started out with him, that we had high
hopes for.

I kept a diary in those days. And the first night I met Cesar, I
wrote in it, "I think I've found the guy I'm looking for." It was
obvious even then.

CHAPTER 2

Are You a Communist?

CESAR CHAVEZ RECALLS

Since I didn't have any regular farm job, I was putting all my time between jobs into the CSO's voter registration project. The June primaries were coming up and the general election. That was the year Eisenhower first ran against Adlai Stevenson. But there were many important local races, too.

When Fred came in to start the registration drive, he had a terrible time getting one deputy registrar deputized. Although they were nonpartisan offices, deputy registrars throughout California were Republicans. They were organized to prevent Chicanos from voting. There were restrictions on everything. We couldn't speak Spanish when we were registering; we couldn't go door to door; we couldn't register except in daylight hours; we couldn't register on Sundays.

Today, the idea of getting everyone to register is accepted. We fought for legislation in Sacramento and helped correct these things. But in those days, there was a lot of resistance. Fred put on a big fight and finally got Jessie De La O whose father owned the little corner grocery in Sal Si Puedes. After Jessie was chosen, Fred took me on as a bird dog to knock on doors and find the people who were not registered.

I'd never done that before, and when I knocked on the first door and a Chicano lady came out, I was so frightened I couldn't talk. She stared at me. She hardly knew me, but she knew my mother.

"Well?" she said looking at me.

I was having a difficult time explaining what we were doing.

Finally she smiled, "Okay, we're going to go register. We know you're registering people."

After leaving her house, I was embarrassed and mad at myself for being so frightened. Instead of going to the next house, I went to a home where there were some rough characters I knew. They started kidding me, but I could communicate with them. Most of them either had been to San Quentin prison or would end up there. When I made a pitch for registration, they laughed and called me "the politician." But I got one of the married sisters and her husband to register.

After that I went back to the second house. Little by little, I got confidence. In about three days I was doing okay. By then it was a challenge. I wouldn't let anybody get away without registering, I'd go into all kinds of arguments, but mostly I'd just sit in the door and not take no for an answer. I had a little game going with myself to beat the other volunteers.

The volunteers were mostly college guys who always had to go to meetings or go study, while I had nothing else to do but register. I couldn't understand why they didn't find it as important as I did.

We began to lose people. After Fred left, I was soon the only one going out. So he made me chairman of the registration drive, and I changed the tactics. Instead of recruiting college guys, I got all my friends, my beer-drinking friends. With them it wasn't a question of civic duty, they helped me because of friendship, and because it was fun. Soon the registration drive was going along very well. One of the men running for the Board of Supervisors became very friendly, and we were able to get five more deputy registrars.

The drive lasted eighty-five days, and I missed only one because Fred insisted that I take off. Part of that time I was working, but even when I worked, I'd take a shower afterward or sometimes just gobble up some food and take off to help register people. I thing we ended up registering about six thousand persons by the November elections.

We had registered so many that the Republican Central Committee decided to intimidate the people that were voting for the first time. Republicans at the polls challenged voters. "Are you a citizen? Read from here!" People were scared away. Fred came to help us, and we tried unsuccessfully to get people to go back and vote. It was a disaster.

After the election, we had an emergency CSO board meeting, and Fred said, "We've got to send a wire to J. Howard McGrath, the U.S. attorney general, to protest the Republican harassment."

Fred asked the president, Herman Gallegos, to sign the wire, but Herman said he couldn't because he was working with the welfare department, and this would jeopardize his job. He went down the line, and everybody said no. They were all professional people except for Mike Aguilar, who worked in a planing mill, and myself. I remember getting very upset. I didn't say anything, but inside of me I lost all respect for them.

Fred didn't even ask me to sign. I was looked upon as probably the least person on the board. Finally I raised my hand and said, "I'll sign it."

Fred looked at me, "You will?"

"Yeah, I'll sign it."

"Okay. Fine! Fine!"

We also put a big blast in the paper. Then the Republicans accused us of registering illegals and dead people. We called them racists. It was a big fight, my first fight with this power structure, and my name started getting in the paper.

At the time I was back working in a lumber yard where we unloaded rough lumber and stored it. I had an Italian foreman who would take me, on company time, over to his house for a drink of wine, cheese, and bread. He liked me because, when he'd ask me for something, I would get the job done.

One day he warned me, "Compagno, you've been getting into a lot of trouble. Campagno, these politics are very bad, you know."

Down at the yard some strange things began to happen, too. Most of the people were Okies, except for one that worked there during the summer. He was an undergraduate who knew what was happening and liked it. But all the others, when I'd come in, would take their hats off and say, "Good morning, politician." It was funny. I wouldn't respond. They weren't being mean, they were just puzzled by what was going on.

Then their attitude toward me began to change. It's a weird thing how the chemistry works. I think this is how the reaction to leadership begins to develop. Leadership many times is only a mental condition, more than anything else. They began to come to me with little problems that they had.

The first was an Anglo and older than I was, but he wanted to tell me that he and his wife were breaking up. I felt so bad and incompetent, as I didn't know what to do. What could I do? Since he wanted to tell me, I worked with him, and listened to all his problems, but I couldn't even make any suggestions. I didn't know how to handle the problem. Then others began coming to me.

There were other signs, too. Often there was good-natured roughhousing, but they began not to roughhouse with me any more.

Then the supervisor, not the Italian foreman but the guy at the top, would come and ask me how things were going. As I look back, I can see he didn't understand very well what I was doing, and I didn't understand why their attitudes were changing either.

One day the FBI came looking for me at work. The foreman came rushing out. "Goddamn! Compagno, you've got your ass in a lot of trouble for fooling around with goddamn politics! Compagno, the FBI wants to see you!"

I was scared. What had I done? I knew I had never done anything wrong, but who knows? These two young guys showed me their FBI credentials in front of everybody. Everyone just stopped working and looked at me.

The agents started asking me a lot of questions about Communism. I said, "You know damn well I'm not a Communist!"

But what they really wanted to talk to me about was the complaint CSO had filed against the Republican Central Committee. So I relaxed, and we talked about a half hour. Then I went back to the line where the guys wanted to know what had happened. I wouldn't tell them.

Later that day the FBI agents took me in their car for a meeting with members of the Republican Central Committee which turned into a shouting match. That's the first time I started shouting at Anglos, shouting back at them.

The agent in charge was trying to work the thing out. Finally he said, "Well, we have enough of these problems in Mississippi and the South, and we don't want to have any of this nonsense here in California."

I felt pretty good then. It was really reassuring. The Republicans were told that they couldn't intimidate people at the polls, and that the investigation would continue. Actually nothing came of the investigation except that the FBI put the heat on the Republicans.

When the agents brought me back to the yard about 3:30, we went into a little diner where most of the plant people came for coffee after work. The workers came by at 4:00, and it became a major story around there.

Then the Republicans started to red-bait me, which made the papers again. That red-baiting was the first time for me, but this was the peak of the Senator Joseph McCarthy era when many people were being accused falsely. When the charges against me hit the press, there were repercussions.

At the plant, one of my very good friends was a poor, illiterate Greek who didn't know how to drive and didn't want to take the bus. I can still see him, very short and with very baggy pants. I went way out of my way to take him home in my car every day, and on Saturdays he would call me to take him and his family shopping.

When someone told him about the attack on me, he came to give me a lesson on how bad Communism was. I stood there, not knowing what he was talking about until he said the paper was charging that I was a Communist or working with a Communist organization.

I was furious at the Republicans that had said that and tried to tell the Greek that I wasn't a Communist. But he wouldn't believe me.

At work he always got his lunch pail and thermos bottle about a half hour before work ended and put it in my car. That day, we were sorting lumber, and he had everything near him. When the whistle blew, he grabbed his stuff, put his head down, and started across the yard to the opposite street where he could catch the bus.

He rode that bus for about two weeks. Then I got some of the Catholic priests in town together with the help of Father McDonnell, and they put out a statement that we weren't Communists. The next day he wanted to ride with me again.

The Chicanos also wouldn't talk to me. They were afraid. The newspaper had a lot of influence during those McCarthy days. Anyone who organized or worked for civil rights was called a Communist. Anyone who talked about police brutality was called a Communist.

Everywhere I went to organize they would bluntly ask, "Are you a Communist?"

I would answer, "No."

"How do we know?"

"You don't know. You know because I tell you."

And we would go around and around on that. If it was somebody who was being smart, I'd tell them to go to hell, but if it was somebody that I wanted to organize, I would have to go through an explanation.

Later I found out that when they learned I was close to the church, they wouldn't question me so much. So I'd get the priests to come out and give me their blessing. In those days, if a priest said something to the Mexicans, they would say fine. It's different now.

Because I was being attacked, the liberals began to seek me out. The few liberals in San Jose asked what they could do. We struck up a friendship which we still have. From then on, every little place I went, I met the liberal lawyer, the liberal teacher, the liberal social worker. We would get together, and I got an education. I was pretty green, and I was impressed by almost anyone. I wanted to learn.

I began to grow and to see a lot of things that I hadn't seen before. My eyes opened, and I paid more attention to political and social events. I also began to read in a more disciplined way, concentrating at first on labor, on biographies of labor organizers like John L. Lewis and Eugene Debs and the Knights of Labor.

CHAPTER 3

Problems and Power

I soon realized that you can't do anything by talking, that you can't do anything if you haven't got the power. I realized that the first time I went to a public office to do battle.

Fred was gone, and we needed more deputy registrars to get ready for the general election. Fred had fought the registrar of voters before the primaries and won. Now it was my turn. Although I was pretty frightened, I got mad right away and lost my fear. I got into a big argument with the registrar and walked out of his office.

That's when I realized you can't do anything by talking. So we began to harass him with telephone calls. I got a lot of people, members of church groups, labor leaders, everyone I could, to call him. Then every single day I called him, came to see him, and had a big argument with him.

I was so frightened and so mad at him at the same time that I just went out on a crusade. When we finally got the deputies, Fred was very pleased. I didn't think it was a great accomplishment, but Fred thought I had done a great thing.

Actually, all I had done was to pay attention to how Fred had done it and copied him. I was so green that I knew nothing about power structures, so I wasn't confused like a few college guys in the CSO leadership who knew too much and were fearful of the power structure.

I always have had, and I guess I always will have, a firm belief that if you muster enough power, you can move things, but it's

all on the basis of power. Now I seldom like to go see my opponent unless I have some power over him. I'll wait if it takes all
my life. And the only way you can generate power is by doing a
lot of work.

It's unfortunate that power is needed to get justice. That suggests a lot about the nature of man. And we also must guard
against too much power, because power corrupts, but that was not
one of our problems then.

We wanted to build power within the community in order to
solve some of its problems. That meant building up political power
by getting the people registered to vote and organizing them. Unfortunately many were not citizens. So Fred started a citizenship
drive that caught fire. We soon had about ten citizenship classes
meeting twice a week in the Mayfair School in East San Jose.

Then we were confronted with people who wanted to become
citizens, but their immigration status was not up to date. Those
cases were a lot of work because documentary evidence was needed
that they had remained in this country since the time they had
arrived.

Proof was needed back to 1924 when the law was passed, but I
would get evidence back to when they entered the country,
whether it was 1924, 1905, or 1890, because it made it easier for
the case. Reconstructing a person's whole life was hard because
people were old, impatient, and couldn't remember. There were
many of those cases, and they took a lot of time.

At first I did this work in the evening, after getting off the job.
But soon I didn't have enough time because there was other help
people needed. I started taking time off work to do it on my own,
a half hour, or one or two hours off. The boss didn't like it, but
I got by with it. Then I'd just take off a whole day. I felt I had
to do it.

When we held a CSO house meeting, there always were one,
two, or three persons that would want to talk to me alone after the
meeting. They'd bring their personal problems. There were many.
They might need a letter written or someone to interpert for them
at the welfare department, the doctor's office, or the police. Maybe
they were not getting enough welfare aid, or their check was
taken away, or their kids were thrown out of school. Maybe they
had been taken by crooked salesmen selling fences, aluminum
siding, or freezers that hold food for a month.

Since I had the inclination and the training, helping people
came naturally. I wasn't thinking in terms of organizing members,
but just a duty I had to do. That goes back to my mother's train-

ing. It was not until later that I realized that this was a good organizing tool, although maybe unconsciously, I was already beginning to understand.

But I was used by people for a long time until I wised up. It wasn't that they wanted to do it, but that I was not prepared or able to tell them what to do in return. My work was just another war on poverty gimmick, which is what happens if people are given everything and don't give anything in return. You can't mold them into any action.

Well, one night it just hit me. Once you helped people, most became very loyal. The people who helped us back when we wanted volunteers were the people we had helped. So I began to get a group of those people around me.

Once I realized helping people was an organizing technique, I increased that work. I was willing to work day and night and go to hell and back for people—provided they also did something for the CSO in return. I never felt bad asking for that. It didn't contradict my parents' teachings, because I wasn't asking for something for myself.

For a long time we didn't know how to put that work together into an organization. But we learned after a while—we learned how to help people by making them responsible. Today it's the same principle with the Union. And it works. We don't get everybody, but we get enough to get that nucleus. I think solving problems for people is the only way to build solid groups.

After there was a layoff at the lumber yard, I lived on unemployment insurance and did this service work full time. As I was wasting so much time driving all over town to see people, I got the idea of opening an office. Saul Alinsky, whose foundation was financing CSO, didn't understand what I was trying to do. He thought anyone who stayed in an office wasn't organizing. He'd say, "No! No! The damn office is an office is an office is an office!" We went around and around with that one.

Finally I said, "The hell with it! I don't have to have your money. I'll do it without money. It's important!" That's how I got him to agree. Fred, of course, also helped me.

So I got an office, a little one with a half-moon shaped window, one of those offices that seemed to have had bad luck, because it would get a new business every month that then went broke. The office is still there today, right in front of the Five Wounds Church on East Santa Clara Street.

We held a raffle to get the first rent money. The first desk and chairs were donated by Alan Cranston, who later became a U.S. senator. At the time he was a young liberal Democrat in Palo Alto who had heard about our voter registration drive and become interested in us.

I think I was the one that started the service center idea in that office, the type of service center we have now in the Union. And I think that work made me very much aware of pressure points. Maybe I would need a letter from a congressman or a telephone call from a priest or a minister to get welfare for someone, for example, or something at the county hospital, or to stop someone from being deported, or to get a crooked contract broken. From those experiences, I learned many ways of applying pressure.

When I first started, many times I didn't know what to do. At first I was just acting as an interpreter at various offices, and I'd end up madder than hell.

Sometimes I'd plead, "Well, could you please help them? They haven't got any food!"

"Well, the book says . . ." the official would answer.

I'd come out of those offices very mad, but I didn't tell anybody anything except Helen. I'd tell her how unfair it was, but I couldn't think that far ahead. I just wanted to help that one particular case.

Of course, Fred got us involved in group actions. Mostly it was neighborhood improvement, but it also included civil rights cases, police brutality cases, and things of that sort. And the more we did, the more I learned how political power could be used to help people and solve problems.

FRED ROSS RECALLS

As Cesar was out of work, I talked to Alinsky to see if he couldn't possibly get some money to hire him. Cesar was very modest about his abilities and frightened that he might not be able to do the job. But I talked him into coming on and assigned him to finish the work I had started in Decoto (what is now Union City in Southern Alameda County) while I moved on to the Salinas Valley. It was tough following in my footsteps, as he had to show them he wasn't just a young, dumb kid. He was very young then, only twenty-five, and looked younger, while I was nearly forty-three.

He learned how to skirt around the opposition to him. One of his little techniques has always been to shame people into doing something by letting them know how hard he and others were working, and how it was going to hurt other people if they didn't help too. I think that was one of the things he learned there.

So Decoto was his baptism, but he wanted to get into a place where he didn't have to follow anybody. Some way he fixed it with a priest, Father Gerald Cox, so that he would be invited to go into Oakland to start a voter registration drive. Of course, he became so indispensable that he really had to stay to organize a CSO chapter. It was really there that he proved himself to himself.

CESAR CHAVEZ RECALLS

Before I left for Oakland, Fred came to a place in San Jose called the Hole-in-the-Wall where we talked for a half hour over coffee. He was in a rush to leave, but I wanted to keep him talking. I was that scared of my assignment.

I had hard times in Oakland. It was a big city, and I'd get lost every time I went anywhere. When Father Cox set up the first house meeting for me, he didn't go, he just called a lady and set it up in West Oakland. I went to the place, but I was so frightened I didn't want to go in, I just kept going around the block. When I got enough courage to stop, I stayed in the car. I couldn't get out of the car.

Finally, I went in and found about ten persons there, mostly women, mostly middle-aged. I just walked in and sat in the corner for about ten, fifteen, maybe twenty minutes.

One lady spoke up, "Well, it's getting late. I wonder where the organizer is."

And I felt I'd die. I just had enough strength to say, "Well, I'm the organizer."

She looked at me and said, "Umph!" I could tell what she meant, a snotty kid, a kid organizer, you're kidding!

That meeting was a disaster, really a disaster. I fumbled all over the place, I was so frightened. But toward the end of the meeting they were listening to me, and I got them to promise to hold house meetings, a lot of house meetings, and to commit themselves. Probably they felt sorry for me more than anything else.

Out of the house meetings we had to get volunteers to become deputies for the registration drive. At that first meeting I did get one, I think Mrs. Castanelli was her name, who became very active.

Then I held a lot of other house meetings. After each one I

would lie awake going over the whole thing, sort of like playing the tape back, trying to see why people laughed at one point, or why they were for one thing and against another.

After about twelve weeks of organizing, we held our first general meeting at the social hall of St. Mary's Church. I'll never forget it because it was very important to me. The suspense was awful. The meeting was called for 7:00 P.M. and I started to worry about 4:00. I wondered, will people show up?

Then the first one arrived. I had everything in order, and I tried to look calm. By 7:00 there were only 20 people, but little by little they filtered in, and gradually I knew it would be a success. We had 368 people.

After the meeting, the first thing I did was sprint to the phone and report to Fred. He was very happy. I had become an organizer, I guess.

At the time, I was getting thirty-five dollars a week and paid my gas and everything out of that. Since I traveled from San Jose to Oakland every day, the money didn't go far, but my brother and sister helped me pay the gas bill. Then Fred sent me to Madera, which is about twenty miles north of Fresno in the San Joaquin Valley, and my pay went up to fifty-eight dollars a week—a hell of a lot of money, I thought.

The plan was to stay about ninety days in a place, ninety days to four months at the most. In those days I moved around with my family as I didn't want to leave them in San Jose and travel back and forth. But as I did more, I had less and less time to spend with them. By then, we had four children, Fernando, Sylvia, Linda, and Eloise.

Of course, being away from my family was a sacrifice, but I knew I had to do it. And Helen has always been very good. She's too strong to complain. So we loaded everything up in the car, got a little house in Madera, and I started organizing.

CHAPTER 4

A Secret Trial

I didn't know it then, but I was in for a special education in Madera. One of the first cases I had was a Pentacostal preacher who was having trouble getting his papers in order. He'd paid a lot of money to many people who handle paperwork for a fee, coyotes we call them, to get his green card from the Immigration Service. He still didn't have it. Both he and his wife needed the green card, which gives them permanent residence status, before they could become citizens. They also had a daughter who was born here but was stuck in Mexico. Immigration wouldn't let her return because she couldn't prove her birth here.

When I went to their home, which was very, very humble, we talked and ate. Then he excused himself to conduct services. "I'll be back in about an hour," he said. "Can you wait for me?" He went into a little room—it hadn't occurred to me that it was a church—I thought it was just a living room.

After they started their service, I asked if I could join them. In those days there was a lot of separation between Protestants and Catholics; in San Jose I was one of the few Catholics who attended Protestant services. When we first came to Sal Si Puedes, Protestants were the ones who gave us lodging and food and invited my mother to go to the service. She wasn't afraid of them.

So in that little Madera church, I observed everything going on about me that could be useful in organizing. Although there were no more than twelve men and women, there was more spirit there than when I went to a mass where there were two hundred. Everybody was happy. They all were singing. These people were really committed in their beliefs, and this made them sing and clap and participate. I liked that.

I think that's where I got the idea of singing at the meetings. That was one of the first things we did when I started the Union. And it was hard for me because I can't carry a tune.

I went to this Pentacostal preacher's home regularly to go over his records, and he would schedule services. We were organizing each other. At the end of the services, it would turn into a house meeting. Eventually the preacher got everybody in his congregation to join CSO.

After a while an Italian priest in Madera started criticizing the CSO, complaining that there were too many Protestants in it. So I made a speech at the CSO meeting that no one on this earth was going to tell us whether there was too much of anything, that this was not a religious movement, and that if anybody wanted to make it so, then they had a fight on their hands.

We lost a few Catholics, but we gained many Protestants. For several years the Protestants, although a minority, were in control of the CSO and provided some excellent leadership.

The priest also red-baited us, and that issue turned out to be a major one in Madera. It taught me a lesson I never forgot.

Red-baiting in Madera was the worst I experienced. Four years earlier, a Chicana married to an Anglo had run for Congress under the Independent Progressive Party, which had put on a registration drive. Chicanos registered under the IPP were getting all kinds of static from the Democrats and the Republicans.

Now people were frightened about registering and voting. They assumed anyone starting a registration drive must be a Communist. They assumed I was, just for registering people and getting them to go to citizenship classes.

It was fantastic how people were frightened. This was the McCarthy era, and they were afraid of their shadows. But I was very naïve. I just kept on plugging and arguing and convincing. I wasn't afraid because I didn't know better.

Eventually we had about three hundred people going to citizenship classes at night, all organized on a volunteer basis. I was the only staff worker, working on a shoestring. I had nothing but an old portable typewriter.

When we started a big registration drive, it was another big fight just to get one deputy registrar. Finally we got a lady who wasn't working and could register day and night. I would leave home at 8:00 in the morning, pick her up, and we'd start work. I'd bird dog for her and she'd register.

By the time we got about three hundred people registered, the county supervisor running for election called, and I think about then we got three more deputies. By the end of the drive we had seven. We just covered Madera from one end to the other, and we registered and registered. At night we'd come back and get the ones that weren't home. We wouldn't let anybody get away.

I worked between fourteen and sixteen hours a day, seven days a week, but I was young. I could go day in and day out. I loved it. At night I'd come home, lie down in bed, and, because Alinsky wanted daily activity reports, I would dictate them to Helen.

I don't know how I did it, and I'd never do it again, but Helen would write longhand as I dictated, just piles of it every single day. Eventually it became a habit. These days I no longer write daily reports down, but at night, the last thing I do is just review what happened that day. I cannot sleep unless I start in the morning and go step by step, through the whole day. I can do that very quickly. Then it's easy for me to go to sleep.

In Madera we soon were holding very large meetings of two or three hundred people, and we developed leadership starting from zero. Fred taught me in organizing never to go to the so-called leadership, but to go right down to the grass roots and develop leaders there. Then we really had people who hadn't sold out. We got a whole crop of leaders just as we did in the Union later.

Because in ninety days we had a whole new set of leaders, all the established leaders were mad at them and jealous. But these new people were going great. There was a guy named Carlos, who was a coyote, conducting a little business where he did translations and immigration papers. Since we helped people with immigration and didn't charge them anything, he was upset. When I started getting newspaper publicity talking about the program, he and his friends attacked me—which we found out is the best way to organize.

He got some Anglos—I don't know who they were—to watch me as I went to the citizenship classes, to spy on me, to protect the country from this dangerous red. They would follow me around, come to meetings, and just sit there and take notes.

At about this time, we began to take on the Immigration Service. The naturalization examiner, J. S. Hemmer, was refusing to let people take the citizenship tests in Spanish, even though the Walter-McCarran Act permitted it. He also was red-baiting the

CSO and taking CSO membership cards away from people before they could become a citizen. Fred already had tangled with Hemmer when he set up the CSO chapter in Fresno, and now it was my turn. Later Hemmer was transferred to Hanford and there, too, another big fight developed.

In Madera, Fred got Bishop William Willinger to help us. He was the bishop who turned against us later during the grape strike; but he helped us in CSO. He called the Immigration Service in Fresno and got an appointment for me and the Madera CSO officers.

When we got to Fresno, Hemmer and I got into a big fight. I raised hell about his not permitting people to take the test in Spanish, and he answered, "If they can't speak English, they shouldn't become citizens, and as long as I'm in charge of this office, I'm not going to have anybody that can't understand the English language be a citizen."

I showed him the letter Bishop Willinger had sent to General Joseph Swing, the general President Eisenhower had appointed immigration director. The bishop wrote Swing that we were not Communists, and that they had better cooperate with us.

Hemmer looked at the CSO officers and answered, "Well, read between the lines. Read between the lines."

Then he started asking the CSO officers how well they knew me, how long they had known me, and if they knew what I did. I caught what he was doing, and I blew my cork. We got into a big argument.

The Madera CSO Executive Board, which was very young, became so frightened and convinced that I was a Communist that they began to side with him. It was probably the biggest shock I ever had, because I wasn't aware how people can change when they are in fear. It taught me the most important lesson in my life about organizing. When people are fearful, when it's their skin, they don't care about anybody.

When I saw my guys were against me and siding with Hemmer, I broke up the meeting. They were so scared they wouldn't walk with me, they wouldn't talk to me. They just went ahead and got in the elevator. Everybody was running for the woods.

I stayed there in the hallway, just hurt and stunned. I wasn't even mad. While I stood there, two huge guys from the immigration office came up. Without saying a word, they stayed one on either side looking at me and rubbing their knuckles. They were huge.

"What do you want?" I asked.

They wouldn't answer. They just looked at me and rubbed their knuckles. I got a little worried. As I got in the elevator, they went down with me, cornering me and rubbing their knuckles. When I left the elevator, they walked right alongside me.

Outside the post office building, the CSO guys were just leaving. I ran to tell them we should have a meeting that night, but they wouldn't even talk to me they were so frightened.

I stood on the sidewalk for maybe five minutes more, but it seemed like an eternity. I just stood there looking across the street at the old courthouse, and those two guys stood right beside me. Finally I got in my car which was parked in front of the post office, and those two stood right by it. I decided to outlast them. It was about 4:00 P.M., and I sat there until about 7:00.

Finally they talked, one went inside, and probably made a phone call, and then they left. When they did, they gave me a dirty look, and I rolled down a window and asked, "Why are you leaving? I'm not leaving yet."

After they were gone, I drove home to Madera where Helen had dinner ready, and the family was waiting for me. I told her what happened. I was disgusted.

Then while I was eating, there was a knock on the door. This lady, a very faithful member, came in and said, "Senor Chavez, something very very bad is happening. Do you know you're being tried? There is a big meeting going on!"

"No, I don't know."

"There is a big meeting somewhere in town to find out if you're a Communist," she said. "I don't care if you're a Communist, I'm with you. If that's Communism, I like what you're doing."

She came in and had some coffee, and I talked to her. I explained what was happening and said, "I've got to know where they're meeting."

"Oh," she said, "I'll find out." She was on the telephone committee, and it didn't take her long. When we learned the meeting was at the CSO president's home, I got a friend named Pinato to find out whose cars were at the meeting. He soon came back to report that all the CSO officers were there, and Carlos and a couple of government cars. I sent him back to find out what was happening.

In about fifteen minutes he was back. "You know," he said, "they're having a hearing, just like when you go to court." They even had a court stenographer. Carlos was acting as a judge and district attorney and everything at the same time.

It was funny—afterward. I just let them get going, then I went out there and right into the meeting.

"Goddamn it," I said. "If you're going to accuse me, you should have me present!"

There were other people there, other members from the different committees.

And I think I said, "It's all right. You can go to hell! I'm going to leave here tomorrow. I never want to come here again!"

Then one lady said, "Well, Mr. Chavez . . ."

I interrupted. "You, too—if you stay here! I thought you really wanted to fight! But you're afraid, and these guys have sold out!"

I accused the officers of selling out for money, which was not true, but it was my ploy. And the people looked around and said, "We didn't know that!"

So I walked out with many of them, members who were poor, who were farm workers. The only ones who stayed were the officers who were all middle class, the court reporter, some guy from the district attorney's office, and that guy Carlos.

Then I called everybody, including the leadership, either by phone or in person, to come to a special meeting. We had about three hundred people in citizenship classes, and I called them all.

At the meeting I turned on the immigration service, which they all hated, and I accused them of being Gestapos. Then I said, "I want you to tell me. I can leave right now, or I can stay and help you guys. But you've got to tell me. I'm not going to work with those banditos, those officers. They're too frightened."

There was a motion to throw the officers out, then a second, then 100 percent. In their place we elected Cirilo Lopez as president. He had been the president of a little local for the beet thinners in Colorado during the depression. They had lost the strike, but he had been active. He had a lot on the ball, a little guy who turned out to be a real lion.

None of the old officers were farm workers. One worked at a store, one at a winery, and another at a cotton compress. These guys were really under a lot of pressure from their employers.

This time we elected nothing but farm workers, and we came up with an all Protestant board. Most of them didn't know how to speak English. Then we started moving. That was one of the best CSOs we had. I radicalized that chapter more than any other chapter, I guess, in that short period of time. They weren't afraid to take on the police or the immigration service. They weren't afraid to fight for their rights.

It turned out to be a very good experience, but it was a very frightening one at the time. People were scared, but not the farm workers, not the poor. It was those guys who have little jobs, who protected their little self-interest. That taught me the best lesson, a good lesson about self-interest. From then on, I had a rule: There would be no more middle-class Chicanos in the leadership.

CHAPTER 5

Negreroes

CESAR CHAVEZ RECALLS

From Madera I moved to Bakersfield, then Hanford, and then on to other cities up and down the state. Everywhere there were problems, there were fights, there were countless cases where we could help people. But no matter what happened, I learned. And I never knew what would be the next lesson.

To meet some of the people's needs there were some laws we wanted passed. That meant going to Sacramento to lobby the state legislature which met every other year.

I went the first time in 1953 as part of a CSO group, but I kept my mouth shut when we went in to talk to our San Jose assemblyman. We talked to several legislators, but we didn't get anywhere that year. After speaking to them, we had a session with Fred Ross to go over what we had done and see how we could improve our techniques.

The whole system in Sacramento is inimical to responding to the people. The legislators protect each other. If a large delegation arrives to speak out on a particular bill, they change the time or the day of the hearing.

I think CSO was most effective in getting laws passed, not through lobbying in Sacramento, but by getting people to call, wire, or write their legislators. But we kept lobbying, too, and we got better and more powerful as we got more and more CSO chapters. At first I did the lobbying because I didn't have anybody else to do it, but eventually Dolores Huerta took over from me, and she was much better.

Even so, progress was slow. It took us eight years to win the fight for old-age pensions to noncitizens and nearly that long for a Fair Employment Practices Commission.

We had a very strong commitment to civil rights. But if we wanted civil rights for us, then we certainly had to respect the rights of blacks, Jews, and other minorities. Fred did a lot of work on this, just pounded and pounded these things into us in his own way.

That's why today we oppose some of this La Raza business so much. We know what it does. When La Raza means or implies racism, we don't support it. But if it means our struggle, our dignity, or our cultural roots, then we're for it. I guess many times people don't know what they mean by La Raza, but we can't be against racism on the one hand and for it on the other.

Fred knew there was discrimination among the Mexicans toward the blacks and others, so he always was pointing it out and eliminating it. In those days the constitution of most groups said members had to be Mexican, but our constitution had no color, race, religion or any other restrictions, and we stuck to it. In San Jose that led to one of our biggest fights.

My sister Rita was president of the San Jose CSO chapter which had about 880 members, a lot of poor people and a lot of middle-class people, but the poor people were in control.

One member was Felix Leon, a tiny guy who owned, as far as Mexican restaurants go, the very best. At every CSO meeting, Leon would come with a donation, get up, and make a speech. We'd say, "Oh, here he goes again!" as he would give us a ten-dollar bill.

We also had perhaps fifty black members then that we had gotten from the NAACP. One of them was Webster Sweet, a University of California student.

One Sunday afternoon he and some of his friends decided to go to Leon's. When they were stopped at the door and told that they couldn't be served, they said, "There must be some misunderstanding. We know Mr. Leon. Why don't you talk to him?"

So the bartender called Mr. Leon, who said, "No, you can't be served here!"

When I heard that later, I didn't believe it. After all, we all were in the CSO, and we preached equality.

Rita went to see Leon, who told her, "It's okay at the CSO, but here it's my business, and I can't have those boys here."

Rita called Ernie Abeytia, the vice-president of CSO, who was a very close friend and a manager for one of the supermarkets. They worked very well together and made a plan. The idea was to call a special meeting, bring up the constitution, and ask if we were going to live by it or not. The intention was to discipline Leon for not permitting the blacks in, and, if he didn't change his policy, to expel him and file a suit against him.

Well, it turned into a big, hot battle. Out of nine officers, seven walked out of the meeting and resigned. Only Rita and Ernie stayed. About 70 percent of the membership, if not more, walked out. A handful of guys stayed, mostly the older people. It was very interesting. It was the poor people, almost all illiterate, many of them from Mexico, who backed the constitution. But most of the middle class walked out.

I think I was in Brawley or Bakersfield at the time of the meeting Friday night. They called me, and I got back to San Jose Saturday. The next day, early Sunday morning, in every Catholic church where Mexicans go, there were stacks of leaflets printed in Mexico in English and Spanish saying, "Rita Chavez and the CSO are a bunch of nigger lovers." But they attacked Ernie and his wife even harder. They called his wife a whore. It was filthy.

Father McDonnell found the leaflets at 5:00 A.M. mass in Guadalupe Church, and called me at the house. I rushed out there.

After reading the leaflet, I called about ten or twelve of the guys that were with us, and we went to every Catholic church in San Jose where Mexicans went. There must have been about ten thousand leaflets stacked there, and we got them. Then we went to all the Mexican stores where there were more stacks of that stuff. We took everything.

Some of these leaflets were mailed—it was very stupid—so we quietly went to the postal inspector, who found they were printed in Tijuana. But they couldn't find out who did it.

The fight raged for a long while. CSO was fighting for its life in San Jose. From about eight hundred members, we went down to less than a hundred. There were members who, every time they'd see us in town would say, "Oh, negreroes!" Negreroes means nigger lovers. It's terrible.

So we fought back. Eventually people began to come back, but it was an awful fight.

CHAPTER 6

Oxnard's Burning Issue

EXCERPT FROM SAUL D. ALINSKY LETTER
TO CESAR CHAVEZ

September 9, 1955

I have your note of September 2nd acknowledging your salary increase to $4,000 per year. I am delighted that you feel as you do, and for the first time in my association with you I find myself in sharp disagreement with your point of view about

(a) You do not expect any more adjustments

(b) That you are being overpaid.

May I say that in the future there will be adjustments and that you most emphatically are not being overpaid. If you want to have an argument with me on the basis of your convictions in this matter I suggest that you have a talk with your wife first. . . .

In making out your expense account it would be helpful if you figured them out yourself. . . .

Also a point of personal curiosity. I note that there is absolutely nothing charged for meals. What were you doing in Fresno at the meeting? Were you on a diet, or did you carry a sandwich from home? May I further suggest that this is an historic event, because it is the first time that I have ever raised the question with an employee of the Industrial Areas Foundation as to whether he did not forget to put things on his expense account! Which all goes to prove that in your own way you are the most outstanding employee we have in the organization!

CESAR CHAVEZ RECALLS

One day in 1958 Fred told me that Alinsky had talked to him about a project in Oxnard. Alinsky was a personal friend of Ralph Hellstein, the president of the Packinghouse Workers Union, which had had a campaign to organize the lemon houses in Oxnard, and in Ventura and Santa Barbara Counties. The union had been very successful in winning the elections in almost all the houses, but they couldn't get contracts. The membership had dissipated, and they were having a difficult time. If the companies refuse to come to an agreement on a contract, the membership becomes discouraged. Hellstein and Alinsky thought that if we could get a lot of community organization going, this would be helpful in some way.

Alinsky told Fred and me that the Packinghouse Workers wanted to give twenty thousand dollars to the project for one year, but I didn't want to go into it. I couldn't see how organizing the CSO would help the plants organize. My big fear was that we would go there and spend their money, and we couldn't produce for them.

Later on when we met with Hellstein, I asked him about my fear of failure. "Oh, well," he said, "You organize the CSO. We're interested in organizing farm workers. Maybe it will help there. If it doesn't help there, hell, it's helping the community anyway."

So I still wasn't too comfortable about that. But I did want some action. When we were migrants, Oxnard was an extremely bad place for us. In the back of my mind I thought that going back would be a little revenge. I just wanted to go back and fight.

DOLORES HUERTA RECALLS

They had a CSO board meeting in Stockton in July 1958, to discuss the Packinghouse Workers' offer. Board meetings were like conventions because all of the chapters sent representatives. There was a lot of discussion about Cesar then.

Cesar was very quiet, very unassuming in every meeting. I mean he never spoke up, although he was an organizer like Fred was. So he was kind of a hard guy to know.

This project meant that Cesar would be hired by the CSO. Prior to this he had been working with Fred under the Industrial Areas Foundation staff money.

So Gilbert Lopez, who was an attorney from Fresno and presi-

dent of the Fresno CSO chapter, got up and made this big spiel asking how do we know what Cesar's going to do, and saying he should have daily reports sent in to the board of directors, and all of this junk.

I remember I got really mad about it, although I didn't know Cesar; just the whole idea that this guy was going to come to work for us, for the CSO, and then to have to be giving everybody daily reports!

There was this big fight about it, and I think Lopez was finally outvoted.

But that time Cesar did get up, and he spoke about the kind of organizing that he would be doing. He also said that he would be willing to do whatever the board wanted him to do, but that it would probably be difficult to see results at first.

I can't remember exactly all the things he said, but he impressed me very much because of the soft-spoken, very gentle way that he had about him in presenting what he thought was his situation. It was kind of like a lamb in the midst of a bunch of lions.

CESAR CHAVEZ RECALLS

After the CSO board meeting decided to hire me for the project, I went back to San Jose, picked up Helen and our seven kids, and went to the state beach at Carpinteria just south of Santa Barbara. It was our favorite little spot, a good place to relax and to think.

In those days we took some vacations, usually camping for a few days. We had a small trailer, a low one with a kitchen, and we could sleep inside. The kids would sleep in the station wagon or in a tent. We spent some good times together.

Once in 1956, we took a few weeks off for a trip to the Grand Canyon, the Painted Desert, and Brice National Park. My dad and my mother went with us on that one. Then another year we did Washington and Oregon and went up to Crater Lake. A good part of the time was spent cooking for the kids, but we also did a lot of hiking on the beach and took lots of pictures. Sometimes I'd just read while they played.

This time I had promised Helen I would stay a week with them in Carpinteria, but I only lasted about two days. I read a little bit, swam with the kids, played with them, and cooked, but by noon of the third day, I had Helen convinced that I should go ahead and see if I could find a house in Oxnard. Although I had promised that I wouldn't leave them alone, she agreed. It was practically the last time I saw them during that vacation.

That same day I found a house in a place called El Rio, about six miles from Oxnard. Then I set up a house meeting that same evening and didn't get back to Carpinteria before 1:00 in the morning. I went to sleep, got up about 8:00, had breakfast, played with the kids for about a half hour so it wouldn't be so obvious, then took off again.

We were going to stay at the beach seven or eight days, but after six we went back to San Jose, loaded up our stuff in a rented trailer, and came right back.

HELEN CHAVEZ RECALLS

When we packed up in San Jose, we were so busy we forgot to go to the bank and get any money. The night before, Cesar had gotten sick and was just burning up with fever. I said, "Let's wait." But we had everything packed, and he had a house meeting that evening. He said, "No, we have to go."

I don't drive, so he had to. Here we get into our beat-up station wagon loaded with this huge rented trailer with all our belongings in it and the kids, and I just had maybe a few dollars.

We had to stop along the way because he was really burning up with fever, and I got a little something for the kids. Then the car stopped completely. We really didn't know what to do. Somebody stopped and helped us, so we gave them our last two dollars. The kids were hungry, but we didn't have any money to buy any food for them.

Finally after that long trip, stopping all along the way, we got to El Rio. There was this little grocery store, and I told Cesar, "Go ask them if they'll cash a check for us because the kids haven't eaten since this morning."

Well, he said, "No, you go," and I said, "No, you go." Finally he said he would, and he got some milk and stuff.

We went up to the little house we had rented, but it was dark, and there was no electricity. I think we had a flashlight. We just threw a few mattresses on the floor so the kids could sleep. I fed them and put them to bed.

Cesar went up to this meeting, sick as he was.

CESAR CHAVEZ RECALLS

Oxnard was probably my worst project of all. Not even the Union has harassed me as much as that one. It started in August of 1958 and lasted through 1959.

The first thing I did was to start house meetings. Then we started a voter registration drive, because the November election was coming up and there was a good Democrat running there against Congressman Charles M. Teague. I began to sign up people for citizenship classes and opened a little office about the third day I was there to service the people.

When I went to Oxnard, I was sure that the biggest issue would be a railroad crossing, because when I was in school, a lot of Mexicans got killed by the train. I remember a school friend of ours got killed, and it stuck with me. I thought this would be a very sensitive issue, but when I mentioned it, people weren't aroused. Instead they began to come at me with the bracero issue. That was an issue that I didn't even suspect.

Braceros are Mexican farm workers who were imported under a federal law passed during the war. Although Ventura is a small county, at one time it had more braceros and more bracero labor camps than any other county in the United States. The biggest bracero camp in the country was in Oxnard, a complex of camps which housed about twenty-eight thousand workers.

At the first house meeting, I went through the whole spiel, then a man got up and mentioned the braceros. By that time I had developed some skill about listening to the issues that people presented. I had learned that people don't come to you with an issue in black and white. Sometimes something hurts them, but they don't know exactly what it is. But in this case it was very clear. He said, "Why is it we can't get any jobs? The braceros have all our jobs. What are you going to do about that?"

At every house meeting, they hit me with the bracero problem, but I would dodge it. I just didn't fathom how big that problem was. I would say, "Well, you know, we really can't do anything about that, but it's a bad problem. Something should be done."

Finally I decided this was the issue I had to tackle. The fact that braceros also were farm workers didn't bother me. There's an old dicho, no puede dejar Dios por Dios—you can't exchange one god for another. This was a question of justice, and I've never had any problem making a decision like that.

The jobs belonged to local workers. The braceros were brought only for exploitation. They were just instruments for the growers. Braceros didn't make any money, and they were exploited viciously, forced to work under conditions the local people wouldn't tolerate. If the braceros spoke up, if they made the minimal complaints, they'd be shipped back to Mexico.

We always felt that ending the program would be the best thing we could do for them and for everybody. So I changed the attack at house meetings to the issue of fighting to get those jobs from the braceros. There was instant reaction.

I studied the issue and learned that, according to the law, braceros could not be used if there was local labor available. But they were being used, and the people could not get jobs. So I decided to find out how the system worked. For the first couple of weeks I'd get up early in the morning, apply for work, and make notes.

When I applied for work at the bracero camp, they would tell me to register at the Farm Placement Service, which was in Ventura, about eight miles from Oxnard. The office opened at 8:00 A.M., and by the time I went there and back, it was almost 9:00. But the bracero camps opened at 4:00 and started dispatching people at 4:30. By 6:00, everybody had been dispatched.

The guy would tell me, "I'm sorry I can't take you because people are gone already. They've been dispatched." So I came back the following morning at 4:00 or 5:00 and the guy told me, "I'm sorry. I can't send you because this referral slip you have from the Farm Placement Office is outdated. It's yesterday's."

That was the gimmick. The whole system was rotten. The Farm Placement Service was in cahoots with the federal government, which was in cahoots with the growers to keep the local workers out of jobs, get all of the braceros in, and then exploit the braceros.

Not only did they pay braceros cheap wages, about seventy-five cents an hour, but they brought in three times as many as they needed and worked them every third day. Since all of the braceros had to pay board, whether they were working or not, and pay insurance and buy cigarettes and other things, whether they were working or not, some people became millionaires just from providing food or insurance or other things for them. But the braceros were poor when they came, and were poor when they went back. It was a vicious racket of the grossest order.

After each refusal I'd go to the CSO office, sit down and type the whole report, just a little story. Then I'd file it. I got a hunch if we used their own medicine and turned it into poison, we might be able to get them.

Meanwhile, I continued to hold house meetings, postponing the first general meeting until I had touched every family there. I wanted to build the chapter really solid. By the time we had our first general meeting, about six hundred came. From then on we held those meetings twice a month for thirteen months, and we never had fewer than four hundred, and several times we had over a thousand.

It was something like Delano later during the grape strike, people coming out of the walls. We had an eleven- or twelve-point program. But the difference between that CSO chapter and any other CSO up to that point was that jobs were the main issue. And I began to see the potential of organizing the Union.

CHAPTER 7

Getting the Proof

CESAR CHAVEZ RECALLS

On January 13, the *Oxnard Press-Courier* announced that Edward Hayes, the head of the Farm Placement Service, was going to install the new executive board of the Ventura County Farm Labor Association two days later. The association was made up of growers who used the braceros.

Hayes was a very powerful figure, a man who could keep thousands of people from getting jobs. It's amazing how you can hate a guy, but before I was through in Oxnard, that was one guy I hated.

We called a big meeting in the park for that night, and about one thousand and five hundred came. We had a radio announcer, an officer of the CSO who had a Spanish-language radio program, covering the Hayes banquet. At 6:00 he told me he thought Hayes was going to be talking about 8:30, so at 6:00 sharp we had maybe one hundred people distribute a leaflet all over Oxnard, in the Chicano barrio, the Anglo barrio, and even in the bracero camps. It took us about one and a half hours.

The banquet was held in the dining hall of the Buena Vista bracero camp. They got all the braceros out, of course, and the braceros were looking through the windows as steaks and drinks were served to the growers. Never before in the history of the camp had steaks and drinks been served. Earlier, while the dinner was being prepared, there was a grease fire that caused three thousand dollars damage. The frosting on a special cake cooked for Hayes was ruined.

Hayes was halfway through his speech when someone showed him our leaflet accusing him of being in collusion with the employers. I'll never forget. He said, "That was a dastardly act!" We demanded that he come to our meeting that night, but he didn't accept the challenge.

The next morning we started hitting the governor's office, raising hell, and they wouldn't talk to us. So I called Alan Cranston, who by this time was state controller. He called the governor's office, and they had John Carr call back. Governor Pat Brown had just taken office and had appointed Carr as director of the Department of Employment, the department in charge of the Farm Placement Service. Carr referred me to somebody. Then I called Carr every day for about a month before I got through to him again.

Meanwhile, I tried to take others with me every day when I went to apply for work at the Farm Placement Service. I begged them to go, but they wouldn't. There was a seventeen-year-old kid named Chavira, a short, handsome kid with black wavy hair —he was my first follower, I guess—and he agreed to go, just as a joke. We went, and we developed a little ritual going into the office.

The farm placement office was at the back of this large building where the Department of Employment was housed. At the back of the employment office was a little corridor where there was one desk. The guy behind the desk was going to sleep—no one had seen him in I don't know how many years. So we went and applied for work.

It took us one and a half hours to get through the application, there were so many questions. They wanted the last time we worked, where we worked, everything. I gave them all they wanted and more. I would fill out two forms, one for them and one for me. After they were filled out, the man gave us referral cards to a grower.

Little by little a few more guys joined me. And after we had gone about four or five times, I had a chance to explain how the plan was working, and how I thought it could be handled. Then it began to work. The numbers who came to the office grew.

I started making it into a sort of game. I'd say, "Let's go to the Farm Placement Service," and we'd start laughing. "We know it's not going to work, but let's go just for the ride. You don't have anything to lose. Let's go." Well, the guys weren't working, so why not?

It started as a game, but after a while it was no longer a game, it was a very serious thing. We would march in, single file, me in front wearing my navy peacoat. At first there were two or three, then four and five, then eight and ten. It kept increasing. Once we got to about twenty, we'd walk in at 8:00 sharp every morning.

We had to march through the entire office and then along one of the walls to the back. The ladies working there, the moment they saw us coming, turned around to look at us. It was a very funny scene as we were playing the game. I didn't care about the women; I was trying to get work for the guys, and, to get them to come, day in and day out, they had to get a kick out of it. It just couldn't be done at that time on the basis of their going to get jobs right then. They just couldn't.

We'd stay there all morning filling out forms, then we'd take time out to eat at 12:00, and sometimes we'd be there until 3:00. We filled out everything they wanted, employment records going back twenty years. I had to fill most of them out in the beginning. Then I began training others to do it. We made two copies, one for them, one for us. The whole idea was, let's use the system and let's make it work against them by documenting cases as they'd never been documented before.

A lot of do-gooder groups that were trying to do something about this bracero program never had evidence of the law violations. They knew what the problem was, talked about it, but they couldn't produce the bodies. I set off to have the evidence, and have it in such overwhelming numbers it couldn't be refuted.

One day, after about a month of trying, I finally talked to Carr again in Sacramento. "I don't believe it," he said, "I want to come out." That's what I wanted. He drove his car down privately, very quietly, and I took him around and showed him everything. Then he said, "It's unbelievable, let's go to work. I want evidence. I don't want just complaints."

Carr, of course, was afraid to move right away. There was tremendous political pressure. Governor Brown also was very frightened. He never did anything on the braceros. He was chicken on it all the way through.

I went to Santa Barbara and met with the Bureau of Employment Security, which was under the Federal Department of Labor. That department, together with the State Farm Placement Service, ran the program. What they would do was pass the buck from one to the other.

We brought the Southern California director of the Farm Placement Service, William Cunningham, to Oxnard for a meeting at the Juanita School, together with the local official in Ventura and a man from the Bureau of Employment Security. The people got so mad they threw them out. Cunningham spoke for about fifteen minutes, about the law giving the workers the right to jobs. He said, "You say there's abuses in the bracero program. Prove it. Anybody can get a job. You want a job? We'll give you a job!"

We opened the floor for questions. It wasn't questions, it was an attack. They stormed him. "Fink! We want jobs!" The people just lashed them. The three ran out of the meeting, visibly shaken.

But the following day we got three guys hired by Japanese-American growers. One worked an hour, then was fired because they said he couldn't do the job even though he had worked cutting celery for seven or eight years. Another got a job irrigating. He'd been irrigating for seventeen years. He was fired after three hours because they said he didn't know how to irrigate. And the guy who lasted the longest lasted about five hours driving a tractor.

So then I called for an investigation. Right away the federal government came, and I gave them five referral cards, only five, because I wanted to see how they were going to play them. I took five that I thought represented some of the most obvious cases.

Then we increased the pressure. We'd go over to the bracero camps and picket at night, then after work just shout at the people who administered the program, "We want jobs!" for a half hour and drive them nuts. We had kids distribute leaflets in the stores saying, "Dear Mr. Merchant, the reason we don't buy here is because the growers won't let us work. They have braceros working, and they take all the money to Mexico."

We also drafted fourteen demands, and out of the fourteen points we got twelve. So I sent a letter to Carr asking for the other two. He answered something like, "What the hell do you want? Blood?"

In answer to one of our demands—and because of pressure from CSO members, other CSO chapters, and supporters—the Farm Placement Service opened an office in a trailer near Oxnard right across the street from the cemetery. Soon after that, the city kicked us out of the city park office which they had let us use.

We rented a little store which we jammed with rummage, and I had my little office in the back. The place was open from 5:00 in the morning until after 10:00 at night seven days a week, and the rummage helped pay for the rent.

Of course, I worked all during the hours the store was open and even longer. At the most I was making eighty dollars a week plus some gas money. It was certainly a far cry from the recent antipoverty programs.

Talk about working on a shoestring. We ran that office, including the telephone, on no more than twenty or thirty dollars a month. I had one man helping me, and the rest were volunteers. That's where the poverty programs failed. They existed because they had money. We had to exist because there was a need, in spite of a lack of money.

Poverty programs didn't organize people the way we did. Their work was superficial. We were gut organizers. We had to organize to exist. We didn't have conferences or seminars, our classes and conferences and seminars were out in the streets and with the people in their homes. And we were completely free. Nobody questioned what we did.

Sometimes today I wonder how we ever did all that we did in Oxnard, because our fight for jobs was only part of the program. Of the other fights, one of the most dramatic was urban renewal —we once got five hundred at a city council meeting to protest an urban renewal project—but there were other fights, like getting deputy registrars, fighting the welfare department, and conducting citizenship classes.

Thirteen hundred people came to class, and we had one class where over seven hundred became citizens in one day. We were holding the classes in schools, homes, on street corners. At night the Ramona School classes were full. Where the kids sat during the day, the parents would sit at night, and we not only taught them the Constitution and basic English, but we also taught them to fill out all the citizenship forms.

After a while in the job drive, we would meet at the CSO office and have coffee and Mexican bread before we went to the employment office. There, the people working started getting worried. They were very nice. They smiled, said, "How are you?" They shook hands before we filled out the forms, but they were very nervous.

By the time we had been doing this a month, we had anywhere from one hundred to two hundred coming in every day. We'd form them single file, and I would shout "March!" and we'd march in. They had to bring in guys from all over the state to take care of us.

We had people referred to all the ranches, so we had something on each of the growers. And, in spite of all that activity, it took us forty-one days before we got one worker placed.

The authorities didn't know it, but I had nineteen hundred

signed affidavits by then, all notarized. Maybe altogether I had fourteen hundred people involved, but some guys had about ten different complaints. We had a guy that came to the Farm Placement Service for something like eighty-five days and couldn't get a job. And we had the referral cards to prove it.

CHAPTER 8

A Victory That Failed

CESAR CHAVEZ RECALLS

One day in April we staged a sit-in at the Jones ranch where twenty-seven braceros were pulling tomato seedlings. It's stoop labor, taking out seedlings from the ground and packing them in little boxes for transplanting in Sacramento and elsewhere.

I went in wearing an old hat and sunglasses and stationed a man opposite each bracero, just facing them sitting down. The braceros were frightened, so they didn't move.

As the foreman didn't know who I was, although he did know my name, my instructions were, "Whatever you do, don't call me by my name." I had left a woman from the Packinghouse Workers outside the field with simple instructions. If any trouble came, I had told her, take my car and go directly to the phone to call Eddy Flores, a farm worker and one of the active leaders, who later became head of the Construction Workers local in Ventura. As a signal, I was going to get out my white handkerchief and wave it if we got arrested.

No sooner were we in the field than the cops arrived, the highway patrol and the sheriff's deputies. They were looking for a leader, but no one was saying anything. Then the lady from the Packinghouse Workers came, with her high heels and her fifty-dollar dress, going through the mud calling, "Cesar, Cesar, I got to tell you something!" I was arrested and so were the others.

But someone called John Carr before they took us in, and the farm placement office radioed the sheriff not to arrest us, that this was something the growers had to work out themselves. Then the federal official arrived and told the grower, "I want these men hired right now. Take those braceros back to the camp!"

We got twenty-seven people working from about 11:00 to about 1:00. They were fired at 4:00, and the next morning the braceros were back at work again. We called Sacramento, got the braceros out again, and our people in. But they started firing them one by one, finding all kinds of excuses, firing them and black-listing them.

After several days, one of the men in the Bureau of Employment Security called me to his room about midnight.

"Cesar, I'm with you," he said. "I think what you're doing is a damn good thing. I want to help." Then he said, "Look, I've got eighteen years in the service. If they find out what I'm doing, I'm going to lose my job. It's up to you. If I can trust you, I'll tell you some things."

I said, "Sure." In fact, I've never mentioned his name.

He told me, "You know, these people don't want any investigations. They don't want anything public because this thing is a time bomb. They don't want any publicity on it, and you've got everybody shook up."

I didn't realize the magnitude of the situation, so I thanked him. I thought, if they don't want any publicity, fine. I knew what to do.

The following morning we marched—about sixty or seventy of us—to the employment office trailer. They registered about eight times each because we wanted to get a lot of cards. We registered until the guy ran out of cards and went to Ventura to get more. Before we were through, we had piles of cards, everybody had eight, ten, twelve, or fifteen referral cards. At lunchtime we sent somebody to the store to bring sodas and food to make sandwiches.

Later that afternoon we gathered more people and started marching from the trailer to the Jones ranch. Besides the people marching, there were maybe forty or fifty cars with mothers and kids, and those that couldn't march.

By that time there were all kinds of cops and TV cameras and newspaper people I had told we were coming. I was marching about the middle of the march. The press wanted to know, "What are you going to do when you get there? Are you going to get into the field?"

I said, "We can't tell you yet. You have to stick around."

When we got up to the gate of the Jones ranch, there was one guy who wanted us to go in, to trespass.

I said no.

"Yeah, we have to trespass. We have to show these guys!" He got up on a car and made a speech.

So I got on another car and said, "I'm not going. If you go, I'm not responsible for what happens."

No one moved, not a single soul. He was by himself. Some people told him, "You go," but he looked around and saw nobody was with him. He didn't go.

Then we got them around the car I was on, and I made a speech. We took a vote not to ever again register to work because registration was a gimmick to keep us from getting jobs.

I burned my referral card, another joined, then another and another and another. Pretty soon everybody joined in. We put them in a big pile and set them on fire. The TV cameras just ate it up.

That night I sent a letter to the local farm placement office and to the state saying, no more registration. And we give you seventy-two hours to give us jobs.

Nothing happened.

A month later, when Secretary of Labor James Mitchell was scheduled to come to Ventura, we decided to picket him. His advance man begged me not to, but I said, "Nothing doing unless we get jobs right now." Since his advance man could not provide jobs, we had about one thousand people picketing the Oxnard airport. Secretary Mitchell landed there, saw all the people, and quickly drove to the Lions Club in Ventura. We followed and picketed him there.

The pickets were yelling, "We want jobs!" We really put on the heat and forced him to have a meeting with us at the Pierpont Inn. I didn't go because I first wanted him to meet some conditions, and he refused. So he met with the Packinghouse Workers representatives.

Later we had a march in town at night with candles. We were at a deadend, and we were just unloading all the pressure on them. It started at one of our regular meetings. I said, "We're not going to meet tonight, we're just going to go into the streets with signs telling people we want jobs." During the day I had had people making signs, so we just picked them up and started marching.

One of our ladies asked, "Can I bring my banner of Our Lady of Guadalupe?" and I said, "Yeah, sure. Bring her." So I set her marching in front. That's where I got the idea that we needed some flag to identify us.

When we went out into the street, instant success! People

parked their cars, women got out, and they started marching. Then we started singing Mexican hymns.

The cops came out right away. They tried to stop us. I said, "You can't stop us!"

"Well, you can't have a parade."

"I don't care."

They said they were going to take me to jail, and I said, "Okay." The people said, "If you take him, then we all go." They meant it.

They didn't take me. Instead, we marched for about two hours, and the cops provided an escort.

That's when I discovered the power of the march. We started with a couple of hundred people in La Colonia, and by the time we got through, we must have had ten thousand people. Everybody was in it. Among Mexicans a march has a very special attraction. It appeals to them—just like a pilgrimage. I had been thinking of a march before that, from Calexico to Sacramento for the old-age pension—I guess for the same reason that marches attract Mexicans, and maybe that attraction was in me—but I had not gone through with that.

Meanwhile, there were more investigations. One day, when Edward Hayes finally came back to Oxnard, I took ten referral cards and threw them on the table. "I want resolutions for these cards. I want answers!" I wanted him to take corrective action and get jobs for these guys.

He looked and started sweating. The most they'd ever received in a three-month period was eight complaints. "There are a lot of complaints here," he protested, and more to that effect. So I gave him sixty more. I was just playing a game with him. He didn't know what to do. Finally he brought people in from different offices, and they set up shop, rented an office at the Packinghouse Workers Union office.

I kept Carr informed of everything I gave Hayes, the time I gave it to him, and his responses. Then I pressed and pressed Hayes. After about three weeks of handling those seventy cards— he still couldn't come up with answers—I dumped another hundred on him.

The head of the federal section from Santa Ana came over, and I told him, "I have a whole stack of cards, and I've got three times more than this. I want a written report on every one." If I had had a legal department as I have now, it would have been beautiful. We didn't have that. I did it without going to the courts or anything.

So then they really started jumping.

Carr also was pushing Hayes and talking to me and saying, "Don't give up. If he doesn't give it to you, you call me." We turned the heat on, we squeezed him, and we got him.

Our biggest break came when we got the growers to agree to hire people at our office. That was the most beautiful victory. We forced the growers' association to come and pick our people up right in front of our office. We became a hiring hall. We had them!

The whole struggle was a thirteen-month fight. I was the only paid organizer, but we had every farm worker family in Oxnard tied into the operation.

People would come and tell us they needed work as irrigators or tractor drivers or in the sheds. I said, "You want to drive a tractor? Okay. You go find me a bracero on a tractor, and you've got a job." That worked like magic. People were going all over the valley.

When they found a bracero, we'd call the federal people and say, we want this job right on the spot.

Then we began to get growers we didn't even know who would call the office for workers. They were paying 65 cents an hour when I went there, and we got the rate up to 90 cents. The grower would call and say, "I need four men," and I'd say, "How much do you pay?"

"Well, whatever the going rate is. I guess seventy-five cents."

"Nothing doing. You want men from this organization, you pay ninety cents."

"Okay. Fine."

There were so many people waiting for jobs in front of our CSO office, they had to block off the street.

Then the police came, brought in six or seven squad cars, and forced the people off the street onto the sidewalk. Then they blocked the streets entirely, so the growers' trucks couldn't come in.

We had to demonstrate against the police. We marched down Main Street, went to the police department, and sat in the station waiting room until the police agreed to reopen the street.

As a result of all the heat, William Cunningham, the Southern California director of the Farm Placement Service, was accused of taking bribes and was canned, only weeks before he was due to retire. He lost his seniority and his pension. Then Hayes also was forced out as head of the Farm Placement Service; because of his ties to the growers, he quickly got a job working for the growers' association in the Imperial Valley. Several others in the Farm Placement Service also lost their jobs. The whole operation was rotten.

We had won a victory, but I didn't realize how short-lived it would be. We could have built a union there, but the CSO wouldn't approve. In fact, the whole project soon fell apart. I wanted to go for a strike and get some contracts, but the CSO wouldn't let me. National headquarters got calls from labor, and the CSO board got frightened. So the CSO president came to try to stop me.

I got angry and told him, "You don't stop me, I quit!" Then I went inside the house and wouldn't let him in.

He stayed there about two hours. Finally he convinced me, and I relented. Not long afterward I was appointed national director of CSO and transferred to Los Angeles.

By the time it was over I was down from 152 to 127 pounds and was averaging about four hours' sleep a night. Not only that, but I nearly lost my youngest son, Birdy, who was born that August.

He got diarrhea when he was about two weeks old, and I was too busy to take him to the doctor. Finally Helen walked with him to an osteopath, who misread the symptoms. She took him home and called me. She was crying. Then I realized how worried she was, and we rushed him to the hospital where the doctors said he wasn't going to live.

In desperation I said, "Doctor, how about getting someone to consult with you."

The doctor got a pediatrician from Ventura who diagnosed the problem and was able to stop the diarrhea. Birdy was saved.

When I left Oxnard, two guys were hired as organizers. But soon after I left, a factional fight started which destroyed the effectiveness of that CSO chapter. We also left the operation to the Packinghouse Workers Union, and in ninety days she blew. In ninety days the whole thing was lost. Talk about factions—there must have been as many factions as there were workers.

When I came back to Oxnard about five or six months later, the guys were out of jobs, and the braceros were all back at work. I came in the morning and talked to a group of workers who had started a little fire by the railroad tracks. They told me, "Oh, it sure went. It's very bad."

I didn't say anything, I was so mad—I don't know at whom,

at the leadership and at the people for not fighting for what I was sure was there. And I thought of all the time and energy that I had put in.

If I had had the support of CSO, I would have built a union there. If anyone from labor had come, we would have had a union. I think if the Union of Organized Devils of America had come, I would have joined them, I was so frustrated.

But then, maybe I wasn't ready. If I had been, I would have done it even though CSO was against it.

CHAPTER 9

"I Resign"

CESAR CHAVEZ RECALLS

I stayed in CSO as director a couple more years, hoping I could persuade the board to organize farm workers. I thought of doing it alone, but I was discouraged by some friends, mostly some of the priests I worked with. They said I couldn't start a union without the help of the AFL-CIO. "That's the only way it's going to be done," they said.

They had good hearts and a lot of interest and gave a lot of themselves, but I didn't know that they knew less about it than I did. When I met with the priests and Dolores, only Dolores encouraged me.

DOLORES HUERTA RECALLS

It was Father Thomas McCullough and Father Donald Mc-Donnell who went back East to talk to Walter Reuther and George Meany about putting money into organizing farm workers. But when they were unsuccessful, Father McCullough said, "Let's start our own group and call it the Agricultural Workers Association."

I made my husband Ventura quit his job to work for AWA. Then my brother quit his job, and both worked full time without pay to organize the union. But Father McCullough didn't want me to be involved. He said that farm labor organizing was no place for a woman. So I kind of worked under cover, doing the work through my husband and my brother.

Father McCullough and Father McDonnell sponsored AWA and wrote the constitution. We did the work. It was difficult for us, too, to work for nothing, because I was having a baby every year. They were hard times! In fact, it ended up in a divorce.

Our group was organized in 1958 to bring the AFL-CIO into farm labor organizing. So, after the Agricultural Workers Organizing Committee was set up by the AFL-CIO the following year, AWA voted itself into AWOC.

My husband Ventura and I wanted to bring Cesar over to Stockton where Norman Smith had set up AWOC headquarters, so that Cesar could explain to AWOC his program of organizing local farm workers and replacing the braceros. We tried to get Father McCullough to use his influence on Smith. But Father McCullough wouldn't go for it. He said, "Well, the AFL-CIO has experienced union organizers, and they know how to organize people."

The next year AWOC got into the big lettuce strike in the Imperial Valley with the Packinghouse Workers. They spent a lot of money. Some of their members started advocating violence in the camps, hoping the Mexican government would pull out the Mexican nationals.

After that, the AFL-CIO pulled out their money, and the AWOC held a convention in Strathmore in the winter of 1961. I got some farm workers who were CSO members down to the convention with me. There, Norman Smith suddenly announced there wasn't any more money, and they didn't know what to do.

So I got up and made this very strange speech that they should go back in cars all the way to Miami where the AFL-CIO was going to have a convention in December and demand that they be given more money to organize workers.

If I'd known we were going to be organizing the farm workers ourselves the following year, I probably wouldn't have said anything.

So a group of farm workers jumped into their car the next morning and drove across the country, pigeonholed all the delegates to the AFL-CIO convention, and got them to vote for the money.

Only three months later, we had a CSO board meeting with Saul Alinsky just before our own convention. Cesar wanted CSO to organize farm workers. He told the board, "If CSO doesn't go for this farm labor project, I'm going to leave the organization."

It was quite obvious to us even then that the AFL-CIO wasn't going to succeed in their drive.

Then Alinsky said, "If the CSO will have to die so that a union for farm workers can be built, it will be a very healthy death. Sometimes an organization has to die." The board agreed to back Cesar's project.

But later, when the vote came at the convention, we were defeated. They said CSO was not a labor organization, it was a civic organization.

We were all so sad. Fred and I were crying, and I guess the only one that was not was Cesar. As the convention ended, he got up and said, "I have an announcement to make. I resign."

He dropped the bombshell on the convention. He had so much guts! Everybody was pressuring him to stay. People were crying. But he didn't bow to the pressure. He left.

Later when Cesar told me, "I'm going to start my own Union," I was just appalled, the thought was so overwhelming. But when the initial shock wore off, I thought it was exciting.

Much later Saul Alinsky told Fred Ross, "Well, you spent fifteen years and around three hundred thousand dollars locating one leader—Cesar Chavez. Pretty expensive find, don't you think?"

CESAR CHAVEZ RECALLS

Fred had to leave before the CSO convention was over, so I drove him to the airport in Imperial. There I met Norman Smith who was then assistant director of AWOC. He offered me a job on the spot. When I refused, he thought I needed more money, so he upped the ante.

He offered me $150 a week, I think, then raised it to $200. I said, "Look, Norm, it's not more money. I can't organize with you guys. You're not going to give me the freedom I need."

Even though I didn't know that much about labor law and about labor history, my fears were really well grounded. I just knew that a big organization was not going to let a little organization get it into trouble. They had too many things at stake, if we started raising hell with strikes and boycotts.

My only hope of success was if no strings were attached.

HELEN CHAVEZ RECALLS

Cesar had always talked about organizing farm workers, even before CSO. After all, we were both farm workers, and my parents and his parents and our whole families.

Finally, he just made a decision that that's what he was going to do. He did discuss it and say that it would be a lot of work and a lot of sacrifice because we wouldn't have any income coming in. But it didn't worry me. It didn't frighten me. I figured we'd manage some way as long as one of us was able to work.

I never had any doubts that he would succeed. I thought a lot of people felt the way we did.

CESAR CHAVEZ RECALLS

I stayed with CSO for two weeks after the convention, then I quit on March 31, my thirty-fifth birthday. I've heard people say that because I was thirty-five, I was getting worried, as I hadn't done too much in my life. But I wasn't worried. I didn't even consider thirty-five to be old.

I didn't care about that. I just knew we needed a Union. What I didn't know was that we would go through hell in the beginning years. There would be lots of frustrations, lots of doubts, and tremendous challenges.

What I didn't know was that we would go through hell because it was all but an impossible task.

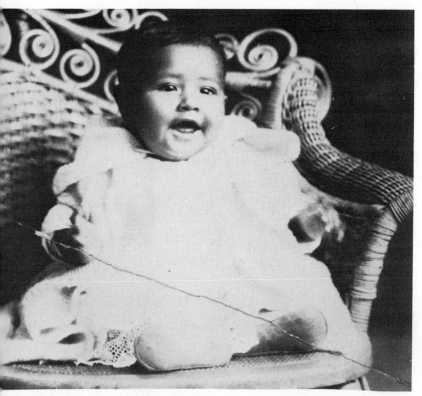

esar Chavez in 1927 when he was confirmed at nine months in
uma, Arizona.

The adobe home built in 1909 by Cesario Chavez and his son Librado in the
Gila Valley was still standing when photographed in 1969 by the author. The
one-room wing at left housed Librado, his wife, and their five children. The
wing to the right of the breezeway is in ruins.

Rita Chavez and her brother Cesar dressed up for their first communion in Yuma.

Cesar Chavez holds his diploma after graduating from the eighth grade in Brawley in 1942 at the age of fifteen. This marked the end of his schooling.

Juana Chavez, the mother of Cesar Chavez, working in the tomatoes at Walnut Grove in 1942.

The short-handle hoe forces workers to remain bent over as they thin a field of celery in Salinas Valley in 1973. Early in 1975 Governor Jerry Brown outlawed its use. Photo: © Bob Fitch.

As a teen-ager Cesar Chavez enjoyed wearing pachuco clothes. This photograph, taken in Delano in 1945, shows, left to right, Richard Chavez, Robert Jiminez, and Cesar Chavez.

Cesar Chavez in the U.S. Navy in 1946 when he was nineteen.

Juana and Librado Chavez, the parents of Cesar Chavez, photographed in April 1947 at a ranch near San Jose when his mother was fifty-five and his father sixty-one.

On his honeymoon in 1948, Cesar Chavez set the timer and took his own picture with his bride Helen.

Cesar Chavez and Herman Gallegos in 1952 when Chavez was first vice-president and Gallegos president of the San Jose CSO chapter. Chavez sported a moustache to look older.

One of the first projects in organizing the Oxnard CSO chapter in 1958 was a get-out-the-vote drive. Cesar Chavez is seen at the right.

Manuel Chavez unveils the first Union flag at the National Farm Workers Association convention in Fresno on September 30, 1962. The scarlet emblem with the black eagle frightened some members away. Photo: Joseph Gunterman.

The first NFWA convention was held in an abandoned Fresno theater. Cesar Chavez and Dolores Huerta are seen on stage. Photo: Joseph Gunterman.

The first corrido about La Causa was written by Rosa Gloria and played from a tape recording to the first NFWA convention. On stage are, left to right, Dolores Huerta, Rosa Gloria, her husband, and Cesar Chavez. Photo: Joseph Gunterman.

Dolores Huerta stands on the roof of a car with other pickets the first week of the grape strike in September 1965. Photo: Harvey Richards.

Singing "De Colores" at a Union meeting in October 1965 are, left to right, The Reverend James Drake, NFWA vice-president Julio Hernandez, Dolores Huerta and three of her children, Vincent, Peanuts, and Emilio. Photo: © George Ballis.

UAW President Walter Reuther marched alongside Cesar Chavez in Delano on his visit there December 18, 1965. Larry Itliong is at left. Photo: © George Ballis.

Cesar Chavez and Senator Robert F. Kennedy in Delano on March 16, 1966.
Photo: © George Ballis.

The long, thin line of marchers threads through the vast expanse of vineyards
in the San Joaquin Valley as they head for Sacramento in April 1966. Photo:
Jon Lewis.

Although his leg is swollen and he runs a high temperature, Cesar Chavez continues marching with the help of a cane on the long road to Sacramento. Photo: © George Ballis.

DiGiorgio strikers stand in the fog next to the shrine built in Cesar Chavez's old station wagon which was parked outside the DiGiorgio vineyards at Sierra Vista near Delano. The vigil continued twenty-four hours a day and a mass and Union meeting were held there daily. Photo: © Paul Fusco.

Cartoons by Andrew Zermeno from *El Malcriado*. The idea for the cartoon at the lower left was suggested by Cesar Chavez.

Senator Robert F. Kennedy, Cesar Chavez, and his mother during mass in Delano at which Chavez ended his twenty-five-day fast. Photo: © George Ballis.

Cesar Chavez receives bread from the Reverend Wayne C. Hartmire at a mass breaking his twenty-five-day Delano fast on March 10, 1968. Next to him are Helen Chavez and Senator Robert F. Kennedy. Photo: Cris Sanchez.

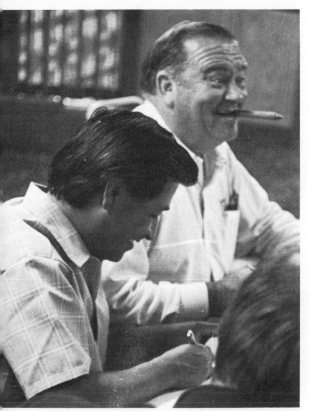

After long and arduous negotiations with the Tenneco conglomerate and S. A. Camp, an agreement is reached in Bakersfield on June 26, 1970. Here Cesar Chavez signs the contract while grower James Camp beams. Photo: © Jacques Levy.

Richard Chavez carries one of the first boxes of Coachella Valley table grapes with the Union label in 1970. Photo: © Bob Fitch.

On July 16, 1970, at Reuther Hall in UFWOC headquarters, Cesar Chavez stands at altar and announces that twenty-three Delano area growers have just asked to start negotiations the next day. The end of a five-year strike appears in sight. Photo: © Jacques Levy.

The five-year grape strike ends at Union headquarters in Delano with the Delano area growers coming to Forty Acres to sign the historic contract. Cesar Chavez smiles as John Giumarra raises both hands. Giumarra's son is at right. Behind them are Bishop Joseph Donnelly, Monsignor George Higgins, and Jerry Sherry, editor of the *Catholic Monitor*. Photo: Cris Sanchez.

Book IV

THE BIRTH OF THE UNION

April 1, 1962–April 10, 1966

The National Farm Workers Association was founded in an abandoned Fresno theater on September 30, 1962, at a convention called by Cesar Chavez.

The plan was to organize workers one member at a time, without hope of contracts until the union became strong enough to strike successfully, a goal perhaps five years or more away. And this plan must be carried out despite families to support, broken-down cars, and lack of funds.

While Chavez worked without money, he was not without friends. One of the strongest was the Reverend C. Wayne Hartmire, head of the California Migrant Ministry. The boyish-looking Chris Hartmire, who had met Chavez in CSO days, organized much of the Protestant support for La Causa and quietly provided help many times over the years.

In sharp contrast to the nearly penniless Chavez effort, the AFL-CIO was heavily financing its own major drive, after assigning veteran labor organizer Al Green in 1962 to head the Agricultural Workers Organizing Committee. Green, following more traditional organizing techniques, distrusted the Chavez style, his unorthodox methods, and his long-haired student supporters.

Then, in January of 1966, AFL-CIO President George Meany, upset by AWOC's lack of success, despite more than a million dollars expended since 1959, assigned William Kircher to oversee AWOC. Kircher, the new national director of organizing for AFL-CIO, was a jovial giant, a United Automobile Worker veteran of the bloody organizing wars against the auto industry. While he knew nothing about *farm labor when he started, he soon became deeply involved in the struggle and came face to face with Cesar Chavez in Delano. Together they made agricultural labor history. For Kircher became a strong advocate of the farm workers' cause.*

CHAPTER 1

The Power
of Agribusiness

In the past 125 years or more, the farm workers' struggles to organize have been smashed repeatedly by the power of agribusiness. It is a story that should be told—how hundreds of strikes
were broken, and everyone destroyed up until now. It's been
nothing but a record of defeat after defeat.

The power of the growers was backed by the power of the
police, the courts, state and federal laws, and the financial power
of the big corporations, the banks, and the utilities.

The first strikes by American Indians more than 120 years ago
were called uprisings and put down by the army; not too long ago
Governor Ronald Reagan referred to one of our strikes as an up-
rising and threatened to call out the national guard.

Since the start of this century, many unions were involved—
the Industrial Workers of the World, or Wobblies, as their members were called; the United Cannery, Agricultural, Packing and
Allied Workers of America; the United Packinghouse Workers of
America; the Food, Tobacco and Agricultural Workers Union;
the AFL; the CIO; and the Teamsters, to name a few. But the
power was stacked against them, and it still is.

There were countless strikes in California, many that were never
recorded, and some that are well known. When I had had about
five years of organizing in CSO, I began to talk to workers and

organizers about strikes and to read farm labor strike reports. I
had stacks of notes that I took after talking to people.

I'd get the stories of the strikes as the workers saw it. Many
times I found them uninformed. I'd ask, "Why do you think
the strike was lost?" And they'd say the leaders sold out—50 or
more percent said that. It would bother me, and I'd say, "How do
you know your leader sold out?"

"Oh, we know."

"How?"

"We know!"

Actually they didn't mean it in the same sense that we see it
as a sellout. They were saying the organizer just didn't have what
it took to do it. When the money stopped coming in—if he was
a paid organizer—he would leave. Or his international would say,
"You've got to go, there's no more money."

And then, of course, violence, terror, and unconstitutional laws
often were used to stop farm workers from organizing, just as they
once were used against industrial workers.

One of the earliest well-known incidents that led to much antiunion repression took place in 1913 on the Ralph Durst hop
ranch near Wheatland. About three thousand workers were recruited by Durst and set up camp there; but conditions were so
bad, the workers drew up a few demands, like having drinking
water brought to the fields twice a day, having one toilet for every
hundred workers, and separate toilets for men and women. They
also wanted higher piece rates and an end to that phony bonus.

When the IWW organizer, Blackie Ford, presented the demands to Durst, the grower struck him across the face with his
glove. A mass meeting held the next day was broken up when
Durst arrived with his attorney—who also happened to be the
district attorney—and several armed deputies and the sheriff. One
of the deputies fired a shot, and a riot started. Before it was over,
two farm workers were killed, and so were a deputy and the district attorney. Many people were injured.

Then, throughout the state, hundreds of Wobblies were arrested, beaten, jailed. Ford and another IWW organizer, Herman
Suhr, who had been in Arizona at the time of the riot, were sentenced to life in prison, and both actually served twelve years.

In 1928 the melon strikes in the Imperial Valley were broken
when the organizers of the Confederación de Uniones Obreras
were arrested and deported. And during the thirties, there were so
many cases of strikebreaking by vigilante groups, deputies, cops,
and highway patrolmen, that it's impossible to count them all.

Organizers were beaten, tarred and feathered, jailed. Some even were killed. On October 10, 1933, Pedro Subia was killed in Arvin and Delores Hernandez and Delfino Davila both died when growers shot up a union hall at Pixley. Seven men and another woman were wounded there. And, although eleven growers were charged with murder, all were acquitted. But 113 workers were arrested and jailed for weeks, and nine children even died of malnutrition during that cotton strike.

During the Salinas lettuce strike in 1936, the sheriff mobilized all men between eighteen and forty-five and deputized them. Those that didn't have guns were given clubs made in the Salinas High School shop. Not only was the strike smashed, but the union, the Vegetable Packers Association, was destroyed. The district attorney at the time was Anthony Brazil who later, as a superior court judge, would rule against us during the 1970 lettuce strike.

It was in the thirties that the Associated Farmers was formed to break up union organizing. Among those who helped finance that organization, according to testimony later given before the Senate LaFollette Committee, were the Farm Bureau, the State Chamber of Commerce, Safeway, Union Pacific, Southern Pacific, and the Bank of America. Violence and terrorism were some of the favorite tactics used by the Associated Farmers.

Many of the workers who were involved in those earlier strikes are pretty old now; we should get their stories. All of them contributed to what is happening to us. Those are our saints, yet we don't even know who many of them are. I see their stories as crucially important to give us a sense of perspective, of history. There is a lot that is hidden, that is just in the heads and hearts of people. But many already are dead.

For example, there was an organizer who left a name—Pat Chambers. He led the big Corcoran and Tulare strikes against the Tagus ranch in the thirties. He was convicted under the Criminal Syndicalism Act and did two years in jail. Not too long ago that act was found to be unconstitutional.

Pat Chambers left a very good name. People remember him. An old-timer in Cutler, where I was trying to organize back in 1962, showed me a little adobe house. "Pat Chambers lived there," he told me. So I asked him how did he live. "Oh, people fed him," he said. I was very impressed. I read a little bit about him, and Fred Ross put together parts of the story. Fred's wife attended some of Chambers's trial when she was a schoolgirl in Sacramento. For years I wanted to meet Pat Chambers, but nobody knew where he was.

Then one day in Delano, after we had won the grape strike,

one of the secretaries came in and told me there was a guy in the office who wanted to shoot the breeze about farm worker organizing. He said that he had done a little organizing in his time, and he didn't want to talk to any big shots, but just anybody in the organization that wanted to talk to him.

"We haven't got the time," I told the secretary. "Try to get one of the organizers to talk with him." Then I forgot about it, until about two hours later when the secretary came back and told me the man was still there. "He says his name is Pat," she said.

"Find out his last name," I told her.

When she told me it was Pat Chambers, I quickly got up. "How old is he?"

"Well, he's an old guy."

"It couldn't be Pat Chambers. Have him come in."

So he came in, and we talked. The husband of one of my cousins, Gonzalo Flores, was once his bodyguard. Pat Chambers didn't remember him, but Gonzalo remembered him the moment he walked in. They got together and cried. Then they embraced and started recalling the strikes.

I asked Pat, "How come you weren't here sooner to support us?"

"Well, I was worried that my coming might hurt you," he said, "but now that you won in Delano, I wanted to come."

He told me that after he got out of prison, he went to San Francisco and joined the Carpenters' Union. He said the opposition was so severe, he couldn't organize farm workers anymore.

When I told him about some of the contracts we had, he just kept saying, "Amazing! Amazing!" He just couldn't believe it. But I couldn't wait to finish with that, so that I could get information from him. At first he was very reluctant to talk about himself, but he came back later, and we got a lot of valuable information from him.

It's from the strikes of others that I've learned some very simple but very meaningful things, very basic things, that have to be taken care of if you're going to exist. I learned that all strikes were decided in the first few weeks. In nearly all cases, the strike was broken in the first eight to thirteen days. A good strike can last about ten days with the emotion and the outrage, but from there on, it's just hard pull. It becomes a lot of hard work.

Some organizers felt, too, that they couldn't organize unless they struck at the same time. That was a big mistake. The first decision we made was that there would be no strikes until we'd organized first. The concept of organizing a union without getting a contract didn't occur to earlier organizers.

Of course, they didn't have much of a chance anyhow, the power was so stacked against them. Besides terror and violence, the power of agribusiness is clear in the history of labor law in our country.

In 1932 the Norris-LaGuardia Act was the first light of hope for labor unions—but not for farm workers. That law was passed to deal with the courts, which were issuing injunctions left and right against labor unions. But because of the power of agribusiness, the law didn't cover farm workers, and today we still have more injunctions than we have letters of the alphabet.

Then the big break for labor came in 1935 when our country was in the depths of the Great Depression, and there were waves of revolution sweeping the country. The Wagner Act was enacted, truly the first Bill of Rights for labor. It gave the industrial unions their start. At that time, General Motors, Ford, and other large employers were extremely powerful, and the unions could not possibly organize without having this kind of legislation. They also needed sufficient economic power under law to be able to wrench signed agreements from the unwilling hands of these employers. It's the same situation we have now with the workers and the growers.

But the Wagner Act specifically excluded farm workers. Again agribusiness was all-powerful in Congress.

When the Wagner Act was passed, it was a remedy to give the laboring people in America the right to have a union. It didn't make any bones about helping unions get organized. The act had no unfair labor practices defined for unions, and no restrictions on union security. Tampering with the securities that unions need to exist and survive is the worst way industrial democracy can be eroded.

After twelve years of organization under the protection of the Wagner Act, the large industrial unions were strong enough to survive all of the antilabor clauses included in the Taft-Hartley Law, the first antilabor law counteracting the things that Norris and Wagner had done. Taft-Hartley placed severe restrictions on union activity, outlawed the secondary boycott, and gave the states the right to enact the so-called "right-to-work" laws which are very antiunion laws. Taft-Hartley also outlawed the closed shop—the security that unions need to be strong and confident, so that they can have the proper relationships with their employer.

Then, exactly twelve years after Taft-Hartley, the Landrum-Griffin Act was passed with more antiunion sections, a ban on recognition and organizational picketing. And the restrictions on secondary boycotts were made worse.

Now, of course, although farm workers were never given the opportunity to form their union under the favorable climate of the Wagner Act, the growers want to impose all the restrictions on the farm workers' union that were later imposed on powerful unions. They want to do that while we are still weak, because that will prevent us from succeeding. They know that putting us under coverage of the present NLRA would not give us the needed economic power to match theirs, and it would take away what little power we have.

That's their position now. But back in 1962, when we started the Union, they didn't think they would need laws to prevent their workers from organizing. There was no union in sight with any chance of success.

So it's against this background of defeats and nearly insurmountable problems that the National Farm Workers Association got started.

CHAPTER 2

How Will We Eat?

CESAR CHAVEZ RECALLS

When I left CSO, we came to Carpinteria, and while the kids played in the sand, I planned my strategy. It was there I had planned the San Jose campaign to revive the CSO chapter after it had disintegrated, and where I later planned the Oxnard project. So it was there I returned to plan the farm workers' Union.

We stayed on the beach in a tent for about a week before going to Delano, Helen's hometown, where I knew that no matter what happened, we always would have a roof over our heads and a place to get a meal.

Those days were lonely days. It took me six months to get over leaving CSO. I was heartbroken. I wasn't angry when I left—if I had left angry, my anger would have sustained me—but I was homesick for a long time. I missed the meetings, I missed being engaged in fights with the power structure and being able to have the tools to help people. Coming to Delano and not having anything to work with was really difficult, but that was one of the things that kept me going. I had to build quickly so that I could get to a level where I could begin to help and be more effective.

I remember going to visit Fred, who was living in Corte Madera then and was just about ready to leave CSO, too. There we were, telling one another our plans, sitting there with long faces, not feeling resentful, just feeling sad that we had come to that.

Once in Delano, the first thing I did was draw a map by hand of all the towns between Arvin and Stockton, eighty-six of them, including farming camps. I decided to hit them all. I wanted to see the San Joaquin Valley as I'd never seen it before, all put together. Of course, I knew the area, but I never had seen it with the idea of organizing it.

I just drove by myself for two and a half days, looking around, crisscrossing the valley, driving by the colonias where the farm workers lived. It was very leisurely, like a vacation. I wanted to see the different crops and take a sampling of some of the workers' reactions to the idea of a Union.

When I saw a crew, I would drive in or go to the fence and ask where the foreman was. If he wasn't there, I would ask how the job was, and whether they were getting enough money. Then I would ask them point-blank "What do you think of a union?"

I would get various reactions, mostly disbelief or fear. Once in a while someone would say, "It's a good idea." But very seldom would someone say, "It's about time, we should do it." So it wasn't encouraging.

Then I started having house meetings, but mostly outside Delano because we wanted to keep it as quiet as possible. We didn't want the growers to know what we were doing, and we thought if we did it extensively in Delano, there were more chances of being identified as the source. To avoid those problems, we'd work Delano for a day and then wouldn't come back until a week or two later.

With the house-meeting approach, in forty to fifty days I could go through a community the size of Delano and really saturate it, really talk to all the poor.

When I talked to people at their homes, it was unbelievable how their attitude changed, how different it was from when I talked to them in the fields. When they overcame their fear, almost all of them would agree a union was a good thing. But almost all of them also thought that it couldn't be done, that the growers were too powerful.

HELEN CHAVEZ RECALLS

While Cesar was organizing, I was picking grapes or doing whatever field work was available. When the grape harvest was pretty heavy, sometimes I'd work ten hours a day, five days a week, for eighty-five cents an hour, I think.

I would get up at 4:00 in the morning. I was so afraid that the children would burn themselves, that I would fix breakfast for them and leave lunch prepared. I would make tortillas, pack my lunch, then go to work, and then come home and cook dinner and try to clean the house. I think the beginning of the Union was the roughest time we had.

Our kids were very good and very understanding. They still are. Our oldest son, Polly, helped. He was thirteen then. I would take him with me sometimes on weekends, because at that time we had to pack our boxes and take them out to the end of the row. That was quite a job after working all day on our knees—having to haul the boxes about a block. Then, when we picked peas, we'd take all the kids with us.

Cesar sometimes would take our youngest son, Birdy, with him. He was nearly three. I couldn't afford a baby-sitter unless my sister Theresa took him, but I really didn't want Cesar to take him a lot of times unless I packed a lunch. There was never any money for Cesar to buy him anything, and sometimes he'd go all day with just a little sandwich that I was able to pack for him and Cesar. But Birdy didn't want to stay with anyone, not even my sister. He wanted to go with Cesar.

CESAR CHAVEZ RECALLS

I remember driving up and down the valley with Birdy. The other kids were in school. I would just take a pillow and some blankets for him, and then I'd teach him to tell from the car what kind of field it was. When he learned to identify cotton, I told him about alfalfa and peaches and grapes.

If I went to Fresno, I'd stop and take him to the zoo. It was relaxed. The pace wasn't what it is today. Sometimes I would have to stay late for a house meeting, and he'd sleep in the car.

There were funny incidents. He must have been about four when I began to attend the funerals of our members. The first one that he went to was in Visalia where we put flowers on the casket. It made an impression on him. Then maybe the following week, we went to a funeral in Hanford where, instead of putting on flowers, they lowered the casket, and we began to put dirt on it, which is the old custom.

Birdy looked, took some dirt, and put it in. Then, in the loud voice of a four year old, he said, "Hey, Dad, how come we're putting dirt on this one, when we put flowers on the last one?"

In the beginning we had a little money we had saved, and I remember stopping at a drive-in and asking what he wanted. He'd just begun speaking, and he'd say, "I want a tote and a ten-burger." Sometimes all we'd get was an order of French fries for both of us. Sometimes I'd have him all day long without eating, but he'd go to sleep and never complain. He was great.

It's very difficult to ask your wife and children to make a sacrifice. And it's unfair to some extent. You must want to do something very badly. But I had no difficulty in that decision, Helen wanted to do it. In that respect I was free. And the kids were a lot smaller. Now they've gotten used to it. They were brought up with the Cause and had to suffer with us.

In the case of other organizers, we later lost some good men because of their wives. As we found out, it's harder for the wife than it is for the man, so we pay a lot of attention to wives in the Movement. We can't be free ourselves if we don't free our women. One of the freedoms is the freedom from fear. We've got to help her overcome that if she's going to be a servant to the Cause and help her husband to be a servant.

It's very difficult I guess to capture the feeling of organizing in a book. I haven't seen a book yet that accurately describes the inside of a guy, how he feels about the conditions, what it's like to be an organizer. I guess it's because there are about a thousand things happening at the same time, so many that you couldn't possibly cover everything and make it readable.

It's not at all dramatic. It's long and drawn out. Most of it is anticipation. The victories come much later.

When we came to Delano, we said, "We're going to organize farm workers. We don't know how, but we have some ideas. We don't have anything planned because even life itself can't be planned, and we're dealing with a lot of lives, we're dealing with human beings."

In organizing, you don't have a detailed plan, like a Farm Worker Organizing Master Plan. It doesn't work that way. You can't say that if you take steps one, two, and three, then everything follows. That would be predicting human nature. No one can do that.

There are guidelines and certain inescapables that you must meet, and then you build around that. But you don't know, for instance, that tomorrow you can have three hundred people at a certain meeting. You just don't know.

And you can't organize by fluttering all over the place or being flighty. That's the worst thing you can do. You must stay with one thing and just hammer away, hammer away, and it will happen.

For example, several years ago we were striking the melons one day, and we didn't get one single worker out of the fields. Everybody was depressed, so I said to them, "Go back again tomorrow. You can't decide a big job like that in one day, keep going, if necessary, to the end of the melon season." You are communicating with people in the fields, and you're making an investment. Even when you think you can't reach them because they're not coming right out, in some way they're going to respond to you, maybe tomorrow, or the day after, or two years or three years later. In fact, we've had six or seven melon strikes and lost most of them. But every year they've gotten bigger, and the workers have gotten wage increases.

You can't do too many other things, either, if you're organizing. You can't organize and have too many other interests. A reporter once told me that I sounded like I was a fanatic, and I said, "I am. There's nothing wrong with being a fanatic. Those are the only ones that get things done."

When it comes to organizing all the farm workers, I'm a fanatic, and I look for other fanatics, the ones that really want to get the job done. The desire to win has got to be very strong, or else you can't do it. An organizer must have a commitment—it's going to be done! I don't know how, but it's got to be done!

There are also some very simple things that have to be done in organizing, certain key things that nobody could get away without doing, like talking to people. If you talk to people, you're going to organize them. But people aren't going to come to you. You have to go to them. It takes a lot of work.

When you pick grapes, you pick a bunch at a time. Eventually you pick the whole vineyard. Organizing is no different. You get in trouble when you begin to get away from the fundamental, when you begin to corrupt organizing by trying to apply all kinds of theories and methods. Then it has no relevance to the whole question of talking to people and dealing with people.

The primitive stage of organizing is like the performer in vaudeville who has sticks and plates. He spins a plate on top of a stick, then spins a plate on top of another and another. Pretty soon he's got nine or ten plates spinning on separate sticks. Well, there's a law of diminishing returns. At a certain point, however good he is, he reaches his peak. He can't spin another plate without having the first one fall.

In organizing, before you reach your peak, you get another spinner to help you spin. Then you hope that he will take another spinner, and pretty soon you'll have many. If you can't do that, you can't operate.

One of the first men to get deeply involved with us was Jim

Drake. I met him the first week I came to Delano, when I was invited by Chris Hartmire, the head of the Migrant Ministry, to attend one of their camps up in the hills. We had established working relationships with the Migrant Ministry several years back, mostly through Fred Ross and Saul Alinsky.

Chris asked me if he could assign Jim, who had just joined the Migrant Ministry staff, to work with me. He started the next Monday and worked with me a while before going over to Goshen and then Porterville where he started the group called the Farm Workers Association. Later David Havens, another Migrant Ministry member, and Gil Padilla, a CSO member who would later become the Union's secretary-treasurer, went over to work with him.

THE REVEREND JAMES DRAKE RECALLS

I really thought Cesar was crazy. Everybody did except Helen. They had so many children and so little to eat, and that old 1953 Mercury station wagon gobbled up gas and oil. Everything he wanted to do seemed impossible. He used his tiny garage as his headquarters, but it was so hot in there, all the ink melted down in the mimeograph machine I lent him.

What impressed me was that even though Cesar was desperate, he didn't want our money, or Teamster money, or AFL-CIO money, or any other money that might compromise him. Right from the start, he made it clear that his organization would be independent. And I was impressed by his perseverance. Building the union was a slow, plodding thing based on hard work and very personal relationships. The growers didn't know he was in town, but the workers knew. After a while, they were coming to his house day and night for help.

The National Farm Workers Association did not just happen. Its development, like everything the Chavez family approached, was mapped out with a design toward success. Workers were not organized in dramatic meetings, but one by one, in a car on the way to a labor commissioner hearing, or while driving to meet an industrial accident referee. And while the new member drove, Cesar talked. He talked clearly and carefully, and the plan was set forth. The trips were not futile either, for a growing number of farm workers passed the word, "If you have trouble, go to Delano. Chavez can help."

Tragedy strikes farm workers in the same ways that it does other families, but there has seldom been a place for a farm worker family to turn. In the NFWA, a knock in the middle of the night at the Chavez home could often materialize quick help. The pains taken by Cesar were never part of an act. They were a very real extension of his philosophy that human beings are subjects to be taken seriously.

CESAR CHAVEZ RECALLS

Slowly we began to build a community. Dolores Huerta came, and I told her, "You have to leave your job. You can't work for a living and fight. You've got to do one or the other. You've got to do this full time. You take your choice."

So she said, "I'll come."

"Okay. If you give up your job."

"How will we eat?"

"I don't know. We'll eat something."

And I didn't know. But as we later found out, somebody in the Cause would never starve. The people would never let you.

We found out many useful things after we began to not be so concerned with ourselves, and how we looked, what we ate, and what we said. And we began to find out a lot of beautiful things, how people really are, how the poorer they are, the more open they are, and the more beautiful they are.

We also found out that while it's not beautiful to be poor if you have no choice, or just for the sake of being poor, it's beautiful to give up material things that take up your time, for the sake of time to help your fellow human beings. I think that has a lot of beauty in it.

So Dolores lived for a while in the house with us. Then, when we got enough money, she got her own house, and my cousin Manuel moved in with me. I would learn a lot from him.

MANUEL CHAVEZ RECALLS

I was making fifteen hundred to two thousand dollars a month, working four hours a day selling cars at Guarantee Chevrolet in San Diego when Cesar called me. It was the Fourth of July of 1962 when I went down to Delano.

He told me about the Union. I said, "Pretty good. How much do we get paid, and who's going to pay us?"

And he said, "Nobody."

I said, "Well, how are we going to live?"

He said, "I don't know."

I said, "You're crazy. You think I'm going to leave my job to come over here. You're crazy, man!"

Then he started telling me about how they treated us in the fields, and I started remembering back.

I was born in Yuma, October 29, 1925. My father and Cesar's father owned a little grocery store. Then in 1939 my mother died, and they were going to migrate to California, so my father and I came with them. Then, in 1943, I volunteered for the navy. I was only seventeen. I was aboard a Seabee 104 and on a converted aircraft carrier. I got a lot of schooling in the navy. Then I took off from the service. They put me in jail and gave me a bad conduct discharge for hitting an officer and going AWOL.

So I came back and started working again in the fields. We all went up north in 1949 to Crescent City in the lumber mills. Then when we came back to San Jose, I split to Phoenix, Arizona. I was selling cars, anything I could do. I kept in touch with Cesar by letter, but I didn't see him again until he called for help.

When I said, "You're crazy, I'm not coming to work for nothing!" Cesar started organizing me. He said, "Don't you remember when they left us in Corcoran, the contractor, and he didn't pay us?"

"Yea, I remember."

"Remember when we were working with D'Arrigo in 1940. He was paying us thirty cents an hour, and that man died because he was all wet?"

I said, "Yea, I remember. We were mad."

He said, "You don't remember that?"

I said, "Yea, but I got out of it! I'm not working in the fields no more. Let them get out like I did!"

And then he said, "Well, that's the thing, why farm workers can't get organized, because of the guys that get out of it instead of helping them."

So then I said, "You know what? I'll come and help you for thirty days. I'll go get a thirty-day leave of absence, and if we don't organize farm workers in thirty days, the hell with your organization, I'll go back."

"No, thirty days is nothing. You can't help me in thirty days."

So he finally convinced me. I said, "I'm not going to do it because I want to help farm workers, I'm going to do it for you, that's all. The hell with the farm workers! I'm going to help you for six months. If in six months we don't organize farm workers, I'm going to leave you."

So I started running around with Cesar. For a while, I had my unemployment insurance, and when that went out, I was broke. I didn't save no money. Money's to roll. That's why they make it round.

We were organizing, talking to people. It wasn't like now— "Cesar Chavez, come on in and eat! Say something!"—They'd say, "You're crazy, man, get out of here!"

I went to Corcoran and tried to make house meetings. I'd get to this guy, and he'd say, "Yea, I'll make a house meeting," and then I'd say, "I'll come about 7:00." And when I come back, not even him was there. They were afraid. Somebody found out he was trying to get a meeting, they called him up, they were going to fire him. It was hard.

I'd have meetings, and I'd tell them I wouldn't do this, I wouldn't do that. We'd have a Union, we'd have a credit union. But we didn't have nothing. So some guy'd get up and say, "Mr. Chavez, when you have that, I'll join. But since you got nothin!" That was tough days!

The reason I didn't leave the Union way back when I could have left was because I was so involved with people then—seeing them the way they were and knowing that something could be done. It's just like a guy is laying down there, and you know you can make him walk because all he has to do is stand up and walk. And the guy doesn't. So, how in hell can you leave him laying down there? You can't just say, "Oh the hell with you!"

And then I guess I had things against the cops and against things that happened to me. And now this is the way I'm paying them back. I feel good when I get a contract, or when I get a grower to his knees. That's my pay. That's more than money.

I've never kept a job over a year. I don't care how much money I made, I didn't like it. Maybe I've been looking for something that I wanted. I never knew what it was. I guess I'm a man of my own. I mean nobody tells me what to do in the Union, not even Cesar!

Well, I guess he does tell me in a sort of a way, but I guess he knows how to tell me.

Now I don't think I'd like any other job. I wouldn't even go work with another union because I don't think it's the same.

CHAPTER 3

We Begin to Grow

CESAR CHAVEZ RECALLS

After my cousin Manuel joined us, we began to form this really close, really tight community. We began to set rules, not written, but understood. We wanted only people with a real commitment. While Dolores and I were the architects of the National Farm Workers Association, Fred helped us, and Manuel played a large role.

In the beginning it was difficult. There were many times we didn't eat. Some people get mad if they don't eat on time. Manuel did at first. I would tell him, "You have to conquer that. You have to get in your mind you're not going to eat many times." So he got used to it.

But he also taught me an important lesson. I remember once I was on the road with Manuel, and he asked, "Are you hungry?"

"Yes, I'm very hungry," I answered. It was about 11:00 in the morning, and we hadn't eaten all day the day before. We had only enough money to buy gas and couldn't go home, or we wouldn't be able to do the job. We had slept in the car that night.

So Manuel said, "I'm going to go ask for food."

"Where?"

"Well, some house."

"Are you crazy?" I said.

"Yeah."

"I wouldn't do that!" To me asking for food was dishonest. I was too caught up with my own pride, my own false pride.

"You're crazy, I'm not going to starve!" Manuel said, "I'm going to show you that I'm a better organizer than you are. I'm going to show you that people will give us food. And I want to show you that you're going to get good food."

For about an hour I argued with him. Finally I said, "Okay, but you do it."

"Ah, you're afraid. I'll do it," he agreed. "You're one of those guys who would starve in a restaurant if you didn't have a penny in your pocket."

And I said, "I suppose you're right."

So we drove around and found a family with a lot of kids outside. It was just a shack. "This is the place that's going to give us food," Manuel said as we knocked on the door.

The kids looked at us, then called their mother. Their father wasn't there. "Sure, I've got something to eat," she said looking at us like we belonged there.

Manuel told her that we were organizing workers, and she said, "I know all about it. We were thrown out of Corcoran six years ago because my husband was in a strike." Actually her husband had been in a strike and had gotten blackballed out of Corcoran some ten or twelve years before.

We went back to the little kitchen, and just as we started to eat, her husband Julio came in and sat down with us. As soon as I stopped worrying about myself, my false pride, I thought, what a beautiful situation.

All the kids gathered around, we started talking about conditions, and we stayed there until 2:00 in the morning. But when we left that house, they were convinced. They began to work with us full time the next day.

Although Julio thought that I was a dreamer, he nevertheless went out. "It can't be done, but it's a good try," he said. But his wife thought it could be done.

After a while Julio changed his mind. He had more memberships in his town than in any other town in the valley, more than three hundred dues-paying members. He was the first full-time convert that we made, and later Julio Hernandez became one of the Union's first vice-presidents.

From then on, asking for food or for help became another tool in organizing. But Manuel said, "Don't think that all the people will give you food." He chose, in the barrio, a brightly painted Mexican-American house with a new car in front. They wouldn't even open the door. They thought we were crazy. But we'd go to the poor homes and never miss. The least they would give us was a taco, and we would eat it outside. We never missed. Or, rather I should say, the people never missed. It was beautiful.

Although we were in very bad shape financially, I didn't worry too much about our own family. I couldn't, I had too many other problems. Richard was a carpenter then, building homes, and Manuel and I would dig the foundations for him. At other times, when we were really short of funds, I worked with Helen in the fields.

Helen did most of the worrying about money for food and clothing. She never wavered, even in the worst periods. She worked in the vineyards or the fields, although she hadn't done work in the fields for maybe fifteen years. For a while she worked in the onions, starting at 5:00 in the morning and working until 6:00 at night. She'd come home exhausted in the evening, so I told her not to go.

"I need to pay the rent," she protested, but I prevailed on her as far as the onions were concerned.

HELEN CHAVEZ RECALLS

I hadn't worked for a while, because at that time of the year you could only pick up maybe a day's or a week's work. There was nothing except peas, and then you had everybody in the whole city out there with their kids picking peas. You just made a few hampers, and that was it.

One day, after Anna had made her first Communion, we stopped at Safeway for a little food. Every time you went into Safeway, they would give you a little coupon that you would run under the faucet. You had to have five of those spelling "money" or something, and a flag. Every time we would go to the store, we saved these.

So when we got one of those little tags, I told the checker, "This is going to be my winner," and he laughed. I was just joking with him. I gave the tag to the kids, and they went out to the car. I think it was one of the girls who put saliva on it, and came in yelling, "Mom, Mom, you got the flag! You won!"

I didn't pay any attention to her, but when we went home, we wiped it off good, and there it was—a winner. I rushed back to Safeway. I was really excited, because I had won $100 and thought, oh, boy, what a lot of food for the kids!

After I got my check, I told Cesar, "Look, we can go get some things."

And he said, "I'm sorry, but this is going toward our gas bill." He said he was about to lose his gasoline credit card because he owed $180.

I was so disappointed, I sat and cried. I had made so many plans for that $100!

CESAR CHAVEZ RECALLS

I used to go out and get Fred once in a while and pour out my heart to him about all the problems I had. He would listen and make suggestions. Then I would feel better and come back. Those were tough times.

I borrowed a hand-cranked mimeograph machine, and we ran a program. The moment my kids were out of school on Friday, I'd give them leaflets, put them in the car, and take off. During the summer we would work until about 9:00 or 9:30, then all day Saturday and half a day Sunday. We would cover Kern, Kings, Tulare, and Fresno Counties distributing leaflets.

I'd put all the kids on one street, then a lot of kids would come out, and we would get through in fifteen minutes with maybe twenty kids helping us. Then we'd take off for the next barrio. Once we went for a week and a half. Dolores started from Sacramento in the north, and I started from Wheeler Ridge in the south. In a week and a half we distributed over a hundred thousand leaflets. With my gang, I got as far as Modesto, but then I had more kids than Dolores and I also had Richard's with me.

The leaflets said anything I could think of, just so I could get the name of the National Farm Workers Association before their eyes. I gave them the address and phone number and something timely like what to do in case they didn't get paid, or if a labor contractor broke his promises. Then I would rush back to Delano. I was sure I would have a whole mailbox full of mail.

Nothing!

To save gas I'd walk to the post office early in the morning and wait there until they got through distributing the mail. I remember the time I got the first letter. No sooner had the mailman put the mail in the box than I grabbed it. That first letter meant so much.

I ran all the way home, sat down to have breakfast, and read it to Helen out loud. It was an inquiry asking "What is the National Farm Workers Association? Is that an association of braceros to take our jobs from us?"

Every two or three days there was maybe one letter. I would answer each and then go see them personally. Then once I got two letters—was I happy!

And the members we recruited were wonderful. During the season they would come thirty, forty miles and bring us beets or celery or carrots or chickens. They knew our condition, not because we told them, but because we were so intimately a part of them. They knew. They'd see the need and come running. The poor are great.

There was one couple in Fresno who had a little room especially for me. They gave me a key, and every time I went by Fresno I could sleep there, open the refrigerator, eat. They gave me the first mimeograph machine I had, a real old machine that looked like it had come to San Francisco around the Horn before the Panama Canal was built.

Once I was going to see Dolores, and I didn't have any money. Manuel said, "Hell, let's just go." I had some friends from the CSO in Madera who gave us a hot meal, got the car lubed and gassed, and gave us about seven dollars. I had a little house meeting with them that night and talked about what we were doing.

That's where the first corrido was written—that's a ballad usually sung to a folk song. There must be more than fifty corridos now about our Movement, but this was the first one. While we were having our meeting, Rosa Gloria just started writing. Then, when I got through, she sang it to the tune of "Corrido de Cananea" which is about a jail, but which was also the scene of some bitter miner strikes. Her corrido was about our Union, and two of the verses went something like this:

> In the year '62
> With effort and uncertainty
> There began a campaign
> For the campesino.
>
> Cesar Chavez started it.
> He became a volunteer
> And went forth as a pilgrim
> To fulfill his destiny.

The theme of the ballad was that I had come, and things were going to be different now. I didn't believe her. But I liked it so much I asked her to sing it at our first Union convention.

After a while we had houses all over the valley with Union representatives. We didn't mention the word *Union*, but when workers came in, we said this was a Union.

They'd ask, "Do you strike?"

"Not yet, but we will strike. That's the only way to win. But we don't want to take you into a suicidal strike. When we're ready for it, we're in for keeps."

That answered their big concern, which was that you can't win a strike. We'd say, "That's right—now. However, the only way to win is through a strike, and you really plan it. Then you can win."

We would come to see the Union representatives every other week, or once a week, or once every four days, depending where the area was. We'd eat and sleep there and service the people from there.

We'd take the big problems that they had, some of the police problems, labor problems like nonpayment of wages, and workmen's compensation cases. We'd service problems at county hospitals, anything that affected them. This was a community Union. When we had to put on the pressure, we knew how to do it from our CSO training.

In Visalia that first winter, I appealed no less than sixty welfare cases and won every single one. I was practically living in that welfare department. I went to administrative hearings on five cases and acted as the spokesman for the person. When the decisions started coming back from Sacramento, I was winning all of them. Then the welfare director called me in to negotiate the rest.

Tulare County is a very cheap county. The welfare director—his name, I think, was Fuot—was an Arab. He got very excited. He was smaller than I am and thin and had a shrill, powerful voice. He would jump up and down and pound on the desk and jump up on the chair and run around the table and pace back and forth. It was really funny. I just sat there and said, "No, Mr. Fuot, no." And I said, "Well, we'll appeal." We got in a big fight, negotiated, and I got most of the things I wanted.

Then we began to set up some services for the members, a death-benefit program, a credit union, and a co-op. Helen would work there at the counter and sell tires and oil to the members cheaper than anywhere in town.

After things got humming, I had to stay in Delano, service the cases, do the correspondence, and write the newsletter. Dolores and Manuel did the field work, and Helen kept the books.

We began to grow. Our house was used as an office, and our door was open twenty-four hours a day. On Sunday, for example, ten, fifteen, twenty cars were parked on the street. The neighbors began to complain.

One day one of our girls came in. She had gotten into a fight with a little neighbor boy up the street who said he knew what we were doing.

"Your mother and your father are running an illegal house," he said.

She didn't know quite what that was—she was very small—but she knew it was bad. She was crying.

CHAPTER 4

The Black Eagle Is Born

CESAR CHAVEZ RECALLS

We needed an emblem for the Union, a flag that people could see. Many ideas were suggested, but we wanted something that the people could make themselves, and something that had some impact. We didn't want a tractor or a crossed shovel and hoe or a guy with a hoe or pruning shears. I liked the Mexican eagle with a snake in its mouth, but it was too hard to draw.

It was Richard who suggested drawing an eagle with square lines, an eagle anyone could make, with five steps in the wings. I chose the colors, red with a black eagle on a white circle.

Red and black flags are used for strikes in Mexico. They mean a union. There were other reasons, too, for those colors. The Nazis were experts at designing symbols with impact. Their flag was red with a black swastika on a white circle. Commercially, the same color combinations were used here by Texaco, Marlboro cigarettes, and by Safeway. Their experts, too, chose those colors because of their impact.

We wanted to have the flag ready for our first convention coming up in Fresno, so Manuel volunteered to make the first one. He's not an artist, but it looked like an eagle, except that the neck looked like a snake. We still kid him about that one.

MANUEL CHAVEZ RECALLS

One time Cesar said, "All right, are you ready to have a convention?" He said, "Manuel, go to Fresno, rent a hall, get some

173

things to eat for the people that are going to come, and set it up."

I said, "Money?"

"No money."

"How am I going to rent a hall?" Nobody knew us. I said, "Give me money for gas."

He said, "I got no money for gas."

So I went to the bar. Some guy said, "Hey, get a beer." And I said, "No, not right now. I got to go to Fresno and rent a hall, and we haven't got no money. Why don't you give me the money so I can get gas?"

Everybody started laughing about it, but they chipped in and gave me about $1.50, and I went to Fresno.

I went to this hall and inquired who it belonged to. They told me there was this bar, so I went to this bar. I had my identification —National Farm Workers Association, secretary-treasurer, Manuel Chavez. But no money.

I said, "Sir, my name is Manuel Chavez, and we want to have a meeting in your hall."

"Oh, fine. Sure."

"How much is the rent?" I think he said fifty dollars, but I said, "I'm secretary-treasurer, but I don't carry the money. The president is the one that holds the money, and he's flying in. We won't have the money until they come in."

He said, "Fine."

So then I went to the store next door to where the hall was, and I told them we needed a lot of baloney and bread for sandwiches. And I told them the same thing, the guys are flying in with the money.

So when Cesar came, I had sandwiches and Cokes, and Cesar said, "Well, are we ready?" And I said, "Nope, let me talk first!"

I went to the delegates and told them what I did. Everybody started laughing. I said, "Before anything starts here, you got to pay. I want to be at this meeting."

So everybody started donating money before the convention started. We had enough money to pay for the rent and for the food and some left over.

CESAR CHAVEZ RECALLS

Our first convention was held on September 30, 1962, in an abandoned theater in Fresno. A week before that I got a letter from Fred wishing me luck. "I'll be keeping all ten fingers crossed," he wrote, "and calling upon the saints of all good agnostics to bring you luck and succor." A few days later he decided to attend.

There was a big screen in the theater, and our huge flag covered most of it. The flag itself was covered with paper. I wanted Manuel to pull the cord, so I could see the reaction of the people as it was unveiled.

When the eagle appeared, everyone gasped. You could hear it. A few were so shocked we lost them. They thought we were Communists. Some commented that the eagle should be gold and the background light blue. Others complained it looked like the Nazi banner. I said, "It's what you want to see in it. To me it looks like a strong, beautiful sign of hope."

Manuel was more eloquent. He explained that the black eagle signified the dark situation in which the worker finds himself, the white circle signified hope and aspirations, and the red background indicated the toil and sacrifice that the Association and its members would have to contribute in order to gain justice for the farm workers.

And then he said, "When that damn eagle flies, the problems of the farm workers will be solved!"

We had about 150 delegates and their families at the convention. Besides adopting the flag, we voted to organize the farm workers, elected temporary officers, agreed to lobby for a minimum wage law covering farm workers, and adopted Viva La Causa— Long Live the Cause—as our motto. We also voted to have dues of $3.50 a month.

Manuel played a very big role in that before the convention. He wanted $5 a month, but I was afraid to go too hard. I wanted $1 or $1.50 a month. Dolores was pretty much with me. We felt that poor farm workers couldn't really afford it. But Manuel argued, "Look, either they pay and we make it, or they don't and we don't. You can't be kidding yourselves."

Manuel taught us some reality. He pounded it into our heads. "If they can't pay to have their own Union, they don't deserve it. They've got to sacrifice to pay. We've got to make them do not as much as we're doing, but they've got to do their share. It must be put up to them in a very frank, direct way." And so we did.

Before the convention, I also worked on the constitution. That was a big job. I had copies of many union constitutions as a guide, but it was a slow process. In the beginning I assigned myself about an hour every day to reading them, trying to understand some of the weaknesses and some of the strong points.

Because of the mobility of the people, I thought that we would need a very strong, centralized administration, and that we could never have a local as other unions have. We couldn't have any geographical restrictions on employment, and I felt the Union would have to be so alike everywhere that workers could recognize that it was, in fact, one Union. But we also wanted local say-so for the workers. Finally, we decided to have each ranch have its own ranch committee that would elect its own officers, its own stewards, and take care of its own problems. At the start, that's the most inefficient way of doing it, but, in time, once they are trained, it's not only the most efficient, but it also is the most representative and has the most involvement.

Then, from the federal law, we lifted the sections on workers' rights, making it part of our constitution—the right to hearings and trials and recalls, the right for members to speak freely, to give testimony to congressional committees.

We presented the preliminary draft at our first convention, but it was not adopted until our next meeting in January. I was still writing it on Helen's birthday, the day before the meeting, when all the family suddenly arrived to give Helen a surprise birthday party. I had to leave the house and go to Richard's home to keep on working.

Her family was very upset and told her, "Cesar must not really like you that much. If he loved you, he'd be here." She defended me, and they argued. When I came home, she was crying, and I said, "Why fight with them? You understand and I understand." Since then that's changed. They, too, understand.

On January 20, 1963, the constitution was formally adopted, and permanent officers elected at a meeting in Pius X Hall in Delano.

Before our first year was up, we knew we were on the right road with the Union. I'm not saying that we had it made, but the hardest bridge had been crossed. We gave ourselves three years of hard work. If we couldn't do it in three years, then we couldn't do it. But we made a firm promise among ourselves that if we couldn't do it, we'd never blame the people, we'd blame ourselves.

MANUEL CHAVEZ RECALLS

After the convention Cesar asked me where I wanted to go organize. I said, give me the toughest city there is. He gave me Corcoran because he said Siler and Boswel owned the damn town, and if you don't work with them, they don't have to run you out of town, they just don't give you a job, and you run yourself out of town. Also, there had been a big strike in Corcoran, and everybody got left stranded. So that was tough.

I went to Corcoran, and I was working, working, working trying to make a member. And I couldn't. Finally I was walking down the street, and somebody honked at me. He said, "I've been hearing you talk about the National Farm Workers Association, and I like it. Why don't you come over to my house?"

So I went to his house and talked to him in the kitchen. I said, "How's your wife?" and he said she was in the bedroom.

He said, "How much do you have to pay?" and I said it was $3.50 a month. "What does it take to join?"

I said, "I've got my stuff in the car." So I made him a member and ran out of there with $3.50 and a receipt. I went to a telephone and called Cesar. Cesar was out organizing somewhere. The next day he wasn't home, and the third day he wasn't. So the fourth day I got him and said, "Cesar, I got a member!"

"Yea, I know."

"What do you mean, you know. I haven't even talked to you."

"Yea, but they talked to us. The wife is dead. We owe five hundred dollars." We had this death-benefit insurance.

So a couple of times I wanted to give up. I'd come to Cesar. I was disgusted, no money, people wouldn't even listen to you. I'd tell Cesar to go to hell. So he'd say, you're exhausted. I'm going to give you five dollars. Go get drunk.

I went and got drunk with five dollars, then the rest of the guys, they knew I never had money, so I wouldn't even spend the five dollars. And the next two days, I'd sleep it out.

"Okay, I'm going to help you another month."

Cesar's pretty smart.

CESAR CHAVEZ RECALLS

We held annual meetings of the Union and the credit union from then on. At one of those meetings they approved our getting an office in the southwest corner of Delano, at First and Albany. My brother, who still was working as a carpenter, donated his evenings to fix it up and paint it. Then we had a party there.

I'll never forget that. People came from maybe seventy, eighty miles, from Fresno, Wasco, Corcoran, Visalia, everywhere, and they brought things, just like a baby shower; but they brought things for the office, paper, pens, pencils, envelopes. We stayed in that office until the strike started, and we had to expand.

There were times, of course, when we didn't know whether we'd survive. We'd get members, and then they would drop out. We might go all day collecting dues and have every single one say, "I can't pay. I'm sorry, but I don't want to belong any more." That happened often. They would come and use us, and after they had gotten what they wanted, they had second thoughts. At times it took a lot of faith and courage not to turn against the people.

All of us would go out and collect the dues. It was hard both physically and mentally because we had to get in a car at night, and we didn't have too much time. It would be raining, and it was cold, and there was a lot of unemployment, and the people had problems.

But we had to do it because we didn't want any money from the outside world. That's the only way the Union can be supported, by its members.

We had two hundred members when we started the dues-paying program. Ninety days later, we were down to twelve paying dues. And from those twelve we began to build steadily. Sometimes we'd lose five, and we'd go back and pick up ten more. But we continued to grow. Of the original twelve, all are still members except two who were killed in accidents. We named the Delano clinic for one of them, Rodrigo Terronez, who was a vice-president.

We began to see that by the time people had been paying dues for six months, we couldn't keep them away. They were right there wanting to know everything. It was quite an experience for me. Then, once a guy had paid a whole year's dues, $42.50, if anybody said anything wrong about the Union or anybody in the Union, that guy was like a lion. He had a commitment.

Sometimes to raise money and get new members, we'd have large fiestas, barbecues, and dances and speeches. We would attract five hundred, six hundred, one thousand people in different towns. I remember one barbecue in the beginning when Helen and I were thinking how to raise money. I wanted to have a lot of people, so I told Helen, "You know what? Let's have a barbecue in Corcoran and invite everybody free."

"Where are you going to get the money?" she asked.

I said, "Well, we'll see."

So we had a free barbecue, and several thousand people came, all farm workers. We sold the beer, and people also contributed. We made more than enough to pay all the expenses. Later we had another one in Lamont and one in Delano that was out of this world. We set up membership booths, signed people up, and gave them *El Malcriado*, the Union paper.

CHAPTER 5

A Strike in the Roses

CESAR CHAVEZ RECALLS

We had our first strike in the spring of 1965. While we didn't win, it gave us a good indication of what to expect in other strikes, how labor contractors and police would be used against us.

Epifanio Camacho, a farm worker from McFarland, just south of Delano, came and told us of all the abuses in the rose industry there. We worked with those workers for more than a month until we had them tightly organized.

Grafting roses is highly skilled work. Grafters crawl on their knees for miles slitting mature rose bushes and inserting buds at top speed. The slightest miscalculation means the bud will not take and the bush will be useless.

Although they were promised $9 a thousand plants, injertadors —grafters of roses—were actually getting between $6.50 and $7 a thousand.

After a series of meetings to prepare the strike, we chose the biggest company, Mount Arbor, which employed about eighty-five workers, not counting the irrigators and supervisors. We voted not to have a picket line, because everyone pledged not to break the strike.

We had a pledge ceremony on Sunday, the day before the strike started. Dolores held the crucifix, and the guys put their hands on it, pledging not to break the strike.

Early Monday morning we sent out ten cars to check the people's homes. We found lights in five or six places and knocked on the doors. The men were getting up.

"Where are you going?" we asked them.

Most of them were embarrassed. "Oh, I was just getting up, you know."

"You're not going to work are you?"

"Of course not!"

The company foreman was very angry when none of the grafters showed up for work. He refused to talk to us. Thinking that maybe a woman would have a better chance, we had Dolores knock on the office door about 10:30.

"Get out, you Communist! Get out," the manager shouted.

I guess they were expecting us, because as Dolores was arguing with him, the cops came and told her to leave.

A day or so later, we had a hunch two or three workers living in one house were going to break the strike. So Dolores drove up to their driveway in a green truck, killed the motor, put it in gear, set the brake, locked the windows and doors, took the keys, and hid them so they couldn't drive out. Even though she was alone, she refused to move.

Then a group of Mexican workers from Tangansiguiero helped break the strike. Everybody was angry, and we sent a letter to the mayor of Tangansiguiero denouncing them. In those little Mexican towns, they have an old building where people go to read the news. On one side they list things like stray animals, and on the other they have a list of criminals.

The mayor was so upset, he put our letter on the side with the criminals, in effect classifying them as such. We got immediate reactions from the workers. People came and said, "Don't be like that. You're giving me a bad name in my community when I go back."

And I said, "Look, you broke the strike. You deserve that and more."

There was a lot of criticism of the Tangansiguieros. Today I think everyone from there is a Union member, and they are all good Union members.

Labor contractors were used to break the strike. Under the California Labor Code, a worker can't be recruited to a strike zone unless he's been warned that a strike is in progress. In this case, they were not told, and we turned the information in to the labor commissioner's office.

His office in Delano did what I thought was a beautiful job of documenting a case where one employer lent all of his crew to Mount Arbor. I went with the agent of the labor commissioner's office to the district attorney in Kern County, who refused to accept the information or issue a citation. So we knew immediately

what would be the pattern from then on. Without labor contractors, we'd win every strike in California.

Because it's so hard to find good rose grafters, however, we were
able to get a wage increase after four days. But we never got a
contract.

About the same time, in the Porterville area, another major
event happened that really helped the Union. When the Tulare
County Housing Authority decided to raise the rents in the Linnel
and Woodville farm labor camps, Jim Drake of the Migrant
Ministry and Gilbert Padilla, who had been active in the CSO,
organized a rent strike.

The housing authority wanted to charge twenty-five dollars a
month for tin shacks built in 1938 that were missing doors and
windows and had no running water. Short of getting into an
agricultural strike, the rent strike, which lasted through the summer, was one of the best ways of educating farm workers that there
was a Union concerned with their economic interests. It was one
of the first demonstrations where the black eagle flew.

And about twenty students who helped there that summer were
even more helpful on their college campuses in the fall when we
were suddenly plunged into the grape strike. They organized support and donations that helped the strikers survive.

CHAPTER 6

The Grape Strike Starts

CESAR CHAVEZ RECALLS

I found out about the grape strike on September 8, 1965, when Manuel Uranday, his wife Esther, and his father came to the office to tell me the Filipinos were on strike.

"Oh, no!" I said.

"What are we going to do?"

"Well, we can't call a strike, because we have to take a vote," I said after we discussed what was happening.

I learned that Filipino workers from a camp at Lucas and Sons had stopped work, and the strike had spread quickly to other growers. Earlier that summer, AWOC had struck in Thermal in the Coachella Valley because the pay was below $1.40 an hour, the prevailing wage for braceros in the Imperial Valley south of Coachella. Actually the bracero law had expired in 1964, but Governor Pat Brown had persuaded Secretary of Labor Willard Wirtz to allow braceros into California at that wage rate. Since growers weren't using braceros in the Coachella Valley, they dropped the wage to $1.10 for Chicano grape pickers and $1.25 for the Filipinos. AWOC called a strike, and in ten days the pay was raised. But AWOC didn't get a contract.

Now in the Delano area, when some of the same growers who paid $1.40 in Coachella would only pay $1.00, AWOC called another strike.

Larry Itliong was in charge for AWOC. He had come to this country from the Philippines in 1929 when he was only fifteen and was involved in his first lettuce strike a year later in Monroe,

Washington. He had been an organizer with AWOC for about five years, but I think I first met him that August when he came to my office with Ben Gines, another AWOC official. Dolores knew Larry well in Stockton, and I knew who he was, but I had never talked to him until then.

He and Gines wanted to know if the NFWA was a Union or a civil rights movement. After I had said it was a Union, they wanted to know if we were going to strike. I said no. Although we met again in our office a week or two later, they didn't tell us whether they were planning to strike, and we never asked.

At the time we had about twelve hundred members, but only about two hundred were paying dues. I didn't feel we were ready for a strike—I figured it would be a couple more years before we would be—but I also knew we weren't going to break a strike.

I thought the growers were powerful and arrogant, and I judged they were going to underestimate us, but I wasn't afraid of them or their power. I was afraid of the weakness of the people. I knew that the only way we could win was to keep fighting a long time, and I didn't see how we could get that determination.

We quickly had a board meeting, discussed the situation, and pretty much decided that this was it. I said it was going to be a long struggle, and the only way we could win was by staying with it. I said that our job was not to get discouraged if we went up like a wave and then came down, that at the point that we came down, we would start with whatever we had left.

We talked about the need to make the strike a public controversy as soon as possible to get it out of the Delano area, not letting the growers choke it there, but publicizing it. I was sure we couldn't win it by ourselves. We needed money. And in order for the growers to come out with what they really thought of Unions, the best way was to put them under pressure and let them express themselves to the public.

We decided to drop everything and start organizing for a mass meeting to get a good strike vote. Well, I was using this for organizing, too. I wanted to have the meeting on September 16, Mexican Independence Day, the great Mexican holiday marking the end of Spanish rule.

There was much to do, finding a meeting place, getting all the members there, and preparing a case for us with the growers, AWOC, and the public. We put out different leaflets every day going door to door in Delano, McFarland, Richgrove, Earlymart, parts of Wasco, Porterville, and Bakersfield.

I sent Dolores to the picket lines to help Larry and feed information back to me on what was happening. I told her, "You know Larry, go there and be helpful to him, and don't interfere with what he's doing, just be helpful."

Larry had so many problems—we all had, but he had many. He welcomed help. Dolores and Larry were in constant touch, and Dolores reported to me every day. We had nothing to give him except our love—we had something like eighty-two dollars in the treasury—while the Filipinos had money and they had a hall and food which they later shared with us, not only because of Union solidarity but because of the Filipino culture. They're beautiful about helping people.

During that first week, the strike spread to about two thousand workers and some twenty farm labor camps. In some places the growers locked the workers out of the camps, camps where they had been living for years. In others, the men refused to leave, and the utilities were shut off. Then the growers added armed security guards, one of whom took a shot at a striker.

So there was a lot of excitement by the time we held our meeting. The hall at Our Lady of Guadalupe Church in Delano was large and had a balcony. We had put up our huge Union flag and posters of Zapata and Jack London's "Definition of a Strike Breaker." By the time the meeting started, the hall and balcony were jam-packed, and people were coming out of the rafters.

There were guys from every ranch in the area. We made sure of that so, when a strike vote was taken, it would be a general strike of all growers. The meeting was very spirited, a band played, and every so often the hall rang out with cries of "Viva La Causa!"

We first talked about the Filipino brothers, about solidarity and the need to have a general strike. When my turn came, I recalled a little history.

"A 155 years ago in the state of Guanajuato in Mexico," I said, "a padre proclaimed the struggle for liberty. He was killed, but ten years later Mexico won its independence." And then I spoke of the present. "We are engaged in another struggle for the freedom and dignity which poverty denies us. But it must not be a violent struggle, even if violence is used against us. Violence can only hurt us and our cause.

"The strike was begun by the Filipinos, but it is not exclusively for them," I said. "Tonight we must decide if we are to join our fellow workers in this great labor struggle."

Then I had several farm workers from different areas like Jalisco and Michoacan get up and give a speech. One of them said he was from Tamaulipas. "It is an honor to come here and we must not abuse it," he said. "We have to aid our brothers the Filipinos. We are all humans. This is a just cause. Let's go out on strike!"

An older farm worker from the valley spoke about some strikes in the thirties. "I saw two strikers murdered before my eyes by a rancher," he recalled. "There was nothing to eat in those days, there was nothing. And we're in the same place today, still submerged, still drowned."

The workers who spoke were eloquent because they spoke from the heart, and they spoke the truth. When the strike vote was taken, it was obvious we would have a general strike. Everyone was for it.

Then everybody signed authorization cards saying they wanted NFWA to represent them. When we counted them a couple of days after the meeting, we had twenty-seven hundred. Of course, not all were signed at the meeting, but more than half must have been signed there.

Before the meeting ended, we voted to have the same demands as AWOC, $1.40 an hour, 25 cents a box, and $12 a gondola.

Then I made a final appeal to keep the strike nonviolent. "Are you in agreement?" I asked.

"Si!" they roared back.

After the strike vote, I asked for several days to try to get the growers to meet with us. I wanted to prepare a case so that if we went to the public, they'd know we tried to meet with the growers. It was also hoping against hope. We knew the growers weren't going to meet with us, but we were hoping that somehow they would.

I called our attorney, Richard Richardson, a young lawyer out of Santa Barbara, and told him he'd better get in a car and go to Stockton, where he met Al Green, the head of AWOC, the next day, and suggested we meet in Delano two days later.

Meanwhile Jim Drake called his boss, Chris Hartmire, who had a friend in Fresno, Ralph Duncan, who worked with the State Conciliation Service. When Duncan came to see us, we asked him to contact the growers and call us back. On Saturday, having heard nothing, we called him. "For God's sake, call us! What happened?"

"The guys don't want to talk," he said. "They wouldn't talk to me."

We sent letters to the growers with return receipt requested. We still have them in the files as evidence. All but one came back unopened. The growers all refused delivery. The only letter that was opened was for a grower who had died. It was a mistake. The property was under trusteeship; the attorney called and said he wasn't authorized to act.

Then we had Dolores call the growers, and Jim Drake call them. We did everything we could, but we didn't succeed. We went to see the mayor of Delano, Dr. Clifford Loader, and told him we thought it was foolish to have a strike, that we could sit down and talk to them. I knew him from CSO days because he was a Democrat. In fact, just before the strike started, I had gotten my first cavity ever, and he had taken care of it.

Mayor Loader issued a call asking the growers to use City Hall to negotiate. He was pretty naïve. The growers really got to him, they were so mad. Since then he's been very much against us.

During the three days before the strike started, we also went to see every labor contractor in Delano, between thirty-five and forty-two of them, asking them not to break the coming strike.

Sunday we met with Al Green in the Stardust Motel in Delano, and I proposed that we have a joint strike committee, a joint finance committee—they had all the money, we didn't have any—and a joint picket line. We said we would recognize him as the leader of the strike.

Al Green would have been the director of the Union, if he had been a little bit smarter. But he turned us down. He said, "I'm just an organizing committee. I'm not authorized to make those kind of deals."

"Well, can you call Washington?" I asked.

"No, I don't want to call Washington," he answered in his low, deep, deliberate voice. "It's not necessary."

So I asked if we could issue a joint press statement.

"No, I don't think that's wise."

There was nothing more to say.

As we were walking out the door, he said, "I'd like to have a picture with you. I've heard a lot about you."

So we had our pictures taken. Then we left to get ready for the next day's strike, a strike that was destined to test our strength and endurance for five painful years.

CHAPTER 7

Where Harassment Backfires

CESAR CHAVEZ RECALLS

We were up before dawn Monday morning. Before the day was over, more than twelve hundred workers had joined the strike in an area covering about four hundred square miles of vineyards.

There was a lot of excitement, a lot of optimism, and a tremendous amount of activity. In those days we didn't know how to organize the people for maximum production, and there was a lot of wasted effort, a lot of people constantly coming and going.

Our office was a little store at the corner of First and Albany, no bigger than 20 by 40 feet, and it was jam-packed. We used it as an office, as a service center, as a dormitory, and as a meeting hall. We never closed. And we were picketing every day, getting up very early each morning and going to bed very late at night.

Ironically, although in the Mexican custom the man is really the boss of the house, once the strike started, women became freer quicker than the men. And it's been our experience everywhere since then. The women are not afraid. They know what they're doing because it means beans and shoes for their kids.

Sometimes pickets asked, "What's the use of picketing?" because they were picketing and couldn't even see the people working deep in the vineyards. The answer was that they affected production.

"Just keep talking to the scabs," I said. "After a while, if it's done

187

the right way, they begin to leave. Somebody else may take their place, or it looks like the job is filled, but it isn't really. There's a loss of time. The grower is getting people who are not experienced, who have never seen grapes in their lives. For the employer that's loss of money."

"We've got to make the grower spend fifty dollars to our one dollar," I said. "We affect production and costs and profit. And if we hold out, we can win."

In addition, to me the picket line is something very special. Unless you have been on a picket line, you just can't understand the feeling you get there, seeing the conflict at its two most acid ends. It's a confrontation that's vivid. It's a real education.

Without knowing it, the workers also had more than just a picket line; they had the nerve to be in a picket line and to be striking.

The growers were very angry at the challenge. How dare they strike the bosses! Both surprised and hurt, they struck back. On the first day, I left two workers to picket the entrance of a ranch near the office. A short time later they were back, breathless.

"What happened?" I asked. "Where's your car?" They had run about a mile to the office.

They said a grower had pointed a shotgun at them and threatened to kill them. He grabbed their picket signs, set them on fire, and when they didn't burn fast enough, he blasted the signs with his shotgun.

The incident was reported to the police, but nothing happened.

A few days later, when we had about six or seven pickets in front of a labor contractor's home, about twenty or thirty growers came over there half-drunk from a party. Julio Hernandez ran to tell me that the growers had beaten one of our men. So I went over and got on the picket line.

The growers were giving us the knee and the elbow, knocking us down and throwing us down. But we remained nonviolent. We weren't afraid of them. We just got up and continued picketing.

A big crowd started forming, booing the growers. Then the Filipinos, who were having a meeting in Filipino Hall, got in their cars and raced over. The growers suddenly were surrounded by angry people. Police, sheriff's deputies, and the fire department arrived.

One of the growers started getting rough with one of the cops, who put him in his patrol car, handcuffed him, and drove him to jail. There they released him. When we finally left, we were bruised, and I had sore ribs and legs and back for a while. Nothing happened to the growers.

As days passed, there was more violence. Growers pushed people around on the picket lines, ran tractors between pickets and the field to cover them with dust and dirt, and drove cars and pickups with guns and dogs dangerously close to pickets at high speeds.

One day, when Episcopal Bishop Sumner Walters joined our pickets, he was a victim of one of those dust attacks. Later, one grower used his sulphur rig to spray the pickets. When he finally was tried, he was acquitted.

Another time Dolores was coming back from a picket line with other people, and their car began to boil over. When they stopped by a house to get water, a grower came charging out of the house with a shotgun, which he fired over their heads.

During the first days of the strike things looked very good—as they usually do—then about the sixth day, did they look bad. From then on it was a seesaw battle.

There were days when we got all kinds of strikebreakers out of the fields. On others we didn't. At times they'd almost drive us out, and we'd regroup our strength and come back again. Sometimes we couldn't even go picketing because there were so many injunctions. We could hardly move. Other times we weren't picketing because we didn't have any gas for the cars—we didn't have any money at all. Our guys went for about six months without getting a bill paid for anything. And we were discouraged.

More than once the authorities threatened to close our office down. Some of the people that were sent to do a job on us obviously didn't like it at all. I don't remember who it was, but I think it was the fire marshall who hated the politics of his assignment and told us so on more than one occasion. But they kept up their investigations under the health and building codes and the fire code. They were just on the verge of knocking us completely out, but we lucked out.

There was constant intimidation and harassment. Every single person who came to our office had his license plate number taken down. If he went to town, he would be stopped and questioned.

Of course, after a while, we welcomed this because every time the cops stopped these people, they'd get madder and help us more.

Those early days were really mean. We had cops stationed at our office and our homes around the clock. Every time I got in the car in Delano, they'd follow me all over, and I wouldn't shake them until I was well past several towns. Then they'd leave me and go back.

One of the first jobs we had to do was to get our people conditioned, so they wouldn't be afraid of the police. If they're not afraid, then they can keep a lot of things cool, but the moment they're uncertain, then anything can happen.

There was other harassment on the picket lines. At one point, after we had been on strike for about five or six weeks, we were stopped constantly by deputies. Every striker was photographed, and a field-report card was filled in on each person. In some cases, it took as much as an hour and a half to go through this process. Then it was repeated every time we moved from one field to another. We have a man in Delano who was photographed, and the same report was filled in on him no less than twelve times.

At first our tactic was total cooperation. Then we started taking their time. In my case, the officer took almost an hour because I went very slowly. I examined the card and the spelling, and I engaged in conversation just to tie him up.

Then we'd go on night picketing, get about thirty cars and go out at night, and they'd have to wake up the cops to follow us. We worked it so they had to have three shifts. If we'd go out of the office at 3:00 in the morning, they'd follow us.

With us, it was a tactic to get them to spend as much money as possible. The county spent thousands of dollars on extra personnel. They'll never spend that much money again. Afterward there were a lot of complaints. A small group of liberals in Bakersfield checked up on the expense and found they had spent thousands of dollars.

Finally we made up our minds we had been harassed enough. We refused to give them any information or to let them take our pictures. We told the inquiring officer from the Kern County Sheriff's Office that if he wanted more information from us or wanted to take our picture, he would first have to arrest us. And at that point we were able to gain some ground.

We found that the opposition has a certain way of responding, a very typical way of responding. That was the case with the growers, but it could be with any opposition. It goes through predictable stages, and they all happened to us.

At the first stage, they ignore us. That happened at the beginning of the Movement when I was running around trying to get it going. Then they ridicule us. People say, "Oh, he's crazy." Next comes the repression. Eventually—after a long time—comes the respect.

We also know that the opposition invariably reacts in a certain way—unless we have a real cool guy as an opponent. We can push a button here or do something there, and we know what the reactions will be, sometimes three or four or five steps ahead. It's natural. They're reacting like human beings with money and with land. They're afraid. They feel threatened.

And I suppose we have a certain way of reacting, though we try not to have patterns. We also try not to say anything we can't carry out, otherwise it becomes an empty threat. That takes a lot of discipline, as one likes to come on very strong.

I remember at the beginning of the strike there was a young fellow who came up to me and said that he didn't like my idea of coming on so soft.

"I come on strong," I said.

"No, you don't. I see you, and you're like a little mouse."

"Well, that's because the truth can't project. Inside of me I'm very strong. Stick around and see." I told him I would be the last one to leave the strike. Afterward, when he had left us, I was inclined to think that he was trying to bolster himself, and this was a reflection of his weakness. I don't like to come down and rattle the saber. I don't think things are done that way.

I think you just tell the opposition what you are going to do. I have some trouble with the people, getting them to understand the advantages of that. It looks like we're disclosing a lot of our tactics or strategy. But in the end, the ones that have been touched by it once know we're not fooling. They know we mean business.

I think it's also important not to get our own personal frustrations mixed up with what we're doing. For instance, on the picket line, the cop is not the one to fight, nor is the scab. It's the grower; it's him we really want to put the heat on. If we get full of anger, we can't think. If we can't think, we can't strategize, and if we can't strategize, we can't win.

One way to get the grower is to go after his scabs. They catch all kinds of hell from us—and I don't mean physical violence. We knew every place they went, and we would just keep after them day and night. We'd get a lot of them to leave, and we would convert a lot of them. Those who weren't converted were immobilized because of the constant pressure.

The Mexican scabs would catch hell from us, but if there was a black scab, we were a little softer on him, and if it was a Filipino, we were even softer. Eventually, though, we got an Okie organizer to get the Okie scabs, a Japanese organizer for the Japanese scabs, a Puerto Rican for the Puerto Ricans, and so on. But once, I remember, there were a few Arab scabs, and the only guy that could speak Arabic was a Jew.

We set the example with the Mexican scabs in terms of pressure—hounding them and educating them. We would take five hundred people and go have a pray-in or a sing-in in front of their homes, or we would put two or three pickets with A Scab Lives Here sign to parade up and down the street for a while.

We would distribute leaflets and put on very simple plays depicting the scabs as something awful. We just put as much pressure as we could, and it worked. Some just quit.

Shortly after the strike started, *El Malcriado* printed Jack London's definition of a scab. It's strong medicine. It starts, "After God had finished the rattlesnake, the toad and the vampire, he he had some awful substance left with which he made a Strikebreaker. A Strikebreaker is a two-legged animal with a corkscrew soul, a waterlogged brain, and a combination backbone made of jelly and glue. Where others have hearts, he carries a tumor of rotten principles." And it ends by saying, "Esau was a traitor to himself. Judas Iscariot was a traitor to his God. Benedict Arnold was a traitor to his country. A Strikebreaker is a traitor to himself, a traitor to his God, a traitor to his country, a traitor to his family and a traitor to his class. There is nothing lower than a Strikebreaker."

When we gave a copy of the definition to one of the deputies, Sergeant Gerald Dodd, he called it vicious and said something like, "I would never let you read this to the people."

"Why?" we asked. "There's nothing wrong with it."

The next day, a Sunday, David Havens of the migrant ministry started reading it on Cecil Avenue near Delano. When Dodd came over and gave him a warning to stop, David just kept on reading. Dodd gave him a second warning, and David kept reading louder. When he got through, Sergeant Dodd placed him under arrest for "disturbing the peace." Much later, the case was thrown out of court.

Dodd was picking us off one at a time—harassment arrests— and we couldn't fight back effectively, so I got together with Jim Drake, Chris Hartmire of the migrant ministry, Dolores, Helen, and the others, and we worked out a plan. As it turned out, it was perfectly set up and executed. It happened two days after David Havens was arrested.

As Sergeant Dodd had his own ideas about how we could picket, I asked for volunteers. I thought it was going to be very difficult, but everybody volunteered. We had more than we needed.

Since I was scheduled to speak at noon the next day on the steps of Sproul Hall at the University of California in Berkeley, we decided to have all our volunteer pickets arrested early in the morning, so that by the time I got to Berkeley, I could make the announcement. This was just a year after the big Free Speech fights there, and the students were politically militant.

Well, the pickets went out to the W. B. Camp ranch, spotted a crew, and started hollering "Huelga! Huelga! Huelga!"—"Strike! Strike! Strike!"— at the scabs. When Sergeant Dodd ordered them to stop, they ignored his command and continued shouting. All were arrested.

The plan was for Chris to hover around and give us reports, but Sergeant Dodd spotted him giving a news release to the reporters there and ordered him to leave. Chris refused, and they put him in the van with the others, standing up all the way to Bakersfield like cattle. Forty-four strikers in all were arrested, including my wife Helen.

Wendy Goepel, a volunteer, drove me that day to Berkeley in a little Volkswagen. After I talked about the strike, I made the announcement of the forty-four arrested just for shouting "Huelga" out in the vineyards, and I asked the students to give me their lunch money for the strikers. It was a big rally, and the response was great.

I had other speaking engagements that day at San Francisco State College, Mills, and Stanford, so I was running from one to the other, but Kathy Murguea and another volunteer stayed in the back of the car counting the money, all those dollar bills in paper bags. We were on the way back to Delano before they completed the count, sixty-seven hundred dollars in one dollar bills.

Besides the money, we got a lot of press, and then, of course, I attacked the sheriff's department bitterly, asking the students to send letters and telegrams and make phone calls to the sheriff.

For about three days the forty-four strikers stayed in jail while Jim Drake was in charge of the demonstrations and pray-ins in front of the jail. We applied a lot of pressure.

In fact, the first two years of the strike I spent most of my speaking engagements and my time getting support to get the growers and cops off of our backs. It worked. We once had over a hundred telegrams and maybe three hundred phone calls to the Delano chief of police in a three-day period. They came from all over the country. Churchmen called him, lawyers, union leaders, government officials, U.S. senators, congressmen.

But we had no other choice. I think in Delano we had over a hundred arrests with only about three convictions. And we had countless other examples of injustice and violence against us.

Some of our pickets were sprayed with pesticides. Others had dogs turned on them, and guns discharged over their heads. We had cases where our cars were turned over, and one case where a grower drove into one of our pickets, and we were never able to get a complaint against him.

So we took every case of violence and publicized what they were doing to us. It works for us, even today, neutralizing many of them. They stop being violent against us. By some strange chemistry, every time the opposition commits an unjust act against our hopes and aspirations, we get tenfold paid back in benefits.

CHAPTER 8

Recruiting Volunteers

CESAR CHAVEZ RECALLS

It's so hard to maintain a nonviolent approach to doing things, but within our Union, we are still succeeding. To explain what I mean, I have to go into another phase of it.

In order for us to have a nonviolent movement, the first thing the leadership must say is, "If we can't organize the farm workers, it's not their fault, it's our own fault." If we start from that premise, I think we're safe, because the easiest thing for organizers to do is to damn the people or damn the opposition.

The second thing we must say is, "We can't win unless we know how to organize." So we need good organizers who are not afraid to act and not afraid to make mistakes. We must give them a lot of freedom and get them to accept other people's ideas. Nonviolence has one big demand, the need to be creative, and the ideas come from the people.

And the third thing we must say is, "We must win in spite of the opposition." We know that every time we knock down one obstacle, we have five more in front of us, because the opposition has got almost everything that society has to offer in terms of structured institutions and power turned against us.

When we encounter obstacles, I don't think our job is to knock them out. I think our job is just to do enough to get them out of our way, so we can keep on going toward our goal.

If someone commits violence against us, it is much better—if we can—not to react against the violence, but to react in such a way as to get closer to our goal. People don't like to see a nonviolent movement subjected to violence, and there's a lot of support across the country for nonviolence. That's the key point we have going for us. We can turn the world if we can do it nonviolently.

So, if we can just show people how they can organize nonviolently, we can't fail. It has never failed when it's been tried. If the effort gets out of hand, it's from lack of discipline.

If we can develop some confidence in an organizer's ability to organize, the organizer's tendency to use violence is much less. Persons who don't have any confidence get discouraged and then get into the trap of thinking that violence is the cure-all. But once that first act of violence is committed, they get on the defensive. And no one wins, that I know of, on the defensive. For example, if they get arrested for violence, then they must redirect their efforts from taking on the opposition to defending themselves.

Many times the leadership, or movements, lose sight of their goal. They are attacked personally and make that the big issue. I've seen the best leaders take off on their own personal problems. It's natural. I don't know how many times I haven't been able to avoid it myself. But we must try, because the people out there are not there because of my problems or because of how I feel, they're there because they want some changes in their lives.

Love is the most important ingredient in nonviolent work— love the opponent—but we really haven't learned yet how to love the growers. I think we've learned how not to hate them, and maybe love comes in stages. If we're full of hatred, we can't really do our work. Hatred saps all that strength and energy we need to plan. Of course, we can learn how to love the growers more easily after they sign contracts.

In the beginning, the staff people didn't thoroughly understand the whole idea of nonviolence, so I sent out the word to get young people who had been in the South and knew how to struggle nonviolently. That's how we got our first volunteers—people from the Congress of Racial Equality and the Student Nonviolent Coordinating Committee who had been in the Civil Rights Movement there. They were very good at teaching nonviolent tactics.

Then about a month after the strike started, we began to get students from the Bay Area to volunteer. They would come down in truckloads and go out with the strikers. Wendy Goepel suggested that there were students politically aroused by the Free Speech Movement there who wanted to come and help.

Wendy had been working with me almost since the beginning

of the Union. She came down to Delano in 1962 to do a study of medical needs, I think. At first she was a summer volunteer at the Migrant Ministry, then she just moved down to work with us. She was a loyal and hard worker until about 1967, when she left and married a doctor.

At the beginning, I was warned not to take volunteers, but I was never afraid of the students. People warned me, "Look what happened to the Civil Rights Movement."

"Well," I said, "sure that could happen to us, and if it does, we'll find out why. But to say, 'No, we're not going to get them' —never!"

Of course, there were problems. When we started the strike, many volunteers were in and out. Some of the volunteers were for ending the Vietnam war above all else, and that shocked the workers because they thought that was unpatriotic. Once, when there was a group more interested in ending the war, I let them have a session with the farm workers. After a real battle, the volunteers came to me astounded. "But they support the war!" they said. "How come?" I told them farm workers are ordinary people, not saints.

I had a set speech when the volunteers came, asking them to focus on the Cause. "You have come to work for the farm workers, so you do what we want you to do if you want to help." I told them to understand that farm workers are human beings. "If you don't understand that, you are going to be mighty disappointed. You have to understand that you may work very hard, and the day will come when they will just boot you out, or they won't appreciate what you are doing." And I warned them not to have any hidden agendas.

If we were nothing but farm workers in the Union now, just Mexican farm workers, we'd only have about 30 percent of all the ideas that we have. There would be no cross-fertilization, no growing. It's beautiful to work with other groups, other ideas, and other customs. It's like the wood is laminated.

Today we have the best-balanced group I know in terms of complementing one another. We have a very good cross-section of Americana here. Some of the kids have pretty wealthy parents, and a lot are middle class, of course. Then there are people like Dolores, other organizers, and me. And there are the farm workers. We have labor people and church people, Protestants like Jim Drake and Chris Hartmire, participating Catholics who came from religious orders, Jewish kids, and agnostics. It's amazing they all work together. That's the miracle of it all.

I only asked a few people to leave. The one that upset me most involved discrimination, someone trying to create friction between the leadership on grounds of race.

On discrimination we spoke up right away. "Black people, brown people, they're all part of the Union," we said. "If you don't like it, then get out, but we're not going to change it." I've been discriminated against, and it's a very horrible feeling. You can't do anything back. Of course, discrimination is bad for all the moral reasons, but it is also bad for reasons of unity. It can quickly destroy the Movement.

Here in the fields, for ages the employers worked the races one against the other in competition for jobs. That was a tactic to keep wages down and keep unions out. They're still doing it. But now there's a force countering that. We just keep telling people, "It's not right. Don't let them divide you." It works.

When it comes to discrimination, I put my leadership on the line, and if they don't like it, then they have to get rid of me. I would go gladly on an issue like that. I'm not going to buy leadership at that expense. I can't.

But our leadership really is committed to the principle that there can't be discrimination in the Union. There can't be, and there won't be.

The farm workers have had a tremendous learning experience from all the volunteers. It hasn't been by accident. We've worked on it hard. But we haven't had a special project, it's just that people learn when they're together.

We've had a lot of people passing through, staying two or three or four months. But the ones that stayed were the real top people of the hundreds that came. It's impossible to mention them all, but I might mention two to show the variety.

Luis Valdez came with the students, was in the picket lines, and stayed for a while. One day he said something about a theater, how important it was, and asked if I thought it could be done. I said, "Yeah, let's try it." So he organized the original El Teatro Campesino with four or five farm workers. They played for the first time at the regular Friday night Union meeting in Delano. Then people began to look forward to the next performance, so the next week they had another one. Then they began to perform on the picket line whenever the occasion lent itself. They were very effective and helpful on many occasions. Eventually they performed also on the campuses and in many cities, publicizing and raising funds for us.

Another volunteer was Marshall Ganz whose father is a rabbi.

When I went to speak in Bakersfield to the Council for Civic Unity, Marshall was there. After my talk, he came up to say hello, and someone told me he had just come from Mississippi. I made a point of talking to him some more.

He had worked for SNCC there and had been in some tight spots, the only white civil rights organizer in Macombe County, where things were pretty rough. I think he dropped out of Harvard to go to the South. I told him we needed a lot of people in Delano, and he soon was working with us. Eventually he became an organizer and took charge of the whole international boycott operation. After that he was elected to the executive board.

Although we recruited many people, probably the one I found the hardest to recruit was my own brother, Richard.

RICHARD CHAVEZ RECALLS

When I came back to the Valley, I was living good. Cesar told me I should quit my job and join him, but I wouldn't do it. I had money to make, and I was doing it, going out and getting better paying jobs.

We used to have our differences at that time. He said there were a lot of people that needed help.

But I was making a very decent living for my family. I had always been a sportsman, I liked fishing and golfing and the outdoors, and I had the time to do it, because I worked five days a week. I had the money, and I was very content.

For a while I forgot about the other people. Cesar kept reminding me about it all the time, but I just wasn't turning, I wasn't listening to him. I'd help him all I could, but I wasn't about to give up the good thing I had going. So he used to scold me quite often.

"Maybe the people don't need as much help as you claim they do," I argued. "Maybe they don't want to work. Maybe they're lazy."

He'd say, "You're wrong! You're wrong! Don't think that way! Not everybody can make it. You're lucky. We were lucky we made it. Not everybody can make it. There's a lot of people who need help. It's our obligation to help people!"

I just couldn't. I would tell him I wouldn't give my life, all of myself to it, because I had my thing going, I had my family.

I really don't know how he finally convinced me. I had this feeling I wanted to help, but I also wanted to help Richard. He started by asking how much money I was making, all this credit buying, spending money golfing. "You spent all this money on a fishing trip, and other people are not getting enough to eat because there is nobody to help them."

Well, he worked on me until I finally did join him. I think he mentioned one time that of all the people he organized, I was the hardest one.

About two or three weeks after the strike started he said, "I want to talk to you very seriously. I want you to quit your job. I need you."

I said, "That's a tough decision to make. I have a wife. I don't know what she is going to say about this. I have an obligation to her, too."

So I talked to my wife. She wasn't very happy about it, naturally, but I said I wasn't happy anymore, because Cesar wanted me to work full time, and there was a strike, and it was really rough for him. He really needed help. So she said okay.

CHAPTER 9

National Spotlight

CESAR CHAVEZ RECALLS

One of our most powerful nonviolent weapons is the economic boycott. Alone, the farm workers have no economic power; but with the help of the public they can develop the economic power to counter that of the growers.

We started the grape boycott helter skelter in October 1965, about a month after the strike started. We had to organize the people first, so they could be more effective and more disciplined. Then, in November, we started putting picket lines wherever the grapes went. We began to send the people to San Francisco and Los Angeles and to have them follow the truckloads of grapes.

When we set up a picket line at one of the piers in San Francisco, all the longshoremen walked out. They, of course, wouldn't go to work unless we left. So we got the ILWU (International Longshoremen's and Warehousemen's Union) in trouble, but they wouldn't tell us to leave.

I especially remember, though, a call from Al Green of AWOC trying to convince me to take the picket line off. I couldn't see any reason why I should, just because it was embarrassing him with the other unions.

"If we must stop embarrassing you at the expense of us not having a Union, we can't do it, and I think it's unfair of you to ask me to do that," I told him.

He got very impatient with me and finally started cussing and threatening me. He said, "I'll take care of you. If you don't take those damn picket lines off of the San Francisco docks, I'm going to take every bit of support, I'm going to take all the money we're giving you, I'm going to pull off all the Filipino brothers, and I'll destroy your damn little Union!"

He was so angry, he cussed me, and I cussed him back. In fact, I not only cussed him back, I went at him on the phone, really tore him up. I was so mad, he finally realized it and pulled back.

"Don't you ever threaten me," I said. "You're not big enough to threaten me, and you're not even big enough to begin to carry out your threats."

We stopped scab grapes from being loaded on the *S.S. President Wilson* which was bound for Asia. Later, longshoremen refused to load scab grapes on the *Burrard*, the *Rio Negro*, and other ships.

As time went on, we began to form a strategy. Experience told us what to do. We decided to concentrate the boycott on Schenley and sent out volunteers to major cities across the country. The Schenley wine boycott started in full earnest the middle of December.

About the same time, the AFL-CIO was having its convention in San Francisco, and Paul Schrade suggested to Walter Reuther that he visit the strike. Reuther was president of the United Automobile Workers. Paul, who was with the UAW in California, knew about the strike but didn't know everything that was happening, all about the two unions.

Two months before this, Roy Reuther, Walter's brother, came to Delano to speak to AWOC and wanted to see me, too, but I was out of town. When Walter sent Paul Schrade and Jack Conway to Delano a day before he came, we were prepared. Both AWOC and NFWA were trying to make an impression. I assigned Wendy Goepel, Jim Drake, and Manuel to work on it. Although Paul and Jack wanted Reuther to help us, they didn't know if he could because we were independent of the AFL-CIO.

When Reuther arrived at the Delano airport, we were there, and AWOC was there. The police chief had given an order that if we marched in Delano without a permit, we would be arrested. Well, the first thing we suggested to Reuther was to march. He took up one of the new plywood NFWA signs Jim Holland, a volunteer, had made the day before, and we marched all the way on Glenwood.

At one spot, the police chief's car had to stop because the march was going through. The guys started shouting, "Arrest us! Come on, take us to jail now!"

Walter looked back and asked, "What's this about jail?" So I told him, and he said, "Okay."

When we went to eat lunch, I was there with Al Green, much to his discomfort. Walter asked us, "How much money are you getting for the strike from labor?" I said, "Not a damned penny, not a damned penny."

Walter looked over and asked Green, "How much are you getting?"

Green began to hedge. Finally Walter got exasperated. "Look, Green, damn it, can't you tell me how much money you're getting?"

Again Green went through all this nonsense. I didn't know at the time that George Meany and Reuther squabbled, and that Green sided with Meany. Green also didn't want to tell Reuther, because he didn't want us to know. Finally, though, Reuther got it out of him. They were getting thirty thousand dollars a month.

Then we went to the city hall because Mayor Clifford Loader wanted to meet with Reuther, the city manager, and a few other people. Reuther gave a very good speech. "You know," he said, "Ford Motor Company once said they'd rather shut their doors than recognize our union. But in time, they did. And in time, that proved to be the best decision for both the company and the workers."

"Look," he told the mayor, "you tell the growers that sooner or later these guys are going to win. I can guarantee you that. So it's foolish to wait all these years. Why not talk now and avoid all the bitterness."

Then Reuther came to speak at a huge meeting we had at Filipino Hall. We were trying to impress people, and Manuel was in charge of our forces. I don't think Green had anybody in charge of his.

I was sitting in front near the stage, as Green didn't want me on stage. It didn't matter to me, but Paul Schrade saw that and went to Reuther, who insisted that I come not only up to the stage but sit by him. They still didn't know the strength of our Movement.

When my turn came to speak, though, there was tremendous applause. People went on shouting for several minutes. Of course, most of the people there were ours. So I spoke, and the people's enthusiasm made an impression. Then Green got up to speak and got a poor reception. It was very noticeable.

Probably from that point on, Reuther knew what was up in terms of support. Earlier we learned that Reuther planned to give five thousand dollars to the strike. He was going to give us one thousand dollars because we were not affiliated with the AFL-CIO and give AWOC the rest. So I told Wendy Goepel to tell Paul Schrade and Jack Conway that if we didn't get half, we didn't want anything.

Well, when Reuther began to speak, the people really got turned on. He made the pledge of five thousand dollars, and when the people came on very strong, he got carried away and said, "Because this is the month of the Prince of Peace, I'm going to make a special contribution of an additional five thousand dollars, or ten thousand dollars divided equally between AWOC and NFWA."

Then a press conference followed in what is now the stock room in Filipino Hall. By this time, Paul saw where the action was, and he was making sure that I was right there by Reuther. Green was at the other corner of the room.

The question was raised whether Reuther would meet alone with the growers. Walter said, "Well, it's not my strike. I can't meet with them by myself unless I get permission from the people. I have to check with the unions first." So he asked Green.

Green looked startled. "What did you say?"

"Shall I meet with the growers? I can't do any harm, I don't think, but it's up to you."

And Al hemmed and hawed and went all over the place, but wouldn't say yes or no. So I saw a clear shot. When Reuther asked me, I said, "Yes, I think it's a wonderful idea to meet with them."

Walter said, "You understand they won't meet with you?"

I said, "I don't care. You go meet with them." That forced Green to say yes. What else could he say? I didn't know all the politics involved at that point, and I didn't care. We were very free and very loose.

So Reuther met with the growers and urged them to recognize the Union. They thanked him but said they couldn't do it, that the Union didn't represent the workers, and the workers were happy. Reuther then reported to us and left.

It was a very significant day. The press played up the visit, and the strike took on national importance. The following day we had three times the number of people willing to come and join the picket line.

Three months later, when the strike had been going on six months, we got more major national publicity. Senator Harrison Williams's Subcommittee on Migratory Labor came to California for three days of hearings, one in Sacramento, one in San Francisco, and one in Delano. They wanted to have it in Fresno, but we fought with them to have it in Delano.

At first Senator Robert Kennedy wasn't going to come, but we wanted him, and he finally agreed. He came for the last hearing in Delano, and that was great, especially when he recognized our Union and came to speak at our meeting.

Shortly before the subcommittee came, about twenty or thirty of our pickets were arrested when scabs threatened to harm them. Our peaceful pickets were arrested instead of the scabs who threatened them. We gave Kennedy that bit of information, and he began to question the old sheriff, Leroy Galyen, who had been elected sheriff way back in 1954 when I first came to Bakersfield to work with the CSO. Galyen was an old captain of the California Highway Patrol.

"What did you arrest them for?" Senator Kennedy asked.

"Well, if I have reason to believe that there's going to be a riot started, and somebody tells me that there's going to be trouble if you don't stop them, it's my duty to stop them."

Kennedy asked the sheriff, "Who told you that they're going to riot?"

"The men right out in the field that they were talking to said, 'If you don't get them out of here, we're going to cut their hearts out.' So rather than let them get out, we removed the cause," the sheriff said.

About this time, California's Senator George Murphy, who obviously approved the sheriff's action, commented, "I think it's a shame you weren't there before the Watts riots."

Finally, as Senator Williams called a lunch recess, Senator Kennedy said firmly, "Can I suggest that in the interim period of time, the luncheon period of time, that the sheriff and the district attorney read the Constitution of the United States?"

CHAPTER 10

Pilgrimage
to Sacramento

CESAR CHAVEZ RECALLS

The day after the Senate subcommittee hearing in Delano, we set out on our march to Sacramento. I had thought of using a march years ago in El Centro when I was with CSO, and I remembered its impact when we had one in Oxnard, but our pilgrimage to Sacramento grew from the ideas of many people.

After some pickets were sprayed with sulphur, someone suggested that five families of strikers make a pilgrimage from Delano to Schenley's national headquarters in New York. Then, in January, a priest came to Delano and talked of the coming Lenten season. It reminded some of the strikers from Mexico of the Lenten pilgrimages they had made.

But more strikers could participate if we stayed in California instead of going cross-country. Some suggested we should march to Mexico to protest the illegal recruitment of strikebreakers. Others suggested marching to San Francisco where Schenley and Di-Giorgio had their West Coast headquarters and where the Longshoremen who had helped us by refusing to load scab grapes, also had their headquarters.

In February, William Bennett, a militant consumer advocate, who was then a member of the State Public Utilities Commission, came to Delano and talked about the California Fair Trade Act which sets a minimum on the price of liquor. Bennett said the

California Legislature guaranteed a high price to Schenley for the liquor it made, but denied farm workers the right to a minimum wage.

That did it. Sacramento became our destination.

I think Jim Drake first went ahead and measured the distance, about three hundred miles. As we didn't know how far people could march in a day, we asked those in the strike who had been in the infantry.

"Oh, thirty miles a day."

"Oh, you can't do it."

"Yea, easy, thirty miles a day." One guy said they once did forty miles in a day by double timing and resting. But I couldn't see it. I thought maybe five, six miles a day, maybe ten.

About a week before the march, we borrowed a home from a friend in Summerland near Carpinteria and took the leadership of the Union there for two days to plan all the details.

We decided to have three teams: one ahead organizing for housing, food, and support; another with the marchers to take care of all the arrangements when we got there; and the third to stay behind to continue organizing and follow-up with the workers. I assigned Manuel to organize ahead of us.

We timed the twenty-five-day march so we'd arrive in Sacramento on Easter Sunday and decided to take the men and leave the women on the picket lines. Dolores had to stay back. Of course, none of the women liked it, but they stayed.

We wanted to use the march for calling attention to the strike, and we wanted to take our case to Governor Pat Brown. But also we wanted to take the strike to the workers outside the Delano area, because they weren't too enthused. They were frightened, and they didn't really know what was happening.

Equally important to me—and I don't know how many shared my thoughts on this—was that this was an excellent way of training ourselves to endure the long, long struggle, which by this time had become evident. So this was a penance more than anything else—and it was quite a penance, because there was an awful lot of suffering involved in this pilgrimage, a great deal of pain.

We wanted to be fit not only physically but also spiritually, and we wanted to stress nonviolence even more, build confidence, and have more visible nonviolent tactics.

"What one thing can we give workers that will make them talk about what we're doing in Delano?" we asked ourselves. And out of that question came El Plan de Delano. Zapata, in the Mexican Revolution, had the Plan of Ayala, which set out what the revolutionists were fighting for. We assigned Luis Valdez to write our plan, and I gave him some of the topics. Then I made some modifications, and after a few corrections by the executive board, we went to the strikers, who approved it.

The march was barely underway when we had a confrontation with the Delano police. After we left the Union office in the southwest corner of Delano, we planned to march east on Garces and then north on Main Street through Delano. But the chief of police refused. He brought out his officers, about thirty men, who locked arms right across Garces to prevent us from marching through.

I was at the head of the march with Father Keith Kenny who had come from Sacramento. We marched right up to the police line and stopped. "We'll stay here if it takes a year," we said, "but we're going to march right through the city."

Since a lot of the press that came for the Senate subcommittee hearings were still in Delano, we called them. They took pictures and began to broadcast the story all over the country. After about three hours, the chief reluctantly gave in, and we marched along the side of the street on through Delano.

Usually we walked single file. The people elected monitors who did a very good job of keeping the marchers off the road and keeping discipline, so people wouldn't respond in kind if there was any harassment.

At the front we had the American flag, the Mexican flag, the flag from the Philippines, and the banner of Our Lady of Guadalupe. People wore hats with red hatbands with the black eagle, and many of the strikers also wore red armbands with the black eagle and carried the huelga flags. Out in the country it was a thin, serpentine line inching its way along the flat valley with lots of red flags silhouetted against the blue sky.

The first day there were more than a hundred marching as some of the wives and kids had come. But I think we had about seventy who planned to walk all the way.

Because Al Green didn't want the Filipinos to join us, he came to Delano; but they told him to go to hell, and they came. Marching has cultural roots for Filipinos as well as Chicanos. Both have some identical roots, the same religion and the same Spanish influence. And the Filipinos' great national hero is Jose Rizal who was a strong advocate of nonviolence. In fact Rizal's picture was in Filipino Hall in Delano.

Larry Itliong told Green, "We're going, we're not staying." He told us, "I'm going to go, and I'm going to make sure you guys have something to drink and some sandwiches." Pretty soon every-body was in the march. That's where I got to know Larry and Andy Imutan and his wife and Philip Vera Cruz, who were all in AWOC. That's where we really began to get a rapport. It's really more to their credit than ours that we're together.

At first the AWOC members didn't know whether we really wanted them in. Our guys were kind of confused, too. Some of the NFWA people wanted only our banners on the march.

"How come they've got the AWOC flag?" they asked.

"What's wrong with it?" I said.

"Well, we should do something!"

"You're damn right. Right now!" I said. "What's wrong? Don't you need your brothers to help?" And I said, "Bring that flag up front!" From then on, the AWOC flag also was at the head of the march.

When we got to Porterville on the second day, Green was mar-shaling his forces, trying to get his workers not to have anything to do with us. But Manuel was out there with a lot more man-power and better organized. Manuel had the membership we had in Porterville from the days when Jim Drake and Gilbert Padilla were organizing there. Maybe a couple hundred farm workers met us at the entrance of town. They brought their guitars and ac-cordions, and we marched, singing, through town to the park.

At the meeting that night, we were asked by the people of Porterville whether they could march with us the next day and act as standard-bearers, carrying the big flags at the head of the march. Of course we thought it was a tremendous idea, and we in-corporated that for the rest of the march. At each meeting, we persuaded people to assume the responsibility of carrying the stan-dards for the next day's march. Sometimes it was difficult, because people were afraid. They liked us and came to our meetings and sang with us, but they were still afraid to be identified openly, for fear of being singled out. Sometimes it was difficult, but we didn't fail once.

Every night we would have a program. We would pass out the Schenley boycott pledge and ask people to send it to the vice-president at Schenley. We told them that Schenley had said a few weeks before that it would not recognize NFWA. So the pledge said, "I will not buy Schenley products for the duration of the Delano farm workers strike. Get with it, Schenley, and negotiate. Recognize the National Farm Workers Association!"

There would be singing and speeches. Luis would do a dramatic reading of El Plan de Delano, and the Teatro would put on a performance. Each morning our advance team would get people to volunteer to take us into their homes and feed us breakfast the next morning. So, at the end of each meeting, those persons who had volunteered would get up and say, I need a couple, or I can take care of a single man, or a family. Sometimes our people had trouble going to sleep, because the hosts kept wanting to know more about the strike and the philosophy. Our people were instructed to talk, and we did an awful lot of educating, real basic stuff.

There's something about a march that is very powerful. It's a powerful weapon, a powerful organizing tool, and it has a powerful influence on those who participate.

There is this anticipation. You have a definite starting place and a definite goal. You're moving, making progress every step. That's very comforting to people. It gives a great sense of calm, because it's peaceable work. You can think much better, and you get a lot of courage. Then there's the sense of personal sacrifice.

The march also generated the spirit which was translated to the boycotters and into boycott action. As the boycotters got reports that we were marching, they got very excited themselves. They intensified the boycott on Schenley.

The march picks up its own cadence, its own spirit, its own history. Every day is accumulated into the following day, so all that happened yesterday is a part of today, and what happened today will be a part of tomorrow. The twenty-five days became lumped one and together.

We had all kinds of reactions from people. On Cecil Avenue between Delano and Richgrove, we were going by growers' homes and began to see little tables outside in the yards, with very nice clean pieces of linen on them and Schenley products. There would be a little sign, "In this house we use Schenley products."

Most of the harassment came from cars. Out of every ten or fifteen cars, one driver would give us the finger; but in most cars, people would wave, and we'd wave back.

People also came out of their houses with food and sodas—supporters, mostly Chicanos. They would come out and want to help. We had some very beautiful demonstrations. One Sunday we passed a little shack sitting in back of a lot, and this man, his wife, and about two or three teen-aged daughters ran across carrying beautiful cups and a beautiful crystal bowl full of punch. As we were going by, they were giving us drinks, the girls running back and forth to fill the cups.

When we saw people working in the fields, we stopped and

talked to them, using a bullhorn. Once we got out of the strike zone, people were very receptive and waved back. Sometimes they came out to say hello.

The further we got, the more publicity the march got, and the more friendly people became. In one case, near Sacramento, there were about eighty people thinning sugar beets. We were on this river levee, high up, looking down at the workers. As we began trying to get them to leave their work and join us, the grower came in a small plane and landed right on the field. The workers had stopped work and were gathering together to make a decision, but when this little plane landed, they went back to work.

We were often surprised at who would come out to join us. We'd get the farm workers, but we would also get a lot of people in the Chicano community and church people. About twenty people from other towns came back with us and joined the strike full time. I hadn't expected that. I hadn't even dreamt that this would happen. I would ask them, "Why are you going?" and they would say, "Well, because I want to help you win Delano, so you can also win for us here." That opened up completely new areas for organizing, new vistas, new horizons. People really teach you a lot.

The first day out we went from Delano to Ducor, about twenty-one miles. There we found a lady in a little two-bedroom cabin who was the only one in this little town that would take us in. Some of us slept inside, and some of us outside on the lawn.

I had a rough and miserable time at the beginning. Before we started, everybody was getting their feet ready for the march. But I was so busy I didn't have time to get ready. I was very tired and out of shape. While others had gotten boots, all I had were some old worn-out low shoes. My back already was bothering me when we started, so I began to favor one foot, which caused blisters on the other. By the time we got to Richgrove, only about seven or eight miles from Delano, my right ankle was swollen like a melon, and the sole of my left foot was just one huge blister.

Since this was a penitential walk, I refused to take any pain-killers. By the time we got to Ducor I was running a temperature. I was so miserable, I thought I was going to die. That little lady gave me her bed, and Peggy McGivern, our nurse, soaked my right foot and popped the blisters on the left one.

I went to sleep, but it was just like a short nap before I was awakened at 4:30 in the morning to continue. The pain was severe. It took me a good ten minutes walking around the house to begin to deaden it. My ankle was still swollen. But I marched all that day, about seventeen miles to Porterville.

By then, my leg was swollen up to just below the knee, and my blisters were beginning to bleed on the left foot. In Porterville I stayed in Jim Drake's house.

The third day was a short march, about twelve miles to Lindsay. I came back in the car that night to Porterville to stay at Jim's house. Then, the following day, we left from Lindsay to Farmersville. By then my leg was swollen way up to my thigh, and I was running a high fever.

I continued walking, but on the seventh day, because I was shaking with fever, the nurse put me in the station wagon. I felt very bad that everybody was marching and I had to ride, so the next morning I tried to march and did for about an hour until Peggy McGivern yanked me in. I stayed in the wagon until about 3:00 or 4:00 in the afternoon.

Somewhere somebody gave me a cane, and as soon as I used it to take some of the weight off, I began to get better. By the time we got to Fresno on the ninth day, I was a little better. The following day in Madera I was much better, and by the time we got to Modesto where I celebrated my birthday on the fifteenth day of the march, I was okay.

The march had really caught on by the time we got to Fresno. We had hundreds, if not thousands, of people marching in the city, mostly nonworkers, Fresno Chicanos. And the city gave us a royal welcome. The mayor, a very decent man named Floyd Hyde, assigned about six or seven officers without uniforms just to run errands for us, and he gave us a special luncheon with some of the Chicano leaders. We had the rally at the Mexican theater, which was jam-packed. From then on, we were in good shape. It got bigger and bigger.

It was on the fourteenth day of the march that I first got to know Bill Kircher, the national director of organizing for the AFL-CIO. Many of our guys, like Jim Drake and Manuel, didn't trust him, but I saw a good chance to make a friend. I was afraid of Green, who had just set up an office in Porterville with the Teamsters and was turning stuff over to them. When I told Bill about that, he didn't say anything. He just got red.

That afternoon while we were walking, Manuel approached Bill. "Hi, Mr. Kircher. You say you're with us?"

"Yea."

"The AFL-CIO is with us?"

"Yea."

"Well, how do you like this?" And Manuel showed him the front page of the local paper which said that the AFL-CIO was boycotting the march.

"Why that dirty son of a bitch," Bill said. "I'll be right back."
He got in his car, went to the next town, and made a call. Later
he told me he asked Green, "Did you put this article in?" and
Green said, "Yes."

Green told him, "Haven't we got more Chicanos and more people in our union? We could make that damn Cesar Chavez's head
spin if we wanted to. We can sink his ship."

So Kircher told him, "You damn fool. That ship sailed a long
time ago, and you were not on it."

WILLIAM KIRCHER RECALLS

We marched into this little town one evening about 5:00 and
Cesar brought me the daily paper from Turlock.

Cesar said, "I'm very sorry, I don't want to criticize, but I think
you want to see this." And he said, "I'm not mad, and you don't
have to do anything."

He pointed out the main story on the front page, a warm story
about the march really, it wasn't antagonistic. It told how this
group was working there to provide housing for people, and that
the auxiliary of some essentially Spanish-speaking organization was
going to cook a meal, that sort of thing.

And in the body of the story was a subhead that said, "AFL-CIO
Boycotts March." Then here was this paragraph or two about a
spokesman for the AFL-CIO that said they were boycotting the
march because it was not really a march, it was a civil rights thing,
a demonstration, no relationship to unionism and so forth.

Christ! Here I am, the director of organization for national AFL-
CIO, right in the middle of this thing, and here's the story. I was
mad as hell!

So the format of the march was that every night there would be
a meeting, and I would always speak for a few minutes, principally
to bring a feeling of trade union solidarity to the thing and visibly
tell Mexican-Americans who were just experiencing this for the
first time how labor felt about this, that their brothers and sisters
were behind them all over the country.

When the meeting was over I remember I had a staff guy who
was there, one of the guys who worked in California, and I said,
"We're going to Stockton." And we got in a car and drove that
night clear to Stockton.

The next morning, I got up early, and I was over in the office
waiting when Green and Dave McCane came in. I said, "I want to
sit down and talk with you fellows. I don't want to talk here."

I took them over to a restaurant and showed them the article. They started hemming and hawing about it, and I said, "Look, I don't even want to discuss the article. I want to tell you something. You fellows have told me how important you are and how much prestige you have in this valley, and particularly in Stanislaus County."

I said, "When this march reaches Modesto tomorrow, I want to see a massive AFL-CIO welcome. That's your home base, that's where you're from. I'll judge how much influence you have in the labor movement by what kind of reception there is for the marchers."

I said, "This is not an arguable position, this is an order. Both of you work for me, and I want to tell you that you better produce!"

That was the end of the meeting. I got back in the car, and I was back on the march by noon.

Man! When we marched into Modesto the next evening, that was the funniest thing. They were lined up—guys with signs— and the funny part was, in the main, guys who had no understanding of what they were doing. They were sort of like paid pickets. They were standing there holding signs, "Asbestos Workers Local 1215, Viva La Huelga!" "Glaziers Union Local 79, Viva La Causa!" Bricklayers, carpenters, painters, all of them.

Really it was a great thing, because you could hear running through the line of march, guys, Mexicans and Filipino marchers, saying, "Hey, look! Bricklayers!" "Hey, look! Painters!" It really had an effect on them.

Actually it was a very positive thing, the way it turned out, but I don't want to take credit for it. To be honest, the reason I did it was I was mad. But the end result I think was a landmark in terms of visible solidarity.

As for the march, by the end of it, my feet had a pancake of blisters. The thing that burned me up was that the biggest blister I had was on a place on my foot where I'll be damned if I could step in anyway without stepping on it. It was right on the middle of the ball of my foot. It took weeks to go away.

CHAPTER 11

Schenley
Signs a Contract

CESAR CHAVEZ RECALLS

The biggest reception we got before reaching Sacramento was in Stockton, two days after our greeting in Modesto. There must have been five thousand people. It took us two hours to do about three and a half miles. People were just getting in front of us with flowers. There were mariachis playing. It was a fiesta.

That evening, as we were getting ready for the rally at St. Mary's Park, I got a telephone call. I told Gilbert Padilla, "You take the message, I can't go." I was just getting ready to start the rally, and there was so much support there I didn't want to leave.

Luis Valdez started a collection—he was very good at it—and there were hundreds of women and kids giving five dollars, two dollars, just a real response to our need for money. I felt bad leaving.

So Gilbert reported to me, "The guy said that he wants to talk to you, because he wants to sign a contract. He says he's from Schenley."

"Oh, the hell with him! I've heard that story before," I said. And I wouldn't go to the phone.

Five minutes later the man called back, and Gilbert said, "Cesar, he's got to talk to you!"

So I went out there. I didn't want to go.

The voice said, "Hello, this is Sidney Korshak," I didn't remember the name. "I want to talk to you about recognizing the Union and signing a contract."

I said, "Oh, yea? What else is new?" And I hung up the phone. I thought it was a prank. I started going out of the building when the phone rang again. I came back. He said, "No, no, look, I'm serious."

So I said, "How serious are you?"

He said, "Well, what do you want me to do to prove it?"

"You come down to Stockton."

"Oh, I can't," he said.

"Okay. If you can't, then forget it."

We didn't know that Schenley was very worried because we had tied up their warehouse in San Francisco with the help of a friendly Teamster local. After I asked a lot of questions, he finally convinced me and gave me the address to meet him in Beverly Hills the next day.

I got ahold of my people, had a meeting, and took a vote to see if they'd let me go to negotiate. Then I took off with Chris Hartmire, who drove while I fell asleep in the back seat. We didn't leave until about 1:00 in the morning, I guess, but we got to Beverly Hills in time.

Korshak had Bill Kircher and the Teamsters there. He had this huge house and all these drinks and food laid out. But Bill wouldn't be caught in the same room with the Teamsters. They had an argument, and I just said, "The hell with it!" I went over to the pool table and started playing pool.

They argued for about an hour. Finally Korshak said, "Damn it, look. You should be making love to me, I'm the company, I'm ready to sign a contract, and you guys can't get together! You get together, and when you do and make up your minds who's going to sign it, then I'll deal with you."

"I'm leaving!" I told him at that point. "There's no reason for me being here. You sign a contract with whomever you want, but the boycott stays on!" And I started to walk out.

"Wait a minute!" he said. "We're going to sign with a union."

"No, talk to me about my Union, not to the AFL-CIO or the Teamsters."

Then the Teamsters came on very strong and supported our position. Apparently somebody was pushing to have the AFL-CIO sign a contract. The fellow in charge of the Federation in Los Angeles came and tried to sweet talk me into signing with AWOC, and I said, "No! You must be kidding. You're trying to tell me to give you a contract, when we fought for it, bled for it, and sweat for it. You must be out of your mind!"

So he got mad, and he said, "Well, if you don't give us the contract, we'll just destroy your Union."

Finally Bill and I hit on a compromise. I didn't care if I was helping him to save face as long as I had the contract.

"We sign it ourselves, it's our contract," I said. "It means a lot to the workers. But I'll let you witness the contract if you want to." So Bill witnessed it.

The preliminary agreement was not even a full legal-sized page. It was only about three-quarters full. The agreement recognized the Union, agreed to the hiring hall, gave us an immediate increase of thirty-five cents an hour, and a checkoff for the Credit Union. Helen had told me, "Don't you come back without that!" The full contract was to be negotiated within ninety days.

The people knew we had met with Schenley, but that night I had the privilege of telling the workers about the contract. I didn't have any particular feeling on the subject in Los Angeles. I knew it was important, but it didn't excite me because the workers weren't there. Driving back, though, I began to understand its importance and its impact as I got closer to them.

Somebody later claimed the Kennedys were influential in getting Schenley to sign, but that wasn't it. It was the boycott. Schenley just wanted the boycott off. It was the first major proof of the power of the boycott.

We didn't actually hurt Schenley in terms of money, but they were very smart, smarter than anybody else. They knew where it was leading. We were doing a lot of damage to their image, which they had spent millions promoting.

For instance, on three successive nights in Harlem we had people from CORE leafleting from store to store against Schenley. Then Schenley hired ballplayer Jackie Robinson as their public relations man. They had a black vice-president who came out to give scholarships to blacks in Los Angeles. We drew up a picket line, told the blacks what was happening, and they wouldn't cross the picket line. Schenley had invited all the black leadership in Los Angeles, but very few crossed our line, and none of the politicians did.

We went into the suburbs at the railroad stations, where the commuters took the train, to the cities in the morning, and gave them a leaflet and a letter. We went to labor unions and churches handing out leaflets—fifty thousand leaflets—just about Schenley. We hit two or three cities a week.

At that time, the boycott was done entirely by volunteers, mostly by students, although we had TV star Steve Allen head the boycott in Los Angeles. All the strikers were in Delano. It wasn't until later that we began to send them out on the boycott. I wanted them to stay on the strike longer and picket longer to get a real feeling of what we were doing. Later we ended up with the most dedicated strikers on the boycott.

We had asked Governor Brown to meet with us when we reached Sacramento, but the governor was deathly afraid of the growers. He wouldn't meet with us. Lieutenant Governor Glenn Anderson met with us two or three days before we got to Sacramento, but Brown was too frightened. Instead, he decided to go spend Easter Sunday with Frank Sinatra, and we got some people from Southern California to go picket him.

When he changed his mind afterward, it was too late. We didn't want him to come. We knew that ultimately he couldn't do anything for us. We wanted the people there, as many people as we could get from other groups, but the governor didn't matter.

As it turned out, we had about ten thousand there on the steps of the capitol on Easter Sunday. It was an exciting end to our pilgrimage. But we knew that it was only the end of the march. We still had an army of growers arrayed against us.

Book V

VICTORY IN
THE VINEYARDS
April 1966–July 29, 1970

Time and again unexpected events determined and changed the union's strategy. When the huge DiGiorgio Corporation turned to the Teamsters for protection, the union faced its greatest challenge. If the growers succeeded in using the Teamsters as a shield against the farm workers' union, the struggle was lost.

The Teamsters were the rogue elephant in the labor movement, the largest and probably the wealthiest union in the world. Because of corruption and ties to the underworld, they were expelled from the AFL-CIO in 1957, despite their massive contributions to the federation's budget and their power to make or break other unions' strikes by honoring or crossing their picket lines.

For years Teamsters had represented cannery and shed workers and truckers, but they had shown no interest in organizing field workers. William Grami, a smooth, soft-spoken, highly intelligent, and ambitious Teamster executive, was the chief strategist and leader of their move into the fields. Over the years, he would tackle Cesar Chavez time and again.

Although Chavez was forced to take on the Teamsters, he knew that the union's major opponents were the growers and that victory would not be won until the union had wrested contracts from the Delano growers, who were the largest and most influential in the table-grape industry. Leader and largest grower of them all was John Giumarra, a small, feisty, gray-haired man of great energy and good humor whose son, John Giumarra, Jr., was a lawyer for the company.

Despite the strike, the union grew, became the United Farm Workers Organizing Committee, and moved its headquarters to the Forty

Acres, a barren, dusty plot by the city dump west of Delano. There more full-time volunteers were drawn to its staff, all willing to work, like Cesar Chavez, for five dollars a week plus room and board.

One of these was LeRoy Chatfield who withdrew from the order of Christian Brothers and left his job as a Catholic high school principal in Bakersfield to tackle an endless series of top-level tasks. Intense, dedicated, bright, and efficient, Chatfield was easily identified by his tall, gaunt frame, blue eyes, and blond hair.

Another key volunteer was Jerry Cohen, an aggressive young attorney who could devastate an opposing lawyer with a quick verbal thrust backed by citings of relevant legal cases. Cohen found the union's freewheeling law practice more to his liking than the War on Poverty's legal assistance program which he had joined after graduating from law school. He was a two hundred-pound six-footer whose trademark was a dusky patch of uncombed hair, a wrinkled sport shirt, and a toothpick between his teeth. Eventually he headed the union's legal staff, which was used to open another front against the growers.

As awareness of the California struggle spread, a fourth group was destined to play a major role. The Conference of Catholic Bishops set up a committee to see if it could resolve the dispute by bringing growers and the union to the bargaining table. Bishop Joseph Donnelly, from Hartford, Connecticut, was elected chairman of this bishops' committee, whose work horse was Monsignor George Higgins, a portly priest stationed in Washington, D.C. Both had extensive knowledge in the field of labor, knowledge that would be severely tested in California.

CHAPTER 1

Praying for DiGiorgio

CESAR CHAVEZ RECALLS

When I thought of organizing workers at DiGiorgio—which I did even before I came to Delano—it seemed like an awesome task. DiGiorgio had a notorious reputation for being antiunion.

In 1939, when more than six hundred farm workers struck their orchards in Yuba City, the company had special antipicketing laws passed by the county, then a sheriff's posse destroyed a strikers' soup kitchen, beat up many strikers, put them in cars, and drove them out of the county. The strike was smashed.

Another strike was broken at Arvin, in 1947, when about thirteen hundred workers struck. DiGiorgio evicted workers from their camps, brought in braceros, and got court injunctions against the strike. Again pickets were beaten, and some people shot up a union meeting. The president of the local, Jimmy Price, was wounded in the head.

In 1960, DiGiorgio not only broke another strike, they were able to get a judge to order the state to provide scabs.

The company always was very aggressive against unions. They used red-baiting very effectively, frightening the workers. They were exceptional in that they knew what they were doing far more than the other growers, and they were among the biggest.

When our strike started in 1965, the company had about forty-seven hundred acres of vineyards in their Sierra Vista ranch near Delano, about nine thousand acres in grapes around Arvin and eighteen hundred acres more at Borrego Springs near San Diego. They had more grapes near Lodi; thousands of acres in pears, plums, and apricots in California, and five thousand acres of citrus in Florida.

We also found out through research that DiGiorgio owned S&W Fine Foods, TreeSweet Products, processing plants, and a sawmill. We learned later that, in 1965, DiGiorgio made more than $231 million and that several of their directors, including Robert DiGiorgio, were also directors of Bank of America and other corporations.

So we were facing a giant whose policy was to break legitimate unions. They had done it before, and they were very comfortable at it. But they met with a very different brand of unionism when they met with us.

As it turned out, I think the DiGiorgio story would make a movie even more exciting than *Salt of the Earth*. Before everything was over the very survival of our Union was at stake.

Helen had worked for DiGiorgio many years before, and she went to work there again to make ends meet when we came back to Delano in 1962. When she'd come home from work, I'd try to get an idea of how things were inside. I'd ask her whether people were dissatisfied, how many crews there were, if there were any tough people there that would become leaders—information that I thought we would need.

Then, about a year before the 1965 strike, we took on DiGiorgio at Sierra Vista. One morning some of our members got laid off and were replaced by braceros. I made a complaint to the personnel office and called some friends I had in the State Division of Labor Law Enforcement. In about two days we were able to get all of the braceros pulled out, about three hundred of them, and the women got their jobs back. It was our first direct challenge of DiGiorgio, but they didn't know we had done the job on the braceros.

When AWOC struck the next year in Delano, they didn't strike DiGiorgio or Schenley because they didn't have any strength there, but when we joined the strike, we went after them and a few others not on the AWOC list. At first we had many workers on our picket lines, but we soon began to lose them because we had no strike funds. That's when we began to develop at DiGiorgio the system that we now use in picketing.

Because people would say, "Look, we'd like to come out, but we haven't got any money," we finally hit on the idea of asking them to stay in there, but to work slower, to do less, to do inferior work, anything that was legal and moral, but that would cost the grower more money.

So we did not hear anything from DiGiorgio from September 1965 until the day we got the Schenley agreement signed seven months later. That same day we turned the boycott against DiGiorgio, S&W Food, and TreeSweet.

We were on the march, walking along the Sacramento River two or three days out of Sacramento, when Paul Schrade told me, "I just heard on the radio that DiGiorgio is willing to have elections." I was very surprised.

Later we found out that they really were not willing to have elections. It was just an offer surrounded by lots of unacceptable preconditions. They wanted an immediate stop to the strike and boycott, compulsory arbitration after thirty days, and they insisted that the strikers couldn't vote, only the scabs. In addition, besides our Union, they also wanted AWOC on the ballot and a company union called the Independent Kern-Tulare Farm Workers Association.

So three days after the march ended Easter Sunday, we started all-out picketing at DiGiorgio. The boycott, too, began to pick up speed right away. There were a lot of people who had fought DiGiorgio in the thirties and the forties and the fifties who started coming out of the woodwork to take them on in Chicago, San Francisco, New York. We had the most effective boycott in the shortest period of time of any of our boycotts. The company quickly set up talks with us about rules and conditions for elections.

The talks didn't last long. While we were negotiating with DiGiorgio Vice-President Bruce Sanborn and their attorney, Donald Connors, in Fresno, I got a call from somebody in the Union saying that while they were picketing at Sierra Vista, a DiGiorgio guard had threatened Ida Cousino with a gun, and another DiGiorgio employee knocked her down. Someone struck Manuel Rosas on the head as he went to her aid. It took thirteen stitches to close his wound. Then our people were arrested.

I came back to the negotiating room. "I'll be damned if I'm going to negotiate with you guys while you're beating and jailing our people!" I said. Then I walked out.

Later, after DiGiorgio agreed to disarm their guards, we met again; but this time the company fired some of our members, including a foreman, Mrs. Ofelia Diaz, who had worked there twenty-four years and was encouraging her crew to join our Union. We broke off the talks.

After a while, the boycott was so effective that DiGiorgio was pleading for mercy. If we had not been influenced by our friends, we would have damaged them severely. But instead, we took the boycott off, which was a mistake, and started talking again about elections.

Then one day the picketers began to bring stories that the Teamsters were in the fields trying to change the affiliation of the workers. Immediately we went out to investigate, and it became apparent what they'd done with us. This was the most dangerous move of all.

Most of the strikers didn't know the full import of it. They weren't frightened like I was, but I knew the complications. I knew, for example, that five years before, an AFL-CIO strike in the Imperial Valley against Bud Antle, the world's largest lettuce grower, was broken when Antle signed a contract with the Teamsters. DiGiorgio knew it, too.

So we researched that and wrote an article in *El Malcriado* alerting our members. The story also reported how, after Antle signed, he obtained a one million dollar loan from the Teamster pension fund.

We began to plan how to get the Teamsters out of the fields, but we also had other problems. DiGiorgio was going all out recruiting scabs, which we countered by visiting their homes and picketing the foremen's homes. Then the company went recruiting to Los Angeles, to Fresno, and to Calexico. Everywhere they went, we followed. When DiGiorgio started going to El Paso in a very concentrated way, we sent Dolores there. As she was invited to speak to a Steel Workers Union meeting, we took advantage of the free trip, and she stayed to organize picketing against the recruiters.

DOLORES HUERTA RECALLS

I was sent to El Paso, Texas, to picket the Chamisal Labor Agency which was recruiting people to break the strike on DiGiorgio. I was there for a whole month picketing the border, passing leaflets in Juarez, Mexico, and asking people not to work for DiGiorgio. Sometimes they were sending two buses every other day to break the strike.

Our work was effective. A lot of the people would get on the bus, and as soon as they got to California, they'd leave the company.

One day, when I was back in Delano, two buses arrived at Sierra Vista. When the bus came in, the workers already had El Malcriado and leaflets, and they carried our flag in the window. All the people were waving to the picket line.

We were worried because workers had to sign Teamster authorization cards as well as the DiGiorgio cards as a condition of employment. So we really wanted to get the message to them not to sign the green Teamster authorization cards which the company then could use to prove their workers were Teamster members.

We had that message on a leaflet, and when the first bus got to the stop sign across from the DiGiorgio Ranch, the people on the picket line passed the leaflets through the windows.

Then the women's bus came and just went through the stop sign.

We had a lot of pickets around DiGiorgio that Sunday, I think about four or five hundred that we got together in about an hour after we got the call from our organizers that the buses were bringing up the workers from Borrego.

We were wondering how we were going to get the word in there to all those women not to sign the green authorization cards.

Then I asked my boy, Emilio, the one with the big eyes, about taking the leaflets in there. "I'll have to think about it," he told me.

He was nine years old then, but he's not an impulsive kid at all. So he went and thought about it and then came back and said, "Okay, I'm ready."

We gave him this big stack of leaflets to take to the women inside the camp which was, I guess, about a quarter of a mile from the road. Then we waited for him to come back out.

Pretty soon here comes Emilio just running as fast as his little legs would carry him, with DiGiorgio's personnel manager, Dick Myers, coming behind him in a car. The poor little boy! When he got to the edge of the road he just collapsed, out of breath. But he wasn't hurt or scared, so it was really funny. And he had gotten the leaflets into the camp.

CESAR CHAVEZ RECALLS

DiGiorgio didn't spend much time fighting us on the picket lines. As they were more mature than other growers, they spent their time gathering information, getting police to do their dirty work, and filing suits against us. Finally, on May 20, they obtained a court order restricting the number of pickets.

We believe that each worker must have the right to protest,

and if he can't be on the picket line to do his own protesting, his right for effective striking is taken away.

We saw this injunction as especially unfair because there had been no violence on the picket line. It also threw all of our strategy into a turmoil, because we couldn't use our source of strength, which was the people. We began to struggle desperately for other ways of putting the pressure on the scabs and on the company.

But after several days of particularly futile picketing, people were getting impatient and discouraged. As I just couldn't come up with any solution, I called a meeting at the American Legion Hall in Delano.

The meeting soon got around to the idea that we were losing because we weren't using violence, that the only solution was to use violence. We spent most of the day discussing that. Then, although we had taken a vote at the beginning of the strike to be nonviolent, we took another vote. Except for one older fellow, all voted to continue nonviolently.

Before ending the meeting, I told them that I had run out of ideas of things to do, but I knew that in them, the people, there were answers, and I needed their help to find those answers.

They said yes, but still they left without suggesting anything.

A couple of hours later, three ladies said they wanted to see me. In those days the question of money was extremely severe. We just didn't have it. So the first thing that came to my mind was that the ladies wanted money for some very special personal need. I asked them to come into my little office.

First they wanted to make sure that I wouldn't be offended by what they wanted to tell me. Then they wanted to assure me that they were not trying to tell me how to run the strike.

After we got over those hurdles, they said, "We don't understand this business of the court order. Does this mean that if we go picket and break the injunctions, we'll go to jail?"

"Well, it means that you go to jail, and that we will be fined," I said.

"What would happen if we met across the street from the DiGiorgio gates, not to picket, not to demonstrate, but to have a prayer, maybe a mass?" they asked. "Do you think the judge would have us arrested?"

By the time they got the last word out, my mind just flashed to all the possibilities.

"You just gave me an idea!" I said, then I was away and running. They didn't know what hit me.

I got Richard and had him take my old station wagon and build a little chapel on it. It was like a shrine with a picture of Our Lady of Guadalupe, some candles, and some flowers. We worked on it until about 2:00 in the morning. Then we parked it across from the DiGiorgio gate where we started a vigil that lasted at least two months. People were there day and night.

The next morning we distributed a leaflet all the way from Bakersfield to Visalia inviting people to a prayer meeting at the DiGiorgio Ranch and made the same announcement on the Spanish radio. People came by the hundreds. You could see cars two miles in either direction.

We brought the loud-speakers and tried to get the people in the camp to come to the mass, but I don't think more than ten came out. Most of them were out at the fence looking and seeing a tremendous number of people. They were very impressed.

There also was so much confusion, our guys found themselves talking to our members inside the camp for the first time in about three weeks.

The next day at noon something very dramatic happened. When the trucks brought the people from the fields to eat at the company mess hall, about eight women decided to come to where we had the vigil instead of going into the mess hall. The supervisors got the trucks in the way to keep them from coming, but the women went way out through the vines and wouldn't be stopped. They knelt down and prayed and then went back.

That was the beginning.

The same evening about fifty women came. The next evening half of the camp was out, and from then on, every single day, they were out there. Every day we had a mass, held a meeting, sang spirituals, and got them to sign authorization cards. Those meetings were responsible in large part for keeping the spirit up of our people inside the camp and helping our organizing for the coming battle.

It was a beautiful demonstration of the power of nonviolence.

CHAPTER 2

A Question of Elections

We did a lot of work getting affidavits to fight DiGiorgio's injunction. Then, at the hearing, we just packed the court with farm workers. Finally, on June 16, Judge Leonard Ginsburg ruled that the Union committed no acts of violence, but that "numerous acts of violence" were committed by DiGiorgio. He dismissed the injunction.

That same week another court dismissed the cases against the forty-four Delano pickets who had been arrested for shouting, "Huelga!"

About the same time, Jimmy Hoffa, the president of the Teamsters, announced that the Teamsters had decided to stop their organizing at DiGiorgio. He was getting a lot of heat from the clergy.

But the announcement wasn't true. It was just a trick to take the pressure off. We were getting reports every day from the inside from Joe Serda, a DiGiorgio foreman. Teamsters were always in the fields with the workers, while DiGiorgio refused to give us access. In fact, when we talked to the workers, company agents were making citizens' arrests against us on charges of trespassing.

Nevertheless, we were still meeting with DiGiorgio. On Monday, June 20, we negotiated all day in San Francisco with their attorney, Donald Connors. Bill Kircher and I were trying to get rules for elections covering all their crops and all their workers, but they only wanted to give us elections in their vineyards at

Sierra Vista in the Delano area and at Borrego Springs in San Diego County.

At 3:00 P.M. we adjourned for two days, agreeing to come back Thursday for more negotiations. But by the time we got to Los Angeles at about 5:00, there was an announcement that DiGiorgio was going to hold an election Friday with our name on the ballot. Afterward we found out that while we were meeting with them in San Francisco trying to get fair rules set up, they already had printed the ballots to run their own election.

We also learned that DiGiorgio had set up a press conference for Wednesday in San Francisco.

WILLIAM KIRCHER RECALLS

I've got a picture—I really wouldn't take five hundred dollars for it—of the guys in the press conference holding their microphones around me, while in the background, with his lips pouting, is Robert DiGiorgio stomping down off his little stage at his press conference. I took that press conference away from him.

DiGiorgio had us in a very bad way. They engaged a public accountant firm, a very prestigious one, Touche Ross and Company, to conduct the election on DiGiorgio property. The workers were going to vote, all the workers, I suppose, including the foremen, and the ballot would be Teamsters, AWOC, NFWA, and "no union."

Well, AWOC had never campaigned in that election. This was an NFWA thing. So we knew what was going to happen to us. It was rigged at this point.

I said to Cesar, "I know what I'm going to do! I'm going to fly to San Francisco and break that goddamn press conference up!"

Cesar's eyes got big, and he says to me, "Really? Would you do that?"

I said, "Goddamn right." So that's what I did.

I went in, and as I started into this big conference room, these two DiGiorgio vice-presidents saw me. One of them took me by the arm and said, "Bill, I want to talk to you."

I just jerked my arm away from him, and I said, "I don't have a goddamn thing to say to you, brother!" He was one of the vice-presidents that had been meeting with us. I just charged right on in.

The room was all set up. They had radio reporters, newspaper reporters, and all three network representatives, ABC, NBC, CBS television. So I just stood right at the line of the cameras. The DiGiorgio people wanted me out of there, but I told them it would take two policemen—big policemen—to get me out.

After I broke the press conference up, I then went right over into court to get an injunction to prevent DiGiorgio's use of the unions' names on the ballot. All of DiGiorgio's lawyers fought the hell out of the injunction, but we finally got it.

But the judge made us post a twenty-five thousand dollar cash bond. Cash! That was rugged because he wouldn't give us any time, and we had to have that cash money there by the end of the day.

It was funny. I got in touch with all of my union friends in the Bay Area. Of course, unions have rules. An officer can't write a check out for something like that. But all of them have attorneys. So they authorized their attorneys to bring, this one two thousand dollars, this one five thousand dollars, and then send them a bill for legal fees so that the attorney was protected, and they were protected.

So here come lawyers carrying money in, and we go over to the court with twenty-five thousand dollars. Of course, when we got the money back, I returned the money to the respective legal firms, the unions tore up the bills, and that was it.

CESAR CHAVEZ RECALLS

We decided to boycott the election. Fred was in charge at Sierra Vista, and I went to Borrego Springs where the election was held in the school, which was out of session. There were a lot of cops who wouldn't let us get in to talk with the workers, but we picketed around the building, shouting at the workers, telling them not to vote. Many gave us friendly signals and didn't get off the buses. We got good support from them, and the boycott was effective.

FRED ROSS RECALLS

On election day at Sierra Vista, we had about four hundred of our people across the street from election hall along the railroad right of way. A majority of the workers refused to vote. We know. We counted.

When the buses were brought up with workers, some wouldn't leave the bus, and others would get out and join us. We had a priest lead us as each bus arrived, and we got down on our knees and prayed, and workers knew who we were.

Then, later, we noticed pickup trucks arriving with three or four workers. DiGiorgio supervisors had gone into the fields and pressured scores of those who refused to vote the first time to come in vote.

The final results showed a majority for the Teamsters, but the voters included stenographers, clerks, and many who were not farm workers and were not involved.

CESAR CHAVEZ RECALLS

The day after that phony election, Dolores went to the Mexican-American Political Association convention in Fresno to ask that they put pressure on Governor Pat Brown to ask for new elections.

The governor was running for re-election against Ronald Reagan, then, and he was in political trouble. He came to meet with the MAPA executive board to talk about their endorsement. Then they hit him with this issue. He said, "No problem, no problem."

We went to see him in Sacramento and, I think, it was during talk between Bill Kircher and the governor that the idea came up of having an independent top labor man come into the field and try to work it out.

Governor Brown asked DiGiorgio to hold off on negotiations with the Teamsters, and so did Senator Robert Kennedy and Senator Harrison Williams, who was chairman of the Senate Subcommittee on Migrant Labor.

Then on Tuesday, the governor appointed Dr. Ronald Haughton of Detroit's Wayne State University and the American Arbitration Association to investigate the election.

On the same day, we asked for a court order to block negotiations between DiGiorgio and the Teamsters.

We organized for a strike at Borrego Springs right after the election. Many workers had left on Saturday and Sunday, so most of those that were for us had gone away, but ten guys walked out, including young Juan Flores who was about sixteen or seventeen, and Jose Renteria.

They had come out on strike early Monday morning, and we kept them with us almost all day, making plans to go into the camp with them to bring their belongings out. Maybe, we thought, while inside the camp we could at least see the other workers.

At first I wanted to have either Father Victor Salandini, a

Catholic priest, or Chris Hartmire go into the camp as witnesses with me and the workers. As the day wore on, though, it became apparent that both of them should go in. There might be trouble. There was another priest there who said he was sent by the bishop in San Diego. He wouldn't leave Father Salandini alone for a minute. By this time, he'd gotten wind that we might be arrested, and he was opposed, because he said this would embarrass the church.

It was getting late, but I didn't know how to get Father Salandini in a car with me. Then the other staff, hearing what the problems were, faked a call. They went over to Borrego Springs and came back and told the other father that somebody was calling from the chancery in San Diego. While he went to get the call, we drove into the camp in the big station wagon—Father Salandini, Chris Hartmire, the workers, and me.

About a hundred yards in, there was a roadblock like in the movies, six or seven armed guards and about two dogs, and parked across the road was a truck they used to transport workers.

At the roadblock we stopped. The guards had their guns trained on us, and they were shaking, they were so frightened.

I got out and said, "Look, we're here in peace. We want to get their clothes. We'll be right back. We won't bother anybody."

"You can't go."

One guard with a helmet came over and pushed me around. He grabbed me by the arm.

"Don't touch me," I said. "If you want me to do something, okay, but don't touch me." He took his hands off.

They ordered Chris, Father Salandini, and me into the closed truck—it had hinged doors in the back—and told the workers they could leave. But the workers said, "No, we'll go with them." So they locked us all in the truck. Then they brought us out to the edge of the desert on the ranch and kept us in the truck parked for hours in the sun.

We must have been there from about 4:00 P.M. to about 8:00. It was hotter than hell, almost suffocating. The truck only had small slits for windows, and the temperature outside was way over a hundred degrees. We could see the guards outside with all kinds of guns. One had two revolvers, a rifle slung on his shoulder, and a shotgun at the ready.

Finally the supervisors came and brought us over to the camp where a lot of workers began to harass the guards. We hadn't organized them. They just knew what had happened.

"Let them out!" they yelled.

Finally they let the workers out one at a time to get their things and come back. The people were pretty upset.

It was about 10:00 at night when they turned us over to the sheriff. We had been kept incommunicado for about five hours.

By this time we were very thirsty, but they wouldn't give us water. Then two station wagons arrived with the sheriff's people. The deputies carried heavy chains.

Chris saw them and said, "Look, what's that? I wonder what they want them for? Maybe some desperadoes."

I said, "No, it's for us."

"Oh, Cesar, they wouldn't do that!"

"Sure, they'll do it. You wait and see."

Sure enough they shackled us. We were sitting down, and they shackled our wrists to our ankles. Then they took the chains off and chained us together in threes, our legs chained to each other and our arms crossed and chained to each other. Then they ordered us to get in the station wagons where the back seats faced backward.

Because of the chains, three guys had to get in simultaneously. It was difficult. We had to turn around, sit on the tailgate, and then jump simultaneously, or we knocked each other down as we tried to get on the seat.

In the back seat I fell asleep right away, I was so disgusted. Although I was happy because of the confrontation, I was disgusted with the so-called justice we were getting.

When I woke up, we were in San Diego. There were all kinds of bright lights in my face and a TV camera poking through the window taking my picture.

In the jail, they stripped us and gave us one of the most thorough examinations I have ever undergone. It was degrading. Then we took a shower, and they gave us prison dungarees and a mattress. Because the tank was full, we slept with the mattresses on the floor.

The next morning, the prisoners gave us a welcome. They made us sit down, served us food, and stood at attention while we ate. We thanked them and asked why?

"Well, because you're fighting the good fight," they said. I was deeply moved.

We were released later on in the day. When we went to trial, the workers were let free, while the three of us were convicted of criminal trespass and given three years probation.

About two weeks after our arrest, Dr. Haughton's report came out recommending that another election be held and setting the rules.

I think it was Fred who negotiated the rules with Haughton and the Teamsters before the report was made. I don't remember being involved directly, we were too busy trying to get the machinery organized to go win the next election.

All sides finally agreed to accept Haughton's proposal. DiGiorgio had to accept because of the pressure, the great cry for elections from the public, and because we had resumed the boycott.

One of the key election rules we won was on eligibility. All workers who were working for DiGiorgio the day before the strike started were eligible to vote. The other key rule was giving us access to talk to the workers. Both we and the Teamsters would have the same opportunity at lunchtime and after work.

August 30 was the date set for the new election. I knew that if we lost this one, we would lose the Union, because the public wouldn't have supported us after that. We hadn't established credibility yet with the public.

Fred was directly in charge of the election campaign. He's the best one to tell that story. After we gave him a team of people, he put them together and worked their butts off. I think they learned a lot. Actually, I never went to the DiGiorgio Ranch once during the campaign, but I met with Fred daily for a report.

FRED ROSS RECALLS

For the first time, we were allowed on DiGiorgio property. The limit was seven organizers at noon and five at night, but after the Teamsters started violating this rule, we soon flooded the place with organizers. We had between twenty and twenty-five and scattered them around the six camps. DiGiorgio had a camp for blacks, and one each for Mexican-Americans, Filipinos, Anglos, Puerto Ricans, and women.

There was a grass "bull ring" under walnut trees across the street from the DiGiorgio commissary where male workers ate lunch. Our organizers would work on workers one at a time. The Teamsters did the same, but they also had brand new Volkswagen station wagons with loudspeakers, and one very witty guy handling the mike.

Inevitably each day's session would end with a big debate and insults exchanged between two organizers. The Teamsters were looking for it, and two or three of our guys wanted to debate and insult also. That's why it was called the bull ring.

I was trying to keep them talking to individuals about the dif-

ference between our contracts with Schenley and Bud Antle's Salinas contract with the Teamsters, and talking about our death benefits, the credit union, co-op, and services—comparing NFWA and the Teamsters.

Then when they started red-baiting us, we brought up the corruption issue—David Beck and Jimmy Hoffa—and it drove them crazy. We would not have used that if they hadn't red-baited us. We got Robert Kennedy's The Enemy Within and handed out hundreds of copies. We also gave out copies of the Communication Workers coloring book on the Teamster Family Tree.

(A sample page from the coloring book: "My name is Dave Beck. I was President of the Teamsters before Hoffa. I am taking a five-year vacation at McNeil Island Federal Penitentiary. This letter contains my pension check for $50,000 which I receive every year. Color my 'touch' golden.")

After the noon bull-ring session, we went back to the Union's pink house to do a post-mortem of that noon meeting. I'd harp constantly on confrontation to get them away from that. Then we would plan for the night operation.

We divided that in two, one group to talk to workers after they finished eating in the camps, from 5:30 to 7:00, and another to call on workers around Delano who lived off the ranch, or those who were on strike. We kept coming back to them even though they got tired of it and told us they would vote for us. We would just put out new leaflets as an excuse to return and give it to them.

We made three-by-five cards on each worker after we got the list from DiGiorgio. I had three persons in charge of the cards, and all organizers were assigned to one of the three. Every night the three would pass out cards to the organizers who would then go talk to those workers.

The AFL-CIO sent about ten to twelve organizers, or maybe fifteen, and they concentrated mainly on Anglos or blacks depending on the race of the organizer. But we duplicated their work because we felt some were too casual. We didn't leave anything to chance.

CESAR CHAVEZ RECALLS

A few days after DiGiorgio agreed to the elections, they laid off 190 of our people. They knew if the people stopped working, they would have to leave and wouldn't vote. Their tactics were dirty. They were one of the most unprincipled companies I've ever dealt with. Then they brought in Anglo high school kids to work and vote against us.

DiGiorgio also had our organizers Pete Cardenas, Eliseo Medina, and Eddie Frankel arrested several times, and each time the cases were thrown out of court. Then the Teamsters brought in their goons and beat up Eliseo, Pete, Marcos Munoz, and Luis Valdez.

So Kircher called the Seafarers in to protect our pickets.

When they came, word got out to the Teamsters that the Seafarers were in town. After that, the Teamsters didn't come near us. The Seafarers were great, beautiful guys who were admired by the workers.

I remember the Teamsters had this goon that came around and scared all of us. One day this guy saw a carload of sailors and started doing his daily gymnastics. The sailors let him go through it all, flexing his biceps, everything. Then they opened the door and came out of their car. This Teamster took a look at them, and his mouth dropped open. He took off, and we never saw him again.

WILLIAM KIRCHER RECALLS

The Teamsters came in and were swaggering around, intimidating people by their presence, and there was some violence.

So I called Paul Hall, president of the Seafarers, and said, "I want some able bodies down here fast!" And he said, "Okay, give me twenty minutes, then you call this number in San Francisco." So I called this good friend of mine—Paul had just called him—a guy named Frankie Drosak, and he said, "We're on our way."

I don't think there were ten hours elapsed between the time I made that phone call and into Delano drove about fourteen SIU members. You should have seen some of them! There was one black fellow who had about a twenty-two-inch waist and about a seventy-inch chest. He looked like a funnel, big shoulders and slender hips. Some of the others were just as impressive, too.

We were going night and day, Cesar and I, and we just didn't have time to do everything. So I just told them quickly what the score was. I said, "Nonviolence, travel in pairs, and make sure that the Teamsters know you are here." I knew the Teamsters well enough to know that the presence of these guys would cool it. And it's true. We never had a minute's violence from the time they got there.

But the next morning Tom Stewart, an AFL-CIO organizer, came over to my motel before I could even get out there and said,

"Look, you'd better come. We've got some problems with the Seafarers."

"What the hell's the problem with the Seafarers?"

What happened was that one of the Seafarers sat down by a Union volunteer who had a sign sewed on his jacket that said, "Ban the Bomb."

The mentality of the volunteers was completely and totally doctrinaire in terms of certain things, among which was their posture against the war in Vietnam.

The Seafarers were involved in the whole business of challenging the loading of Communist ships, so they were essentially anti-Communists, and to them Vietnam was a war against Communism. So they were cast doctrinally almost in the opposite direction from the volunteers. It was almost down to the wholly simplified position that anybody who was against the war in Vietnam was a Communist. Almost that.

So this Seafarer sat down next to this volunteer who had a sign that said, "Ban the Bomb" and said something to him. This fellow answered that he was a member of some anti-Vietnam committee, or whatever it was.

The Seafarer jumped up and went in the next room where there was a girl. He said to her, "Hey, we've got to do something about it. We've been infiltrated!"

She said, "What do you mean?"

"There's a guy in there from such and such an organization"— he named this peace organization—"and we got to get rid of him!"

She said, "Hell, I won't help you get rid of him, I'm a member of the same organization."

A few Seafarers were really upset. They said, "We've got to do something."

I never had anticipated this. But I quickly rounded them up, set them down, and said, "In a battle there are priorities and priorities. And the priorities here are this. These people are dedicated, devoted friends, and the fact that you got different points of view on something not related to this is just too goddamn bad. So you just forget about that!"

And they said, "Okay, okay," and we never had another problem about it.

CESAR CHAVEZ RECALLS

Ten days before the election, DiGiorgio sent a letter to all their employees. It said that the June 24 vote showed that 284 wanted a union, and 60 did not. So, the letter said, "We think that a vote for 'no union' would be a wasted vote." The company concluded, "As we have said in the past, we think the Teamsters Farm Workers Union is your best bet, but it is your choice to make."

CHAPTER 3

A Merger and a Vote

CESAR CHAVEZ RECALLS

The time had come to take a major step—merging our Union and AWOC into one AFL-CIO union. Actually the merger would have taken place even if the Teamsters hadn't moved in. The only question was when to do it. Now we thought it would be best to merge before the election.

When Bill Kircher initiated the idea shortly after I met him, I favored it. We already had gone to Al Green of AWOC, but we had been turned down. So when Bill said we should merge, I said, "Wonderful—except that we have many problems, a lot of education to be done."

The education went on for months and months. I would call Bill in Washington and tell him, "We're having another meeting!" And he would come.

He'd sit there, for example, in a room at the Bakersfield Inn, and Dolores would ask questions. Dolores had never been anti-AFL-CIO, but she had a lot of questions. I also remember Bill coming up once from Hollywood to speak to the volunteers. There was a very cute girl, very beautiful girl, who told me, "You goddamn fink! You sold out!"

And I said, "Don't say that. I didn't sell out." I said, "You know what? We have no place to go. You're leaving tonight. You're going to forget about us. We've got to stay here." And she left the Cause. Much later she wrote a letter to apologize. "I don't understand it, but I left, and you didn't."

It was interesting. We had the two extremes, those for a merger and those opposed, and they could be as radical, one as the other. For example there was Marshall Ganz, "You're goddamn right we need the AFL-CIO. We've got to beat those bastards!" And there was Jim Drake who was against it, and one girl who cried at the thought. I went for months with a lot of bruises down my back.

I told people, "Look, I hear you don't like what we're proposing. We've got to think about the future of the Union, whether we are going to build a Union. We need strength. We need allies."

What eventually convinced Jim Drake was Bill Kircher coming in and just taking his coat off, writing leaflets, and giving his talents to us, distributing leaflets, taking on the Teamsters. That was what really counted.

The Migrant Ministry was involved. They had their staff, their future, their money tied to us, and Chris Hartmire is such a beautiful guy. He said, "Cesar, whatever you think is right, we'll do it. Let's win this strike!"

One day, about a month before the election, I walked into Bill's room and said, "Bill, I think we better do it right now, let's announce the merger right now." And we sent a wire to George Meany.

We took a vote, and the only people who voted against the merger were maybe 10 or 15 percent of the volunteers. Even though they were nonmembers, we gave them a vote. Everybody who was eligible to vote in DiGiorgio voted for it. There wasn't a farm worker's vote against it.

WILLIAM KIRCHER RECALLS

We had open meetings, two big meetings, giving a complete explanation of the merger. We also had meetings of the leadership. I'll bet that the top leadership of the United Farm Workers, at the point the merger took place, knew more about union structure and autonomy and constitutional relationships than 75 percent of the leadership of the labor movement below the national level today.

I don't think I have really a better friend, I mean this in the context of real principle, than Jim Drake. I think that it is a friendship that is built on great respect for honesty and integrity on both sides. The same goes for Chris Hartmire and David Havens.

I remember I made up my mind that these were guys that you can not sweet talk. So I just told them, "You've heard the old saying, as ministers, that many of the greatest sins against charity are committed in the name of charity."

And I said, "Guys like you run around committing many of the greatest sins of prejudice in the context of fighting for tolerance."

They said, "What do you mean?"

"Just what I said. You're all victims of an internal battle in your own machinery where you are always fighting the hierarchy which you have just classified as backward. Then you equate hierarchy with structure and establishment. From that point on, anything that relates to structure, establishment, you're against. If you see me in the context of structure or establishment, you're against me without even knowing me." I said, "You're a victim of your own prejudices."

One night Jim got really mad at me. It was a meeting shortly after the march, and the march actually made the organizational work blossom. Cesar was having trouble delegating work, so he developed some departments. He had a great big chart listing these departments. Someone was going to be in charge of this, and someone in charge of that. And he and Jim were holding the chart up there explaining.

So after the meeting, I got Jim outside and said, "Gee, Jim, I feel sorry for you. My heart goes out to you."

"What do you mean?"

And I said, "This must be a real sad night for you."

"I don't understand," he said.

"All of this unstructured freedom that you love went right down the goddamn drain!" I said. "And you're being made to be a party to building up bureaucracy."

"Goddamn it, get off my back!" he said.

"No, Jim," I said, "I'm serious. You know, in my union, the Auto Workers, which is the biggest, we must have had a couple hundred thousand members before we got this bureaucratized." And Jim got so mad he turned around and stomped away.

But this was the kind of game that went on in those early days. That's what you had to do with a guy as bright and as dedicated as Jim Drake. You could never con Jim Drake into a drink of ice water. You had to, number one, be doing all of the things he was doing and, number two, you had to show that you had as much pride in what you were representing as he had in the things which he was representing. When he reached the point where he saw these two things, then you had a friend, then you had cooperation, and then you started making some progress. I consider him one of the finest men I ever knew in my life.

It happened that the Executive Council of the AFL-CIO had a meeting in Chicago on August 23. We were in this meeting in San Francisco a few weeks earlier when the merger decision was made. So I called, and we got an exchange of telegrams that we could release in the context of the news conference that we held announcing the coming merger, what would now be the United Farm Workers Organizing Committee, AFL-CIO. The UFWOC charter then was approved when the Executive Council met.

CESAR CHAVEZ RECALLS

When I took over as director of UFWOC, my first official act was making our position clear on labor contractors. The merger meeting was in Chicago, and within seventy-two hours of the time I was named director, I came to Delano, got in my car, went to Stockton, and just ended AWOC's contracts with the contractors.

The AWOC organizers were complaining they couldn't go to where the workers were, at the pickup point, because people were cussing at them and cussing the Union. I knew that was because the organizers had a little combination between themselves and the contractors.

So I said, "Beginning tomorrow morning, you dissolve every goddamn contract with the contractors. They're not worth the paper they're written on." And those organizers tried to argue with me.

All the organizers quit except Larry Itliong. They were making something like $125 a week, but I wanted them to suffer with the strikers. I demanded full commitment. One guy had a Cadillac. I said, "You're not going to organize with me with a damn Cadillac! You either get rid of the Cadillac or leave the Union." So he left the Union.

The job can't be done unless there is a commitment. If we're going to lead people and ask them to starve and to really sacrifice, we've got to do it first, do it more than anybody else, because it isn't the orders, it isn't the pronouncements, it's the deeds that count.

When we merged, we had other problems, too. There was muttering all over the place that the members didn't like the Filipinos coming in.

As we had other entities—the co-op, the credit union, the clinic, the service center, and so on—I told our members, "You have to give the Filipinos representation not only in the Union, but in all the other services that we have."

There was this group of about twenty who didn't like the idea.

They came in a delegation after we had voted on it and talked to me for about two hours. I just let them talk.

Then I said, "You're kidding yourselves. What are you doing this for? It's just lost time, your time and mine. You know what the policy is. You know how I feel. It's not going to change."

"Well, we'll leave."

"Fine, leave," I said. "It's not going to change." But they really didn't want to leave.

So I said, "Okay, I'll leave then." I made a proposal. "Let me leave, and I'll go work for the Filipinos, and you can have your Union."

No, they didn't want me to leave either.

"Well, you're going to have to accept this," I said. "And now go back and think it over, and you better be prepared to defend yourselves because I'm going to take you on. Or be ready to throw me out!"

I was very hurt that they should have come up with this. I thought we had trained them not to feel this way. Luckily a lot of people didn't see it their way.

About six months later, we were having a meeting when I suddenly proposed that we should get rid of all the Filipinos from the credit union. I did that with a straight face.

The Filipinos just stared, but the Mexicans—the same ones that were arguing before to keep them out—reacted angrily.

I knew what kind of an effect I was going to get, but I wanted to make it a learning experience. The same Mexicans who, six months ago, were saying the Filipinos should be thrown out started arguing to keep them in "because they work like hell, they really are good."

So I started laughing, and I said, "Of course, I don't want them out. I just wanted to get your opinion on them."

While all this and the election campaign were going on, we also were putting on another major effort. The election rules said that anyone working at DiGiorgio the day before the strike started was eligible to vote. Since most of those workers were gone, we sent out people to scout for them all over the state. Then we went into Arizona, Texas, and, I think, Oregon and Washington. We sent teams of people into El Paso, San Antonio—all over creation. We even went into Mexico. Then we put out publicity on Spanish-speaking radio stations asking people to contact us, or, if they couldn't find us, to come to Delano to vote on August 30.

Two days before the election, Harry Bernstein, the top labor reporter of the *Los Angeles Times*, came and told us we were going to lose.

I already was very worried. This was the end of us if we lost. It was not like losing just another election, it was like losing the whole thing.

Harry Bernstein said, "You haven't got a chance." He told me they were betting in Las Vegas with odds of about three to one against us.

Then both major television networks came out on their news shows the day before the election with reports that it was a foregone conclusion that, while there had been a heroic battle, the farm worker forces could not make it.

Saul Alinksy also said that the Teamsters were going to beat us. He said, "You're going to be decimated. The Teamsters are too strong."

The night before the election, I had trouble sleeping. Finally I went to sleep about 3:00 A.M. I told myself, "Well, what the hell. We didn't have anything when we started. Here we go!"

For election day we had organized all the names, broken them down by street address and organizers. We made sure that our supporters voted. I was at the office talking to people, thanking them if they voted for us, and if they hadn't voted yet, encouraging them to go vote and get others to vote.

A lot of people would come to our office where we would shuttle them to DiGiorgio. One man came all the way from Mexico, and when he got to the polls, they told him he couldn't vote because they couldn't find him on the list. One of our organizers, Gene Boutelier, brought a family of four from El Paso, and their car broke down just between Delano and McFarland. Gene got a ride to Delano and ran into the office for another car. But when he finally got them to the voting place, it was closed. He had driven them all the way from El Paso and missed the election by ten minutes.

A Spaniard was there as arbitrator. He had a lot of guts, just a little guy who wasn't afraid to stand up to the Teamsters. He kept very neutral, and we didn't know where he stood.

But about an hour after the election results were announced, he came in, tears in his eyes, and said, "The only thing more important than this is getting Franco out of Spain. This is second!"

FRED ROSS RECALLS

The election was from 6:00 A.M. to 8:00 P.M. We had it organized so a long line of cars was ready at 5:00 A.M. to pick up workers.

"Oh, you don't have to come," they'd say.

"Oh, we want to so we can put your name on the board as having voted."

We had already found out what time they'd be ready to go, in the morning, afternoon, or night. So many workers were showing up to vote, it drove DiGiorgio crazy. Some workers never had worked for the firm, but they had heard about the election, and they wanted to vote anyway. Of course, they couldn't.

The choices on the ballot were UFWOC, Teamsters, or "no union." The "no union" vote was practically nonexistent. Each union had its own observers who worked in shifts during the day. We had decided who we'd challenge ahead of time, such as foremen who were supervisory personnel.

Each observer had a book with all the names in it. The observers checked the name off of each person who voted, and although they were not allowed to take the book out, when they were spelled at the end of a shift, they took the book with them. We would pour over it to find the weak spots and send out people to get out the vote.

The last person that came to our office arrived at 7:50 P.M. We didn't have time to check to see if he was eligible, but we rushed him to the polls.

Then the ballots were put in a box and put in a trunk of a California Highway Patrol car. A representative of DiGiorgio, the Teamsters, and UFWOC got in the back of the car, and Dolores and a lawyer followed them to San Francisco. But the CHP outdistanced and lost them.

Dolores was afraid of foul play, so she gave our man a Dexidrin tablet so he wouldn't fall asleep. And even after the ballots were counted, he couldn't sleep all night.

CESAR CHAVEZ RECALLS

They started counting the ballots the next day in San Francisco.

Everybody in the Union was gathered in Delano at Filipino Hall. That was an emotional day, more, I guess, than any other I've seen. People were crying. The picket line was there, our friends that had voted, and a lot of friends that were just there to visit us.

I was in Delano, too, making plans on what to do in case we lost, how to deal with the strikers. Then Dolores called from San

Francisco and said, "Hey, Cesar, I think we've won this damn thing."

I said, "Don't say, you think. You'd better be sure."

"Let me call you back."

In ten minutes she called back and said, "I think we won."

I said, "No, no! Be sure! The count will come pretty soon."

After the count, the Arbitration Association didn't want to make it public. So Bill Kircher said, "Okay, if you don't want to make it public, just give us the figures." Then, when they gave him the figures, Bill said, "The hell with you, I'll make it public."

As soon as they got the word in Delano, the merchants began to close down for the rest of that day. For them it was a day of mourning. We got the word that we had won about 10:30 in the morning and had a celebration at Filipino Hall. There was a lot of singing, clapping, and shouting.

Then I said, "Okay, we've won, but we can't sit on our laurels. Let's go get another one." We ate lunch early and then went right back to picket at another ranch. We're a tough little Union!

We beat the Teamsters 530 to 331 in the fields. Only 12 voted for "no union." The Teamsters won the sheds, 97 to 45.

As I look back, I see that the way the Teamsters acted at Di-Giorgio was inescapable. They operate out of deceit and contempt, and out of positions of unchecked power. How else can they operate, except coming to the back door and making those sweetheart deals with the employers? This was the first time they had done that to us, but it wouldn't be the last. And every time they did it, it was the same way, the only way they could do it.

TELEGRAM FROM MARTIN LUTHER KING, JR.

As brothers in the fight for equality, I extend the hand of fellowship and good will and wish continuing success to you and your members. The fight for equality must be fought on many fronts— in the urban slums, in the sweat shops of the factories and fields. Our separate struggles are really one—a struggle for freedom, for dignity, and for humanity. You and your valiant fellow workers have demonstrated your commitment to righting grievous wrongs forced upon exploited people. We are together with you in spirit and in determination that our dreams for a better tomorrow will be realized.

CHAPTER 4

The Arvin Story

CESAR CHAVEZ RECALLS

Even though we had won the election, our battles with DiGiorgio were not over. We now wanted to hold elections at their big Arvin ranch southeast of Bakersfield.

Mack Lyons, a black farm worker from Texas, played a very important part in that fight. He was aggressive, worked hard, and got caught on fire. The blacks were a very small percentage of workers at Arvin, but the Chicanos, Puerto Ricans, and whites responded to him so well that they elected him their leader.

MACK LYONS RECALLS

About a month or more after I went to work at DiGiorgio at Arvin, I saw Richard Flowers passing out leaflets when the trucks came out of the yards. He'd put a bunch of leaflets on the truck, and we'd read them. And that was the first time that I had ever read anything about the farm workers' Union.

I don't know why I was so interested. I guess I just wanted to find out a lot of things. Maybe it was because I did some farm work back in Texas, and it was real hard. I would be in the field and, man, I would be thinking, I wonder why in the hell do people have to work this hard. I was a little kid. I was wishing, how come the hell something can't happen to help people like this, to make their lives a little bit easier, a little bit better. And I wondered, could anything ever happen?

Like I remember, I used to go to the fields with my mother when I was too little to work, but she would be picking cotton. And I would ride the cotton sack, and like a couple of times I fell off the cotton sack, and I was really scared because I was lost. She didn't know I had rolled off. And I remember like when I got a little bigger, I had a little sack, one of those burlap sacks that you pick cotton in. When I was really small, like four, five, six, and seven.

Well, I came to California in 1965 when I was twenty-five, and I went to Bakersfield where there were a lot of people I met from Texas, little towns thirty, forty miles from Dallas, and they happened to be working in Delano picking peaches at that time.

I hadn't picked grapes or peaches before, and I decided to go and work with these guys. When the grape season came, we were working for a labor contractor in Delano. His name was Manuel Jiminez.

One morning we saw these guys standing alongside of the road. Most of them were Mexican, and I didn't speak any Spanish. Nobody knew what was going on. We went on to the field; we just didn't pay any attention to the guys that were standing alongside of the road.

The next day we came by, and people were still out there with picket signs saying Huelga. Nobody knew what it meant. I mean, we had no idea of what was going on.

One of the people that was checking for the labor contractor was a lady. When we asked her, what was these people doing? she told us, well, that was that farm workers' Union, and that they were supposed to be out on strike, "But just go to work. It don't mean nothing."

From what she told us, I figured we shouldn't be here. But the guys I was working for, they said, "Well, she's right, they're wrong."

After we went back home, we talked about the strike and figured that we should find something else to do. We left that whole area, and we looked for jobs for about three days. Finally two guys found jobs at a dairy. I finally found a job driving a cotton picker. Later I went to work at DiGiorgio at Arvin. There was no strike there.

I didn't know at the time that people got fired for union activity or for talking about the Union, and I started asking people, what about the Union? What about these people on strike?

Well, this particular afternoon, Richard Flowers and Marshall Ganz were standing at the gate passing out leaflets. We stopped and talked. I gave Marshall my address, and I asked him if he could come by my house that night. He and Richard Flowers almost beat me there.

I didn't join the first night, but I told them that the next meeting I would join, and that way maybe some of the other guys would join also.

Then the organizing activities kind of increased. They would come to ranches at noontime, and they would give us some leaflets, and I would help them pass them out.

What we were going to do was ask for an election. Well, we asked. A telegram was sent to DiGiorgio. He didn't answer it.

Finally we had to do more than just ask for elections, so everybody got together and signed a petition to Governor Pat Brown. We got signatures from about 90 percent of the people that were working there, and we got a delegation together, and we went to Los Angeles.

I think there was about twenty of us that was picked. Like we went to the governor's house in Los Angeles, and we gave him the petition.

Some of the people that went started getting pressure from their supervisors—if you don't stop, you're going to get fired. Some of them was fired.

And like nobody never pushed me. I think they just thought I was a little crazy, or a little stupid. I knew what the consequences would be, but I figured that I could get back to driving a cotton picker or go back to doing something else.

FRED ROSS RECALLS

We fought for elections at Arvin, but the Teamsters opposed it. So the majority of the workers signed a petition asking for an election, and we got on statewide TV and presented Governor Brown with the petition. But it did no good.

So Cesar called us together—it was near the end of the harvest— and made the statement, "Well, we've got to come up with an idea. I know I could if I were down there, so why can't you?"

I had been flirting around with an idea for a couple of weeks. I felt something more could be done with those petitions, but the idea kept eluding me. So when Cesar said this, it hit me. If we could get the governor to write a letter to the people who signed the petition telling them he had done all he could, but maybe they could take it up with DiGiorgio, I felt that the governor's letter would give them the courage to leave their job to see DiGiorgio.

We had to spin wheels to get Brown to do this. We had a letter all ready in English and Spanish. Then I went to his Los Angeles campaign headquarters. The governor was traveling, campaigning against Ronald Reagan, but finally they tracked him down. When we showed him the letter, he said, "I don't see anything wrong with that. Okay, let her go."

This was planned Sunday so the workers would get the letters on Monday. I picked out the names of forty workers, had that letter typed, and then had the letters mailed special delivery from each town.

On Monday, we called those workers and suggested a meeting for that night. About thirty-five of the forty were invited, and we sent organizers to bring them to the meeting.

We wanted the workers to come to San Francisco to Sansome Street in the financial district where DiGiorgio's office was. We also planned to get the picket line there at noon, and the Teatro Campesino on a flat-bed truck outside the office chanting and singing.

MACK LYONS RECALLS

We picked a delegation to go to San Francisco to Robert DiGiorgio's office, and they picked me to be like the spokesman for the group.

When we got there, DiGiorgio wasn't in. Just his receptionist. She told us that he was out to lunch, and we said we'd wait until he came back. And then around 1:00 or 1:30, she told us that he wouldn't be back in that afternoon.

Some cameras and some press were there, and we told them we was going to stay there until we met with DiGiorgio, and he agreed to let us have elections.

Finally, someone got ahold of DiGiorgio, and he said that he would meet with us the next day.

When we met with Robert DiGiorgio and two of his assistants the next day, he told us about how happy the rest of the people were down at DiGiorgio, and that some of the people at Sierra Vista didn't want to work, like they joined the outside agitators, and he couldn't agree to have no elections. And he had another meeting that he had to go to, but he left his public relations guy to answer any questions.

We decided that we was just going to stay there until he agreed to have elections. Then this public relations man told us that if we didn't leave, we was going to be arrested for trespassing. Finally we got arrested. We went to jail for a few hours, along with some of the top labor people in San Francisco who had joined us.

We got out of jail that night. The next day we went right back to his office and got arrested again. Finally he agreed to have elections on November 4.

Then is when the problems came, like the guy that run the camp hired some goons to go around scaring people and beating up people that he thought was going to vote for the Union, that was living in the camp. He was sort of weeding the people out before the elections, firing some, threatening some, beating up some.

And every day, the assistant superintendent, Harold Rhodes, he would go around and make two speeches to every crew about how the Union was bad, they wasn't nothing but a bunch of Communists, and we've been treating you boys fine all these years, we don't want you to vote for that Communist Union 'cause we're all happy here. If you want a raise, we'll pay you just as much as the Union is asking for, and you won't have to pay Union dues. All that stuff.

Harold Rhodes's speeches got on my nerves so bad that I started making speeches also. I was driving a truck, me and three other guys, and we had the opportunity to see three or four or five crews. We was picking up grapes for them, and like every time we would get to a crew, I'd tell them like, Harold Rhodes has been over here, and you and I know how the conditions is here, what we want, and how we're going to do something about our conditions. Like you know Harold Rhodes, you know he's for the company, he's the assistant supervisor, he is doing all he can for them, he don't want us to be able to do anything for ourselves.

And like Harold Rhodes and Jesse Marcus started making signs that said, Vote No, and a couple of the anti-Union truck drivers wrote on their trucks, Vote No.

So I started putting signs up, writing all over the place, Vote Yes. I put it on my truck. I'd go around all of the crews, Vote Yes, like I wasn't scared, trying to get them not to be scared and doing the same thing.

The company got on my back. I had the Vote Yes sign on a day and a half before they said anything about it. Then Harold Rhodes came to me one morning when we was picking up grapes. He told me to get that thing off the truck. I told him to get it off, if he wanted to get it off. So he got some grape leaves, and he rubbed it off.

I told him that I was going to put it back on. And, man, he was really mad. And I put it back on, and he rubbed it back off again. Finally he left. The workers was getting a kick out of that! Like I was writing it back on, and he was taking it off, and he was assistant supervisor, and like he could fire me. Well, he didn't.

Probably one of the reasons why is because of something that happened earlier. When we met with Robert DiGiorgio, one of the first things we said was, "Okay, whatever comes out of this meeting here that we have with you, we know that we're not going to have a job when we get back. We know that we're going to get fired. And what we want you to do is write a letter to your supervisors down there, and we'll carry it to them, with the names of the people that's here, so we'll be sure we have a job when we get back."

And like they was glad to do that publicly, I mean so it would look like they was good guys, and they didn't fire people for this. That's the thing that saved my neck, I think.

There are a lot of things that happened, that have really been inspirational—as long as I've been with the Farm Workers— incidents, people, and all kinds of events that have taken place that really make you feel more dedicated, really feel good about what you're doing. The most touching was the night of the election at Arvin.

I saw people cry, and they was crying because they was happy, and they was crying because they saw that something was happening, and they had been a part of it. It was just a real feeling.

The people—you had white, black, Mexicans, Puerto Rican people—everybody was crowded around this little room where we was counting the ballots, and everybody was trying to look in the window, and you'd look up, and you'd see three or four black faces, white faces, Mexican-American faces. That was a really beautiful sight, to see the hope that was in people. I mean you just see their faces. You was looking at those ballots, and you'd look up at them, and they'd smile, and they'd cross their fingers, and they'd do something, some gesture of encouragement.

And then, when we announced that we had won, everybody started hugging everybody. Before then, on the ranches, they always kept all these people separated. This was the first time I ever saw all these people being happy about the same things. You could see that all of these people had something in common. And that was probably the most inspirational, the most heart-warming, the greatest thing that ever happened to me.

And then the fact that I was elected to be chairman of the DiGiorgio Ranch Committee where the majority of the people was Mexican-American and Puerto Rican and Anglo, and the minority was black.

I was aware of people wondering like, okay, you're black, so you've got something in common with another black person, you supposed to do special favors for him, or it could be the other way around. Like you're really conscious of this, so you're not going to do anything for him. You're going to do everything for an Anglo or Mexican-American. And I could see all of these questions in people's minds, but nobody never said anything about it.

And when I was elected, I was trying to figure out all of these things. And finally I decided, okay, all you have to do is just do whatever is right. And then there was no more problems about it. Every once in a while, a question would come up in my mind, am I favoring anybody? I'd ask myself, and I would like search back to see. And I wasn't, I was just doing what was right, and I didn't try to balance right and wrong according to the races or any sort of proportion. And I really learned something from that. And I gained the respect of all of those people, and it really made me feel good.

DOLORES HUERTA RECALLS

We wouldn't have won the Arvin election if it hadn't been for the Okie and black votes, because DiGiorgio brought in a whole bunch of guys from Mexicali to vote against the Union.

It's cheaper for them to bring in guys like that and pay them five hundred dollars apiece than it is to get a Union, in the long run. They brought in some guys from Mexicali that just scared the hell out of me. They sent a chill through my spine just to see them. They were brought in specifically to break the strike, and they were told, if the Union wins, the guys that had these jobs before will get them back, and you're out of a job, and they'll send you back to Mexico.

MACK LYONS RECALLS

After we won the election, then we had the problem of getting the contract. Like we won the election, but that just gave us the right to negotiate, and all that couldn't be settled in negotiations had to be sent to arbitration.

We picked a negotiating committee, and we started to negotiate. I was chairman of the commitee, but I had never had any experience before in negotiating. Well, before we had the contract, there were all kinds of grievances about water and the price of vines. I got a little experience there. And we knew what we wanted, and we just asked for it, and give them all the reasons why we should have it. I didn't have no experience except, I guess, just natural experience that comes from getting denied something.

When we started negotiating, that was one of the toughest, I mean, that was the most disgusting thing that I have ever experienced. I mean, when people know that they're wrong, and they know that what you're asking for is reasonable, and like the excuses that they give, I mean, the excuses wasn't convincing enough to convince anybody!

The ice water for instance. They didn't see why they should be required to put ice in the water in the summertime, or to buy cups, so we would have individual drinking cups. Just one of the smallest things.

I've experienced some very sad moments when it comes to the treatment that the farm workers have gotten. I remember once a guy got hit in the eye with a piece of wire. He was cutting it, and it snapped back and hit him. One of the crew bosses was in the field, and like the guy told the crew boss that he got hit in the eye, and that he wanted to go see the doctor. And like one of the supervisors was coming to the field, and the crew boss told the guy to get under the vine so the superintendent wouldn't see him. That was really sad.

The saddest part of that was this damn crew boss. I don't know what would have to be wrong with the guy for him to be that damn scared of something.

And then another instance. A guy was run over with one of those juice trailers that's got about seven or eight tons of grapes on it. He got his leg run over, and they took him to the company doctor, and that damn doctor just gave him some pills and told the guy to go home and come back to work tomorrow. And the guy's leg was swollen up, and it was blue, and it was really screwed up. And later, he came to our office, and we took him to the hospital, Kern General Hospital. They didn't want to treat the guy. They didn't want to wait on him out there, because he wasn't going to be able to pay anything, because he wasn't making anything. The company was supposed to be carrying workmen's compensation, but like they was scared to treat the guy for fear that the company's insurance wouldn't pay off.

There are millions of things like that.

Anyway, we negotiated for three or four months. Then everything went to the arbitrator.

One of the things that we were really afraid of, we knew that they was going to sell their land, and they knew that they was going to sell their land because of the acreage limitations, and the government giving them cheap water for only ten years. And we talked about a successor clause. That was one of the things that we really wanted, a successor clause, so we.wouldn't have to have the same problem once they sold, so that the contract would still be binding on the company that bought the land. And somehow they convinced the arbitrator that they wasn't going to sell, like according to the agreement that they had made with the government.

They had to sell their land, but the arbitrator said, no successor clause. He called us up, I guess to make us feel good by saying that if the company sold the ranch, it would continue to operate under the contract.

Then, after we finally got the contract back from the arbitrator, we had the problem of enforcing the contract, and that got to be the big problem.

We set up a hiring hall in Lamont. First of all the company had to give us a seniority list; and it turns out that the people that the company felt voted for them, they put on top of the seniority list. Now this was designed to make the rest of the people mad and to cause some dissention.

The fight with the seniority list began when we got the contract, and it ended when they sold the ranch. We started straightening it out little by little, but we never did get it completely straightened out.

And like in the first three months of the contract, we had over a hundred grievances, and it was impossible to get them settled with the company—I mean just any kind of grievance. Like they fired people for taking some asparagus home. All the years before, people could get asparagus or any kind of stuff that they picked and just take it home. But they stopped people from taking anything home to eat. They started wanting people to work faster. They started setting quotas for people, and I mean they started really harassing people. They harassed them more after we got the contract, just trying to discourage people. We just had constant problems with DiGiorgio. That was a full-time job trying to administer the contract.

After we got the contract, I decided to go to work for the Union. That's when I started administrating and running the hiring hall.

I started getting five dollars a week and the rent paid, just the regular Union benefits.

I used to think that money was very important in the lives of people. But I don't think so. I think money is just something that people have gotten used to having, like you can trade for something you want. Money is unimportant. We just need to have the money to get some of the things that you can't get any other way.

NOTE: By December of 1967, DiGiorgio began the sale of 4,700 acres in the Delano area because of the federal reclamation law that prohibits individual owners from getting federally subsidized water for more than 160 acres for more than ten years. By the end of 1968, the company had sold all its holdings—and the Union had lost its contracts.

CHAPTER 5

Teamster Coup

CESAR CHAVEZ RECALLS

Ten days after we won our first election at DiGiorgio and before the campaign had really started at Arvin, the Perelli-Minetti workers, who had been agitating for a strike for a long time, finally went out on their own when a supervisor fired a crew. Then they came to see us. Although we had more strikes than we could shake a stick at, we took on that one, too.

Six crews struck that Tuesday—forty-eight workers who harvested the wine grapes on the twenty-six-hundred-acre ranch near Delano, the only ranch that had not been struck in 1965.

On Friday, Dolores and our attorney, Alex Hoffman, went into negotiations with the three Perelli-Minettis—Fred, Jean, and Bill —and came back very encouraged, thinking the company was going to want to move. After negotiating all day, the Perelli-Minettis said they would consult their lawyers Tuesday and notify the Union in a few days whether they would extend signed recognition or not. We recommended either an election or a card check.

But unknown to us, the company went directly to the Teamsters, and on Monday three busloads of scabs from as far away as the Mexican border came through our picket line escorted by Teamsters. Then the company put out a press release saying that because they had "written proof" that the Teamsters represented the majority of their workers, they had signed a contract with them.

We had to make a decision. We got the key people together in the Union, came up to Santa Barbara at St. Anthony's Seminary, locked ourselves up for about three days, and analyzed the whole situation. We felt that if we didn't fight now, every time we got our grower ready to sign, he would go to the Teamsters.

By the time we got through our sessions, we were convinced that if we put pressure on the company, they would get the Teamsters out. So we all but forgot the fresh grapes and turned the boycott on Perelli-Minetti.

Month after month, the Perelli-Minetti boycott continued. We followed their wines all over, to stores in the San Francisco Bay Area and in Los Angeles.

The company pressured the Teamsters, telling them, "Okay, you told us that you'd take care of this problem. Now there's a strike, and there's a boycott, and we want you to help us with the boycott."

The Teamsters couldn't help them, but all of a sudden they became very concerned about the representation of the workers. They got a guy from San Jose, Oscar Gonzales, and made him the head of all their field operations.

A lot of people in the Union got very upset, but some of us didn't because we thought that was a sign. Generally the Teamsters are fighting the Chicanos and the blacks to keep them from leadership. For example in the canneries—60 to 80 percent Chicanos—the people can't get leadership. So why would the Teamsters give it to them in the fields? We thought it was their first step toward backing out.

ALBERT ROJAS, FARM WORKER AND ORGANIZER, RECALLS

I first met Oscar Gonzales in 1964 when I was working with the War on Poverty in Oxnard. Oscar had started an independent union called the United Farm Workers Union, with little committees in Watsonville, Salinas, Hollister, Gilroy, San Jose, and Santa Clara. He had no contracts, with the exception of one toward the latter part of his organizing.

Two years later, Oscar called me in Oxnard and told me Bill Grami, the Teamster in charge of farm worker organizing, wanted him to work with the Teamsters to help organize farm workers throughout the state. They were offering him some good money, at least ten thousand dollars a month as far as expenses and gas and office equipment, hiring staff, whatever.

In the meantime, I had started to organize farm workers in my own area, Ventura County, organizing about four hundred farm workers at a large chicken ranch. We also were signing up workers in the strawberries industry, and we were doing very well with the base that we had.

Well, Oscar joined the Teamsters, UFWU became Teamster Local 964. In the beginning, Bill Grami did a lot of convincing about how much power Oscar was going to have, how much leverage they were going to give him. And they really convinced him.

Oscar said he needed me very badly to organize in my area, and I agreed, although I warned him that the Teamsters would eventually dump us. I thought that what was happening to Cesar in Delano would probably happen to us, too; the Teamsters were so damn powerful, that they wouldn't leave us the autonomy that we would want to have. We were giving a charter by the Teamsters, and I was one of the vice-presidents of the local.

After a while, I didn't think the Teamsters were really wanting us to organize farm workers in our own area. I felt that if they did, then the best way that they could prove it to us, other than being tied up in Delano, was to stop the trucks when we called the strike on the strawberry industry.

We were dealing with operations that went all the way from Salinas into the Oxnard-Ventura area and all the way down to the San Diego area. Oscar asked me to send him reports on the names of the trucks that were hauling those strawberries, and I think he approached Grami. But the Teamsters didn't want to help us out on that effort.

It was the same at Goldman's Egg City Ranch. We had a strike there for about two weeks and were very close to getting a contract. Oscar called Bill Grami to stop the trucks that were carrying eggs out of there, but Grami didn't try. Grami felt that it was necessary that we should go into Delano and take over the whole operation there.

I was against it. I told Oscar, as far as I'm concerned, if there's any real concern with the Teamsters to organize farm workers, they'd organize in the areas that we've already done some work. And the Teamsters haven't given us the support that we've asked them for.

So Oscar decided not to go to Delano and got involved in organizing a strike in the tomato industry in San Jose. That strike lasted a good eight weeks, but he got no help from the Teamsters. The Teamsters were hauling the tomatoes out.

CESAR CHAVEZ RECALLS

We went after Perelli-Minetti for ten and a half months, until they were almost bankrupt. We chased them all over. Finally, we got them in New York, closing their last outlet, and they came literally on their knees to us and said, "We'd like to sign a contract with you, but we've got the Teamsters."

We said, "Don't talk to us about the Teamsters, we're not interested."

Finally the Teamsters called, saying they wanted to meet with us and Perelli-Minetti, that there were some things we had to talk about.

First we met with the Teamsters alone and demanded that they end all their farm labor organizing activities. So they just cut Oscar Gonzales's neck off. I've never seen anything like it. Bill Grami called him in from an anteroom and said cold-bloodedly, "We don't need you any more." Just like that. "As of now, no more money. We want you to hand the farm workers the key so they can go to your office and get some of the stuff that they need."

After that was done, we worked out a no-raiding and jurisdiction agreement with Father Eugene Boyle, Episcopal minister Richard Byfield, and Rabbi Joseph Glazer as mediators. UFWOC would represent all field workers, while the Teamsters would represent workers in the commercial sheds and canneries.

ALBERT ROJAS RECALLS

Oscar really felt he got shafted. Before Bill Grami negotiated the pact with Cesar, Grami met with Oscar and some of the other organizers from the Watsonville, Gilroy, and Salinas area. Grami was sitting behind a fairly small desk, kind of reclining back.

Oscar got into a heated debate calling Grami a son of a bitch and pulling out a knife. At that point I asked Oscar to cool it, and asked Grami, "Why is it that the Teamsters were so desperately concerned in the very beginning to convince Oscar and to convince us that you guys really were interested in organizing farm workers?"

Grami didn't say nothing to that question, but he just came back saying, "Well, Al, honestly, the Teamsters are looking for a way to merge, and there's a possibility that the Teamsters might merge with the AFL-CIO someday."

Then after the Teamsters signed the pact with Cesar, Oscar was a hurt man. He went his way, and I went my way. I joined UFWOC as an organizer.

CESAR CHAVEZ RECALLS

When we met with the Teamsters and the growers at the Teamsters' headquarters in Burlingame, the Perelli-Minetti brothers had too much pride to face up to reality. Although we sat across from each other at a huge conference table, they sat facing the side, refusing to talk to me. They talked to their attorney, who talked to our attorney, Jerry Cohen, who then talked to me. After about the third time, Jerry and I began to make a game of it.

"Now, Cesar, Mr. Perelli-Minetti tells his attorney to tell me to tell you that they want to know from you through me through the attorney back to them . . ."

The situation was ridiculous, but they still wouldn't talk to me.

Eventually we agreed to give Perelli-Minetti the Teamster contract with some modifications, I think, in wages. We had to take a contract that wasn't as good as Dolores thought it should be, but we made that up two years later when we renegotiated.

When we left Burlingame that Friday, everything was ready to be signed on Tuesday. My prayers were answered, I thought, how can I give thanks? I decided fasting would be a good way, from Friday to Tuesday when the contract would be signed.

What started as a thanksgiving fast—giving thanks for saving the Union—changed when the signing was delayed.

"I can't eat until he signs," I thought. At that point, although Perelli-Minetti didn't know about it, the fast became more like a hunger strike. I didn't tell anyone I was fasting. I continued working.

Day followed day, and the next weekend came around, but they still hadn't signed. I was sick, both mentally and physically, as I hadn't prepared myself mentally for a fast. Before they signed on the thirteenth day, I thought I would die. But after a couple of days in bed, I was okay.

DOLORES HUERTA RECALLS

During that fight with the Teamsters, we lost a tremendous amount of momentum. We went into a slump for nearly a year.

We finally settled the agreement with Perelli-Minetti on July 10, 1967, but we got stuck with their lousy contract.

During the same period, I was negotiating with Christian Brothers and Almaden. The Christian Brothers wanted to sign the DiGiorgio contract, but there were too many bad things in it. My big fight was to get rid of the DiGiorgio albatross.

We had very painful negotiations with Christian Brothers. We only got a nickel increase a year, instead of ten cents, as in other contracts. And we only were able to get three paid holidays by telling them that we wanted the religious days of Good Friday, New Years, and All Saints Day. Of course, after we got the contract, we changed that to the Fourth of July and Labor Day, but at least we embarrassed them into it.

We also had lengthy negotiations with the Almaden Winery. At the end, I think Mack Lyons went up with me and organizers Marshall Ganz and Jose Luna to San Francisco, and we finished negotiating the contract about 4:00 in the morning.

The next day I ended up in the hospital. I fainted. I can't remember what had happened a couple of nights before, but I know we had a meeting with DiGiorgio in the morning, and I hadn't slept for about two nights.

So I just fainted dead away, and I had to stay in bed for about three days.

CHAPTER 6

Boycott Grapes!

CESAR CHAVEZ RECALLS

Since I was being constantly asked by the staff and the leadership, "What are we going to do next?" I did what has to be done in this situation. I answered, "Go and bring some suggestions of what we ought to do."

After a study and many soul-searching meetings, we finally decided to go after Giumarra, the largest table-grape grower, because his workers had lots of grievances and made less money. Giumarra's piece rates were the same as other growers, but because of company restrictions and insistence on quality, workers picked less boxes an hour.

We put it to the membership in Delano, voted to go after Giumarra, but decided not to strike him right away, because we didn't know how strong we were going to be.

I wasn't too hot on just going after Giumarra. I was afraid we'd establish a pattern of going after growers one at a time, and if the domino theory didn't work, it would take us thirty years to get all the Delano growers.

Problems developed later which proved that going after Giumarra alone wasn't the ticket. But once it was decided, I put Fred Ross in charge of the organizing campaign, and he did a beautiful job. We organized like fools, talked to every worker, and won many over.

After we started feeling our strength with the people, we wrote about seven letters to Giumarra asking for meetings. He refused.

Finally Ralph Duncan, of the State Conciliation Service, got

Giumarra to send employer representative Philip Feick to a meeting at the Caravan Inn in Bakersfield. We had a committee of
about fifteen or twenty workers elected by the people, but Feick
wouldn't speak to us. There he sat, across the table from us, facing
Duncan at one end of the table and talking only to him.

"We represent the workers," we said. "Why don't we have an
election?"

Feick refused. In fact, he told us to go to hell.

Earlier, we had talked to other labor leaders who explained to
us the quandary we were in about elections. We solved it by their
experience. We told Feick we couldn't offer him two bites from
the same apple. If we didn't have elections before a strike, we
would not be willing to have elections after a strike.

Soon after that meeting, we held a huge rally at the Bakersfield
fairgrounds and took a strike vote. When we struck, almost everybody came out, very close to sixteen or eighteen hundred workers.

A few days later, we were all picketing at the Giumarra entrance
when Feick walked across to the picket line and told me, "Well,
Cesar, if you prove to me you've got the strength, I'll talk to you."

I said to myself, "Oh, my God. I know it's impossible to keep
the people out, we just don't have any money." I knew that the
ranks would sag. But there are so many subtleties involved. It's
amazing how we can keep the people, even if they go back to
work.

I told Feick, "Okay! It'll take some time, but we'll do it!"

DOLORES HUERTA RECALLS

As we started the strike with Giumarra on August 3, 1967,
DiGiorgio was going to start their harvest. But they refused to
increase the rates according to the arbitration award. They were
supposed to go from $1.40 and hour to $1.65 plus the incentive.

Instead they wanted to increase the piece rate, which was against
the contract. Mack Lyons and Marshall Ganz had several meetings
with DiGiorgio, but they couldn't settle the thing.

I knew the reason was political. DiGiorgio wanted to beat us in
the strike. They were going to use that against us in the strike
with Giumarra by paying us the same as Giumarra was planning
to pay.

Cesar and I have a lot of personal fights, usually over strategy or
personalities. I don't think Cesar himself understands why he
fights with me. We have these heart-to-heart talks every six months
or so on how we're not going to fight anymore, and how demoral-

izing it is to everybody else that we do. But then, like the next day, we'll have another fight.

This time Cesar said, "I don't want you to go into arbitration."

Since we had gotten the DiGiorgio contract arbitration award April 3, we already had been in arbitration about three times. Not only was this costing the Union a lot of money, but Cesar felt that going into arbitration wouldn't resolve the real issue, which was that the workers had to assert themselves to make the contract work.

However, I had called the arbitrator at about 11:00 the night before and had gotten the meeting set for the following morning in San Francisco, as the workers had started a work stoppage over the issue. I was utterly confident that we would win the arbitration and get an immediate decision.

Poor Mack and Marshall were with me when I said, "Let's go!" Cesar said, "Don't go!"

And I said, "We're going! Goodby," and we went.

I called Cesar from San Francisco after we won the decision. I forgot what he told me, but it was something very snotty to let me know he was still mad, even though I had won.

We got into the Giumarra strike after that, so we forgot about that one, but this happens all the time.

It wasn't until I first came to Delano that Cesar became very quarrelsome with me, right after I started working with the Union. I think the reason was that he was under a lot of pressure. He still gets that way when he's under a lot of tension, and uses me to let off steam, as I would do with my own family. He says, "I know that I treat you very mean, like I treat Richard and treat Manuel and Helen, all very mean." But I understand it. He knows I might get angry or feel bad about it, but I'm not going to leave the Union.

He can't do that with the attorneys. He certainly can't do it with the strikers or the staff, because everybody else is on a voluntary basis, and if Cesar gives them a bad time, they'll just split. Of course, he can't go too far with Helen either because she won't take it. He knows that. Helen is pretty tough.

But I've never seen Cesar harsh with a worker. Despotic people who get into a position of authority take it down on the most defenseless persons. Cesar isn't that way at all. He is a very gentle guy—a very gentle guy in many ways.

He worries about my health, and bugs me all the time. I do get myself worked up and tense, but I'm better now than I used to be. I can relax more.

I used to work Saturday nights and Sundays, and Cesar would

say, "Look, why don't you go home and spend the day with your kids today?" I felt I had to be there working every minute. He'd give me gentle hints, sometimes not so gentle. Like he'd really get shook if he'd come into the office at midnight or 1:00 in the morning, and I'd be doing some work.

Of course, this was before the strike started. After the strike, I had to do a lot of necessary work.

CESAR CHAVEZ RECALLS

We kept the workers out on strike for four days. Then the crippling injunction came which permitted only two men at each entrance and prevented us from having masses of people at the avenues between the vineyards where the workers could see us.

If we had known then what we know now about injunctions, we would have beaten Giumarra right then, because we needed two or three more days to beat him. But the injunction contributed to breaking the strike, as did our lack of money for strike benefits.

The workers started deserting. They went back to work, or they moved. We kept the Giumarra battle going by using the Delano strikers and members of the staff. Then we sent people out on the boycott.

Actually some people were sent out earlier. Delano striker Eliseo Medina was sent by plane to Chicago the day we took the strike vote. But it wasn't until the winter that we sent out a large number of boycotters to New York in our yellow bus. This was a new experience, and we wanted to train them before sending them out to other cities.

DOLORES HUERTA RECALLS

Cesar called a boycott conference in Delano in December 1967. Then he sent me to New York. I was there about ten days. Then we all came back and got together again.

I got in a big fight with Cesar and Jim Drake about what I thought had to be done. I thought we had to work much more with the labor unions and other groups to get the boycott going. I also thought that we should send a carload of people to every city. Cesar and Jim Drake didn't agree. They had the idea of sending fifty farm workers to New York City in the yellow bus. So that's what they did.

Then Fred Ross said, "Well, I'm not going to go back to New York without Dolores." So I ended up on the boycott myself. I should have kept my mouth shut. My job wasn't on the boycott, it was supposed to be on negotiations.

I took my kids to New York with me. It was really healthy for them, even though it was miserable for them there. After that there was a big difference in my relationship with my daughter Lori, compared to the year before when I left her alone for five months.

Fred assigned me to work with labor. So I got labor to get the Teamsters to stop the grapes. The farm workers picketed at the terminal market, and we were able to get those hardened produce buyers to stop buying grapes.

When we got to New York, it was something like four or five degrees above zero. The first day we went out on the picket line, one of the Filipino women fell down and hit her head on some ice and had amnesia for about an hour. Everybody was slipping on the ice and falling. But they had a heck of a lot of spirit.

CESAR CHAVEZ RECALLS

When the boycott began to make a dent, Giumarra started changing their labels. First they had six. Then in less than sixty days they had about sixty. Soon we were dealing with over a hundred. Although it was against the law, they were using the labels of all the California growers against us.

We had great difficulty in boycotting labels, because the labels many times were not attached to the grapes. When the grapes go to the serving trays in the market, the boxes aren't with them.

Our own troops were confused. They didn't know which labels to boycott, which not to boycott. People who wanted to help also were confused. And out of all this confusion came the idea.

Fred and Dolores found how to attack the riddle. They said, "Look, all the growers are now involved, right? Let's boycott all of them!"

I immediately rejected the idea.

They explained to me that was the only way you could do it, because then the grapes became the label itself. That made it clear to me.

Then it was just a question of the principles and the morals involved. I still wouldn't do it, because I felt that we had to actually be involved with the growers in a strike.

So we organized in the other areas and tried to get the growers to negotiate with us. When they wouldn't, we struck them again.

After that, we just said, "Boycott California fresh grapes," and we began to have success. In thirty days we began to see a change.

FRED ROSS RECALLS

It's amazing the tremendous effectiveness of the boycott, considering the small size of the staff that was involved. We never had too many full-time people on it.

That first busload to New York had about forty farm workers and ten young volunteers, students and ex-students. We all were paid five dollars a week and room and board.

Gradually the boycott spread to other cities. We pulled out everyone from New York except about seven young volunteers from the Bay Area in California and turned over the New York office to them. Eliseo Medina took people to Chicago, Marcos Munoz took others to Boston. We only had enough people for about four cities, Boston, Chicago, Los Angeles, and Detroit.

Then boycotters had to be sent from the West Coast, from Delano mainly, to open up other cities. There were both farm workers and volunteers sent, but none of them were trained. They just learned as they went along, doing the same thing we had done in New York.

They contacted various organizations—labor, churches, students, civic groups, women's groups—made speeches, and passed around lists for people to sign up for picketing and to give financial support. Then they picketed the chain stores. The heavy emphasis was placed on cracking the big chains, getting them not to handle table grapes. To do that we were using the secondary boycott, asking people not to shop there until the grapes were removed. But there also was a lot of primary boycott pressure that can't be measured, support generated by all the publicity about the many things that were happening. More and more people were refusing to buy grapes.

CHAPTER 7

The Power of Nonviolence

CESAR CHAVEZ RECALLS

To us the boycott of grapes was the most near-perfect of nonviolent struggles, because nonviolence also requires mass involvement. The boycott demonstrated to the whole country, the whole world, what people can do by nonviolent action.

Nonviolence in the abstract is a very difficult thing to comprehend or explain. I'd read a lot, but all of it was in the abstract. It's difficult to carry the message to people who aren't involved. Nonviolence must be explained in context.

People equate nonviolence with inaction—with not doing anything—and it's not that at all. It's exactly the opposite.

In his autobiography, Malcolm X said, "I believe it's a crime for anyone who is being brutalized to continue to accept that brutality without doing something to defend himself. If that's how Christian philosophy is interpreted, if that's what Gandhian philosophy teaches, well then I will call them criminal philosophies."

But Gandhi never said not to do anything. He said exactly the opposite. He said, "Do something! Offer your life!" He said, "If you really want to do something, be willing to die for it." That's asking for the maximum contribution.

Often only talk results when a person with social concern wants to do something for the underdog nonviolently. But just talking about change is not going to bring it about. Talk just gives people an out. Generally what happens is that people will study nonviolence, read books, go to seminars where they discuss nonviolence, and attend endless meetings. In most cases, they find some satisfaction in this and think they somehow are accomplishing something. But all the while, and right across town, the pot is brewing.

Reading is not bad, but thinking they made a great accomplishment is bad. They're kidding themselves. These people can't be effective. Nonviolence becomes just an ideology, something to write about, or read about, or talk about while still being very comfortable. The ideology becomes a luxury, not a way of life. And nothing can be changed while being comfortable. Life is not made that way.

Nonviolence is action. Like anything else, though, it's got to be organized. There must be rules. There must be people following.

The whole essence of nonviolent action is getting a lot of people involved, vast numbers doing little things. It's difficult to get people involved in a picket line, because it takes their time. But any time a person can be persuaded not to eat a grape—and we persuaded millions not to eat grapes—that's involvement, that's the most direct action, and it's set up in such a way that everybody can participate.

Nonviolence also has one big demand—the need to be creative, to develop strategy. Gandhi described it as moral jujitsu. Always hit the opposition off balance, but keep your principles.

Strategy for nonviolence takes a tremendous amount of our time —strategy against the opposition, and strategy to strengthen our support. We can't let people get discouraged. If there's no progress, they say nonviolence doesn't work. They begin to go each and everywhere. And it's only when they are desperate that people think violence is necessary.

Of course, it isn't. If any movement is on the move, violence is the last thing that's wanted.

Naturally, nonviolence takes time. But poverty has been with us since the beginning of time. We just have to work for improvement. I despise exploitation and I want change, but I'm willing to pay the price in terms of time. There's a Mexican saying, "Hay más tiempo que vida"—There's more time than life. We've got all the time in the world.

Some great nonviolent successes have been achieved in history. Moses is about the best example, and the first one. Christ also is a beautiful example, as is the way the Christians overcame tyranny. They needed over three hundred years, but they did it. The most recent example is Gandhi. To me that's the most beautiful one.

We can examine it more closely because it happened during our lifetime. It's fantastic how he got so many people to do things, which is the whole essence of nonviolent action.

Nonviolence has the power to attract people and to generate power. That's what happened to Gandhi. Besides millions of Indians, he had many Englishmen, both in England and even India siding with him.

By and large, people oppose violence. So when government or growers use violence against us, we strategize around it. We can respond nonviolently, because that swings people to our side, and that gives us our strength.

First, of course, the workers have to understand nonviolence. Gandhi once said he'd rather have a man be violent than be a coward. I agree. If he's a coward, then what good is he for anyone? But it is our job to see he's not a coward. That's really the beginning point of our training.

And while the philosophy of nonviolence covers physical, verbal, and moral behavior, we haven't achieved that goal. If we can achieve it, we're saints—which we're not. We're still working on eliminating physical violence, though that isn't all, by any stretch of the imagination. After workers begin to understand physical nonviolence among people, then we also apply it to property and go on from there.

It's like a leader marching at the head of a column, going up and down hills. Pretty soon there are forks and cross-streets, and the leader can't be followed because they can't see him. They don't know where he went. The important thing is to bring them along. The important thing is not to get lost.

There came a point in 1968 when we were in danger of losing part of our column. Because of a sudden increase in violence against us, and an apparent lack of progress after more than two years of striking, there were those who felt that the time had come to overcome violence by violence.

CHAPTER 8

The Miracle of the Fast

CESAR CHAVEZ RECALLS

There was demoralization in the ranks, people becoming desperate, more and more talk about violence. People meant it, even when they talked to me. They would say, "Hey, we've got to burn these sons of bitches down. We've got to kill a few of them."

Several packing sheds had been burned. We had a very narrow escape when one of our guys was run over by a truck. The people there wanted to do the truck driver in. I even had to confiscate a few guns off the picket line.

I thought that I had to bring the Movement to a halt, do something that would force them and me to deal with the whole question of violence and ourselves. We had to stop long enough to take account of what we were doing.

So I stopped eating. It was a Thursday. Then I didn't eat on Friday or Saturday or Sunday. LeRoy Chatfield, a former Christian Brother, who was, I guess, the only one who knew I was fasting, started coming with me and helping me through the first few days. He would drive me home and pick me up and hear about all the pains I had and all the nightmares about food.

Those first three days LeRoy brought me Diet Rite, but I was worried whether Diet Rite had any food value, because then that wasn't a clean fast. After that I took only water.

I didn't know how long I was going to fast.

After four days, I called a meeting of all the strikers and the staff at Filipino Hall to announce what I was doing. I just made a short speech. I told them I thought they were discouraged, be-

272

cause they were talking about short cuts, about violence. They were getting so mad with the growers, they couldn't be effective anymore.

Then I talked about violence. How could they oppose the violence of the war in Vietnam, I asked, but propose that we use violence for our Cause? When the Civil Rights Movement turned to violence, I said, it was the blacks who suffered, who were killed, who had their homes burned. If we turned to violence, it would be the poor who would suffer.

"But," I said, "it's not enough to say, 'I'm not going to be violent.' We have to show our commitment by working harder." I said that our work habits had been destroyed. People were bitching, they were staying in the office, they weren't going out to the picket lines.

Then I said I was going to stop eating until such time as everyone in the strike either ignored me or made up their minds that they were not going to be committing violence. I didn't wait for reactions, I just walked out of Filipino Hall and headed for the co-op building at the Forty Acres.

I thought that if I fasted at home, Helen would be burdened with people coming to the house at all hours. That decision was hard on both of us—I liked Helen to be with me all the time, and she was split two ways, either away from the kids or from me. But fasting at Forty Acres was a good decision for other reasons that I didn't know then, but that became obvious as the fast continued.

While I was walking the few miles to the Forty Acres, Bob Bustos joined me. Helen stayed at the meeting for a while, then caught up by car and walked the rest of the way with me.

She told me I was crazy, and nobody would appreciate what I was doing. I said I didn't want anybody to appreciate it.

"What about the family? Don't you think that we count?"

"Well, that's not going to work," I told her. "I made up my mind, and the best thing you can do is to support me and help me out."

After we argued a while, it hit her that I was really serious. "Well, I should know when you make up your mind, you're stubborn, nothing will change it. I might as well just go along with it," she said. "But remember I don't like the whole idea. I think it's ridiculous."

I didn't realize it then, because I was too worried about myself, but Helen was stunned. She thought I was going to die because of the fast.

Meanwhile, at Filipino Hall, the meeting was thrown into an

uproar. After I walked out, people began to fight among themselves. LeRoy finally said, "The hell with it. I'm not going to stay here fighting while we have a guy fasting. He needs a place to stay, he doesn't even have a bed. He doesn't have any water. You know the damn place is as hot as hell. He needs a fan in there. I don't know about you guys, but I'm going to go out there and help him." And he left.

Andy Imutan, one of the Filipino leaders, got up and began trying to bring the two sides together. We lost several persons who felt I was playing Jesus Christ, but we pulled all the others together.

JERRY COHEN RECALLS

LeRoy told us the night before the meeting that Cesar was fasting, and I got pissed off because of the Perelli-Minetti experience. We didn't know then that he was fasting, so I went up to Marysville to negotiate a contract before completing the Perelli-Minetti agreement. If I had known, I could have completed the agreement a lot sooner.

So now, when we heard he was fasting, about three of us cooked up this idea—the only way to get him off it was not to eat until he started eating. We figured we could get everybody in the offices involved.

Cesar had no way of knowing our plan. But at the Filipino Hall meeting, he gave us two examples. He said, "Now this is a fast, which means that I'm not doing it to put pressure on anybody." If we were negotiating with the growers, he said that he'd ask that the negotiations be stopped during the fast because they might take it as pressure.

"Another example," he said, "is if any of you were"—and I don't know if he said "chicken shit enough to," but some words like that—"for instance, tell me that you weren't going to eat until I started eating, that would be a hunger strike, and I wouldn't agree to pressure like that. This is not a hunger strike in the sense that that would be a hunger strike."

That really shocked me, because he psyched out the scene. He's very smart. He just took the sails right out of our plan.

CESAR CHAVEZ RECALLS

At the Forty Acres, I stayed in bed most of the time to conserve my energy. Every little drop counts. I also wanted to change the atmosphere, but I didn't want to stop working. Lying down I could still do a lot of work and see a lot of people. And, as I also wanted to receive Communion every day, we had a daily mass and meeting.

After about three or four days, the spirit was definitely there. The Filipino women and the strikers painted the co-op windows with bright colors. They looked like stained glass. Things began to get cleaned up. Everybody began to get things done on their own. They began to think how to help.

The rest was just like a miracle—not the fast, but the things that it did to people. It jolted everybody around. We got more than I ever bargained for. The good effects were way beyond my dreams. The work schedule began to pick up, dedication increased, and the whole question of using violence ended immediately. Of course, the sheds continued to burn, but we found out later some volunteer firemen were burning them.

There were many other effects. The reaction from the opposition was ridiculous. People in town, the opponents, were saying, "Oh, that man's not fasting, he's just fooling everybody. We know he has a nurse there, and she feeds him." They said Marion Moses, one of my nurses, had gone out and chased jack rabbits at night and fried them for me.

I thought their comments were a compliment. Their reaction proved to me that a fast was powerful, and by refusing to admit I was fasting, they were admitting that fasting was a good thing.

The fast also affected the grape boycott, which became stronger. And a lot of people on the boycott also fasted. So did many others. Marshall Ganz fasted for ten days. Dolores fasted, Richard fasted. Besides fasting, they also saw all kinds of work that had to be done, and they did it.

Then the fast affected other people. There was a very good response from the church and some of the labor leaders. Walter Reuther came and gave us fifty thousand dollars for a building.

Once we started with the religious service, the fast affected our members in a very religious way, supporting me. They brought many offerings, the largest number being crucifixes and Christ in many forms. Many others brought the Virgin of Guadalupe, while the third most popular gift was St. Martinas Pores, the black saint from Peru, who is the most popular saint in Latin America.

There was a lot of personal communication in the fast. The people came, and I would say one word or two, and they understood. To some it was very emotional. They were very worried about my dying.

While the fast had tremendous effect and developed strength in many ways, very few people supported me—wanted me to keep fasting. Most people were worried, though for different reasons. The doctor was worried because he was in charge if something happened to me. The staff was concerned because of friendship, and because they felt many things had to stop while I fasted. Very few people could see all the spiritual and psychological and political good that was coming out of it, good which I had no idea was going to happen.

As the days passed, the pressures increased for me to stop fasting. Helen and Richard were very worried. They tried to argue me out of it. "You can't do this," Richard would say. "What happens if you die?" And any time there was an opening, Helen would take a good shot at me, wanting me to stop. She began to organize pressure against me—not consciously—but by expressing her fears.

LeRoy, however, really saw the opportunity, saw what it was going to do for the Union. He wasn't that worried about my health.

I went through different stages. In the beginning I had nightmares about food, about eating chicken or good vegetables. Then I would wake up to find I hadn't eaten anything, and I was still hungry. Then I went through the hunger pains, the headaches, cleaning myself out. It was a very difficult period.

After about seven days, I got away from all the physical pain. I did not want food. I saw it and rejected it. And I was surprised how little sleep I needed, only two or three hours of it at one time. I spent more time awake than sleeping.

It wasn't until later that the other pains came, the leg pains and back pains. I think that because of a lack of calcium, I began to draw calcium from my bones. The pains in my joints were horrible. But that was later, after more than two weeks of not eating.

After seven days it was like going into a different dimension. I began to see things in a different perspective, to retain a lot more, to develop tremendous powers of concentration.

I had a lot of time to examine my past, and I was able to develop self-criticism and examination. I began to see that there were more important things than some of the problems that upset me, such as my administrative problems. I lost most of my emotional attachment to them.

It wasn't that saving my soul was more important than the strike. On the contrary, I said to myself, if I'm going to save my soul, it's going to be through the struggle for social justice.

DOLORES HUERTA RECALLS

We arrived in New York about January 20, and Cesar went on the fast February 15. We all got hit with it suddenly, because he didn't tell anybody until he had been fasting for about five days. When I heard about it, I vomited, and I know the women on the boycott in New York broke down and started crying. I think I lost eight pounds the first week of his fast. All of us understood the religious aspect of it, so we had a priest come over from Brooklyn the next Sunday and give us this special mass.

Fred reacted very strongly, too, because I think Fred probably loves Cesar more than anybody in the world—maybe even more than his wife and children.

Some people reacted the other way, they just missed the whole point of the thing. A lot of people thought Cesar was trying to play God, that this guy really was trying to pull a saintly act.

Poor Cesar! They just couldn't accept it for what it was. I know it's hard for people who are not Mexican to understand, but this is part of the Mexican culture—the penance, the whole idea of suffering for something, of self-inflicted punishment. It's a tradition of very long standing. In fact, Cesar has often mentioned in speeches that we will not win through violence, we will win through fasting and prayer.

I wasn't in Delano at all during the fast, but a lot of unpleasant things happened there at that time in terms of the organization. Tony Orendain, who was the secretary-treasurer of the Union, was very cynical against the church. He was one of the guys that was a leader in all of the conflicts that took place when Cesar went on the fast. There's an awful lot of bigotry even among Mexicans, especially the ones from Mexico.

But the reaction was widespread. Sometime after the fast started, Fred and I were talking on the phone to Saul Alinsky, who said he had told Cesar how embarrassing it was to the Industrial Areas Foundation for Cesar to go on that fast.

And I said, "Well, you should be glad that he didn't do it while he was still working for you."

Alinsky said, "We've had a terrible time trying to explain it."

And then Fred—you just can't say anything against Cesar without Fred reacting—said, "Yea, Saul, but you don't know what a good organizing technique that was, because by that fast he was able to unify the farm workers all over the state of California. Prior to that fast, there had been a lot of bickering and backbiting and fighting and little attempts at violence. But Cesar brought everybody together and really established himself as the leader of the farm workers."

And Saul was at a loss for words.

But that was the reaction of many liberals and radicals. Cesar feels that liberals are liberal right up to the steps of the Catholic church. Guys can be liberal about homosexuality, about dope, about capital punishment, about everything but the Catholic church. There the liberalism ends. So he doesn't want to feed the bigotry that the average person has against the church. He tries to overcome that bigotry by his example.

CHAPTER 9

"To Be a Man Is to Suffer for Others"

CESAR CHAVEZ RECALLS

It's hard to remember all that happened during the fast, but I remember this group of farm workers who came from a long ways to visit, really perplexed by the whole thing and very worried. I was having a meeting with Manuel when somebody knocked on the door.

"Don't bother him, he's eating right now," Manuel joked. And I can imagine their reaction.

Then there was a worker from Merced who was sent to Delano commissioned to make me eat, he said. When he came to see me the first time, I noticed he'd had a few drinks. He wouldn't talk to me until everybody was gone. He waited about three hours.

During the day there was a person at my door, but about 2:00 in the morning there wasn't. I was reading. So the worker came in carrying a bag and said, "I'm representing a committee in Merced. I have strict instructions to make you eat, because if you don't, you are going to die, and you don't do us any good dead."

He had a bag full of tacos and ordered me to eat.

Politely I said I couldn't right now, but when I started eating, I would eat everything he had in his bag.

He insisted. Then he got desperate. He tried to push the tortilla in my mouth, but I kept moving. Finally he got on top of me, trying to hold my arms with his knees—which was easy because I

279

was so weak—and he held my head still with one hand while he tried to force the taco into me. He was a big guy, but he failed.

Then Richard saw what was happening, thought the guy was trying to kill me, and called for help. Everybody rushed in and dragged the poor guy out.

"Leave him alone, leave him alone," I shouted. "He's not trying to hurt me. Leave him alone." Finally I had to get up and scream at them, "Leave him alone." I explained what was happening. So they apologized to him and let him go.

On the twelfth day of the fast, I was scheduled to go to court in Bakersfield on a contempt of court charge. I was in bad shape. They had to literally drag me up there and back, two days in a row. By then, Jerry Cohen was our attorney, in charge of my defense.

JERRY COHEN RECALLS

Cesar was charged with contempt of a court order that permitted only one picket the length of a football field and three pickets at an entrance. It banned almost everything except breathing. Giumarra alleged massing on various occasions when more than three pickets would gather.

Now the twelfth day of his fast, Cesar had to go to Bakersfield. On that day I went over to the office just to look at some material one last time. It was my first contempt hearing, and I was pretty up tight.

It was foggy, and I remember driving out to the old pink house and coming down Garces. All of a sudden, these lights started coming out of the fog. It was the workers in their cars. I parked there and just watched all those cars come. It was a great feeling. There must have been five hundred cars full of workers.

Marshall Ganz had gone down one day just to see the physical layout of the courthouse, and representatives of the various ranch committees came with him. They saw about how many workers it could hold, where they could go, and how the stairs were. The ranch committees worked on it together. Guys from up north got to know the guys that worked at DiGiorgio and they worked with the guys from Schenley.

So when we got to the courthouse, there must have been three to four thousand workers there, workers all around the building, workers lining every wall of the courthouse.

The clerks were very surprised that farm workers could be so well-behaved. "When we have ten to twelve high school students," the clerks told me, "they make more noise than all the workers you have in here." They also were astounded at how many workers there were, and at what they were doing, because the workers were singing softly, and they were praying.

Before Cesar arrived, Giumarra's attorneys got there, and we went up into the judge's chambers. We hadn't been having too much luck in that courthouse before, because it's really the growers' courthouse. But I think everybody that morning knew it was our courthouse. Giumarra's attorneys made all their arguments that the workers had to be kicked out of the court, that to have these workers as pressure on the court had no place in jurisprudence.

I went through my little bit with the cases I had, but it wasn't the cases that counted. After William Quinlan finished his argument, presiding judge Walter Osborne said, "If I kick these workers out of this courthouse, that will be just another example of goddamn gringo justice. I can't do it."

That was the first time we have ever won anything in that courthouse, and just because the workers were there. Every time I had ever been in that courthouse before, it was like going on enemy territory. But after that demonstration, it was a lot different.

We had to come back the next day because the judge continued the case, and we had just as many workers there. That put more pressure on that judge than anything else we could have done. He continued the case because of Cesar's condition, but then he later continued it again, even though we were ready to go. Finally after about a year, the case was dropped. Giumarra dismissed it out. In the first place, their case was weak, and in the second place, they didn't want those workers in the courthouse.

CESAR CHAVEZ RECALLS

During the early part of the fast, I had a very embarrassing experience. The supervisor from Almaden sent a case of wine to me with one of the organizers who brought it in and opened it— six or eight beautiful bottles of choice wine.

"Close it and take it back to him and thank him," I said, "but tell him that I don't accept gifts from the employers, and that none of the organizers are to accept gifts. If he wants to give us anything, he can give it to us in the contract."

And so that passed. But about four and a half months later, a committee from Almaden, two carloads of people, came to the house on a Sunday. They had a lot of complaints. Their crews were not being handled right.

A couple of the guys said, "We came to see you, but of course, we know that you can't do too much." And they had a little snicker that I caught.

"Wait a minute," I said, "tell me exactly what you mean by that gesture."

They wanted to skip the subject, but I pinned them down. "Well, there's a rumor at Almaden that you're taking wine from the employer," one said.

"When?"

"Well, during the fast."

I went blind, I was so embarrassed. Then I got in the car, and they took me to the Forty Acres where the organizer was.

"What happened to the wine you brought down during the fast?"

"Oh, it's there."

And I got mad! "Let me see it!"

He brought it.

"There are only three bottles! Where are the other bottles?"

"Oh," he said, "the guys drank it."

I was so mad, I sent him on a special trip to Almaden to return the wine and told him, "Don't you come back until you've got a receipt from him."

The workers apologized to me, and I said, "No, don't apologize. I appreciate what you did." Then I sent them a really warm letter thanking them for telling me.

JERRY COHEN RECALLS

The fast was a very complicated act, because Cesar is a very complicated guy, and people reacted to it in a very complicated way.

It's strange how some people react who profess to believe in freedom of speech and freedom of religion. They tolerate anything except religion. A lot of liberals and radicals were pissed. For example Tony Orendain, when he came in to see Cesar about some Union business, would sit facing away from him, facing the wall. A lot of people working in the legal department were mad at me, because I wasn't in the legal office every day licking the stamps, putting them on the envelopes, organizing the thing at the courthouse. Instead I spent a lot of time at the Forty Acres talking to Cesar.

The petty reaction that a few had came to a head in Filipino

Hall about the fourteenth day of the fast. Emotions were really deep, with a strange thread of intolerance running in some people. A supposedly very tolerant liberal got up and said that this religiosity out at the Forty Acres was phony and was taking away from work.

"My only religion is work!" he said.

I got up. "Well, that's what Calvin Coolidge said, 'Go to your factories and pray.'" I thought that put them right where they belonged. We really got into it. Some of those people ended up leaving.

I'm not religious at all, but I would go to those masses at the Forty Acres every night. No matter what their religious background, anyone interested in farm workers, or with any sense about people, could see that something was going on that was changing a lot of people. The feeling of the workers was obvious. They talked at those masses about their own experiences, about what the fast meant in terms of what the Union was going to mean to them. That was a really deep feeling, but it wasn't religious in the sense that somebody like me couldn't relate to it.

Before the fast, there were nine ranch committees, one for each winery. The fast, for the first time, made a Union out of those ranch committees, because they had some common things to work on—what was happening there, and how they were going to organize to go down to the courthouse. Everybody worked together.

Some people that were within traveling distance would go home and come back every day, but many stayed at the Forty Acres, bringing their own tents, asking others to help pitch tents. As they came to LeRoy Chatfield for help, cynical people thought it was being manipulated by LeRoy. That was nonsense. The workers were moved, they wanted to do something, and the best thing they could do was help, start building the Union, and stay nonviolent.

It was ironic. People who were supposed to be good organizers were so blinded by their intolerance of the religious aspects that they could not see what a great organizing tool the fast was, and that, in a way, it was there for everybody to make of it what they could.

What Cesar did was a fantastic gamble. He didn't know how people were going to react. When he walked out to the Forty Acres after announcing the fast, he was basically by himself. They could have said, "You're nuts," and just left him there. But the fast grew in intensity and picked up momentum. As the days went by, the feeling of the workers really increased, and their numbers grew from the hundreds to the thousands.

CESAR CHAVEZ RECALLS

About the twenty-first day of the fast, Helen, Richard, his wife Sally, and one or two of the kids were with me. They were very worried about my health. While we were talking, all of a sudden I said, "Oh, do you hear the music?"

"We don't hear anything."

"Yea, there's music."

When I said it the third time, "Yea, that's really nice music. Where's it coming from?" they all looked at me and at each other as if I were crazy.

I demanded that they investigate.

Richard went out and just looked around a little bit. "No, there's nobody playing."

"Richard, somebody is singing Mexican songs, and they are playing."

"Oh, you're crazy."

"I know there's somebody doing it." Then I began to wonder, am I really going crazy? So I said, "You have to go out there and look."

He went way over by the dump at the other end of Forty Acres, and there were a group of guys there drinking and singing.

And I could hear it that far away, while in the room behind the closed metal door and in spite of adobe walls eight to ten inches thick.

Every day the pressure on me increased to end the fast. It came from all directions. Members talked one to the other, then there were constant delegations. "You've got to stop! You've got to stop!" The fast began to really affect them emotionally.

Senator Robert Kennedy sent me a wire of concern. He asked me to consider the consequences of what would happen to the Movement if my health failed. There were many other telegrams and letters. The pressures were a tremendous drain on me.

My doctors were extremely worried about my lack of proteins. At first I didn't want to let them examine me. Finally I agreed that a doctor could check me, but that he couldn't X-ray or take blood out of me.

The doctor found it very hard to accept those restrictions. But I felt that if he examined me and said I was in very bad shape, and I then stopped the fast, there would be no risks. I also would feel I stopped because I didn't want to make much of a sacrifice. And if he told me I was in perfect shape, there still would be no risk. Without the element of risk, I would be hypocritical. The whole essence of penance—which I'm a fool for because I think it works—would be taken away.

Maybe I was in bad shape, but I thought I could go for a few days more, and since I wasn't hungry, I had no intentions of eating.

DOLORES HUERTA RECALLS

At one point I talked to Congressman Philip Burton's assistant, Chuck Hurley, who is a very good friend. Chuck told me LeRoy Chatfield called him. "He wants the congressman to send Cesar a telegram asking him to stop the fast," he said.

I called Jim Drake to find out what was going on. "Well, Dolores," Jim said, "all I can say is I think if Cesar wants to fast, that's his business, and I happen to agree with him on it, but I'm in the minority."

I think LeRoy thought Cesar was damaging his health, and, of course, he was right. In fact, I later apologized to Leroy for criticizing his actions.

Peggy McGivern, who was the other nurse taking care of Cesar, was worried about his health, too, but Peggy also is a very strong Catholic. She told me she just felt Cesar wasn't being told the truth about what was happening to him, and that they were just trying to scare him off the fast.

She was right, really, because they were worried about Cesar's spine degenerating, and that never really did happen. He had muscle problems which the fast aggravated because he wasn't getting protein or the proper exercise.

When Cesar finally decided to end the fast, Kennedy was asked to come. It took quite a bit of work. He wanted to come, but I think that he was afraid people might interpret it as a political expediency. At the time, the political scene was tight. Senator Eugene McCarthy had announced that he was running for president against President Lyndon Johnson, and there was a lot of pressure on Kennedy to enter the race.

We went down to see his assistant in New York and asked him to ask Kennedy to come. Carter Burden's reaction was, "I don't think he should go. I think it's terrible to use a religious ceremony like a mass for that purpose."

But in the end, he did come.

CESAR CHAVEZ RECALLS

I think my biggest success in life was being able to go without food for twenty-five days. I don't think I could top that.

On the day I broke my fast, I was pretty much out of it, I was so weak. We had a mass at the county park and used a flat-bed truck for the altar.

Kennedy arrived at Union headquarters at Forty Acres before the mass started. He was uneasy. "What do you say to a guy who's on a fast?" he asked someone before he came into my room. He was in there only briefly, and neither of us had much to say.

At the park, I was so much out of it, all I felt was a lot of people pushing and trying to get closer to the altar. It was hot. I remember arriving, a lot of people trying to say hello, trying to hug me while I was being held up because my legs were so weak.

The mass was said by many priests, and many nuns came to distribute the bread. I couldn't see the crowd because I was sitting down, but it was certainly one of the largest gatherings in Delano at the county park.

I remember the TV people were there, and one cameraman couldn't get in while Kennedy was giving me a piece of bread. When he finally did, he told Kennedy, "This is probably the most ridiculous request I have ever made. Could you give him a piece of bread again?"

Because I was too weak, I couldn't even speak my thanks, but Jim Drake expressed my thoughts which I had put down earlier.

"Our struggle is not easy," I wrote. "Those who oppose our cause are rich and powerful, and they have many allies in high places. We are poor. Our allies are few. But we have something the rich do not own. We have our own bodies and spirits and the justice of our cause as our weapons."

"When we are really honest with ourselves," I concluded, "we must admit that our lives are all that really belong to us. So it is how we use our lives that determines what kind of men we are. It is my deepest belief that only by giving our lives do we find life.

"I am convinced that the truest act of courage, the strongest act of manliness is to sacrifice ourselves for others in a totally non-violent struggle for justice. To be a man is to suffer for others. God help us to be men!"

When it was over, they put me on a mattress in the station wagon. I had been up about two hours, so the moment I hit that mattress, I went to sleep.

Jim Drake told me that after the mass, the people crowded

around Kennedy, telling him he had to run for president. Kennedy was really moved. When he got in Jim's car to be driven to the airport, he turned to Jim and said, "You know, I might just do that." It was the first indication we had that he might run.

CHAPTER 10

The Spirit of Martyrs

CESAR CHAVEZ RECALLS

Six days after the fast ended, Robert Kennedy announced he was a candidate for president.

I had first met him at 2:00 in the morning in Los Angeles back in 1959 to talk about voter registration for his brother. He was very straightforward, and I was impressed, but we just talked about voter registration, and I didn't meet him again until he came to Delano for the Senate Subcommittee hearings in 1966—three years after President John Kennedy had been shot.

This was a time when nearly everybody was against us; about the only people for us were ourselves. Then Kennedy came and did something heroic—he endorsed us, but in a clear-cut manner.

Even then, I had an idea he was going to be a candidate for the presidency, and I was concerned because he endorsed us so straightforwardly, without straddling the line. I was sitting next to Dolores, and we both had the same thought—that he didn't have to go that far. Instead of that awful feeling against politicians who don't commit themselves, we felt protective.

So when Paul Schrade—just after Kennedy announced—called to ask if I would endorse Kennedy and be a delegate for him at the Democratic Convention, I knew it would not be honorable to ask for something in return. With most politicians this would have been all right, but not with this man who had already helped us so much.

Our members voted unanimously that I should be a Kennedy

delegate. The only question raised was about the AFL-CIO's position in strong support of President Johnson. I told them that while we respected the AFL-CIO position, we had our own political decisions to make.

We immediately began a voter registration drive, assigning some of the leadership to work in sections until we had all meaningful rural counties and each assembly district in Los Angeles covered. Then I began to hit the universities to get students who were for Kennedy.

On April 4 I was due to speak at Our Lady of Guadalupe Church in Sacramento when the news came that Martin Luther King had been shot. It hit me hard.

I had followed King's actions from the beginning of the bus boycott in Montgomery, when I was organizing the CSO, and he gave me hope and ideas. When the bus boycott was victorious, I thought then of applying boycotts to organizing the Union. Then every time something came out in the newspapers, his civil rights struggle would just jump out of the pages at me.

Although I met some of the people that were working with King and saw him on television, I never talked with him except on the phone. But Martin Luther King definitely influenced me, and much more after his death. The spirit doesn't die, the ideas remain. I read them, and they're alive.

We worked right up to the last minute on Kennedy's campaign. It was just like organizing a strike—hectic.

I made a swing, speaking to farm workers, making as many as six appearances a day all over the state, places like Soledad and Salinas and Stockton. We called rallies, and it seemed like the whole town attended.

In East Los Angeles we recruited people to visit all registered voters. We set up telephone and walking committees, and the last thing we did was organize thousands of little kids to leaflet people.

I'm proud of the work we did. It wasn't new to me, it was something I'd been doing for many years. What was new was that we had a good candidate and lots of resources that I never had had at my disposal before.

The drive was a tremendous success. Some Chicano precincts turned out 100 percent and went 100 percent for Kennedy. We played a major role in getting his victory in California.

But on election night I was very tired, and I felt embarrassed when my name was called at the rally at the Ambassador Hotel.

So I left early, before the senator came downstairs. I must have sensed something wrong. I was happy until the time I got to the Ambassador, and then I began to feel melancholy.

I dropped in briefly at Richard Calderon's party—he had run for the legislature—which was in a small building, and very noisy. When we heard Kennedy had been shot, there was great fear. The Chicano kids immediately got around me and took me home. Some of the women were crying, and some of the men were very angry, cursing because it had happened.

It was so senseless, so useless! We felt it closer than most people because we were so involved with him. I was convinced he would have gotten the nomination, and I was pretty sure he could have won. Kennedy was by far the real force for change, and he was willing to take in the poor, and make the poor part of his campaign. It was a tremendous setback. A vacuum was created when he died.

Later Nixon was elected, and we saw an immediate change, hostile and not caring. The Executive Department ceased completely to involve us in anything. We were completely shut off.

Three months after Kennedy's death, I arrived home from a UAW Labor Day picnic, walked in the door, and turned to close it when I had a severe pain like a knife through my back. I couldn't move, I wanted to die. For a good twenty minutes I stood frozen. Finally I was given some aspirin and was able to go to bed.

After twenty-some days in the hospital without getting better, I came home. Nothing could be done. The doctors didn't know what was wrong, but they believed there was something wrong with my spine.

That was when I began to understand what pain was, one thing missing before in my life. Even in the fast, the pain was nothing like this.

From September until about February, I just lay there, still working, but miserable. Some of the people around me were discouraged. As I was losing a lot of weight, they thought I had cancer.

When Marion Moses, the nurse, came back from the boycott and took a look at me, she really got upset. So did the UAW's Jack Conway and Paul Schrade. They called Senator Edward Kennedy, asking him to send Dr. Janet Travell who had treated President Kennedy's back.

Dr. Travell quickly diagnosed what was wrong. First she asked me to get up, walk around, sit, and stand. Then she told me I had one leg longer than the other, and told me a little bit about referred pain. When she gave me the first treatment, I was able to sit up. In fact, after the treatment I felt so good I went to the regular Friday night Union meeting at Filipino Hall for the first time in months. It was painful, but I made it.

JERRY COHEN RECALLS

In January 1969, we got a call from a guy named Monares in Marysville who said he had information about somebody about to shoot Cesar. He wanted to meet with someone right away.

Richard Chavez, David Averbuck, and I left Delano that night and arrived in Marysville about 1:00 Sunday morning. We went to Monares's house and found out that he'd been checked into a local hospital in an extreme nervous condition. When we could not get access to him, we decided to call the authorities.

"If you don't give us access to the guy, and if anything happens to Cesar," we said, "everybody involved is responsible." Besides wanting to talk to Monares, we wanted to get the word to people that we knew, and that we were on the trail. We wanted to blow the scheme out of the water.

The authorities got us into the hospital in the middle of the night, but Monares had been sedated, and we had to wait. When we finally talked to him, the gist of his story was that there had been a meeting of labor contractors, that the subject had come up of somebody going down to shoot that son of a bitch Chavez, and that they had approached somebody who Monares characterized as a sexually deviate sharpshooter. This, of course, scared the hell out of us.

To this day we really don't know if the story was true, but we were upset, because here was a physical manifestation of somebody's state of mind that had ended him up in the hospital. We had received a lot of threats before on Cesar's life, but that was the first time where we ever really talked to someone involved. I had the impression that something had gone on at a meeting, but I don't know how definite it was, or how far it got.

DOLORES HUERTA RECALLS

When I first got back from New York, Cesar was very sick, and the security was lousy. His cousin Manuel had just arrived to take over Cesar's security, and we sent for Mack Lyons and two others who were on the boycott.

Earlier I talked to Cesar on the phone from New York. He told me about the threats, and said, "I've just made up my mind that I know it's going to happen sooner or later. There's nothing I can do."

When I first came back, he was just so damn morbid. In fact, when I got in the office, I sat there crying, because I just felt that he had resigned himself.

Not only was there the Marysville plot, but I learned of other meetings with labor contractors, and we found out that a guy in Napa was talking about killing Cesar, as was another guy in Santa Maria.

But as Cesar's health and the security improved, his state of mind did, too. Since then, the Union has always insisted that he have guards. He doesn't really want them, but, at the same time, I think he wants to stick around a while if he can. It's not a personal thing with him. It's because he wants to work. It's like a paradox even with himself.

CESAR CHAVEZ RECALLS

There isn't anything that can be done about protection except to make sure that the Union is based not only on myself but on others—and it is. The only way they could protect me is to put me in a bullet-proof tube, or to put me thirty feet underground in a silo. And what work could I do then?

I got my German Shepherd, Boycott, in 1969 to help with security. He became a very close companion. All I did was talk about my dog. I never did that with my children. I don't play golf or fish, so he became my hobby. When I'm tired I got out with him, and ten minutes later I'm relaxed. I never thought I could like a dog so much.

Later that year, we got a second German Shepherd I called Huelga. Of course, the other side quickly started saying mean things about them. The *Delano Record* reported that I got my "vicious" dogs to scare the workers into signing up with the Union.

But the people like Boycott. At one of our meetings I asked them to declare Boycott officially as one of the negotiating consultants.

"Every time we take him we get good luck," I said. Then I looked down at the dog and asked, "Right, Boycott?"

The dog, who was lying down under the table, leaped up and put his paws on the podium. The vote was unanimous. It's better to have the dog as a guard than men. If anything happened to me, the men would become scapegoats in the Union. It could destroy them, and I don't want that to happen. If we can insulate the officers, that's the most important thing we can try to do. This way, the dogs will be blamed.

It's not me who counts, it's the Movement. And I think that in terms of stopping the Movement—this one or other movements by poor people around the country—the possibility is very remote, unless major social changes are made, or force is used to repress us. The tide for change now has gone too far.

FROM JACQUES LEVY'S NOTEBOOK

February 6, 1969—From early morning to late at night, Cesar handles union business from his bed, holding meeting after meeting. It is his regular routine. His face is drawn with fatigue and etched with pain. During our interview, I ask him about his sudden incapacitation, about the severe muscle spasms which are the result of a lifetime of trying to compensate for the unequal length of his legs.

"At first I counted the days without pain," he says, "but as I got better, I started counting the days with pain."

His office is a tiny bedroom filled with a large hospital bed and a standing blackboard. The walls are orange-pink, his electric blanket a deep orange. To the right, behind his bed are a wooden crucifix and a photograph of a Bufano statue of St. Francis; on the right wall, a huge picture of Gandhi, a smaller portrait of Robert Kennedy, and a woodcut of a family buring their dead. Behind his bed, to the left, there is a black poster featuring three heads— those of President John Kennedy, Martin Luther King, Jr., and Senator Robert Kennedy—and one word in red letters—"WHY?" There is also a small cloth hanging with the word "Love."

The spirit of martyrs fills the room.

CHAPTER 11

Perils and Pressures

CESAR CHAVEZ RECALLS

A large-scale attempt to organize a company union that would fight us and confuse the public was made in 1968 by the growers, who put a lot of money into it. Their efforts had the backing of the John Birch Society and the National Right to Work Committee.

First, they set up a dummy outfit called Mexican-American Democrats for Republican Action and made money transfers to that group. Then MADRA turned the money over to AWFWA, the Agriculture Workers Freedom to Work Association.

We investigated it, and Jerry Cohen worked with the government people. Finally the fear of federal investigation made AWFWA give up in 1969, but not before its officers, Gilbert Rubio and Shirley Fetalvero, filed a report required under the Landrum-Griffin Act.

The report told how the growers hired Jose Mendoza and Rubio for $120 a week "to start opposing Chavez." It said that AWFWA was started at a meeting at Sambo's restaurant in Bakersfield, attended by both John Giumarra senior and junior, Delano grower Jack Pandol, DiGiorgio personnel manager Robert Flores, and Jess Marquez who ran one of the DiGiorgio camps.

According to the report, the Giumarras furnished office space, typewriters, and office supplies to AWFWA, and "John Giumarra, Jr., Robert Sabovich, and Jack Pandol gave orders to Mendoza and AWFWA."

The report also listed more than four thousand dollars in checks given by growers to MADRA and AWFWA.

Mendoza went all over the country speaking against us. He was even given an award for his work "to help farm workers" by Illinois Senator Everett Dirksen, at a banquet of the National Right to Work Committee in Washington. Later Cornelio Macias, who eventually joined the Teamsters, replaced Mendoza as director of the company union.

AWFWA was troublesome to us. It did hurt, but it was never threatening to the extent that it would destroy the Union. AWFWA, though, did indicate where we were at with the growers. It showed their unwillingness to accept the workers' organization.

This wasn't the growers' first attempt against us, nor was it their last. First came the Citizens' Committee for Farm Labor, then the Kern-Tulare Independent Farm Workers Association. And always, it seems, it's been the Teamsters Union—certainly the gravest threat of all. Growers' attempts to manipulate the workers always have been there, and probably will be there for a long time.

By 1969 I felt the growers were worse off than we were, though we weren't in very good shape. The leadership was depressed, and the rest of the workers felt it. I'd been bedridden for a long time, and we were in the fourth year of the strike.

By this time, we were fighting on four fronts, and each was taking a lot of manpower. There was the strike, the boycott, the legal cases, and the whole propaganda front. It was pretty confusing for the opposition. But then we're just a little mouse; so we can't fight the lion face to face.

By then our actions were more deliberate than at the start, because we had alternatives. We could strike or not strike; we could slow a grower down or infiltrate him; we could boycott, or we could sue. Whatever we did drained our opponents financially, to the point where they would finally find it less costly to just sit down and negotiate.

For example, our legal staff spent months researching the way growers got around the law to get cheap water from the federal government, despite the 160-acre limitation. Finally we sued the growers, the water district, and the government, a suit that would cost the growers a cool million to defend.

But our most effective weapon was the boycott. As it became more effective, there were indications that the growers' united front might crack. One of the first hints occurred during the California primary campaign in 1968 when Congressman Phil Burton called me from Washington to ask if I would like to meet with Lionel Steinberg, the largest table-grape grower in the

Coachella Valley. I said yes, but the meeting produced nothing.

Then in 1969, Steinberg and a group of growers asked to meet with us. What I didn't know at the time was that the growers also were turning to the Teamsters for help. They were in contact with both Einar Mohn, director of the Western Conference of Teamsters, and Bill Grami, who led the Teamsters in all their fights against us.

LIONEL STEINBERG, COACHELLA VALLEY GROWER, RECALLS

When Cesar Chavez commenced a boycott of table grapes—because he found he was not too effective in removing the workers from the fields—it surprised some growers. This social, political boycott effort, which is unparalleled in American history, literally closed Boston, New York, Philadelphia, Chicago, Detroit, Montreal, Toronto completely from handling table grapes.

It took several years for the boycott to be that effective. It just gradually closed in like a noose around the necks of the vineyardists. While before the strike, we had in this little Coachella Valley some two hundred grape growers, in five years we were down to about sixty growers, and where there was once thirteen thousand acres, we were down to seventy-five hundred acres.

During this boycott period, I was forced to sell some other land that we owned and to heavily mortgage my property to stay in business. But I felt that we would eventually resolve the grape controversy satisfactorily for both sides. Consequently—I'm most fond of grape growing, I've been in it since I was fifteen—I decided that I was going to be tenacious and stay with grape growing rather than go into something else.

Back in May and June of 1968, when I was serving as president of the Desert Grape Advisory Board, I forced a vote at a grape growers' meeting hoping that there would be enough grower support for negotiations with Chavez. But I was outvoted about 8 to 1. And since I was the chairman, I felt that I should abide by the majority wishes.

Then I received a telephone call from Washington from an old friend who helped me when I reorganized the California Young Democrats in 1948. Congressman Phillip Burton called me in late spring of 1968 and said that Cesar Chavez had indicated to him an interest in meeting Lionel Steinberg.

I did speedily agree to meet with Chavez. This was done very privately, because the grape growers had voted not to meet with him. We set up a rendezvous at Sambo's Pancake House in Palm Springs.

I went into the restaurant on a Saturday morning, and I saw Chavez drive up with two of his lieutenants. He came in by himself and came over to the table and sat down and talked, but the place was so filled with teen-agers and tourists—and Chavez is rather an introverted person and in some respects rather shy—that I quickly perceived that we were not going to get very well acquainted in a waffle house. So I invited him to go up to my house. He went out and told his two aides that he was leaving with me, that we would be back in an hour or two.

We talked about our mutual friend Phil Burton, about the late President John Kennedy, Bob Kennedy, politics. This was the end of May 1968, just before the California primary.

My wife and I have had a lifelong interest in art as well as farming. We had a great interest in pre-Columbian art and have a small collection and interesting artifacts from Vera Cruz. Chavez seemed to be looking around the room, and he pointed out some of the pre-Columbian objects. I mentioned that we were collecting them.

The reason I'm mentioning this is because, about two weeks later, it was brought back to my vivid attention by a man they call Reverend Jim Drake.

So Chavez asked me to sign a unilateral agreement which he alleged that he would develop with me, one that could be worked out and lived with on both sides.

I told him that I was just not able to do it in 1968, as much as I would like to, and I took him back to his car.

Since I was unable to make a union agreement with him, apparently some of the Chavez group, either using recognized union tactics that you strike the so-called weakest link or the most friendly link, turned their entire fury and vigor on me personally.

I think that in 1968 I bore the brunt of their attack on the picket lines, and in the vineyards surrounding my crops, and the harassment, and the antagonism, and the threats against some of my employees, and the rock throwing, the name calling, and all the cowboy and Indian tactics that were used in attempting to shut down the grape industry of the Coachella Valley.

So I came out to this one field that was the center of the battleground. We badly needed to pick these grapes because of the tremendous heat. It was about 110 degrees that day, and the crop was imperiled. And I saw Reverend Jim Drake on the picket lines, imploring his people to come out of the fields and leave these awful farmers and these awful people, in particular Steinberg.

So I went up to Jim Drake and said, "Aren't you aware that I have at least been trying to resolve this thing, that Chavez has been at my house, and we had this long conference, and at least we attempted to set some sort of ground rules for a future meeting?"

So Drake very curtly replied to me, "Chavez is not interested in pre-Columbian art!"

That was the only comment that he made about this very important meeting that was held very secretly and under the friendly auspices of Congressman Phil Burton.

So, if his observation were true, apparently Chavez didn't appreciate the effort. He was only interested in the end result, which was a contract. And anything else was not helpful. And he had his mind set on one thing—that was winning the battle, winning the strike, not making friends.

In January of 1969, John Kovacevich of Kern County and I felt that a resolution of the strike and the boycott was extremely important to the welfare of the workers as well as to the growers. Possibly our political orientation as lifelong Democrats made us more interested in the right to organize labor.

John Kovacevich and I were cochairmen of the Farmers for Kennedy and Johnson in 1960, and I served as national treasurer of farmers for the late President John Kennedy, and held two appointments for President Kennedy during his administration. I was Governor Pat Brown's first appointee to the California State Board of Agriculture, and Kovacevich likewise served on that board.

So in 1969 we made plans to try to invite a group of growers to sit down with us privately, and I was going to invite Chavez to meet with us and attempt to determine if a reconciliation or an agreement of some sort couldn't be put together.

The weeks sped by—January, February, and March—and another group of growers felt that Chavez and his group couldn't be lived with, and said that under no circumstances would they sit down with the Chavez group.

They said they wanted to start talking to the Teamsters. And some of them did. And they implored me to also meet with some Teamster leaders.

I really couldn't accurately say whether several of these growers made the telephone call to the Teamsters, or the Teamsters were aware that the problem was on, and they met by mutual interests. But the fact remains that the growers were open with the Teamsters in the early spring of 1969, and I met with two Teamster leaders in Palm Springs for about an hour in February or March. They indicated that if the growers were interested in a Teamster's agreement, they were interested in putting one together for them.

Subsequently I received a call from another grower in the San Joaquin Valley who said that he had invited about twenty-five or thirty of the leading grape growers of the state to meet with two of the top California Teamster leaders.

There were thirty grape growers present at this meeting at the Century Plaza Hotel in West Los Angeles. Many of them indicated that they felt it was utterly impossible to get a livable, workable agreement with the UFWOC. They urged the Teamsters to intervene and step in and come up with an agreement that would be fair to the workers and to the growers.

Some of the growers there had had previous experience with the Teamsters which they alleged was satisfactory. They felt that they could be more comfortable with the Teamsters Union than they would with this social movement that was being led by Cesar Chavez.

These two union leaders from the Teamsters said very clearly and unequivocally that they didn't want a repeat of the Perelli-Minetti episode where they were invited in, and then kicked out.

So this leader of the union unequivocally stated that he felt this matter was so controversial and so complex that he wanted nothing less than a full-scale meeting in the office of the governor of the state of California, Ronald Reagan, and that he wanted some indication that the state of California and the governor felt that it was important that peace be brought to the vineyards of California, and that they have some assurance that this was not going to be a fiasco. They would then determine that the Teamsters should enter the table-grape industry.

So one or two of the grape growers who were prominent Republicans are alleged to have made the contact with the governor and the president of the State Board of Agriculture, Allan Grant, who also heads the California Farm Bureau.

Much to their surprise, the governor refused to intervene, and Allan Grant was furious, I understand, and felt that the meeting was unnecessary, shouldn't have been held, and didn't want to lend any encouragement to it.

So the Teamsters, finding there was no official support and seeing disunity in the ranks of even these thirty prominent grape growers, backed away and made the decision apparently not to intervene with the table-grape situation. That was about mid-March of 1969.

Meanwhile Kovacevich and I continued our talks to try to get a group together and meet with Chavez. By mid-May I had six or seven prominent table-grape growers of the Coachella Valley who were holding meetings and who hired labor consultant Al Kaplan. And Kovacevich had four or five San Joaquin Valley grape growers.

We reached the point where I was in daily communication with Senator Ted Kennedy who was also assisting in attempting to get some sort of a rapport set up, and with Congressman John Tunney who represented our district here in Coachella Valley. In fact, we were in daily conversations with former Governor Brown, Kennedy, Tunney, and Phil Burton.

FROM JACQUES LEVY'S NOTEBOOK

One day in June 1969—"Funny thing about these growers," comments Bill Kircher to Cesar. "If you don't get them talking while the heat is on, you don't get them to talk. I'll bet if you look at my itinerary, my coming out to Delano, it's in May, June, and July. The peak occurs each year at the same time. The greenness of the vines and the increase in adrenalin works the same way. They can't bargain when the vines are dormant."

LIONEL STEINBERG RECALLS

We decided that we needed a governmental body to bring the two groups together—the Chavez group and this group of ten or eleven growers. Finally it was proposed that we try to get the Federal Mediation and Conciliation Service.

We went through some three or four frantic days to get Curtis Counts, its director, involved. Senator Ted Kennedy spoke to him, urging him to step in, but at first, Counts said legally he had no right to enter into an agricultural labor matter. I think it even went to the White House before permission was granted by someone at the White House level to permit Counts to intervene.

By this time it was late May or early June, and the grapes were being harvested. After some fourteen, fifteen days of meetings, the meetings were deadlocked. With a great deal of personal disappointment and reluctance, I saw the meetings dissipate and gradually go downhill to where there was more bitterness on both sides than perhaps even existed before. Most of the growers felt that this just proved that Chavez was impossible. He wouldn't even come to the meetings.

There were claims his back was bothering him, and it may well be true that he was ill. But he certainly was on the picket lines a few days before, and he had been up and down out of sickbeds before.

FROM JACQUES LEVY'S NOTEBOOK

July 4, 1969—Los Angeles Times news item: Table-grape growers file a seventy-five million dollar suit against UFWOC claiming "the boycott has caused losses of twenty-five million dollars to grape growers. The suit asks for treble damages."

Five days later, UFWOC demands state and federal tax returns and all financial records from the growers who are suing. Under rules of discovery, the union is entitled to the information which will cost the growers a substantial amount to compile.

LIONEL STEINBERG RECALLS

So I came back to Coachella Valley to call Ted Kennedy and call Tunney and say, "Look, I went to the meetings, and I thought we were going to sign an agreement. The boycott is still on, and I still would like to see if I can't unilaterally solve this matter." I said, "Chavez has said all along—and he did to the federal conciliator—'I'll sign an agreement with just one grower. It doesn't have to be everybody, or ten growers.'"

So I called Chavez, and with great reluctance they agreed to meet with me with their committee. But we still didn't reach an end.

FROM JACQUES LEVY'S NOTEBOOK

July 9, 1969—At union headquarters the talk is about the negotiations with the Coachella growers that broke off two days ago. Dolores Huerta was negotiating with Steinberg until 3:00 this morning. During lunch at the communal kitchen in Filipino Hall, strikers and staff discuss the situation.

News that the growers were negotiating for the first time has damaged the effectiveness of the boycott, some say. If victory is in sight, why not eat grapes again?

It's obvious that Cesar is under tremendous pressures. Any contract would be interpreted as victory, but the only contract the growers would sign would not materially improve the plight of farm workers. It would not protect them from the abuses of labor contractors, or from the exposure to poisonous pesticides.

There are those who argue that signing the contract is the major break-through, that contracts can be strengthened when they are renewed. And if this chance is missed, the union will be weaker next year. There may be no second chance.

Now that the talks are broken off, word has spread that George Meany and Bill Kircher are angry, some of the church support is miffed, Harry Bernstein, the Los Angeles Times labor reporter, has been critical. Calls have come from Senator Edward Kennedy, among others, and Paul Schrade of the UAW.

Is Cesar wrong? Can he withstand the pressure? Does he know what he is doing?

CESAR CHAVEZ RECALLS

1969 hurt the growers badly, but they needed more. We were miles apart, they weren't hurting enough. We already had contracts in wine, and we knew what we needed in terms of contract language. Steinberg thought that because he was willing to talk to us, he was doing us a favor.

He forgot about those four years of badgering us, disregarding the wishes of the people, and the strikers, and putting people out of a job, and bringing in strikebreakers.

FROM JACQUES LEVY'S NOTEBOOK

July 16, 1969—Los Angeles Times news item: At a Senate labor subcommiteee hearing in Washington, Dale Babione, deputy executive director of procurement in the Defense Supply Agency testifies that the Defense Department bought 2.4 million pounds of table grapes for Vietnam in fiscal 1969 compared with 555,000 pounds in fiscal 1968. Total table-grape purchases by the department were 6.9 million pounds in 1968 and jumped to 9.69 million pounds in 1969.

Senators Walter Mondale, Alan Cranston, and Harold Hughes charge that the Defense Department policy favors grape growers and violates its policy of neutrality in a labor dispute.

CHAPTER 12

The Eagle Is Flying

FROM JACQUES LEVY'S NOTEBOOK

December 18, 1969—San Francisco Chronicle news item: The State Board of Agriculture voted to wage a privately financed national publicity campaign to try to counteract the UFWOC grape boycott. The decision was made at the suggestion of board president Allan Grant, who is also president of the California Farm Bureau Federation.

CESAR CHAVEZ RECALLS

We began to hear a lot of stories about the effectiveness of the boycott, a lot of talk about the growers being in trouble. From all the signs, we were pretty certain that victory was right around the corner. In December, Jim Drake and I took pictures of packed boxes of table grapes being opened and the grapes thrown into gondolas to be taken to the winery. That meant tremendous losses.

Some of the people working with the Lucas Company told us that the cold storage sheds were full of grapes they couldn't sell, and that the grapes were rotting. Then we heard Lucas picked up all the leftover shook—the boards used for making boxes—put them in a pickup and asked for fifty-two dollars credit. In the past they'd leave thousands of dollars worth of shook out there for use the next year.

It was about that time that the bishops got involved.

MONSIGNOR GEORGE HIGGINS RECALLS

Before the bishops conference met in November of 1969, I helped draft a possible statement on the farm labor problem including, as I recall it, a specific reference supporting the boycott.

At the November meeting, two of the California bishops—Bishop Hugh Donohoe of Fresno and Archbishop Timothy Manning of Los Angeles—said they thought that the bishops, at that stage, could perform a better service if they would withhold a statement on the boycott and offer their services in some way as mediators trying to bring the parties together.

I suggested that Bishop Donohoe meet with Bill Kircher. After that meeting Donohoe suggested that the body of bishops appoint a committee to go out there and look into it.

Appointed were Manning, Donohoe, Bishop Joseph Donnelly of Hartford, Connecticut, who had experience in the labor field, Bishop Humberto Medeiros of Brownsville, Texas, who worked among Chicano farm workers, and Bishop Walter Curtis of Bridgeport, Connecticut, who was an active member of our Social Action Committee.

The committee organized itself and selected Bishop Donnelly as its chairman. As I had known him for many years, it was just natural for him to say, "You're going to work with us." I just became the staff man, making phone calls, writing letters and statements.

Since the beginning, the committee was, in effect, Bishop Donnelly, myself, and Monsignor Roger Mahoney of Fresno, who became our local secretary because he had the contacts in California which we didn't have.

While I had never done much labor mediation, I was always in one way or another on the fringes of the labor movement, keeping in touch with labor problems. I had taken my degree in labor economics at Catholic University, and for almost thirty years I worked in the social action field with the United States Catholic Conference, a kind of secretariat to the National Conference of Catholic Bishops.

Donohoe and Manning were the ones who said, "Let's not rush in with an immediate, dramatic statement on the boycott. Let's see if we can't bring the parties together."

So in January, Donnelly asked me to find out what they had done, and when I told him they had done nothing, he said, "Well, that's all I need to know. I didn't want to move in unless these two California bishops weren't going to do anything."

Within a matter of a week or two, he called a meeting of the whole committee in California. Then we had endless meetings with any number of growers up and down the San Joaquin Valley, individually or in small groups. Roger Mahoney brought them together. We also met with Cesar and his people.

We must have been out there six or eight times or more, sometimes for three or four days, sometimes for a week, just going around talking to growers and talking to Cesar.

In the beginning the reception was hesitant—friendly, no blood, but no action either. They just wanted to hear us out.

We said, "We are interested in bringing the parties together. We believe in trade unionism, and we believe in collective bargaining. We're not neutral in that sense. We're here to tell you, very frankly, that we think you should negotiate. We are offering our services, if we can bring you together."

Some of them had been burned, from their point of view, by the negotiations which broke down the year before. But eventually one or two said, "Maybe we could start this over again, but we don't want to go through that process again, you know, with people shouting at one another and counterpropaganda and so forth. If we're going to negotiate, it will have to be done a little more seriously, and maybe we could agree to meet again in smaller groups if you people would sit in with us as observers."

The first one who finally made a firm request of that kind was Steinberg. In March, Steinberg said he was willing to go—if we would sit in. We took the position all along that we weren't interested in sitting in on anybody's negotiations or acting as mediators, but if the parties wanted us to sit in, why we would.

So we went to the union and told them his position. They said, "All right, if that's what he wants, it's all right with us."

That led to that first settlement down in Coachella, the one that was signed in Los Angeles at a big press conference. From then on in, we just kept doing the same thing. We met with more growers.

FROM JACQUES LEVY'S NOTEBOOK

April 2, 1970—San Francisco Chronicle news item: Two Coachella Valley growers yesterday signed a union contract with UFWOC. The contract covers three vineyards owned principally by David and Charles Freedman and managed and owned partially by Lionel Steinberg.

The vineyards employ about 750 workers at harvest peak and

cover seventy-eight hundred acres, about 15 percent of all grapes produced in the Coachella Valley, but only about 1.4 percent of the state's total output of table grapes.

The contract calls for $1.75 an hour plus 25 cents for each box of grapes picked, in contrast to the current rate of $1.65 an hour and 15 cents a box. In addition the growers will put 10 cents an hour into a health and welfare fund and 2 cents into an economic development fund to help workers who lose their jobs because of old age or mechanization.

The contract also sets up a hiring hall run by the union, and provides safeguards in the use of pesticides.

CESAR CHAVEZ RECALLS

After we signed Steinberg, we went to Coachella and began to negotiate at Reverend Lloyd Saatjian's church with the two Larson brothers. At some point they said they didn't think we represented the workers.

"Well, let's have an election," I said.

They didn't want to, but they were trapped. They insisted on negotiating, but I said, "No, you say that we don't represent your workers, and I want to prove that we do."

Our position was no two bites at the same apple, but we made an exception with Larson because he had been touring the country saying we didn't represent his workers. K. K. Larson was probably the most active guy against us, speaking all over the country.

It wasn't a hard campaign, the companies didn't fight us. I talked to the workers only once at a big meeting about an hour or so before the election. Manuel already had talked to each worker individually.

Early in the morning, just before the election, I stopped to get something at a grocery store. As we got across the street, my dog Boycott jumped out of the car and started after me. But there was a car coming, going about forty miles an hour, and he was hit and flung way across the road. When he landed, he was in shock and took off, running into the desert.

I had to make a choice, going to find the dog, or going to the elections. But people come first, so I went to the election. Afterward, I went back to the motel and was lying on my bed worrying about Boycott.

Suddenly I had a vision of where Boycott was. We went dashing out in the car to the desert and, sure enough, there was the dog. When I ran toward him, he started running deeper into the desert. Although I called him, he ran further away. The more I called, the more he ran.

Finally I yelled the command, "Boycott, come!" and he did, still in shock, his pads worn out from running across the sand. We took him to a veterinarian who said he had no broken bones. It was just a miracle.

We won the election at both Larson ranches by a vote of 152 to 2.

Earlier, the Coachella growers had formed a new committee called the Growers Committee to Protect Workers' Rights and put out a leaflet in Spanish and English saying that the workers didn't want the Union. So we went on TV April 15 and challenged all the growers in Coachella to have elections on the spot. They wouldn't respond, of course.

Actually there were only about three influential growers holding everything back in Coachella. They were under pressure from the big Delano growers who felt that a break in Coachella would hurt them.

But other growers were in trouble. In May, about a month after the Larson vote, we signed up Bruno Dispoto and the Bianco Fruit Corporation. Dispoto had vineyards all the way from Coachella and Arvin to Delano and Modesto. Bianco had vineyards in both Delano and Arizona.

With our victories, strike fever was spreading in Modesto and Stockton, Madera and Fresno. There also were some melon strikes, and people in the oranges wanted to strike in Yuma.

One day a strike started at a peach ranch in Kingsburg, about twenty miles south of Fresno. I think it started over someone being fired. Then it developed into a community strike. People came from town, put up tents next to the road by the orchards, and set up stoves. Women cooked, and men came day and night to eat there. The spirit was so strong, the strike was still going after a week.

When we investigated and learned the orchard belonged to Hollis Roberts, Dolores went to talk to him. We almost flipped when he agreed to negotiate. We thought we were fishing for trout, and we caught a whale.

Roberts operated more than forty-six thousand acres spread over five San Joaquin Valley counties, and he employed more than four thousand workers. Later the press reported that he grew about eighteen fruit and nut crops; that he was the largest producer of walnuts, almonds, persimmons, and canned figs; and that he had more acres of citrus than any other grower in the country.

I met Hollis Roberts during the negotiations, a huge man about six feet six inches tall. He was an Okie who came with his wife to California during the depression. They were so poor they worked together in the fields picking cotton and other crops.

Then they made it. He's some sort of an organizing genius in business. Now they live in a huge, fancy house. I remember having to use the phone there, and Roberts leading me into his bedroom. The house seemed to go on and on and on.

Roberts was very honest, and I felt like I was dealing with a rich farm worker—no pretense or anything. But he had a rough way of talking. At different times he talked about those "niggers" in the fields and he called the Mexicans "my boys."

I finally shook my head and said, "That's all. No more!" I told him, "These are grown men. Why do you keep calling them boys?"

He couldn't understand what was wrong. "Well, I've always called them that, and they don't mind, so why should you care?"

"Even if it's all right with you and your men, it's not all right with the Union. So we will no longer call them boys or niggers." It was the same education we seem to go through with everybody.

After the contract was signed covering all his crops, Roberts told me, "Cesar, you're a big man now. You got to get yourself a Cadillac. Don't play around with those Fords." And when I complimented him on his huge office, he said, "Well, you should have one this size, maybe even bigger. You're a big man now. You gotta have a bar, all these things." And he meant it. He wanted me to buy a Cadillac right away.

He became very helpful, very active rounding up other growers to sign up. For a while I felt like making him my number one organizer. But I learned long ago you can't get too close to those you have to deal with across the table.

After Steinberg and Larson signed, we wondered what would happen to the boycott. The boycotters and some of the leadership feared that Union grapes would weaken it and open up markets for scab grapes.

For about ten days it was touch and go. Then the domino theory materialized. Salesmen are smart. They offered less money for scab grapes, telling non-Union growers, "If I buy your grapes, I buy a picket line with it."

We heard the story of one grower, Lucie Titwell, who had one hundred thousand boxes of grapes she couldn't sell. She called her

San Francisco broker in tears asking him to take her grapes. "I can't sell them," was his answer.

Then eight hundred boxes of Bagdasarian grapes hit San Francisco, but the Teamsters wouldn't unload them. They said they had no time. We had strong support among their members in that local.

As the season developed, another thing happened. The growers with contracts were helping the Union, tipping us off to where non-Union grapes were going. They were ready to cut each other's throats just to help themselves.

Marshall Ganz came up with the instant boycott, concentrating on the growers we wanted, getting on the phone and closing all their distribution points. We could close their markets within twelve to twenty-four hours.

LeRoy Chatfield worked on supermarket chains. Their choice was getting publicized for having Union grapes, or picket lines if they didn't. Many agreed to handle only Union grapes.

We got one large grower, Karahadian, when we reached an agreement with the Mayfair chain which we knew was his principal market. When he came to us, he wanted a contract retroactive to that day he lost Mayfair. We already had the word he was using twenty-six salesmen in twenty-six different areas of the country, but that he was not selling more than fifteen hundred boxes per day.

The day after he signed a contract, he sold ten thousand boxes in five hours. In three days he emptied his cold storage. Not only that, but Union grapes with our Eagle on them were selling from fifty cents to seventy-five cents more a box.

We started getting an average of five to ten calls a day from growers asking, "What do I have to do to get the bird on my grapes?"

We told them, "If you sign the contract, we'll give you the bird!" The eagle was flying.

We ended up getting all of Coachella and the Arvin growers. We also went after the giant Tenneco conglomerate, which was buying up vineyards so fast it looked like they would soon own about 50 percent of the table grapes. The company already owned more than a million agricultural acres in five states and owned oil all over the world.

About that time we lost a good friend when Walter Reuther was killed in a tragic plane crash. After his funeral in Detroit, I met some people from Canada, Latin America, Asia, and Europe who were interested in world-wide cooperation and were willing to take on Tenneco. There were guys from the Chemical Workers Union, Plantation Workers, Transport Workers, and Metal Workers.

The World Council of Churches also wanted to do something like this, take a world-wide conglomerate and deal with it on a world-wide basis instead of country by country.

As it turned out, Tenneco was so terrified at the thought of an international boycott, we were able to negotiate a contract.

When it looked like everything was going to break, we started after the lettuce in Santa Maria and Salinas. Hy Balen from the Cab Drivers Union in New York was assigned to Santa Maria to help the local people organize. Since we already had been doing some work there for about two years, we also sent out letters to all the growers in Santa Maria asking for recognition.

As it turned out, that triggered the Teamsters and the growers, and the most dangerous fight of our lives. But we didn't know it then. All we knew was that we still had to contend with the Delano growers.

CHAPTER 13

First Cracks in Delano

CESAR CHAVEZ RECALLS

One day in June, I got ahold of the grower, Hollis Roberts, whom I figured loved to do these things. I told him, "Hollis, you know it's to your advantage to have peace in agriculture."

"Sure," he said.

"I think you're the man to do something. I think you could get the big boys in agriculture to get all the growers that are not in now and get them in so we can turn the boycott into a great promotional campaign for grapes."

I said, "We're willing to do it. We're committed to do it. We'll do it if you can get them!"

"What do I do?"

I suggested he talk to Allan Grant who was both chairman of the State Board of Agriculture and president of the California Farm Bureau.

After about a week, Roberts said Allan Grant didn't want to answer the phone.

"Why don't you get Russell Kennedy?" I said. Kennedy was one of the biggest cotton men in Kern County, president of Calco Compress. He and Allan Grant were close friends.

I knew that Roberts knew Kennedy because Roberts mentioned that before signing the contract, he went and touched base with some of the big guys, including Russell Kennedy who told him, "You're a fool of you don't sign. I fought the compress workers, and it just doesn't pay. We wouldn't know what to do without the union."

Kennedy got ahold of Allan Grant who was somewhere in Louisiana, and Grant flew right back. They had a meeting in Las Vegas. I don't know whether Kennedy was there, but Roberts brought Earl Coke, who was state secretary of agriculture; Jerry Fielder, the head of the state Department of Human Resources Development, and a few other men.

Roberts just laid the cards on the table. This was on June 25, one of the days we were negotiating with Tenneco in Fresno. Roberts kept in contact with me by phone.

After the meeting, Grant sent out his staff to organize the growers. Four days later, Governor Reagan announced he was offering the use of the State Conciliation Service to hold elections in the vineyards.

I never thought that the offer was sincere. It was more like a diversionary tactic. And I felt the governor never would have made that offer until the growers agreed to it. If my reading was correct, all they needed now was a little push. I felt the most crucial part of our drive would take place in the next two weeks. We'd either get them, or we'd probably have to fight another year. But we weren't about to accept the governor's offer. No Union strikes for elections. There would be no two bites from the same apple.

As if to confirm my suspicions, John Giumarra, Jr. accepted the governor's offer the next day. He also called for a moratorium on the boycott until the elections were held.

I think Giumarra was under a lot of pressure and wanted to bring his friends along, not just come in by himself. We had most of Los Angeles closed off to him, where he sold 50 percent of his grapes. We also had all of Canada closed off to him, shut tight, and he sold a lot there. It was very easy to boycott him, as his labels were well known in boycott circles. After all, that's where we started.

During the next few days, as the pace became more hectic, I got irritable. I was going too fast and not doing anything. So I started to fast. The weather was very hot, way over a hundred, and in the next three days, I lost 10 pounds, dropping from 168 to 158 pounds.

But I didn't have any privacy, and I couldn't work. There were so many things to do which I didn't want to do because I was too weak, that I decided to postpone that fast for another time. It wasn't fair to the Movement.

Nine days after Governor Reagan makes his election offer, Cesar discusses strategy with Jerry Cohen and Dolores Huerta. Because Delano is oven-hot, and his back continues its stabbing pains, he has come to my cramped, air-conditioned room at the Stardust Motel where he can lie on the bed.

"We are not begging anyone. We could blow the whole thing now," he tells Jerry, as Dolores sits on the floor talking on the phone.

A short time later he comments, "There is such a big plum hanging there in front of us, and it's so tempting to pluck it!"

But the temptation is resisted. The union rejects the offer on July 9. The next day, word gets around union headquarters that Philip Feick of the Western Employers Council will make a major announcement at 6:00 P.M. on TV.

"Does the TV work at home?" Cesar asks his daughter Linda, who is working at the office as his secretary.

"It does sometimes," she answers. "It's temperamental."

So Cesar decides to go back to my motel room. Just before the broadcast, he arrives with Manuel Chavez, Marshall Ganz, three guards, and Boycott.

I tape Feick's statement as he accepts the State Conciliation Service offer for immediate talks. "The prime consideration of both sides should be to assure secret ballot elections," Feick says. And his statement offers both a stick and a carrot.

If the union turns down the offer, the growers may withdraw their acceptance. If it accepts, "Perhaps the balance of the entire industry would be involved" in negotiations and an agreement, Feick says.

After the broadcast, the tape is replayed and discussed. The conversation centers on Giumarra.

"We sweated for five years, let him sweat a little," Cesar says. But the others are not so sure.

Because his back is throbbing, Cesar lies flat on the bed. The others are sitting on the two chairs and on the floor. Boycott is curled by the door. The talk is far-ranging, but there is no agreement.

Then Cesar notices the dog and asks, "Boycott, what should we do?"

Boycott stretches, comes up to him and puts his paw on Cesar's arm.

"You see, he says, 'Sign!' " says Manuel who is in the armchair beside the bed.

Cesar smiles. "No, he's putting his paw up. That means, 'Stop, don't move!' "

He knows the union's strength. There are many reports, including one that the Lucas company of Delano already has ordered seven hundred fifty thousand union labels printed.

Nor does Cesar trust Ralph Duncan, director of the State Conciliation Service. He feels that Duncan double-crossed the union before the strike started in 1965 when he failed to get the growers to even talk to the union. And he has been told that Duncan made several talks to college students that were obviously biased against the union.

Cesar wants the Catholic bishops as mediators and feels his bargaining position will be stronger if the growers ask for the talks rather than come to the table at the request of a third party.

So he meets that night with Monsignor Roger Mahoney to see if the bishops will act.

CESAR CHAVEZ RECALLS

On July 16, Bishop Joseph Donnelly called and said Feick was in the room with him. I insisted he get on the phone. Feick began kind of funny. "Well, I guess we want to meet, unh?"

"What do you mean, you guess? Do you want to negotiate?"

"Well, the bishop here was suggesting,"

And I said, "No, I want to hear it from you!"

"Well, yea."

"Yea, what?" I meant it to sound that I wanted him to say that he wanted to negotiate. He said it.

"Okay, that's all I wanted to hear," I said. It was small of me to do that, but I really wanted to hear him say it.

FROM JACQUES LEVY'S NOTEBOOK

Cesar calls a meeting for 2:00 P.M. Thursday, July 16, at Reuther Hall. He is very secretive, excited. No one knows what it's about, but the hall is set up for a mass. About a hundred are there, members of the staff, the people from the kitchen at Filipino Hall, a few mothers with infants, and several volunteers with guitars.

A portable plywood altar is set up in the center of the hall with wooden chairs placed in a square around it. Father David Duran puts on his scarlet chasuble with the symbol of the Holy Spirit represented by the union's black eagle across the chest and a white dove on the back.

After the mass, Cesar gets up. "I just wanted to say these few words," he starts out. Then he makes a few announcements. The opposition "Grape Eaters Local" is meeting at VFW Hall tomorrow; 550 lemon and orange pickers struck in the Santa Paula-Fillmore district near Oxnard three days ago; lettuce pickers have joined lettuce thinners on strike in the San Luis Valley, Colorado.

He pauses, conscious of the drama, conscious, too, that this is a historic moment.

Bishop Donnelly has given him a message, he says dramatically. He looks at a slip of paper. "This is July 16, 1970. Quote: The table-grape growers listed below have authorized Philip J. Feick, Jr., Western Employers Council, Bakersfield, California, to negotiate on their behalf with United Farm Workers Organization Committee for the purpose of effecting a labor agreement between the parties. Unquote."

He reads the list of twenty-three companies. Giumarra's name brings a loud cheer. So does Caratan's, Pandol's, and several others. The men they have fought so bitterly for five long years are finally willing to talk. The negotiations start tomorrow in Bakersfield.

He tells everyone the union has a commitment not to make the names of the growers public.

"These growers represent about 42 percent of all the grapes in California, maybe about forty thousand acres, and we are going to get on the phone right now and start calling the boycotters.

"But let me ask," he pleads in his most plaintive tone, "please don't call them! Let me call them for once, huh? So I can give them the good news, because I hate to call them and hear, 'Oh, we know all about it!' "

And he warns, "So the boycott is still on until the contracts are signed. Full steam ahead!"

After the mass, Cesar goes to the union's pink house where he stays until after 10:30 P.M. calling the boycotters everywhere—New York, Minnesota, Texas, Denver, Seattle, New Orleans, San Francisco, and on and on. Helping him are Larry Itliong and Marshall Ganz. For dinner he eats matzos, Monterey Jack cheese, and water.

During each call he reads the names of the growers slowly, keeping the biggest names for the end. The joyous reactions are intoxicating. And in the next room, I am recording them from an extension phone for the labor archives.

The next morning at union headquarters, Dolores asks Cesar, "Did you sleep last night?"

"Hell, no, how could I sleep? I worked out our tactics."

"I couldn't sleep either," Dolores says.

At 11:00 A.M., the union negotiating team is in Bakersfield at the Isabella Room of the Holiday Inn. Cesar, Dolores, Jerry Cohen, Bill Kircher, Larry Itliong, Marshall Ganz, UFWOC Executive Board member Philip Vera Cruz, and Irwin De Shettler, an AFL-CIO representative, sit down along one side of tables set up to form three sides of a rectangle. A number of Delano farm workers sit along the wall behind them.

Bishop Joseph Donnelly and Monsignors George Higgins and Roger Mahoney are there when three young growers in sport clothes walk in with Feick, the man who nearly three years earlier had refused to talk directly to Cesar until "you prove to me you've got the strength."

Feick smiles broadly as he heads directly for Cesar.

"Here's a gentleman I haven't seen for a long time," he says smoothly and shakes hands. The growers, John Giumarra, Jr., Louis Lucas, and Louis Caratan also shake hands all around.

The bishop opens the meeting, then Kircher breaks the ice, talking of the strong emotional feelings on both sides. "If we are to turn the corner on these past three years, and actually do a good job, we cannot sign a paper truce and have the battle continue. We are anxious to have a total peace, or no peace."

Caratan sits looking angry and cynical. Giumarra appears earnest, while Cesar and Dolores are very stern. The others seem more relaxed.

For some twenty minutes Kircher lectures, then concludes, "We'll never love each other, we know that. But we want to understand each other."

"I don't know how there could be any response other than the other team—our team—must have reached the same conclusion, or we wouldn't be here," Feick answers. "We are here to try and bring as near to total peace in the industry as we can."

As Feick talks, Jerry and Dolores take copious notes. Cesar sits back and listens.

Kircher goes over some of the demands the union will present, including the request that when a contract is reached, it will be signed at union headquarters.

"You may hate it now, but we want to put a large emblem in the very floor for what we consider a real crossroad in the life of this union," he says. Caratan sneers.

The preliminaries over, a recess is called before the union presents its proposed contract. Then the talks adjourn until the next day when the growers hope to have counterproposals. It's 1:30 P.M.

Cesar, Kircher, and I then drive some hundred miles southwest to Fillmore where Cesar meets with the leaders of the citrus strike.

A hundred families have walked out, but they have no money, and since they live in company housing, they face eviction. Cesar estimates it would cost sixty thousand dollars a month to finance the strike, and chances of winning are slim. The workers need more organizing.

If he decides to take on citrus, it would be a major battle, he explains, as citrus is the second largest crop in terms of manhours. He tries to convince the leaders to end the strike.

That night, when he talks to the strikers who have filled Lady of Guadalupe Church, the spirit is militant and enthusiastic. It's obvious the strike will continue.

By the time we are back in Delano, it's 1:45 A.M.

The grape negotiations resume later that day, but Cesar stays away. Sunday, too, he is absent as the talks falter. The two sides are in separate rooms with Kircher, somehow, taking on the role of mediator. By evening, the talks break down.

When Bishop Donnelly persuades both sides to resume negotiations the next afternoon, he takes over as mediator, going from one room to the other. But Feick's position hardens. He insists on taking the Tenneco contract and diluting it, a suggestion the union rejects.

Finally, Feick walks in dramatically on the union negotiating team.

"We are going home," he says curtly. "If the union wants to get in touch with us, they know where to reach us."

Later Jerry comments that Feick is bluffing. "We can wait," he says. "We're about a week early."

MARSHALL GANZ RECALLS

We had a tracking operation against Giumarra. We found out where the grapes were going in different ways, from some of the other growers, from truck drivers, and from other sources. Once we got this information, we would call the boycott cities. It was very effective. We stopped Giumarra in Portland, in San Francisco, and in other cities.

The boycotters would go see the buyer and say, "I understand that you have a shipment of Giumarra arriving on X day. I just want you to know that there are going to be five hundred pickets here waiting for it." That way we rerouted a bunch of Giumarra grapes and plums in shipment.

One day we got a report that there was a truckload of Giumarra grapes going to Appleton, Wisconsin. We knew what time the truck left, figured out that it would arrive in Appleton sometime between midnight and 5:00 A.M. on the following day, and called the people up in Milwaukee who got to work on it. I got the report the next day.

This truck driver arrived in Appleton at 2:00 in the morning. Waiting for him were about forty or fifty pickets. The truck driver was beside himself.

"Jesus Christ!" he said, "you picket me down there when I go in; you picket me when I'm coming out; and now here in goddamn Appleton, Wisconsin, at 2:00 in the morning, here's thirty, forty more of ya!"

And they said, "Well, we're going to be wherever you go."

So he just turned the truck around and took off for Montana. I don't know whatever happened to the grapes after that.

CHAPTER 14

A Surrender
and a Challenge

CESAR CHAVEZ RECALLS

Since I couldn't stop the citrus strike, I was back in Fillmore the
day after the grape talks collapsed, helping the strikers and walking their picket line.

The next day in Delano, I got a call from Salinas alerting me
that the Teamsters were in the lettuce fields signing up workers
and telling them they were going to sign contracts with the
growers. I had to act fast.

FROM JACQUES LEVY'S NOTEBOOK

When the union executive board meets at 2:00 P.M., Friday,
July 24, Cesar asks for permission to turn the meeting into an
emergency session. A few hours earlier, he tells the board, he got
a call from Salinas where Teamster truckers have just ended an
eight-day strike against lettuce growers. The Teamsters may extend
their contracts to cover the farm workers, he says.

Cesar decides to drive directly to Salinas and hold a press conference. Meanwhile the board will send telegrams to the major
growers' associations in the area asking for immediate recognition
of UFWOC and negotiations for a contract.

"How long will it take to drive to Salinas?" Cesar asks.

No one is sure, and we check a road map. We estimate it's a four-hour drive. So Dolores is asked to call union organizer Jose Luna in Hollister, ask him to set up a press conference for 8:00 P.M. in Salinas, find a suitable location, and notify the press.

Then a hitch develops. Cesar's guards have taken off in the car and can't be found. He asks me to drive him, and we take off, leaving a message for the guards to catch up.

Twice on the drive north, we stop to call union headquarters to learn what arrangements have been made in Salinas. But Luna hasn't called.

When we reach Salinas at 7:30 P.M., we find a public phone booth at a closed Standard station, and Cesar calls the union. This time the union switchboard doesn't answer. Apparently everyone is at the regular Friday night union meeting at Filipino Hall. Cesar calls Helen there and learns there's been no word from Luna. He asks her to check around and call him back.

While we wait in the dark, I call a local radio station to find out if they know of a Chavez press conference. They don't.

It's after 8:00 P.M. when the phone finally rings. Helen, who has found Luna, gives Cesar an address on Market Street, a big shell of a building that was probably once a recreation hall.

Outside are Cesar's guards, and as Cesar walks in, there is a deafening cheer. The place is jammed with farm workers, one television crew, and a reporter for the Salinas Californian. The number and spirit of the farm workers surprises me.

It is not until later that I learn that four years earlier in the Imperial Valley and Calexico, Manuel Chavez started organizing workers who then moved north to harvest the Salinas and Santa Maria area lettuce crops. He defied the experts then to do what they thought was impossible. Jose Luna, too, has been busy organizing the six thousand strawberry workers at the giant Pic 'N Pac Company in Salinas, and the workers in other row crops in the Salinas Valley area.

Following the press conference, where he makes public his demands to the lettuce growers, Cesar goes to a lettuce worker's home for a strategy session. He suggests a march through the Salinas Valley. The Teamsters must be met head on.

It's well past midnight when Cesar heads north for San Jose to see his parents. Early the next morning he is due to march and speak at a rally in San Rafael, north of San Francisco, where typographical workers are striking the San Rafael Independent Journal. Since the typographical workers have been sending milk the past five years to the children of striking farm workers, Cesar wants to help.

We have no idea how strangely this thousand-mile round trip journey will end.

CESAR CHAVEZ RECALLS

Coming back from that typographical union meeting Saturday night, I called my house, and Helen said Jerry Cohen wanted to talk to me, that it was very important.

When we got to Delano after midnight, I had all kinds of notes. The guard outside the house gave one to me, Helen had one for me, and there also was one by the telephone saying, "Call Jerry!"

"Giumarra wants to talk," Jerry told me.

"You're kidding!"

"No, he wants to talk."

"Okay. We'll meet him at 10:00 in the morning then." I was tired. In fact, I was beat. From the time I had left Delano Friday afternoon, I had had only about three hours sleep.

Jerry insisted. "No, he wants to talk now."

"It's almost 1:00 in the morning!" I argued, but I finally agreed and told Helen, "Well, it's not every day that Giumarra wants to negotiate."

I knew that the giant Acme chain had taken off all Giumarra produce, and the Kroeger Food stores canceled their grape order in Cincinnati Friday. About the only major city where Giumarra was moving any grapes was Detroit, but that very morning Giumarra's broker there had announced no more Giumarra grapes.

So Jerry and I went over to the Stardust Motel. We were in room forty-four trying to relax when John Giumarra, senior and junior, both arrived from Bakersfield.

"Well, I'm here!" said John Giumarra, senior, smiling as he walked in.

I said something like, "How are you?" and he said, "Well, you've gone after me so much, you must like me a lot!"

Because of my back, I have a special rocking chair which we had brought into the room. He's got a bum back, too, so we first talked about that and the chair and the doctors. Then we started an all-night discussion.

Dolores had been in Fresno all day Saturday taking care of three different negotiations. She left Fresno at 1:00 in the morning and joined us in Delano.

We went over the whole contract, explaining everything and answering all his questions. I told him I didn't want to sign a contract with him until I was sure that all the growers wanted to really have peace. I asked him to get all the growers together.

Since, by then it was about 9:00 in the morning, I suggested we meet at 6:00 that evening.

Even though it was Sunday, Giumarra had all the growers together by noon, about thirty or forty of them, all of the tough ones that had fought us so hard.

We got hold of all the workers on the negotiating committee and started the meeting in the big hall of St. Mary's Catholic School shortly after noon.

The workers sat behind some long tables the length of the hall, and the growers sat facing them in several rows of school desk chairs. They asked a lot of questions, which we answered. It's amazing how much of their own propaganda they believed about the hiring hall and everything else.

I didn't stay there too long, but the negotiations continued until late Monday night, when everything was settled except some technical language which Jerry and Giumarra, junior, were going to work out. We were getting the hiring hall, protection against pesticides, $1.80 an hour going up to $2.05 in 1972, 10 cents an hour for the Robert F. Kennedy Health and Welfare fund, and 2 cents a box for the economic development fund.

FROM JACQUES LEVY'S NOTEBOOK

It seems hard to believe that the five-year strike is about over. When the negotiations end, a few members of the negotiating team decide to celebrate over a glass of beer at the Delano Motel. From there, Marshall Ganz phones Vivian Levine, who is in charge of the San Francisco boycott, to tell her the good news.

She asks him, "Have you heard the radio?"

"What's on the radio?"

"The Teamsters have just signed thirty contracts in Salinas!"

That ends the celebration.

CESAR CHAVEZ RECALLS

I knew if we let the Teamsters get away with this one, we wouldn't have a Union. So I called another press conference in Salinas Tuesday morning and challenged the Teamsters and growers. I told the press I suspected that the top architects of this conspiracy were Einar Mohn, the West Coast Teamster leader, and Governor Ronald Reagan.

"For all we know, they may want to sign up the rest of the farm workers in California in the same back-door manner that they did this in the Salinas Valley," I said.

After the press conference, I met with some of our organizers and lettuce workers to set our plans. I also wanted to re-emphasize the need for nonviolence.

I told them I expected the Teamsters to buy people off or to try to intimidate us. "But we're not afraid of them. Nonviolence becomes more powerful as violence becomes more pronounced. You'll see how our tactics work."

FROM JACQUES LEVY'S NOTEBOOK

Meeting with the workers at one of their homes in Salinas, Cesar stresses three points:

—"The Teamsters shouldn't frighten any of us, because if we're frightened, we can't fight."

—"We shouldn't get mad, because then we might do something not consistent with our philosophy of nonviolence, and we have many nonviolent means at our disposal."

—"It's going to be a long struggle, and we must be prepared for that."

Several workers express their fears for his safety, but Cesar shrugs that off. "There's too much work to be done," he says. And he steers the talk to plans for a march through the Salinas Valley. Maps are brought out, and the details worked out. The march will start in two days.

That evening, Cesar and Bill Kircher drive out to a rally outside three labor camps. The workers straggle out and listen quietly as Cesar talks to them in Spanish from the back of a flat-bed truck. The guards worry about his safety, whether the Teamsters will react.

After the rally, Kircher tells me, "The workers were awfully quiet. There's none of the spirit like in Delano. I wonder what it means?" I, too, am struck by the subdued atmosphere.

Back in the car, Cesar tells Kircher, "The first question the workers ask is, 'If we strike, how do we feed our families?'"

"Well," answers Kircher, "if you need a strike fund, I'll raise it. I did it before, and I will again."

We drive the long four-hour drive back to Delano. On the way, Cesar stops to phone headquarters and learns there's been a hitch. Jerry Cohen and Giumarra can't agree on the contract language.

It's 1:00 A.M. before we arrive in Delano, where Cesar is met at his home by Jerry, Dolores, and Marshall Ganz. The problems with the contract wording have been ironed out, and the signing ceremony will take place tomorrow at the Forty Acres.

A five-year battle has been won, but instead of joy, Cesar looks tired and glum.

"What a shame that when we were tasting such sweet victory, the Teamsters had to come in and spoil it," someone comments.

Cesar straightens out. Noticing that his mood is demoralizing the others, his expression changes.

"We shouldn't worry so much about the Teamsters," he answers. "They shouldn't frighten us. Actually we were going to have to fight the Teamsters sooner or later, and it's a very good thing that it happened this way."

As he speaks, his enthusiasm returns. "Every time, we find two steps have to be taken. The first is to get the growers to accept the idea that they must work with a union. Then they have to determine which union. Now that the Teamsters have taken care of the first step, we are left with only one. And we can really put that to them in many ways."

Perhaps his optimism is catching, but everyone is so tired, it's hard to say. We all stumble off to bed. In a few hours the Delano growers will be coming to the Forty Acres to sign a contract.

RICHARD CHAVEZ RECALLS

The growers went to the Forty Acres, but even at the parking lot, they were still trying for last-minute changes on something that they thought wasn't clear. We were arguing in the parking lot before we came in to sign the contract in Reuther Hall.

The growers came in through the back door because the hall was full of people. The only empty seats were at the head table where there were microphones. So they filed in one by one, some-one from each company, and sat down facing the people. They were very up tight. They looked pretty sick. But Giumarra was very cheerful. He made a speech that finally peace had come to the valley, that we were going to work together.

It was a great thing. People were very happy, singing and cheering. The hall was so crowded, it was just solid bodies, and there were more people outside that couldn't get in.

There were twenty-nine contracts signed that day.

FROM JACQUES LEVY'S NOTEBOOK

The younger John Giumarra speaks for the growers. "I hope that with this foundation you can move on to greater things, and we'll prosper and so will you." He speaks of peace and good will and the start of a long journey.

Cesar, wearing a barong Tagalog, a Filipino shirt, first thanks those who helped prove that "through nonviolent action in this nation and across the world, that social justice can be gotten."

"The strikers and the people involved in the struggle sacrificed a lot, sacrificed all of their worldly possessions," he says. "Ninety-five per cent of the strikers lost their homes and their cars. But I think that in losing those worldly possessions they found themselves, and they found that only through dedication, through serving mankind, and, in this case, serving the poor and those who were struggling for justice, only in that way could they really find themselves."

CESAR CHAVEZ RECALLS

After we and the growers had signed the contract, the reporters asked a lot of questions. They wanted to know what we were going to do about the Teamsters.

We hadn't made any plans on our next moves, but events already had taken the choice out of our hands. Despite our great victory, the very existence of the Union was again threatened.

Jacques Levy with Cesar Chavéz. Photo: © Bob Fitch.

Cesar Chavez, on top of truck, addresses lettuce workers outside a Salinas labor camp on July 28, 1970. But the spirit of Delano is absent. Photo: © Jacques Levy.

Marshall Ganz reports to Cesar Chavez in Salinas before one of the many farm worker rallies that were held in 1970. Photo: © Bob Fitch.

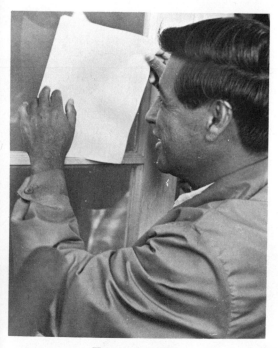

Locked out of the Freshpict office, Cesar Chavez holds up a sign reading, "I am here to be served the order. Cesar Chavez." In Salinas on August 11, 1970. Photo: © Jacques Levy.

Teamster William Grami and Cesar Chavez sign another jurisdictional pact in Salinas on August 12, 1970. Looking on are, left to right, Monsignor Roger Mahoney, *Catholic Monitor* editor Jerry Sherry, and Monsignor George Higgins. Photo: © Jacques Levy.

Taking time off from negotiations with Inter Harvest, Dolores Huerta speaks to some three thousand farm workers at a rally in Salinas August 23, 1970. Photo: © Jacques Levy.

Hoping to get arrested for violating a court injunction which the higher courts later found to be illegal, Cesar Chavez and other volunteers form a picket line at a Gonzales ranch on September 9, 1970, while a sheriff's deputy just watches. Photo: © Jacques Levy.

Cesar Chavez works at his battered desk in his secret office in Salinas. Photo: ©
Bob Fitch.

One of the many conferences between Fred Ross and Cesar Chavez during the
Salinas battle in 1970. Photo: © Jacques Levy.

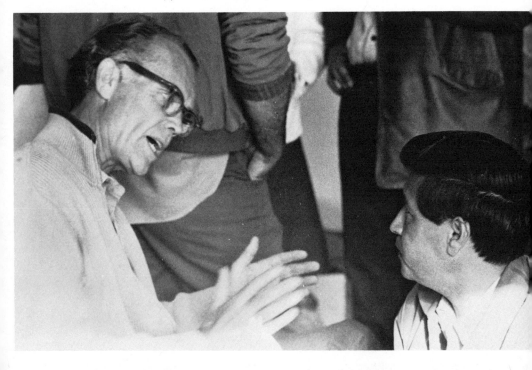

UFWOC negotiations with Freshpict and D'Arrigo held in Salinas in September 1970. The workers at the companies elected their own representatives to participate in the negotiations. At left is Dolores Huerta shown addressing representatives who are seated behind the table at right, facing the workers. Next to Mrs. Huerta is Irwin De Shettler, an AFL-CIO representative. Photo: © Jacques Levy.

Dolores Huerta and Cesar Chavez, backed by farm workers, hold a press conference to announce the start of the lettuce boycott on September 17, 1970. Photo: © Jacques Levy.

Seated on the floor in the hall of the Salinas courthouse, Cesar Chavez awaits the start of his trial for contempt of court with his wife Helen on December 4, 1970. Photo: © Jacques Levy.

Farm workers in the courtyard of the Salinas courthouse are told that Cesar Chavez has just been jailed for contempt of court on December 4, 1970. Photo: © Jacques Levy.

Ethel Kennedy, widow of Senator Robert F. Kennedy, marches to the Salinas jail to visit Cesar Chavez. Next to her is Dolores Huerta, while UFWOC Vice-President Larry Itliong holds her left arm. Photo: © Gene Daniels.

anuel Chavez stands toe to toe with an Im-
rial County deputy sheriff during the annual
elon strike in 1972. Each year the melon
ikes have become more effective, but growers
date have refused to negotiate. Photo: Cris
nchez.

Coretta King, widow of the Reverend Martin Luther King, Jr., comes to Phoenix on the nineteenth day of Cesar Chavez's Arizona fast in 1972. Chavez, seated in his armchair, was hospitalized the next day, but did not end his fast until five days later. Photo: © Sue Levy.

Cesar Chavez ends his twenty-four day fast on June 4, 1972, at a mass in Phoenix. Giving him comfort is folk singer Joan Baez. Photo: © Jacques Levy.

The Reverend Frank Plaisted reads a prayer while pickets kneel in front of a Tenneco vineyard in the Coachella Valley April 19, 1973. Deputies and Teamster guards look on. Then deputies arrested the minister and 134 pickets for violating an antipicketing injunction. Photo: © Jacques Levy.

Cesar Chavez takes a closer look at Teamsters sitting across the road on what UFW pickets called "the garbage truck" in the Coachella Valley. A few days later, men on the garbage truck stoned Chavez's car with twenty-pound rocks. Photo: © Jacques Levy.

Top AFL-CIO leaders on a fact-finding mission for George Meany visited Coachella Valley picket lines on June 8, 1973. Shown, left to right, with Cesar Chavez on a flat-bed truck addressing strikers are Albert Woll, the national AFL-CIO's general counsel; Joseph Keenan, secretary-treasurer of the International Brotherhood of Electrical Workers; John F. Henning, executive secretary-treasurer of the California AFL-CIO; and Paul Hall, President of the Seafarers International Union. Photo: © Jacques Levy.

In the spring and summer of 1973, Cesar Chavez traveled up and down the state of California spending much time talking to strikers whose contracts had been taken over by the Teamsters. Photo: © Jacques Levy.

Kern County Sheriff Charles Dodge patrols a picket line, while Cesar Chavez talks to strikers in the background. Photo: © Jacques Levy.

Defiant Lamont strikers in 1973 being carted off to jail in a paddy wagon. Photo: © Jacques Levy.

Frank Valenzuela, former mayor of Hollister, is attacked by Kern County deputies as he offers to calm Marta Rodriguez in front of the Giumarra ranch near Arvin. Photo: © Bob Fitch.

Beaten and maced by Kern County deputies are Frank Valenzuela and Marta Rodriguez, whom he had tried to help. Photo: © Bob Fitch.

Seventy-six-year-old Dorothy Day, editor of the *Catholic Worker*, waits to be arrested on a UFW picket line. Photo: © Bob Fitch.

Farm workers pass by Nagi Daifullah's casket in Delano on August 17, 1973. Dolores Huerta is at rear. Photo: © Bob Fitch.

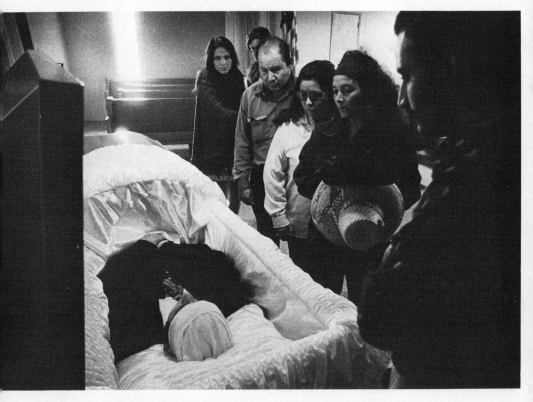

Senator Edward F. Kennedy addresses the UFW convention in Fresno on September 22, 1973. Photo: Courtesy of William Soltero.

UFW delegates at the Fresno Convention Center during the Union's constitutional convention on September 23, 1973. Photo: © Bob Fitch.

After being elected at the 1973 constitutional convention, the new UFW National Executive Board takes the oath of office. Left to right are, Cesar Chavez, Gilbert Padilla, Dolores Huerta, Philip Vera Cruz, Pete Velasco, Mack Lyons, Richard Chavez, Eliseo Medina, and Marshall Ganz. Photo: Frank Greer.

At their fiftieth wedding anniversary in San Jose on June 15, 1974, Juana and Librado Chavez pose with, left to right, Vicky, Cesar, Richard, Lenny, and Rita. Photo: © Jacques Levy.

In Covent Gardens, during his visit to Europe in September 1974 to promote the boycott of California grapes and iceberg lettuce, Cesar Chavez looks over some Italian grapes with British union officials. Photo: © Jacques Levy.

Pope Paul VI greets Cesar Chavez at a private audience on September 25, 1974. Looking on is Bishop Joseph Donnelly of Connecticut. Vatican photo by Felici.

Book VI

NEW FIELDS, OLD ENEMIES

July 30, 1970–November 1971

After nearly a century of fighting unions, lettuce growers stampeded to sign with the Teamsters. First to sign was a group in Salinas. Then others followed from King City and Santa Maria south to the Imperial Valley and east in the San Joaquin Valley and Arizona—growers that produce the bulk of the nation's lettuce, a good share of its strawberries, and a salad of other vegetables.

UFWOC's strategy was to retaliate with economic pressure, using both strikes and boycotts. As with DiGiorgio and Perelli-Minetti, Cesar Chavez believed that sufficient economic pressure on the growers would force them to rid themselves of the Teamsters with the same dispatch with which they had linked up with them. And he decided the biggest companies were the most vulnerable, particularly since they had easily identifiable trade-marks.

One of those was Inter Harvest; growers of lettuce, celery, and other crops the year around. Inter Harvest was owned by United Fruit, a company with a notorious reputation for its repressive policies in Latin America, where it owned vast banana plantations, if not entire countries. United Fruit now was part of the conglomerate United Brands.

Equally vulnerable to a boycott was Purex, a household word in bleaches. Purex owned the Freshpict Corporation, growers of lettuce and other crops. Then there was the Pic 'N Pac Corporation, largest strawberry growers in the world, which was owned by the S.S. Pierce Company, noted for its gourmet products.

Now the farm workers' struggle was stabbing deeper into the fiber of corporate America, a David unafraid to take on both the Goliaths of unions and conglomerates. Such temerity was bound to have repercussions.

But in the fields, there was no time to consider the consequences. Manuel Chavez, Fred Ross, Marshall Ganz, and others were working around the clock with the workers, organizing ranch committees on ranches with Teamster contracts, developing the union's strength, and then running the largest strike in California agricultural history.

On the other side, the growers and Teamsters were organizing countertactics. By now, the stakes were higher, both sides more sophisticated, and the battle more complex.

United Fruit chose one of its vice-presidents, W. W. Lauer, to handle UFWOC. Lauer, an expert in labor-management relations, appeared gentle; but his urbane exterior masked a toughness and nerves that never seemed to ruffle. He was a likable man with a dry wit, who championed his company's position with skill and the coolness of a chess player.

Heading the other growers' opposition was Herbert Fleming, a Westerner more comfortable among Kiwanians than Wall Streeters. Tall, sociable, and also quiet-spoken, he looked like a close-cropped, gray-haired collegian, an unlikely actor in a bitter labor battle. But Fleming was president of the Grower-Shipper Vegetable Association as well as president of his own lettuce-producing firm. And he had every intention of keeping the members of the association united.

As for the Teamsters, William Grami took personal charge of this campaign, setting up his headquarters in one of Salinas's most expensive motels, the Towne House. There he would be joined by a sinister figure, a rough, tough man named Ted Gonsalves, who ran the big Teamster cannery local in Modesto. And Gonsalves would fill the Towne House with tough, burly men spoiling for battle.

CHAPTER 1

Message at a Wedding

FROM JACQUES LEVY'S NOTEBOOK

Thursday, July 30, 1970—San Francisco Chronicle news items: The Council of California Growers announces that 80 percent of the Santa Maria area signed five-year contracts with the Teamsters yesterday. More than sixteen hundred workers are affected.

"Details on wages, working conditions, health and welfare programs, and unemployment insurance will be worked out in supplemental agreements for the various crops."

Governor Ronald Reagan charged Wednesday that it is "tragic" that the grape workers affected by grower contracts with Cesar Chavez's union "had no choice in determining whether or not they want to join the union."

"I would now hope that the workers would be given the right to determine—by secret ballot—whether they want to join or be represented by this union," Reagan said.

CESAR CHAVEZ RECALLS

I knew the whole row-crop industry had to be taken on. So Thursday, the day after the Delano growers signed, a four-day march to Salinas started from Greenfield in the south, Gilroy in the north, Aptos in the west, and Hollister in the east.

The question was, do we really represent the workers and, if we do, how do we manifest it? I had to get people involved in a large way and demonstrate it—but it had to be something that builds up, not just a rally.

The week before, I had set up a committee of workers and townspeople. Because I know the people, I knew a march would be the easiest and best way. The problem was that Salinas was in the middle of the valley. So the committee decided to have four marches converging on Salinas where they would march through town together for a big Sunday rally.

I visited the lines and marched for two or three hours, but in a couple of cases I had to get in the car and quit because I couldn't walk—my back hurt me so.

Friday night, when I spoke to five hundred farm workers in Watsonville, I challenged Reagan to set up elections. "UFWOC is willing to submit to this election immediately," I said. "Of late Reagan seems very concerned about farm workers' rights. Now he has a swell opportunity to demonstrate his interest."

And I repeated that if the growers didn't accept elections now, we would be unwilling to hold them a year later.

When the march ended Sunday, more than three thousand workers at the Salinas rally voted to strike and boycott if necessary. We hadn't made our plans yet, or decided who to go after. But I mentioned that there were three big companies that would be good boycott targets—Inter Harvest owned by United Fruit, Freshpict owned by Purex, and Pic 'N Pac owned by S.S. Pierce.

And I announced that we were moving our Union headquarters from Delano to Salinas.

FROM JACQUES LEVY'S NOTEBOOK

At the rally, Cesar accuses the Teamsters and growers of a "great treason against the aspirations of those men and women who have sacrificed their lives for so many years to make a few men rich in this valley.

"It's tragic that these men have not yet come to understand that we are in a new age, a new era," he says, "that no longer can a couple of white men sit together and write the destinies of all of the Chicanos and Filipino workers in this valley!"

The workers, massed by large crimson union banners bearing their companies' names, punctuate the meeting with cheers and cries of "Huelga!" Their singing vibrates with militancy. The spirit of Delano flares in Salinas.

Later in the afternoon, the executive board and a few others meet in a crowded bedroom at the downtown TraveLodge Motel. Some sit on the beds and others on the floor along the walls.

Cesar reports that the Fillmore citrus workers have agreed to call off their strike and wait their turn; that when Manuel Chavez talked to some two hundred strawberry workers in Santa Maria about the new Teamster contracts, they struck and joined UFWOC; and that 659 workers signed UFWOC authorization cards at the rally today.

But they face serious problems. It will cost a hundred twenty-five thousand dollars a week to pay strikers twenty-five dollars a week strike benefits, or about seven hundred fifty thousand dollars for five or six weeks.

"Strike now, pay later," he jokes before assigning several persons to find funds. He will attend the AFL-CIO Executive Board meeting in Chicago Wednesday, where Kircher may make a pitch for support.

Marshall Ganz, looking more like a plump storekeeper than a union organizer, enthusiastically reports what he has learned about Inter Harvest and chuckles through his moustache at the company's vulnerability to a boycott.

The company was set up in 1968 when United Fruit, known nationwide for its Chiquita-brand bananas, bought nine Salinas-based produce firms. They now own twenty-two thousand acres in California and Arizona. Not only are Chiquita bananas famous, but the company has just spent millions promoting the Chiquita label for its lettuce, celery, and artichokes.

Sixty percent of United Fruit's profit is in bananas, which are highly vulnerable to boycotts. "They ripen quickly and generate heat as they ripen. If a banana ship is not unloaded quickly, it can blow up."

"United Fruit's headquarters are in Boston where we have strong support," Marshall laughs. "And the company owns fifty ships, eleven of which were rented for use in Vietnam—a perfect target for the Peace Movement."

A few joke at the prospects, but Cesar's mind is on crucial questions. Should the union risk an election? Can it win? Should the union now make that a major issue?

"You have to understand that if we lose the elections," he says somberly, while standing in the middle of the room, "the only honorable thing to do is not to try again. If the Teamsters win, then we have to give up in that area for good, not contest it or try again later. It's all or nothing."

He looks hard at Marshall, Fred Ross, Dolores, and the others in turn. Finally he asks for a vote. They all support elections.

After more discussion, Inter Harvest is chosen as the first target.

CESAR CHAVEZ RECALLS

It was hectic. There was more work being done on more fronts in that period than at any time in the history of the Union, but I wasn't feeling the pinch as much as at the beginning of the Delano strike because, by this time, we had developed a lot of organizers.

The amazing thing was that even though we swore we couldn't spread ourselves that thin, the vacuum was filled. It forced the Union to develop more leadership and to give people more responsibilities.

We had to take care of all the grape contracts and all our new members. Then I assigned organizers to other lettuce-growing areas like Santa Maria, Oxnard, Brentwood, and the major areas in Colorado and Arizona, because, while Salinas was producing maybe 95 percent of all the iceberg lettuce at that time, we wanted to be prepared in case of a strike or an election.

We didn't fully understand in the beginning that we were involved in all of Salinas, not only lettuce, but tomatoes, strawberries, artichokes, celery, almost everything in sight in the valley. We had to deal with those workers coming to us, pressuring us to support them in a strike. Santa Maria, too, was all up in arms.

I was frantically trying to raise money. After we got the idea of borrowing it, we contacted the Franciscans, who then contacted other religious orders. Over a period of time I think we finally borrowed three hundred eighty thousand dollars which we were able to pay back in eighteen months.

We also started putting a little pressure on United Fruit. LeRoy Chatfield presented his famous preboycott stage, calling in the Chiquita distributors and outlining the plan we had developed for a world-wide boycott of Chiquita bananas. I knew that if we ever started a public boycott against them, it would be very hard to turn off—too many disliked the company. But there were other ways of applying pressure.

For example, one of LeRoy's friends, who purchased produce for a two hundred-store supermarket chain, told Jim Pollis, the Western region United Fruit distributor, that he would stop buying Chiquita products when the boycott started.

Then I asked LeRoy to get Anna Puharich to call on Eli Black.

In our research, we found out that Black, a former rabbinical student, was the president of United Brands which had recently acquired United Fruit in a financial coup.

LeRoy first met Anna in 1968 in New York when she was executive director of the foundation Spectemur Agendo, and I met her when I went to Bobby Kennedy's funeral. By 1970 she was working full time with us.

Well, she met with Maurice Kaplan, the chairman of the Executive Committee of United Brands. I'm not sure what Kaplan expected when he was asked to meet with one of our representatives, but I'm sure he didn't expect to met someone as sophisticated as Anna and as beautiful, or that they had a number of mutual friends.

Anna explained the entire background of the Teamster affair and got Kaplan's home phone number, so the Union could contact him before we did anything.

ANNA PUHARICH RECALLS

When I called Mr. Black, they told me he was in Europe and gave me his assistant, Burke Wright, who suggested we meet the next week.

"No, because it's happening right now," I said. And I knew I had to put in a little something extra; so I said, "When I left Salinas, they were having a meeting about boycotting Chiquita."

As soon as I said that, he said, "May I have your phone number, and I'll get back to you."

About a half hour later they called back and said that the chief executive, Maury Kaplan, would like to see me the next day.

Wright and Kaplan got put off completely when they saw me. I don't know what they expected, but they didn't expect me, and they said so.

"We understand that you guys sitting back here don't know what's happening in Salinas, because you have people there you trust," I said, explaining the situation. "We don't want to boycott, really, but what can we do? I mean what would you do, if you were in our place? Especially because Chiquita is so easy, it would be a natural! I mean you, as businessmen, know that. That's how it is." They listened.

Maury Kaplan was funny—by this time he was calling me Anna. He said, "You know, Anna, our guys in Salinas know all about lettuce, and they're very good. But it's probably true they haven't had their heads out of a head of lettuce for years."

Then Kaplan called Black in Europe and explained everything to him on the phone. Black told him, "Investigate immediately, and if it's true what she's saying, then let's sit down and let's work, do everything we can to negotiate and sign with them. We'll worry about fighting the Teamsters later."

Later Black and Kaplan told me about how they had been boycotting grapes. Their children were in college and were very into it, too, especially Black's. When Black brought home to the table what was happening, I mean his children apparently—really! Like he'd better sign!"

They never expected it to hit them.

CESAR CHAVEZ RECALLS

I flew out to the AFL-CIO meeting in Chicago to get the endorsement of the board. Kircher had talked to George Meany, and it looked like there was going to be a strong statement supporting us and condemning the Teamsters.

Then someone told Teamster President Frank Fitzsimmons this was about to take place. Fitzsimmons called Meany and said, "Don't do anything. We're going to get out of this mess. We don't want any part of it." So the Council held up.

Bill Kircher was really upset. He and I knew that the Teamsters were stalling, but there was no way to tell Meany that they were. Meany didn't want to get into an unnecessary fight unless he had to.

While I was in Chicago, I met with most of our boycotters from throughout the East.

"Are we ever going back to the farm workers?" they asked me, "or are we going to be here forever?"

I told them I thought the grape boycott would be over pretty soon, and they could all come home by the end of the month.

We had a commitment to them, and we had to live up to it. But I was aware that that meant dismantling our most powerful weapon and replacing the boycotters with new, inexperienced volunteers.

FROM JACQUES LEVY'S NOTEBOOK

August 4, 1970—Governor Ronald Reagan today turned down Cesar Chavez's challenge to set up elections for farm workers in the Salinas and Santa Maria areas.

In answer to a question at his regular weekly press conference, Reagan said, "I'm a little puzzled by his sudden conversion to a belief in balloting for the workers now with regard to another union in another area when he has denied this for the people he's been organizing in the San Joaquin Valley. I personally believe in the right of workers every place to vote . . . and I just don't think that it is something that you can decide to have for one group . . . and not agree to the rightness of it all over."

CESAR CHAVEZ RECALLS

Soon there were widespread work stoppages in Salinas, Santa Maria, and Oxnard that lasted one, two, or three hours, or one afternoon. Workers would go home, or put up a picket line and then take it off. Most of the stoppages were spontaneous, but we had done an awful lot of agitating and organizing already. When Teamsters came, trying to sign up workers, they would rebel and respond with slowdowns and walkouts.

Most of the stoppages took place in the Santa Maria area, where Manuel was. He was a little more advanced than we were in Salinas because of his outstanding job in the border area over the past two years. Had that not happened, we would have been dead, but now we had a base and a membership.

Then growers started firing workers for refusing to sign up with the Teamsters, so we went after them. The people wanted to strike, but I kept holding Manuel back until all the farms were firing people. The more people got a taste of the pressure on them, the easier it would be for us to organize. And we were just not ready for a strike. It takes a long time to get ready, to know people, and to train them. Besides, the expectation of a strike is very damaging to the grower.

On Friday, just two days after my Chicago meeting with the boycotters, about 150 workers at Freshpict were fired for refusing to join the Teamsters. We hadn't thought of Freshpict as the company to go after first, but they made a target of themselves. The workers met that night at a little grocery store on William Street in Salinas and voted to strike. Saturday morning, more than three hundred walked off their jobs. By the start of the next week, the strike had spread to Freshpict ranches from Castroville to King City.

Teamster Bill Grami had been after us for a meeting for a couple of days, but we decided to let him stew while we organized the workers and showed him our support. The day before the

Freshpict strike, he tried to call both Dolores and me, then reached Jerry Cohen, who set up a meeting for the next week. But Grami called back after the Freshpict strike started, saying he felt that it would be important if we could meet sooner.

"Like when?" Jerry asked.

"Like right now," Grami answered.

Jerry told him I was at Eloise's wedding in Delano.

Eloise, we call her Tota, was my second daughter to get married. Both were married when there was a lot of pressure on me, so Helen had been after me every single day the last two months reminding me, "Don't forget Tota gets married on August 8!"

"I won't forget."

But she'd leave me notes. "Just make sure!" She knew I was up to my head in work.

When I started walking Tota down the aisle, I saw Jerry in one of the pews about the middle of the church. He looked up at me and motioned with his eyes that he wanted to see me.

I took Tota to the altar, came back, and knelt by Jerry.

"Guess what. Grami and Andrade want to talk to us about Salinas."

"What do they want, just to talk or do they want to deal?" I whispered.

"Well, they said they wanted to talk."

"Call back and ask them. If they're in a mood for dealing, we'll come. If they just want to talk, I can't leave my daughter's wedding. Tell them I can meet with them tomorrow."

By the time Jerry returned, we were already out of church.

"They want to deal, and it has to be done tonight. They're meeting us halfway. They're waiting for us at Paso Robles."

"Oh, my God!"

After about an hour at the wedding reception, I called Helen aside and told her what the problem was. She looked pretty upset. She didn't say, "Don't go," she just said, "Can you stay a little longer? At least until you can dance with Tota."

So we stayed and ate, the presents were opened, and the cake cut. When the dance started, Tota danced first with her husband, then I danced the second piece with her.

After that Dolores, Manuel, Jerry, Richard, and I got in the cars and raced over to the Black Oak Inn to meet with Grami and Pete Andrade, who headed the Teamsters' cannery division.

CHAPTER 2

A Secret Letter

CESAR CHAVEZ RECALLS

Every time we met with Grami he acted as if nothing has ever happened before, he was just so damn friendly. Well, we did the same thing. I wasn't really mad at him. I was very relaxed, and I think all our side was. But Pete Andrade was very tense.

Grami started by saying that he didn't think we would have any problems with the jurisdiction, that they definitely wanted to get out and wanted to renew our jurisdiction agreement.

By this time, I didn't trust them, but I'll always negotiate. We didn't ask why they broke the pact they signed with us after Perelli-Minetti. We didn't want to appear like cry babies in front of them.

In his clever way, I understood Grami to say the machines would be no problem, and all the things we thought would be problems wouldn't be any problem. The only thing he was worried about was processing going into the field.

Dolores asked him for an example, and he mentioned there were now experiments with a machine that picks tomatoes, washes them, makes juice, and cans it out in the field.

We said we would agree to disagree on that one, so it was put aside. I was only half-listening, trying to get behind them, trying to analyze what they were trying to say. Because they weren't really saying what they wanted to say.

Grami tried in the beginning to get us to call off the strikes, but we told him that we couldn't. We said that if we saw that there was some definite movement toward a solution, we might.

337

We tried to get him to get the growers to recognize our Union, but he said that he couldn't because there were a lot of independent local growers that didn't like us at all and would resist us. But he thought he might be able to get some of the large corporations.

He said he didn't want the Teamster contract used as a springboard for negotiations. We answered that we felt that once they were out, they had nothing to say about what we negotiated. They finally agreed, but said this was going to become a problem.

In his own very clever way, Grami was telling us that if we accepted their contracts, then we'd be able to get recognition.

We finally proposed that the bishops' committee call a meeting of the three parties—the Teamsters, the growers, and us—to resolve the matter, and Grami agreed.

After our talks ended, Andrade relaxed a little. He told us about his early days of organizing in Salinas, and a funny story about a guy who wanted to shoot him. Pete is always telling stories about guns. This theme seems to go with him. He said his favorite pastime was to shoot insulators on power poles with a hand gun.

Finally Manuel asked him, "Will you please tell your guy over in Santa Maria to buzz off. I've had diarrhea for the last two weeks!"

MARSHALL GANZ RECALLS

Monday morning, while we were contemplating what place we should strike next, I got a call from Pic 'N Pac, the largest strawberry grower in the country.

It seems that a car had gone by with a loudspeaker saying, "Huelga Freshpict! Huelga Freshpict!" So the committee at La Posada, the trailer camp where many of the Pic 'N Pac workers lived, took that to mean huelga and wouldn't let any worker out of the camp. The whole La Posada—seven to eight hundred people—was just shut.

We went there and told them to come back in a couple of hours with all the other Pic 'N Pac workers. So they went out all over the place to pull people out of the fields who came from town, from Soledad, and other places, and brought them back for a meeting.

Cesar talked to them, and they voted to go out on strike.

Then the workers from Oshita came in Tuesday and said they had to strike, that they were being forced to join the Teamsters.

We said we weren't sure whether we should authorize that strike or not, because we weren't sure how well organized they had their workers, and we weren't authorizing strikes unless we saw about 80 percent of the work force organized and ready to come out.

So they came in that night and pleaded for authorization. It was the following morning that the Oshita strike started.

FROM JACQUES LEVY'S NOTEBOOK

Monday, August 10, 1970—Except for his visit to La Posada—where no one guessed how badly his back hurts him—Cesar stays in bed at the Salinas apartment a friend loaned him. "I must have a candy back, it seems to melt with the sun," he complains. But he doesn't let up on his work.

During the day, Dolores and Jerry negotiate with Bill Grami. That night the talks collapse.

Dolores returns to the apartment, unhappy with her performance. UFWOC acted too belligerently, she feels, and she had no planned strategy. She says Grami tried to trick her into a no-strike agreement when she thought she was approving a news release.

When Grami got a phone call—which was often—he would say, "I'll call you back," then hang up and say, "Another grower."

Dolores's words tumble out. "Grami kept talking about 'protecting the industry,' and I kept repeating, 'Unions represent workers, not industry.'"

When she tells Cesar she didn't like the way things went, he answers lightly that the Teamsters will call tomorrow.

"What have we got to lose? We can beat them, even if it takes twenty years. All it takes is work, and we know how to do that. We're not afraid of work," Cesar reassures her.

Dolores is looking for outside pressure to put on the Teamsters. They can't think of any, but Cesar is very cool.

CESAR CHAVEZ RECALLS

Tuesday, at a meeting at our new headquarters on South Wood Street, I told the people how, on Saturday, a local judge in a local court issued a temporary restraining order to stop all picketing at Freshpict without notifying the Union or giving us a chance to present our case. That's pretty much what they do down South. I said I could not obey this unconstitutional act, and I was starting a fast to protest the order.

That fast was not like a spiritual fast. It was mostly because I was distressed, and I needed strength. Because the Teamsters had broken their agreement, there was a lot of hatred building up. It wasn't clear in my mind what I would do in case violence broke out on our side. I also wanted to try and get the proper perspective of what was happening in Salinas.

That afternoon, when word came that the Court of Appeals in San Francisco had turned down our appeal on the Freshpict injunction, I decided we'd better put a little heat on the company and publicize the restraining order.

Since I knew that Freshpict was looking for me to serve me with the injunction order, I thought of going to their office and saying, "Here I am, serve me." Before leaving the office, I told the press where I was going.

FROM JACQUES LEVY'S NOTEBOOK

Tuesday, August 11, 1970—No movie director could have improved on the scene.

Cesar and Jerry Cohen get in my car, and I make a dash for the Freshpict headquarters. But I make a wrong turn, and the press arrives before we do.

When Cesar walks through the crowd of reporters, TV cameras, and farm workers to stride into enemy territory, he finds the door locked. A few worried-looking secretaries stare out through closed windows.

Cesar calmly borrows a yellow sheet from Jerry's legal pad and writes, "I am here to be served the order. Cesar Chavez." Then he presses the message against the glass front door.

When nothing happens, he shows the message to the TV cameras, sits on the steps. and waits, a lone still figure sitting quietly among the milling newsmen.

"They've looked for me all over. Now they run away," he plaintively tells a reporter.

The police arrive, then Freshpict President Howard Leach. Jerry suggests that Leach serve the court order, but Leach answers that he can't, as he is a party to the suit. Politely he declines Jerry's offer to waive objection on that point.

Policeman Larry Myers also refuses to serve the order. That's the sheriff's office job, he says.

The court order takes on the aspect of a poisoned potion that no one wants to serve Cesar, and the TV cameras keep running, much to Leach's embarrassment. "If you'd told us you were coming, we'd have been ready," he tells Jerry.

Finally Leach gets someone in an adjoining business to serve Cesar. But as the cameras whir, Jerry gets Leach to sign as a witness that the order is properly served.

CESAR CHAVEZ RECALLS

While we were engaged with Freshpict, Monsignor George Higgins was busy, too. As none of the bishops were available, he was representing the bishops' committee and arranged for the Teamsters and us to get together again.

The talks started about 11:00 P.M. when our attorneys, Jerry Cohen and Bill Carder, met with Grami and Higgins. It was dawn before they reached agreement—another jurisdictional pact.

The Teamsters agreed we had jurisdiction over all field workers, and Grami agreed secretly to get out. We asked Grami to go to the ranchers who had signed up with the Teamsters to get them to negotiate with us.

In turn, he asked that we hold up the strike for a six-day period so that the ranchers would be able to tear up their old contracts and get together on the new one.

We also came to an understanding that if progress was being made during those six days, we would be willing to extend the strike moratorium another four days.

If there were any disagreements over the pact, the dispute was to be referred to the bishops' committee.

JERRY COHEN RECALLS

There were a whole series of secret agreements that were signed that Grami would not put into the pact for political and legal reasons.

I got on the phone to Cesar, and he said, "Look, we're in a fight. If Grami is being untrustworthy, we're still going to be in a fight. But if he won't put it into the agreement, get what you can get, any way you can get it."

So those secret agreements went to the extent that the Teamsters committed themselves to giving us individual rescissions of their contracts and to helping us in organizational activities. They said they had guys who could help us, and they agreed to honor our picket lines.

MONSIGNOR GEORGE HIGGINS RECALLS

Bishop Joseph Donnelly was not able to come, so Monsignor Roger Mahoney and I met in Grami's suite upstairs at the Towne House with Jerry Cohen, Bill Carder, and Bill Grami.

For the first couple of hours, we kind of sat there as witnesses while they batted it around. After several hours, they finally agreed on the terms of the jurisdictional agreement which they agreed would be put in writing in lawyers' language.

That wasn't too hard to get. The Teamsters must have been prepared to give that when they came. The problem was what to do about these existing lettuce contracts.

They finally agreed that the side agreement concerning the existing pacts would be put in a separate letter given to Monsignor Mahoney and myself for safekeeping. There would be no copies of that kept, and it would be kept secret.

That agreement was that the Teamsters would use their best efforts to get the growers to ask that the contracts be rescinded within a period of six days plus four—the four to be granted by me at my discretion if I thought they needed more time.

Now only history will be able to determine whether the Teamsters used their best efforts.

CESAR CHAVEZ RECALLS

We were trying to get the Teamsters out, at least publicly, so that, in the minds of people, there would not be two unions fighting on jurisdiction, but one Union fighting the growers.

And while we'd had enough experience with Grami to believe that he wasn't going to honor the agreement, we had nothing to lose by signing it. If we didn't, the AFL-CIO and the bishops would feel that we were in bad faith, and we wanted to keep them as allies.

On the other side, some people feared that if Grami didn't come through, we were losing time by stopping the strike. But we always say that we have more time than money, and I wasn't really concerned if we lost a week or ten days.

I reported our agreement to the workers that morning, and they agreed with it. They voted to stop their strike against Freshpict and the others for six days.

I also told the workers I was going to continue my fast until we saw how the ranchers reacted.

When the bishops' committee called a press conference at the Towne House later that day, so that Grami and I could sign the pact, I made another pitch urging that the growers let the workers decide which union should represent them.

"We're telling the employers that we don't want to get into another prolonged dispute similar to the Delano thing," I told the press. "And we're hopeful that they will want to meet with us and see if we can resolve the issues."

But there are so many times when we speak, and the other side does not listen. As it turned out, the moratorium turned into an intense period of action and intrigue.

CHAPTER 3

A Fast That Failed

FROM JACQUES LEVY'S NOTEBOOK

Wednesday, August 12, 1970—Cesar's been in great pain for days now. His fast continues, and after attending the press conference at the Towne House, he returns to bed, exhausted, having been awake all night keeping in touch with Jerry Cohen. He quickly falls asleep, but Marion Moses, his nurse, wakes him when LeRoy Chatfield calls from Los Angeles.

Cesar opens his eyes, weakly answers a question, and falls asleep again, the phone drifting from his head to the pillow. Marion pushes the receiver back to his ear, and he talks briefly to LeRoy before falling into a deep sleep again.

LeRoy, who has set up a meeting in Salinas for 9:00 tonight with Will Lauer, United Fruit's vice-president of corporate industrial relations, flies in and reports to Cesar before the session.

Since Anna Puharich had given him Maurice Kaplan's home phone, LeRoy called the chairman of United Brands' Executive Committee at midnight to tell him the strike will start at 5:00 A.M. Kaplan, hoping to stop the strike, tried to call his negotiator, Lauer, and both the president of United Brands and the president of Inter Harvest, but couldn't reach any of them. Kaplan then called LeRoy back to say he was still trying, that the company wanted to settle quickly, and Lauer would be given two weeks to settle with UFWOC.

"About an hour later, Lauer calls and asks, 'You want to speak to me?' cool as a cucumber," LeRoy tells Cesar. "He tried to stall the meeting until tomorrow, but I said, 'No, it must be tonight.'"

LeRoy also has learned that United Fruit is taking every possible step to protect itself against a boycott. In every port where their ships land, they have notified every union local involved in the handling of bananas that the company expects them to honor their contracts to the letter, or they will be sued.

"That must have been a major logistic enterprise," LeRoy says in awe, as so many ports and unions handle the fruit from ship to supermarket.

At the strategy session before the meeting, Cesar is wide awake, his mind keen. Jerry, Marshall Ganz, and LeRoy gather around his bed.

"Monsignor Higgins has set up a 4:00 P.M. meeting tomorrow with growers," Cesar says. "Whatever we tell Lauer tonight is done to influence the meeting of the growers tomorrow. They're not going to do anything until then. Remind them we have not struck or boycotted them."

Lauer must be told that Inter Harvest is the leader of the industry—"You got them to sign with the Teamsters, now get them to sign with us. We want you to move fast. There is tremendous pressure from the workers to strike," Cesar rehearses the approach.

"Come in tougher than hell! 'Either you have good relations with us, or all hell breaks loose!' Keep asking, 'How come you did it for the Teamsters?' "

The minimum demands must be rescission of the Teamster contract, recognition of UFWOC, and a contract. Cesar agrees elections are no problem. But they must get in writing from Lauer that the company and its supervisors won't campaign against the union. "And they must police their guys themselves."

Fortified by the strategy session, the union team drives to the Highway Center Lodge at the south end of Salinas, off Freeway 101. They find Lauer and two other company men sitting in an upstairs bedroom, their pressed business suits and ties in sharp contrast to the wrinkled sport shirts and slacks worn by the negotiating team. The turbulent world of union organizing is face to face with the polished urbanity of corporate life.

"Now that the Teamsters have withdrawn, UFWOC is interested in dealing with United Fruit," LeRoy starts off after the introductions.

But Lauer challenges the premise. "The Teamsters have not rescinded the contract," he says, and he has been unsuccessful in trying to reach Grami. He only is here because LeRoy insisted on meeting tonight, but he is not prepared to negotiate until he meets with Grami. His voice is soft, cultured, masking toughness.

Jerry gets angry, accusing Lauer of playing games. "Grami is at the Towne House. I just came from a meeting with Grami in which he said he'd grant a rescission to anybody."

Lauer parries the thrust. He can't find Grami. He tried. Then turning to the attack, he wants to know where Cesar is. He only agreed to this meeting because it was requested by Chavez, and he wants to meet him. "This is not the meeting that was promised."

After the first mild skirmish, Lauer explores the scope of the proposed negotiations. They seem to disagree on everything. On elections, the union says they must be supervised by the bishops. Lauer doesn't object, but wants the Federal Mediation Service included. He says it would be easier for some of the other growers to agree.

"We'd like other growers involved, and your leadership would help," Marshall pushes, sensing an opening.

"Not now! Not today," Lauer replies. "The very fact we're meeting with you doesn't make us very popular. You do have a problem. I don't know the best way to handle it. There is great opposition—most passionately so—to your union among some growers. I doubt we have influence now."

Marshall attacks. "Who brought in the Teamsters?"

Lauer denies United Fruit did. "We didn't take the lead. The Teamsters came in on their own."

When LeRoy challenges that, Lauer maintains his position.

Marshall makes another thrust, complaining that many workers are being intimidated by Inter Harvest supervisors. Robert Nunes, Inter Harvest vice-president, asks for details and promises to take care of it.

"I assume your union will withhold strikes and boycotts," Lauer asks. Each attack brings a counterattack. Lauer may be outnumbered, but he is not outclassed.

"For a time," Jerry answers.

"How long?"

When he is told six days, Lauer objects. "I think it'll take several weeks, even with good faith." He estimates it actually will take two months.

"That's a lot of bullshit!" explodes Marshall. "You signed with the Teamsters like, boom!" Two months will take it past harvest time. "That's just unreal to our workers. We have to represent your workers!"

It won't take long to negotiate "if we explain what our contract means, and not Allan Grant," Jerry needles Lauer, telling him the union only needed two days with John Giumarra with the workers involved in the negotiations.

Lauer remains tough. They expect to use the Teamster agreement as the basis for negotiations. "It has substantial economic concessions, though I'm not suggesting the wording should be the same."

"It's an insult to tell us we're going to start with a sweetheart contract as a basis for negotiating," snaps Jerry.

"You can make life hard or easy," Lauer answers softly. "The fact is the growers identified themselves with wage changes that are going to cost a lot of dough. You're going to get tremendous resistance. You've already seen it!"

"Some of the growers are preparing suits against the Teamsters. And there will be suits against us," he says.

The talk briefly returns to elections, with Marshall asking whether they can be held either Saturday or Monday. Lauer wants to get the Teamster rescission first.

Lauer is then asked to get Freshpict, Pic 'N Pac, and Oshita in line. LeRoy says Purex President William Tincher received ten thousand protest telegrams and is coming tomorrow.

"Don't hold your breath," Lauer warns.

When the meeting ends at 10:30, the team goes back to report to Cesar.

"They're trapped in their own cesspool and the Teamsters," Cesar comments.

CESAR CHAVEZ RECALLS

We were begining to apply the heat on Purex, too, and their president, William Tincher, really blew.

LeRoy made calls to some of the stores telling them a Purex boycott might be next. Of course, the word got back to Tincher. Then we picketed his office in Los Angeles. He took it very personally. He thought what we were doing was underhanded, illegal, and immoral. But what he had done about recognizing the Teamsters against the will of the Freshpict workers never crossed his mind. So we gave him a little reminder, more than anything else.

He ended up flying to Salinas.

FROM JACQUES LEVY'S NOTEBOOK

Thursday, August 13, 1970—Fifteen minutes before the growers are scheduled to meet, Jerry Cohen and Marshall Ganz return from a meeting with Tincher and Freshpict President Howard Leach.

As Cesar lies in bed, weak, his head aching, Jerry describes how Tincher was so upset, his body shook as he screamed, with a Southern accent, about the boycott and said he would never negotiate with a gun at his head. Tincher wants the boycott stopped in exchange for one meeting.

Cesar remains silent a few minutes then suggests, "How about the suit?"

Both Marshall and Jerry jump. That's a perfect counter, they agree. Jerry goes to the phone and calls Leach. "We'll call all the boycotters and tell them to stop all activities for six days, if you'll cancel the restraining order, the suit, and the charges against us." A number of pickets already have been cited for violating Freshpict's injunction.

"Our boycotters are very angry about the lost jobs and the citations," Jerry goes on. He asks that the company reinstate the workers who were fired, and that there be a meeting in a day or so.

Leach answers that he will make the union proposal known at the growers' meeting.

Shortly after the phone call, someone comes in with a copy of the Teamster contract wage rates. Cesar looks at them in disbelief. "The dirty bastards!" he exclaims softly.

Then he and Marshall set up meetings for the next three nights with workers in each of the crops to determine their contract demands and needs. They want their proposals ready should negotiations start.

CESAR CHAVEZ RECALLS

Before I knew the new Teamster wage rates, I remember teasing the workers, asking, "How much do you think the Teamsters are going to get?"

And they answered, "Well, even though we know they're crooks, at the worst they would at least get five cents increase a year."

Then we learned they had accepted a half a cent a year increase, only two and a half cents increase in the piece rates in five years. Of course, when we told the workers that, they just exploded. From then on, organizing was just like taking candy away from a baby.

Just learning that the Teamsters signed their contract before negotiating the wage rates was like putting the frosting on the cake. It made it obvious that this was just an out-and-out conspiracy with the growers to form a company union. Who in the world would sign a contract without wages.

We couldn't believe how crass they were, or how dumb, leaving their flank with the workers completely open. But then, that was the only way they could get a contract. Either you have the company, or you have the workers. You can't have both. So it wasn't hard to turn the workers against them, to have them understand what was happening.

The day after we signed the jurisdictional pact, growers from El Centro and the San Joaquin Valley, as well as Salinas met with Grami and Higgins for about ninety minutes. Herb Fleming, the president of the Grower-Shipper Vegetable Association and head of one of the large Salinas companies, was to try to get power of attorney from all the growers with Teamster contracts by Tuesday, when the six-day strike moratorium ran out.

The only thing that I knew about Fleming was that he was visible only through the media. We hadn't had any direct dealings with him, though we would have many later.

As I recall, the report came back to us that Grami told the growers something to the effect that the pact doesn't really mean anything. Grami is very good at double-talking.

And during the six-day moratorium, the growers and the Teamsters still were forcing the workers to sign up, threatening to fire them if they didn't, and even firing some of them.

FROM JACQUES LEVY'S NOTEBOOK

Friday, August 14, 1970—The fourth day of his fast, Cesar has cramps throughout his body and is so weak he can't stand by himself. His weight has dropped 14 pounds to 148, leaving his face strangely thin. As he lies in bed, knees up, his eyes closed, he looks ten years younger. Beside the bed are two books about Gandhi and the Nuevo Testamento.

During the morning, Jerry Cohen, Marshall Ganz and Larry Itliong, who have been up all night, report that Purex still has not agreed to drop its suit; so Cesar calls LeRoy Chatfield to put on more heat.

LeRoy sends pickets to forty-seven Thrifty stores in the Los Angeles area and talks to one Thrifty and three Purex shareholders who are sympathetic. Later Thrifty's president calls Tincher to say that if Purex's labor problems aren't resolved, Thrifty will shop elsewhere, a meaningful threat since Thrifty has more than three hundred stores.

Although Cesar must drink three quarts of water a day, he hasn't been doing so and gives Marion Moses a hard time when she brings him a glass.

"Get on your knees," he teases the nurse.

"Bullshit!" she snaps. And Cesar drinks the water complaining that it tastes awful.

Someone asks him if his fast will again last twenty-five days. "I'll be dead halfway through that," he smiles weakly.

Later that afternoon, Dr. Jerome Lackner arrives from San Jose, a paradoxical sight in his conservative grey business suit complete with vest, his ferocious Zapata moustache, and his peace and Huelga buttons on both his vest and jacket.

Dr. Lackner, who treated Cesar during the Delano fast, is shocked at Cesar's condition. The fast only started Tuesday after a glass of milk and two slices of cantaloupe for breakfast, but Cesar now is so weak his voice is hardly audible. His skin has an unhealthy palor, and as he lies in bed with his eyes closed, it's hard to tell if he is breathing.

Dr. Lackner says he is much sicker after four days than he was after two or three weeks of the Delano fast. "As far as I'm concerned, if I believed in force and violence, it would be ended right now!" he says. But he knows Cesar won't follow his advice.

CESAR CHAVEZ RECALLS

Sometimes you must withstand pressures from your friends and your family as well as from your enemies. And when it comes to fasting, I don't negotiate. Once I'm on a fast, I'm on a different level. Patience is infinite. I could say no and no and no a thousand times and not get sick about saying no.

Some people have died from fasting in fifteen days, some in twenty, but I don't know if they died because they were unable to assess the situation. Yet you're not afraid of that, either. Maybe what happens is you go on a fast, and get feeling so great you're not even afraid of death.

However, I could tell I could not last much longer, so I broke the fast on Sunday, the sixth day, with semita, the Mexican bread of the poor, at a small mass we held in the parking lot behind Union headquarters.

The fast was a flop. It backfired. Generally when I go on a fast I develop amazing vitality. But I was worn out, and I think I was too preoccupied with what was going on. So the whole idea of coming back with a lot of vitality just didn't work. I went to a Franciscan retreat near San Juan Bautista to recuperate.

Although I was isolated there, I could still remain in contact. I was getting about twenty calls a day.

CHAPTER 4

"The True
Teamster Position"

CESAR CHAVEZ RECALLS

On Monday, Jerry Cohen, Dolores Huerta, and Marshall Ganz met separately with Freshpict and United Fruit to try to set up the ground rules for negotiations. They got nowhere with Freshpict.

As for United Fruit, Lauer told us he couldn't understand the Teamsters' position. When he gave Bill Grami a written proposal asking to have their contract rescinded, Grami told him he would take it to the Teamsters' attorney.

"I smell a hang-up," Will Lauer said.

FROM JACQUES LEVY'S NOTEBOOK

Tuesday, August 18, 1970—This is the last day of the six-day moratorium, a day of such intense maneuvering it is hard to assess the situation.

This morning Bill Kircher asks Larry Itliong to get the boycotters home. Apparently there are repercussions within the AFL-CIO to their activities against either United Fruit or Purex. But Larry will stall.

When the growers and Teamsters meet with Monsignor George

352

Higgins from 9:00 to noon, everyone just assumes the moratorium must last ten days, even though there's been no progress.

At 12:35, the union meets with United Fruit's Will Lauer and Monsignor Higgins, who says there are "very severe" problems among the growers. Some not only want legal action taken, but they want Higgins out of the picture.

"Even though we get a release from the Teamsters," Lauer says, "we still take a risk of a suit from other growers. We're willing to take that risk." But the Teamsters still haven't given United Fruit a rescission.

The constant reference to suits if any grower gives up his Teamster contract suggests some secret agreement would be broken, but Lauer does not explain, and no one asks him.

About an hour later, hoping to find out just what the "true Teamster position" is, Jerry Cohen and Dolores Huerta decide to see Bill Grami. My curiosity to learn how he walks the tightrope is greater than my reluctance to have him aware of my project. So I join them.

More than fourteen years before, Grami and I were on friendly terms when he first came to Sonoma County to organize the Sebastopol apple canneries.

At that time, as a reporter for the Press Democrat, I was covering Grami's activities. I thought him to be one of the young Turks in the Teamsters—well-educated, anti-Hoffa, anticorruption.

Then, after he won the cannery strikes and took over Local 980, throwing out the secretary-treasurer and his wife who had been entrenched in that local for years, an incident occurred that I never forgot.

I was given a tip that Grami had pocketed strike funds earmarked for local strikers. Although I distrusted my source, who was obviously out to get Grami, I decided to check with some of the women strikers.

Then Grami called me at the newsroom. "Hey, Jacques, I understand you are trying to talk to some of my people."

"Yea, Bill, that's right."

"Well," he said, laughing softly as he said it, "you remember what happened to Victor Reisel!" And then he smoothly changed the subject.

I knew that Victor Reisel, a labor columnist, was blinded for life by acid thrown in his face while exposing underworld ties to labor unions.

When we enter Grami's suite at the Towne House, Bill gives us *all friendly handshakes. He is no longer as I remembered him, trim and clean-cut. His face is jowly, his chin melts into his thick neck, and his paunch droops over his belt. His mouth smiles, but his dark eyes conceal his thoughts.*

He appears relaxed, unperturbed, as he sits down cross-legged, showing off his shiny cowboy boots. His voice is soft and sincere, but one of his first statements confirms that the Teamsters have changed their position, in apparent violation of the pact.

The Teamsters now want all their contracts rescinded—or none. Of course, he says smoothly, that position could change within the hour. He explains that he believes that Herb Fleming, the president of the growers' association, can keep all the industry together, so he supports him. But yesterday Fleming ran into two solid walls, one serious, the other, he feels, just talk.

Fleming "went in yesterday and said, 'Support UFWOC.' The Executive Committee reversed him, and he was surprised. I feel I must support Fleming," Grami continues.

If the industry position hardens against rescissions, he says, then the Teamsters' policy could change to grant individual releases. But that would be after the ten-day moratorium.

"We're technically liable if they leave singly," he says without explanation.

Fleming told him two companies will file suit, charging a Teamster-UFWOC conspiracy. "Fleming says some really believe that I'm part of it. He has to get out of the position where he's suspected," Grami says.

Then he dangles a carrot. "There are over two hundred growers involved, over fifty thousand people involved in this deal!" That's the highest figure we have yet heard.

"I'm not convinced we're in trouble," Grami says a little later, "I feel there is a strong element in the industry pushing it toward a resolution."

With a smile, he says he thinks the industry is trying to find out the "true Teamster position." They already know UFWOC's position, and that UFWOC will act.

"The question is, what will the Teamsters do if you act? I was speaking in riddles this morning. I was asked a hundred times, 'Is your word any good?'

"We're trying to avoid answering that! We'll fight to the death to prove our word is good. If this becomes the issue, the whole Teamsters will unite behind that. It's not really the issue. The Teamsters have said they're not interested in organizing farm work-

ers. UFWOC said it is. The pact is signed. The real question is, is it to the advantage or disadvantage of all parties concerned to adhere to the agreement."

Rather than a statement of "the real question," I sense a threat behind Grami's remarks. He can rally the Teamsters behind the issue of standing by their contracts.

That suspicion is strengthened when Grami says flatly he won't sign any rescission. Einar Mohn, the head of the Western Conference of Teamsters, or someone else in the Teamsters will have to sign. "My name is on those contracts. I feel an obligation to that." And a little later he comments, "I know someone is leaving after this is over."

Grami has dropped another hint, whether intentional or not. He is building a power base within the Teamsters and is looking forward to next July's Teamster national convention. With Jimmy Hoffa still in the penitentiary, challenges are being mounted against Frank Fitzsimmons, Hoffa's hand-picked successor as president. Grami wants to consolidate his local base, get credit for signing up the farm workers, and shift the blame to Einar Mohn if he loses them. While Mohn is head of the Western Conference, Grami is allied to another faction within the Teamsters, an Eastern faction that eventually hopes to capture control of the giant union.

But Grami is not about to disclose his plans. Instead he says the Teamsters must be practical. Besides being exposed to a suit if they give individual rescissions, he explains, they face another problem because some of the growers are members of cooperatives in processing plants with Teamster contracts.

Some food processors are saying the Teamsters better be prepared to break their processing, frozen food, and trucking agreements if they break the farm workers' agreement. "They're saying it in enough places to cause our organization some pause," he says.

Dolores asks him what happens if a grower signs with UFWOC?

"I don't know. It depends if we contest it. I don't think we would, as a practical matter, but you must cross the bridge, too. If you remove those most for UFWOC from the growers' group, you may be in a worse position, too."

He says he's received "tremendous criticism" as well as support from within the Teamsters. "The issue to avoid," he repeats, "is to get Teamster pride in our agreement."

And he concludes, "I'll stay right here till it's over." There is as much threat as reassurance in that statement.

JERRY COHEN RECALLS

When we left that meeting, we didn't know what the hell Grami had said. We had the distinct impression that he was giving us a line of crap. We did know he had gone to the growers' meeting and told them he wasn't going to let them out. I think it was an immediate double-cross on his part.

FROM JACQUES LEVY'S NOTEBOOK

Tuesday (continued)—After another meeting with Freshpict which breaks up in discord, Dolores Huerta, Jerry Cohen, Fred Ross, Marshall Ganz, and I drive to the Franciscan retreat to see Cesar. It appears an oasis of peace compared to the bedlam at union headquarters.

Cesar looks in pain, but he sits in a rocking chair for the strategy session. After ideas are bounced around, he decides to zero in on United Fruit's Inter Harvest. "They are the most vulnerable and can buy off the Teamsters if necessary to get a rescission," he says.

"You should just walk in unannounced and tell Lauer, 'We want recognition, and we want to start negotiating within twenty-four hours. If you don't, you're going to get it.'"

"That's right!" Dolores agrees.

"He's going to say, 'What about our agreement to have elections?'" Jerry says.

"Tough, you know," Cesar answers. "The agreement is past now. 'If you want us to show you we represent the people, we'll pull them out on strike.' There are three ways of demonstration, so we say we want to take the easiest one for us. We want to pull all the people out on strike."

Often in the past, he has said there are three valid ways to prove representation—by secret ballot, by card check, and by a strike.

Cesar also wants to open up another front, putting added pressure on the Teamsters. He assigns Dolores and Fred to go after Bud Antle, the big lettuce-growing company which has had a Teamster contract since that AWOC strike in 1960. But as Cesar points out, that contract covered only about fifty out of seventeen hundred workers. And a portion of the one million dollar Teamster loan to Antle is still outstanding.

They discuss the end of the six-day moratorium, angry that Monsignor Higgins has let the growers assume from the start that it will last ten days. But despite the lack of progress, Cesar thinks the strike should not be resumed tomorrow.

It's up to the workers, however, and when Dolores gets back to the Salinas headquarters, she finds them in a militant mood. The hall is packed, everyone standing shoulder to shoulder.

Although now forty years old, Dolores looks much younger as she stands on a chair confronting them. When she says that Cesar has urged that they not strike, her voice is drowned by cries of "Huelga!"

A Bruce Church worker argues against extending the moratorium even twenty-four more hours. "We gave them six days!" The workers cheer. Others fan the flames, and strike fever blazes.

Dolores signals for silence. The growers thought they had ten days, her words spill out in rapid torrent. Not only that, but the boycott machinery must be set in motion if they strike. They need time to prepare.

"Huelga" signs go up. The workers stir uncomfortably. Dolores keeps talking and finally asks for an extension—just one more day. She agrees they should only give the growers six hours and then strike, but she asks for twenty-four hours.

After more spirited debate, they vote to extend the moratorium twenty-four hours.

With a sigh of relief, Dolores goes with Marshall and me to see Monsignor Higgins at the Towne House. It's 10:15 P.M. and the priest is in bed.

Higgins is upset when Dolores presses for action, but she tells him the workers will strike if there is no progress.

"I can go home tomorrow. I'm doing everything I can to see if something can be worked out." He says Fleming needs more time to get the growers' proxies. "If you want my frank opinion, I think there will be a major break in this by the end of the ten days. If I'm wrong, you can still do what you have to do. My own reading is that something is going to break before the four days are up. I can work all night again, but I can't make decisions for them."

Marshall says that workers tell him growers gave them ten minutes to sign a Teamster card or be fired. He warns that some workers may start wildcat strikes.

Higgins wearily promises to convey that message to the growers.

CHAPTER 5

Bedlam in Delano

CESAR CHAVEZ RECALLS

Besides the chess game going on with the Teamsters and the growers, and the pressures of impending strikes, I had tremendous administrative pressures.

We were desperately trying to raise money. There were the pressures of the boycott people wanting to come back, and I had to figure out how we could bring them back and still not lose them.

A lot of grape growers were refusing to sign up, though Dolores was negotiating with them in Fresno. I was telling the boycotters to go after them, but they wanted to come home. So I decided to sacrifice the grape growers, knowing we were going to get involved in a long lettuce strike. Except for the tokay in the Lodi area, we had about 95 percent of the fresh grapes signed up.

In Delano the situation was just as hectic. For the first time there was a hiring hall, but the grape was late, and the workers were blaming us for not having work. I guess that's normal. If it rains, they complain that since the Union came, it's always raining.

But we also were having our problems with the hiring hall. We had eleven thousand workers coming in, and no cooperation from the employers. Because the leadership was in Salinas, we were not organized to deal with it. The best I could do was leave Richard in charge and put a lot of inexperienced people on him. That's all we had.

And Richard had his hands full because the growers suddenly realized that a contract was not everything, that they could still try to do what they wanted. We began to get that awful feeling

that the only thing they really wanted was to get rid of the boycott. Labor contractors and foremen were the first problems. Under the contract they should have been eliminated, but they
started fighting for their positions.

I didn't have the skills in administration that I developed later,
so my biggest headache was administrative. And we had so many
administrative problems.

RICHARD CHAVEZ RECALLS

*When Cesar left for Salinas, he took the whole crew—I mean
everybody—and I was left in charge of getting all the Delano area
contracts ratified. That meant going out there, talking to the crews,
explaining all the terms of the contract, and getting them to vote
on it.*

*The growers couldn't get the union stamp until the contracts
were ratified.*

*There were twenty-nine ranches, and I don't know how many
hundreds of crews of thirty to forty workers each. Altogether, I
think there were something like nine thousand workers. Picking
had just started and not all the people were there yet.*

*We had to go to each crew on each ranch and pass out little
cards. If they approved the contract, they would sign them. Almost
everybody signed, almost 100 percent. The companies already had
told them that the Union had come to terms with the company,
and that now it was up to them to vote on the terms of the contract.*

*I think the only organizer left with me was Robert Bustos, then
I got some help. Chris Hartmire sent me about twenty volunteers,
mostly young college kids from Los Angeles, and we got more from
the Bay Area. But we really didn't know what we were doing, to
be truthful, and all kinds of things happened.*

*We had a day-long session with the volunteers, going over every-
thing. "We want everything filled out exactly," I said—the worker's name; permanent address in Texas, Mexico, or wherever; the
local address; social security; age; date of birth; number of depen-
dents; and the beneficiary in case of death. We needed all that information for the medical plan, the death benefits, and taxes. Then
we divided the volunteers who were ratifying the crews out in the
fields into ten or twelve teams of about five or six people.*

But even though we explained it to them, some didn't follow in-

structions. Because it was a lot of writing, they thought that they would just abbreviate. That's when we really got into trouble. For example, they would go to a Caratan ranch and put just Caratan. But there are two Caratans, M. and Anton.

Because there was so much confusion, they were coming in and just dumping cards for us to file in the office. When it just said Caratan, people filing didn't know which Caratan. And then, to top it all, some wouldn't even write Caratan, just the first three letters, "Car." But we also had Louis Caric, and they put "Car" for Caric. It was just a complete mess.

And then Zaninovich. There are five Zaninoviches—two of them with the same first name, Vincent B. and Vincent V. All they put was Zaninovich.

Then, because there were so many crews, and it was going to take weeks to do it, some kids from Berkeley just gave the cards to the foremen, so the foremen could do the contract ratifying instead of doing it themselves.

So that fell apart. There was no way that I could put it together. They didn't know who they left the cards with or anything. They had to take me and show me where, and once I knew the ranch, I'd go talk to the foreman and ask for all the cards back. Some I got back, some I didn't. I had to go crew by crew. Sometimes I went to crews that had already been ratified, and they'd complain, "You guys crazy or something? We already had somebody here yesterday."

And some volunteers weren't taking street numbers or crew numbers, or who they were working with. Just nothing. It was disastrous. I've never seen anything like it.

While that was happening in the fields, at the same time there was no organization at headquarters. It was all too sudden. There were thousands of cards that we had to file, and nobody knew where they belonged.

Esther Uranday was running the hiring hall, but we only had had the Schenley contract before, just a few cards. Now there were thousands. So the cards were just thrown around. There were tables all over the place with boxes of cards on them, cards on the floor, cards in the hiring hall, boxes here, and boxes there.

I'd get a filing crew working. Then they'd leave to go eat or something, and somebody would come in and move the cards. They would be misplaced. All of a sudden, everybody lost control of where everything went.

Then there were duplicates, and we had to take them out. Sometimes there were three cards for one worker. Sometimes there were none. Some cards were incomplete, or had misinformation, and we had to go back to the crews, walk the rows until we found the persons.

There was more confusion to add to the confusion at the hiring hall. The workers had to come there to get a dispatch. We weren't even smart enough to say, "Continue working, we'll give the dispatches after all this is over."

There were thousands of people waiting, everybody wanting to get dispatched at the same time. No one could work because there were people just squeezed in there. We would be announcing all day long, sign over here, and get dispatch cards over there. Then the hiring hall had to match the worker with the card already signed in the field. But there were so many cards, they couldn't find them.

Other workers, who didn't want to lose picking time, would come after work. So we had about thirty to forty crews waiting outside, everybody wanting to go home, confusion to add to confusion. I don't know how I kept my sanity.

Finally we said, "Don't go to the hiring hall to get your dispatch, continue working." And that's how we eliminated people from the hiring hall, until we got things straightened out.

There was a young professor, another guy with him, and a girl who thought that we weren't dispatching people fast enough. They just took it upon themselves to ask people how long they had been waiting. Some had been there for two to three hours. The three thought it was undemocratic, that people shouldn't wait that long. They said people don't even wait that long at the welfare.

So these three went to the Department of Employment and said, "We're from the Farm Workers, helping over there, and it's total confusion. We don't know what we're doing. Could you please tell us how to dispatch people."

The guy that worked there is a good friend of mine and called me to ask what it was we wanted. When I hung up, I went looking for those three.

Not only had they gone to the Department of Employment, but they had gone to some of the growers, telling them to please forgive us because we weren't selling the guys out, we were trying.

I told them they couldn't do these things, and they argued that we should have a meeting and do it democratically. We ought to vote on it.

I really got pissed off and told them to get the hell out, but they didn't. They continued to play politics.

Finally I stopped everything and called another session. After that, it started working a little better. After about two and a half weeks, we kind of started seeing daylight. But it was quite an experience, what with the politics that went on, the confusion, not knowing what we were doing, and the growers putting pressure. They wanted that union stamp and didn't give a damn what happened. They just wanted that rubber stamp to put on the boxes, so they could sell their grapes.

It was the most terrible two weeks in my whole life. The pressure was just terrible, coming from about four or five sides.

Finally, after two and a half weeks, things started to become more normal. Then, slowly, we started going back to the crews and checking. By that time some people had left and were working with other crews. So that meant more problems.

Before the Union, many people would just pick the cream of the crop at one vineyard, then move to another. But this time, if this guy worked for Giumarra, they would deduct $3.50 dues. Then he'd go work on another ranch which would deduct another $3.50.

After they received their second paycheck, those workers would come into the hiring hall just raving mad, ready to hit somebody. "This goddamn Union is no good. That's all they wanted, was just the money." Of course, not everybody was that way. But the bookkeeping required to make refunds created more problems for us still.

During all this time, everyone was in Salinas. I would call Cesar, but nobody was paying attention. A young guy from back East, who didn't like the way things were in Delano, disappeared one day. I didn't know where he was and didn't care because I had too many other things to worry about. He made a trip to Salinas and told Cesar things in Delano were no good, that Richard just didn't know what he was doing, which was true. I didn't know.

So Cesar called me. I've got all of this pressure about to the cracking point. I think I'm going to have a nervous breakdown, and Cesar calls me and just gets on me. I had just finished that day, it was about 11:00 at night, and he just didn't even wait for me to explain anything. He just got on me. Of course, he was pretty nervous in Salinas himself. He had all that pressure.

But I blew up. "You can have your goddamn Union. You and your Union can go to hell as far as I'm concerned. You take this son of a bitch. I quit right now. I quit!"

I got it out of him. "I've got a written report here," he said, "a twenty-page report of the way you've been messing up."

I said, "I told you. I called you three days ago, that it was very bad, but I'm trying to work at it."

And I finally hung up on him.

The next day we made peace. Finally things started getting better. They sent me two guys from Salinas who knew what they were doing. After about three or four weeks, it was down to normal.

CHAPTER 6

War Is Declared

FROM JACQUES LEVY'S NOTEBOOK

Wednesday, August 19, 1970—Early this morning Dolores Huerta visits Monsignor Higgins to ask that he attend tonight's union meeting. The priest hesitates, but agrees on one condition— that he does not do so to rouse the workers to strike.

"All I'm saying is that during this ten-day period, I must do all I can to prevent war," he says. "The people talking the loudest do not really represent the industry. This I know from the inside. And an authorized strike would be a very bad mistake!"

But the union seems headed for a strike. At the Franciscan retreat an hour later, Cesar tells Dolores, "Unless a big miracle happens, there will be a big strike in Salinas tomorrow. I feel confident about Santa Maria, but I'm leery about the enthusiasm in Salinas. They haven't been tested."

Dolores replies that most are migrants, ready to leave the area. Father David Duran estimates 90 percent are green-carders.

Cesar shakes his head. They can't stop a strike tonight, he thinks. Dolores again agrees, except if there are talks, or talks are about to start.

Then focusing on Purex's Freshpict, she says, "I think it would be very bad to stall. It would be a politically stupid error on our part. The workers would never forgive us. We should strike the bastards." When Jerry Cohen calls in to report that he will meet United Fruit's Will Lauer at 1:00, Cesar tells him to say that the union is striking at 5:00 A.M. Then Dolores goes to Bud Antle in the afternoon to warn the company that their workers, too, will strike unless negotiations start.

After talking to Antle, who protests he has had a contract with the Teamsters since 1960, she goes to the union's room at the Towne House where she learns that Monsignor Higgins called a half hour ago to say there is no word from the growers, yet, but if the union calls a strike, he will go home.

At 5:05 P.M., Jerry Cohen gets a call from Freshpict and tells them of last night's union meeting. The workers are set to strike, he warns. Shortly after, a call comes in from Andrew Church, attorney for the growers' group, who says progress is being made, that Herb Fleming has been on the phone all day talking to San Joaquin Valley growers.

Both Jerry and Dolores have splitting headaches. It's after 6:00 when she goes up to see Higgins in his room.

"What will happen at the union meeting tonight?" Higgins asks anxiously. He doesn't want the union to strike and repeats that the growers still are trying to put something together.

Dolores blames him for the misunderstanding that the moratorium would last ten days, regardless of progress. Higgins apologizes.

"Apparently I'm the obstacle, and I better get out," he says, feeling the hostility in her voice.

"You're not an obstacle, but . . ." her voice trails off.

"I don't think ten days is long to iron out such a serious problem," Higgins says defensively. "You have the workers. The Teamsters have a program." He says that the Teamsters have been meeting with growers individually all this time.

"I think the Teamsters intend to tear up the contracts. Some growers threaten collusion," he says. Then, seeing the skepticism in Dolores's face, he says, "If I'm in the way, I want to know it."

The phone interrupts. It's Cesar asking if Higgins will go to the meeting tonight to ask the workers not to strike.

"I'll give them my best judgment," the priest promises, and the tension in the room eases.

Not only are the headquarters jammed with workers an hour later, but many are milling about the sidewalk and parking lot, unable to get in, as Dolores asks Higgins to speak first. It's up to him to put out the fire.

Higgins starts off defensively, faced by hundreds of hushed, expectant faces, dark faces weathered by sun and toil, determined faces that reflect centuries of endless waiting without hope.

This is his fifteenth trip to California for farm workers, he says. He helped settle the war between the Teamsters and UFWOC and get the pact signed. He has been meeting almost around the clock to try to settle this.

"I'm here as a mediator. During these four or five days, I petitioned for an extension of time. I was convinced there was substantial hope."

"I am the first to admit there was some misunderstanding," he apologizes. "I acted as a friend of the farm workers, in the hope that it will be best for all workers. I've come here to ask you to give me until Saturday. I'm speaking to you as man to man. If I'm wrong, there are no restrictions of the steps you can engage in. I'm asking you as strongly as I can to wait until Saturday!"

Cries of "No! No! No!" interrupt him.

"I'm asking you to accept my good faith," he pleads. "I've done the best I can. If there is a strike, my good faith as a mediator is destroyed. If my good faith is destroyed, I can no longer act as a mediator. If I made a mistake, I'm sorry."

He seems shaken, standing there as Father Duran translates. The faces before him are grim.

"Are there any questions?" Higgins asks hopefully. The silence is punctured by shouts of "Huelga! Huelga!" Then in various ways, the questioners ask whether the growers understand the urgency.

"They know we are just thirty-six hours away from deadline," Higgins assures them. "Don't ask me to do a miracle!"

Dolores jumps up on a chair and starts her rapid-fire talk. She has a message from Cesar. As all those dark eyes focus on her, she reads.

"I recommend strongly that we support the bishop's committee. The only thing we have to lose by waiting is the loss of our chains."

She says the union wants to hold a meeting tomorrow afternoon with representatives from each ranch. She asks that they elect a representative to be part of the negotiating committee.

"We're ready! We're here!" shout some.

"Cesar also warns us to be prepared," Dolores continues. "If we must, be ready to strike. Bring all the workers at noon Sunday. We want all workers! And bring posters and banners to represent each ranch."

"We want a demonstration of force on Sunday!"

"But all the growers want is more time," one worker argues. "Either we have a strike, or there is no strike!"

"All of us have this feeling, but it is a matter of timing," counters Dolores. "It's not just for ourselves, but for all. If we can win by waiting, let's do it. We're not afraid of anybody!"

"Let's get the bishop to give us a little more help, rather than time," another shouts.

Father Duran, the union priest, answers. "You all know I'm al-

ways ready for a fight if necessary. But Higgins is a good man. I'm
ready to fight! I came to the valley because we need to help farm
workers. But we choose our own battelfield! Battles are won only
with perfect time and place. We're not fighting for just one. I believe each one of us is fighting for dignity, and we must prepare
ourselves, and if one of us is not prepared, that may be our down-
fall."

A farm worker agrees, his eloquence, the eloquence of generations of peasants. "Let us support Cesar Chavez whom we have
forgotten for a moment. He has dedicated his entire life for us.
When he fasted, how many fasted? Now is the time to back our
organization. Isn't Mr. Chavez suffering for us? Sacrificing for us?
We must sacrifice, too. These fields have been watered by the
sweat of our brow, and the crops have been fertilized by our toil.
Let us not forget our 'De Colores' principles."

"Can Monsignor guarantee negotiations will be completed by
Saturday?" a voice challenges.

"No."

"Then strike!"

"Cesar, of course, is doing the best he can to support us, and so
it's important to support him," another argues.

Dolores breaks in. "We need your faith, because it's your faith
that supports us."

The debate continues, intense as only it can be when sheer survival is at stake. Many arguments rival in power the words of poets.

Finally, there is a call for a vote. The question is whether to
postpone a strike vote until Sunday. Those in favor raise their
hands. And then those opposed.

The strike has been postponed.

The meeting ends with the singing of "De Colores."

But not all the workers are in agreement.

CESAR CHAVEZ RECALLS

The AFL-CIO and the church thought that we could get something if we extended the agreement, but the workers wanted to
strike right now. We were in a bind. We had to keep our allies
with us. I knew that we had to, beyond any doubt, prove that we
were reasonable people. While the AFL-CIO liked us and knew
we were right, I think they still didn't know if we were reasonable.
All the propaganda that came out of the grape strike was still
hanging in the air.

There also were other reasons for delay. The reports that I was getting from Marshall Ganz were that we still didn't have all the ranches put together. Some didn't have committees. They hadn't met, or if they had, the meetings were slipshod. On some of the ranches in the Watsonville area, we couldn't even identify the workers, there was such a mess up of support.

I was worried, too, that we wouldn't have enough leadership to go around, and that some of the workers wouldn't stay out long enough because they weren't well organized. They had the enthusiasm, but they weren't structured yet for the strike.

FROM JACQUES LEVY'S NOTEBOOK

Thursday, August 20, 1970—Late in the afternoon, Monsignor Higgins calls Jerry Cohen to set up a 7:00 P.M. meeting with Freshpict. Earlier in the day, both Bill Grami and Monsignor Higgins were asked to leave a growers' meeting at the Towne House, a meeting that then continued for hours in the offices of the Grower-Shipper Vegetable Association.

Promptly at 7:00, Dolores, Jerry, and seven Freshpict workers are ushered into a conference room at Freshpict headquarters. Maps of company ranches decorate the walls.

The air of expectation is heightened when Monsignor Higgins looks in and walks out without a word. After the delay has become oppressive, Freshpict President Howard Leach appears and asks to speak alone with either Dolores or Jerry. Dolores refuses. Anything that is said must be said before the entire committee. Leach disappears.

And still nothing happens. A few jokes release the tension while the waiting continues. Then Monsignor Higgins reappears. The company would prefer to meet alone with the officers, he explains, as these are just prenegotiations. The company hasn't yet agreed to recognize the union.

The workers understand that, Dolores answers, refusing the request. After Higgins leaves, Jerry comments, "This is what it's all about. They don't want to talk to their workers."

Thirty minutes have elapsed before Leach walks in with his labor relations attorney, William Spalding, and Monsignor Higgins. The talks continue for some time, with Spalding in nearly constant acrimonius debate with Dolores. Only Higgins prevents the two sides from breaking off talks permanently. But no time is set to resume them.

Outside in the Freshpict parking lot, the workers talk over their impressions. "They're talking loud, but inside they're scared," one says. The others agree.

Back at the Towne House, Dolores is depressed. "As I told Cesar," she remarks, "we were not destined to get anything easy." As if to confirm it, Jerry calls United Fruit's Lauer and learns that Grami has taken his stand. Either all companies get rescissions, or none.

Then at 9:30 P.M., TV Channel 11 calls. The growers have called a press conference for noon tomorrow, and the reporter wants to know why.

By 10:30 we're at Cesar's retreat. Told of the press conference, Cesar says, "If it's a press conference, it's bad news." Then he asks, "Why would the growers want to fight some more?"

"I don't know," Jerry answers.

The meeting is interrupted by Dr. Jerome Lackner, who has arrived from San Jose to examine Cesar. The two go into the bedroom.

Jerry's eyes sparkle. "It's war! We're going to win this war fast. We're going to get United Fruit fast, and Purex. Then we've got union lettuce and get the chains."

Helen Chavez walks in, and Jerry turns to her. "We're going to be in a fight, Helen!"

"We've been in a fight for five years," Helen says quietly. "We're so used to fights that if we weren't in one, we wouldn't know what to do."

In the kitchen, Cesar's sons Paul and Birdy giggle and play. One of the guards is snoring, asleep while sitting against the front door.

It's midnight before the meeting breaks up, and we drive the twenty miles back to the Towne House. There we learn Monsignor Higgins called five minutes ago. Dolores calls him back and writes down Freshpict's latest proposal.

After calling Cesar, Dolores goes up to see Higgins, who looks weary and is wearing green pajamas.

"Should you also get Inter Harvest?" Dolores asks.

"As I read it, they're both going to go," Higgins answers. "And if there is a press conference, there's going to be war." He looks grim. "I got the feeling there was friction. Inter Harvest walked out of the secret growers' meeting."

Freshpict said to hell with rescinding the Teamster contract. He spent one and a half hours with them. "They don't want war. They asked me to come up with a proposal. I think it's symbolism, a precedent of the bishops' committee being involved."

And Lauer called him tonight. "We do not want war. We want out," the United Fruit vice-president told him.

Then Higgins asks whether farm workers will be at the negotiations. He prefers they wouldn't. But Dolores says that after a strike situation, there is tension, and this helps break the tension.

"I'm scared," Higgins confesses. "I don't want this thing to break down."

"I'm not afraid. Their behavior was excellent," Dolores insists.

"Is there a compromise so you can consult your committee, and if necessary have them here?" Higgins presses.

"We did it at Steinberg, and had lots of trouble afterward," Dolores answers. "You can't do it here." She says that from now on, workers are involved in the negotiations. Speaking of the growers, she says, "It's good for their souls!"

"I don't want to worry about people's souls at this point," Monsignor Higgins argues. "If we run into snags, call a caucus. You know what's involved. My pride is involved."

We return to the union's room, and Dolores and Marshall start debating. It's 1:30 A.M. before we all head off for bed.

Friday, August 21, 1970—In the growers' headquarters, TV cameramen and reporters swarm all over the modern office, setting up for the press conference. Grower representatives are friendly and solicitous. The president of the association, Herb Fleming, wearing a yellow sport shirt, jokes with the reporters. He is slender, handsome, personable.

"I'm a farmer, not an entertainer," he apologizes as they ask him to say a few words into the mikes. Then he reads a prepared statement.

"We have negotiated proper and legal contracts with the Teamsters Union. They have assured us that they will honor these contracts, and we intend to do the same."

When asked if the workers can refuse to join the Teamsters, he answers, "They're going to go along like any employe who works for an employer with a contract."

Do workers have a right to elections?

"No, no more than they did with UFWOC. Elections were insignificant," Fleming says.

There are more questions, but the story is clear. War has been declared.

CESAR CHAVEZ RECALLS

I didn't like the growers' decision, but I expected it. I didn't ever have any illusions that they would leave the Teamsters voluntarily.

The worst thing was to know that the Teamsters had gone back on their word again. Bill Grami didn't know that that was the nail on his own coffin. He didn't know that by refusing to rescind all the contracts, he was looking at the present, and we were looking at the future.

FROM JACQUES LEVY'S NOTEBOOK

When the Freshpict talks resume Friday afternoon, they come to a compromise on some issues, but there is no meeting of minds on the foreman issue. The union wants them covered by the contract, but the company doesn't.

During a caucus, Dolores calls Cesar. She sees little hope for the Freshpict talks, she says, and they turn their attention to United Fruit, deciding to go for immediate negotiations at 9:00 the next morning, or to break off talks with them completely.

When the caucus ends, Freshpict states it won't budge on the foreman issue, and the union restates its position.

"Monsignor, it's your ball game," the company negotiator says.

"You can see it in my face. I'm terribly disappointed," Higgins replies. "I'll be available."

The talks with Freshpict have collapsed.

CHAPTER 7

A Fork in the Road

Saturday, August 22, 1970—The Teamsters will rescind their contract Monday, United Fruit Vice-President Will Lauer reports happily when Jerry Cohen and Dolores Huerta meet with Inter Harvest at the Highway Center Lodge. Now they can set up elections.

It's too late, Jerry answers. Negotiations must start immediately —by noon.

Lauer looks surprised. "I understand there was a commitment that a vote was fundamental. From our standpoint it's critical."

"Certainly the growers didn't see a need for elections when they took the Teamsters in," Dolores answers. The union waited a week. "The only thing we have is a lot of farm workers mad at us. We have to depend on their support for organizing."

"If you take that out of the picture, it presents a very serious internal problem within United Brands and Inter Harvest," Lauer argues, promising to do all possible to expedite the vote.

"Impossible," Dolores tells him, "we just ran out of time. We gave the growers until Saturday noon. The Teamsters have no doubts we represent the workers."

After more futile arguments, Lauer suggests Monsignor George Higgins be brought in as mediator. It's 10:40 A.M. as Jerry and Dolores amble down to the parking lot and stand in the sunshine until Inter Harvest's personnel manager Cal Watkins provides them a motel room.

At 12:35, Higgins walks into the union's room to propose that a card check be held while negotiations go on concurrently.

"Here's the sticky problem," he says. "What happens if you don't have a majority?"

"That's unreal," Marshall Ganz laughs. "We do."

"Okay, but I don't want any misinterpretations. I told them time is of the absolute essence," Higgins says nervously. "But suppose you don't?"

"We stop negotiating," Dolores answers. She then brings up another hitch. "That's not exactly what Cesar wanted. He told me no card check."

Higgins looks more worried.

"I'll take the responsibility," she says.

"He didn't mean it," Jerry suggests.

"Yes, he did," Dolores says earnestly.

"Then we'll fight him. We'll all fight him," Jerry answers firmly.

Marshall calls union headquarters and reports they have 856 signed authorization cards from machine and ground crews at Inter Harvest. That's 95 percent, he says.

When they return to Lauer's room, Lauer says, "If you don't have a majority, you have mud on your face. Do you realize you are talking in the neighborhood of eight hundred to one thousand employes?"

"Yes," says Marshall.

"What happens if they don't have a majority?" Higgins asks Lauer.

Lauer says he would break off the talks.

"You signed with the Teamsters without a majority," Dolores snaps.

"That was a mistake," Lauer answers softly. "We won't make that same mistake twice. We need elections for a matter of morality and principle."

"It's late for that," Dolores sneers.

"It sure is," Lauer admits.

"It's redemption," Jerry quips, and Lauer smiles at him.

The two sides agree to caucus briefly. It's 1:45. On the way to the room, Jerry grabs an egg sandwich from his car. A few minutes later, Fred Ross arrives. "We've got the cards alphabetized," he says. "All 656 of them."

"656?" Marshall asks in surprise.

"856," Fred corrects himself.

When the talks resume at 2:09, Higgins volunteers to do the

card check. They nail down the final details. "I suggest we break for lunch," Lauer says.

"We just ate," Jerry says lightly. "If you want egg salad and peanut butter and jelly sandwiches, we'll be happy to share them with you."

Lauer prefers to start the negotiations at 3:30. "Can you wait that long, Jerry?" he asks.

"You can't!" Jerry needles back.

MONSIGNOR GEORGE HIGGINS RECALLS

Dolores did me the worst disservice any human being has ever done when she agreed to a card check but said, "You must conduct it alone. Nobody else in the room."

I had never conducted a card check on that scale. It took me fourteen hours! United Fruit had two high-powered secretaries in the office who stayed up all night just to show me where things were. They stayed in their own office. They could have done that card check in two hours, I'm sure.

After three hours, I'm still plowing through these names. I'm going blind. Beverly Hackman, the vice-president in charge of industrial relations, wanders in. "How are you doing, buddy? You want any coffee?"

Well, I thought, you'd better get out of here! If Dolores sees you here, there's going to be trouble.

"No," I said, "I'm fine."

"Well, fine. I just thought I'd ask if you need any coffee, or you want a drink or something." And about an hour later, he comes back again. He came back three times.

I finally said, "Look, what's up? What are you looking for? I know you're not here to influence the vote because you can't. There's no way you can do that! But," I said, "what are you after?"

"Well," he said, "for God's sake, brother, they've got to win! We've got to negotiate!" He said, "I'm not asking you to sell your soul, but they've got to win!"

And here was Dolores saying, "If you let the company in, they'll cheat on you!"

FROM JACQUES LEVY'S NOTEBOOK

It's 4:00 P.M. Saturday when the workers' committee piles into four cars and heads for the Inter Harvest offices. But there are too many people, and the negotiations are moved to a lunchroom in one of the huge lettuce sheds.

The room has cold, ice-white walls stretching some twenty feet high with a corrugated iron roof peaking toward the center of the building. Two tables covered with red oilcloth are end to end stretching some thirty feet or more. Plain, green, wooden benches flank them. The room and tables are so narrow, the negotiators are literally nose to nose, eyeball to eyeball.

Lauer is accompanied by seven men, while the union is represented by Jerry Cohen, Dolores Huerta, sixteen men, three women, and a little girl about one and a half, wearing green slacks and shirt and shiny red shoes. Her mother has pink curlers in her hair, covered by white netting.

"How many votes does she have?" Lauer jests, pointing to the little girl.

"We're doing this not only for the workers, but for her," Dolores answers earnestly.

As Dolores goes through the basic contract, explaining its provisions, she translates what she says into Spanish.

Lauer quickly raises the issue of including crew foremen. "This could be a very difficult part of the contract," he says.

Dolores tells him that in Coachella the workers showed an increase in production two weeks after the contract was signed. And at Schenley, where the crew foremen are still included, they are renegotiating their third contract. Schenley produced 960 tons more grapes last year with 9,000 less man hours, she says.

"That's why we find it so important," she explains. "When we sign, we don't want continual war. We don't want to make that man the enemy of people. There's a primitive attitude in agriculture that you discipline workers by firing them. This is what we are trying to eradicate."

When she goes into a long explanation of the hiring hall, Lauer has many questions. One of the company men wants to know what happens if a field is condemned because it is not up to minimum standards.

"The field should be checked first," Dolores says.

"We call them out in the hopes we can provide them work," one of the Nunes brothers, an Inter Harvest executive, remarks.

"Maybe they prefer the day off," Dolores snaps.

She asks the workers what the practice is. They answer in Spanish which she translates. "The brother says they have a field man that checks the field. If it is no good, they don't get paid for the work done."

"We hear you loud and clear," Lauer says, playing with his glasses as he stares at Dolores.

At times Jerry and Lauer spar jovially about the contract language. Then the question of breaking for dinner arises. Lauer wants one hour or more, the workers suggest a half hour or less. They continue negotiating.

At 7:00 P.M., they finally break for dinner. Then Jerry and I return to his room to rest until the talks resume at 9:00. I ask him his plans for the future, and he says he hopes to stay with Cesar— provided Cesar survives.

"You ought to see my file of letters," he says glumly. "Some are real dangerous."

He recalls the Marysville plot, then tells of another time in Coachella when there was a July 4 party. To protect Cesar, Jerry took him to Palm Springs to see The Graduate. But they got out of the movie early and decided to see how the party was going.

"We both let our guard down," Jerry says. "We walked into the room full of people. Then the lights went out. I saw a flashlight moving across the faces toward Cesar, and I pushed people aside to get to him. And the flashlight hit me.

"Then the lights went on, and there was a cop, gun in one hand and the flashlight in the other! He said he was afraid for Cesar's safety and had heard a commotion in the crowd.

"You know how Kennedy mistrusted the cops. If the lights had not gone on, would he have shot Cesar? Or did he think I was a threat—moving in as I did?

"Thinking about it later, I was really shook up."

Briefly we discuss the possibilities of danger in a fight with the Teamsters. Then we head on back to the negotiations.

The night fog has enveloped Salinas, and the room is cold. Lauer wears a green carcoat with leather buttons and a hood. Nine men are with him.

On the union's side are twenty-four workers, Dolores, Jerry, and Vivian Levine of the San Francisco boycott. Jerry, his hair as disheveled as ever, chews his toothpick at a furious rate.

As the night drags on, the lines of fatigue grow more visible on everyone, but Dolores continues tirelessly. The discussion turns to pesticides. Several types are mentioned.

One of the scientists working for the company protests the union's request to ban certain chemicals. "What are you going to do when you have nothing else to use?"

"What are you going to do when you have no more people?" Dolores answers.

When Dolores mentions the restrictions on Parathion, Lauer says the company wants a three-day limit before the workers can go back into the fields treated with the chemical.

"The law says fourteen days, it's so dangerous," Jerry counters.

A woman worker asks why lettuce pickers get a rash on their hands.

"I'd like to ask you to first accept the proposition that our company has approached this on a sound and humane basis," Lauer says. "If you would give us references on the claims you make, we will study them."

A company man argues that it's standard practice in the area for farm workers to go into the field three days after Parathion has been used.

"If three days is the practice in this valley, we're going to have a ball," Jerry responds.

It's 1:00 A.M. before the talks recess until later Sunday morning.

CESAR CHAVEZ RECALLS

Besides being weak, I think that one of the reasons I went to the Franciscan retreat was because I wanted to plan strategy. I don't think I did this consciously, but that's what happened. It was a good place for me to be to meditate and pray. I was able to reflect on what was happening, to shed all of those million little problems, and to look at things a little more dispassionately.

I also could rest there, as Helen was with me. I can rest when she's around. It's a strange thing. I don't tell her I want her to help me, and if I ask her, she never tells me what to do. But she forces me to say what I want to say. So having her there was good.

The key question was whether we could pull off another boycott. I was worried that we might not be able to, because the people had been out there three or four years. I knew no one wants to go on a boycott, as was proved a little later, but I also knew we would need the boycott.

I wasn't worried about the strike. That was like putting a train on the track and it's rolling. It's going to get there. Or like putting something on to cook. With a match, enough gas, and enough heat, it's going to happen.

So I wasn't surprised at the success of the big strike rally in Salinas Sunday. I was sick and had to get the report on the phone from Dolores and Marshall. They told me it was fantastic, but we expected that.

More than three thousand farm workers voted to strike.

FROM JACQUES LEVY'S NOTEBOOK

Sunday, August 23, 1970—After the strike rally, the Inter Harvest workers go back to the secret negotiations. During the talks, Jerry brings up a news story that just broke. Three farm workers died in North Carolina after being sent into the fields five days after it was sprayed with Parathion.

Now the union will insist on twenty-one days before a worker can enter a sprayed field, he says.

"Our company has a set policy not just on product safety, but also on employes' safety," Lauer answers quietly. "We won't have a problem, Jerry, if we approach it on a technical level."

The negotiations continue at a snail's pace through the evening, into the night, and on into the first hour of Monday morning. Then they recess for eight hours.

Monday, August 24, 1970—It's a very wet, foggy morning, and there's been tremendous activity at union headquarters since well before dawn. Strikers are going out to picket, and reports keep coming in either by phone or workers.

Father David Duran emptied all the buses at the day haul location. Although the center usually sends out from five to six hundred workers, not one worker went out between 4:45 and 5:45 A.M. This is confirmed both by day haul center manager Charlie Silva and TV reporter Rick Davis.

At about 7:00 A.M., UFWOC headquarters has about thirty to fifty people. Dolores arrives. She didn't sleep well and got called when some Inter Harvest crews struck. She is worried.

We go see Cesar, wondering if he will be awake, and find him at mass. When he returns, he is obviously in pain. "Are you getting any rest?" he is asked.

"How can I? When I know all this is going on! I woke up at 4:30 this morning and thought, 'They're just arriving at headquarters now on the way to strike.'"

Earlier Dolores told me she slept badly and realized today, for the first time, she was sleeping on box springs without a mattress. She is staying in the home of union supporters.

When we get back to headquarters, the telephone lines are flashing like a pinball machine. Calls from press, radio, TV, and workers. Strike headquarters is a beehive.

When the talks resume with Inter Harvest at 9:50 A.M., Lauer opens on the attack. "Before we begin the negotiations," he says, "I would like to understand what happened in the field this morning. We had promises of no economic action. No matter what the circumstance, no matter what the event!"

Dolores is apologetic, but Lauer doesn't want excuses. He stands up for the first time to talk, aiming his words at the workers. The company and the union will have a relationship for a long time, he says, and agreements must be observed by each side.

Finally one of the workers speaks up. "I'm David Gonzales," he says. "I represent some of the crews. Last night I did my best and talked to some of them and told them it was all right to go to work. This morning some of the men and buses were stopped by other people not from the company, and we're not going to fight."

"I'm not expecting that," Lauer says. "I accept that." And the serious business of negotiations is resumed.

But by mid-afternoon an impasse appears near. The two sides are in separate rooms. Bishop Joseph Donnelly, who flew in from the East the night before, joins the union negotiators again after consulting with the company.

"We've been talking to the company since we left you," he says. "We're pretty well persuaded they are very close to the end of the line economically."

He says the company is willing to move the machine lettuce cutters up from $1.75 to $1.91½ cents an hour, provided the issues of working foremen and hiring hall can be worked out. They are also willing to guarantee an increase in July 1971.

Dolores is suspicious. "I have a strong feeling politics are involved. The $1.91½ is the Bud Antle figure," she says. "I have a feeling a deal has been made not to exceed the Teamster rate."

She tells the bishop she talked with Cesar. "I feared something like this would happen. I can tell you we would not have a single worker supporting us, if we accepted this, and Cesar said the contract must be approved by the workers."

"I hate to see this. It would be a break-through contract," Bishop Donnelly says glumly. He looks unhappy as he goes to report to Lauer.

"They're going to test our strength," Jerry predicts. It means a general strike, injunctions, and the union must disregard them. "If we reject that proposal, we've got to keep that strength going," he warns. "Once we show our strength for a period of time, they'll have to deal with us regardless of the Teamsters."

The two sides are asked to meet together.

Lauer says he wants to review the situation because "I'm afraid we're coming to an end in the road or a fork in the road."

"If we come to an impasse," he says a little later, "I can only say I'm sorry about it. If the union at any time is able to resume talks, this committee will be ready to do that."

Dolores restates the union's position and concludes, "While we do want an agreement, we don't want it at the expense of the workers."

Everyone shakes hands, still friendly, though talks are breaking up. It's 3:35 P.M.

After the company has left, Bishop Donnelly makes one final try. He suggests accepting $1.92 now, and an additional 7 cents in January.

"Too low," says Dolores. "Bruce Church pays $2 an hour right now."

"Well, I'm sorry to see it," the bishop says.

"We'll be around," Monsignor Higgins promises.

We return to union headquarters, where we find out much has happened.

There have been maybe two thousand pickets striking between thirty and forty growers whose fields are scattered all over the Salinas Valley area. It is impossible to keep an accurate count, but the afternoon paper confirms the union's claims with quotes from Louis Larsen, marketing specialist for the Federal-State Market News Service, probably the only neutral source available.

"Things are pretty well shut down," Larsen told the paper, "with only Bud Antle, Inter Harvest, and Sears of Watsonville working. No lettuce markets are being quoted out of Salinas," he said, "because of the scarcity of the produce."

The strike also has affected the production of strawberries, celery, carrots, and tomatoes.

Not only are ranches shut down in the Salinas area, but the strike is as effective in King City, fifty miles to the south, and on down another hundred miles to Santa Maria, where another two thousand workers closed sixty-two ranches.

Despite the magnitude of the strike, incidents were few. Marshall Ganz reports that pickets were threatened with loaded guns at two ranches. Several pickets were arrested on trespass charges at the Crossetti ranch. And reports came into union headquarters of armed guards seen on various ranches.

The Salinas Californian reports that the mood of the pickets is reflected by Howard Pipes, a Pic 'N Pac strawberry worker from La Posada labor camp.

"We don't want the Teamsters. It's all a big racket," Pipes told a reporter. Asked how he would feel about a prolonged strike, Pipes answered, "Chavez went twenty-five days without eating. If we have to, we can do the same."

Anthony Grcich, president of Pic 'N Pac, reports the company plans to renew its injunction suit again UFWOC.

Both Bud Antle and the Mann Packing Company obtained temporary restraining orders from Superior Court Judge Stanley Lawson to halt picketing at their fields and coolers.

And Attorney Andrew Church, representing the Grower-Shipper Vegetable Association, promises to file similar suits tomorrow for the rest of the growers.

CHAPTER 8

Violence

FROM JACQUES LEVY'S NOTEBOOK

Tuesday, August 25, 1970—I am at union headquarters at 8:00 A.M. when Jerry Cohen tells me the broccoli workers at the Mann Packing Company are going on a sit-down strike.

The idea has been discussed before. If the workers can't picket because of the injunction, they can go to work, then suddenly sit down and refuse to move, keeping strikebreakers out of the field. Perhaps it is a tactic that can spread throughout the valley, a giant sit-down strike reminiscent of the automobile workers' efforts in the thirties.

When Jerry says he is going out to see what happened, I go along, anxious to get pictures of what could be the first major sit-down strike in agricultural history. With us are Venustiano Olguin, twenty-four, a college graduate who worked in the Coachella Valley fields as a child, and his fiancée, Kathie Kozak, nineteen, a volunteer.

Venustiano shows us the way to the field, where we see a sheriff's car at the far end. As we start down the dirt road toward it, the workers head our way wearing bright yellow rain gear and boots and yellow rain hats.

They have been served with copies of the court order which they give Jerry. Then they tell him other workers also are going on a sit-down strike at the Hansen ranch.

Again Venustiano directs us there. At one closed and guarded ranch gate, Jerry asks some pickets whether the workers are still in the fields. When told they are, we drive around the perimeter of the ranch to find them. On the opposite side we find an unguarded dirt road leading to the ranch house about a half-mile away.

We leave the car and walk, four abreast, down the road, flanked on each side by tilled fields reeking of herbicides. After we have walked some distance, a pickup heads toward us. The driver is uncommunicative when Jerry identifies himself as the UFWOC general counsel and tells him he is going in to check the workers. The pickup just turns around and heads back to the ranch headquarters.

The road lies straight and flat through the bare fields to a gentle rise in the distance on which sit several white buildings shaded by trees. The road goes up the grade then turns right toward the buildings.

As we get closer, a half-dozen green and yellow pickups head out from the buildings, drive to the bend, and stop, blocking the road. The maneuver strikes us as ridiculous—all those vehicles used to block the path of three men and a girl. Jerry is armed with his yellow legal pad, while I carry a notebook and a camera around my neck.

As we walk up the rise, men pour out of the trucks, big burly men who gather in the middle of the road, looking anything but friendly, their brawny arms folded across their chests.

Standing some distance in front of them is a middle-aged man, thin, nervous, in slacks and sport shirt. He is obviously in charge.

Jerry walks up to him, introduces himself, and asks his name. The man refuses to give it.

"Are you in charge?" Jerry asks.

The man nods.

Jerry says he has come to see the workers and asks where they are. As he does so, I step over to one side to take pictures of this strange scene—Jerry and the man standing face to face, the group of toughs some fifteen feet behind them, and the green and yellow pickups in the background.

The man tells Jerry the workers are gone and asks Jerry to leave.

Knowing the workers are still there, Jerry asks, "How did they leave? Did they go by car? By bus? Or did they just walk out?"

The man looks nervous. He insists the workers are gone.

"Where are they?" Jerry asks again.

This time, the man doesn't answer. Instead, still looking at Jerry, he yells, "Okay, boys, go get 'em!"

Obviously outmatched, we all turn to go. We are a good half-mile from our car, and there is no one to help us.

As we walk rapidly away, the largest man there jumps Jerry from the rear and gets a strangle hold around his neck. Although Jerry weighs more than two hundred pounds, the thug lifts him off the ground with little effort and bounces him forward in front of him.

As I look back, Jerry's head is grotesquely twisted to one side, seemingly separated from his body by a thick arm and fist. His eyes squint upward as he calls out, "Hey, Jacques, take a picture of this!"

I turn and, while walking backward, focus the camera. Someone yells out, "You take that picture, and I'll smash your camera."

I finish focusing, snap the shutter, then start walking quickly down the dirt road again, too proud to run, but not about to linger either.

Suddenly I am struck from behind and sent sprawling. Expecting blows, I bring my knees up against my chest and cover my head with my hands. But nothing happens.

As I scramble to my feet, I notice my notebook at the side of the road behind me. When I step toward it, one of the men moves up threateningly.

I look to my left and see Jerry now on the other side of the road, still held in the choke grip. Next to him stands a giant of a man, muscles bulging, his hands inside black leather gloves.

As I watch, the black leather glove swings back and low to the ground, then comes around hard and fast in a swift, graceful and deadly curve up to Jerry's temple.

Both Jerry and his captor fall to the ground, but the grip around his neck doesn't loosen, and he is brought back to his feet. Again the giant swings and again the blow smashes into Jerry's skull. This time Jerry alone falls.

He lies dazed for a minute before rising. Shaken, we all slowly head down that long dirt road.

Later I learn that Venustiano, who could not weigh more than 150 pounds, had leaped toward the goons when Jerry was grabbed.

"Hey, you can't do that! He's an attorney!" he yelled. Someone knocked him down and kicked him in the head. Then as he rose, he was knocked down again and smashed in the chest.

Kathy, who saw me fall, saw my camera strap break, and the camera skid along the dirt. The man who jumped me leaped after it, smashed it with his boot and kicked it into the bushes along the road.

Shortly after the incident, deputies identify the man in charge as the ranch owner, Albert Hansen, and the three-hundred-pounder who grabbed Jerry as Jimmy Plemmens from Teamster Local 890.

It isn't until much later that I realize that the notebook I left behind contains Cesar's phone number at the retreat—a location that up to now has been kept secret for obvious security reasons.

JERRY COHEN RECALLS

One thing I have a clear recollection of is a funny thing. After we got off the ranch and were back with the pickets, I went down on the ground, and I felt like I was going to throw up. I felt dizzy, and I remember a captain of the sheriff's office bending over me and saying, "Hey, Cohen, there's too many pickets at this entrance."

And then the ambulance came, and I went to the hospital.

CESAR CHAVEZ RECALLS

Jerry's beating signaled the beginning of Teamster violence against us. And it was pretty much a pattern of what they did in Delano and other places.

There were Teamsters coming and intimidating people, some beatings, some shootings. They beat up four or five lonely pickets where they found them by themselves. They tried to run some people off the road. They threw objects from moving automobiles into the picket lines.

On the same day Jerry was beaten, a grower in Gonzales ran a bulldozer into one of the pickets' pickup. But there also was a bad incident in Santa Maria involving one of our own pickets. Because he was very aggressive, the Teamsters picked on him and harassed him. They went to his home and harassed his wife a couple of times when he wasn't there. But this picket was not afraid of them.

One day he and his wife were at a restaurant with two or three other huelgistas, and about six or seven Teamsters came in and beat him up. Later the police came and arrested him, but the Teamsters were let go, even though they were the attackers.

Up to that point, I am told this picket was nonviolent. But about two days later—the day Jerry was beaten—he was coming from a picket line to get some water or something, met two or three Teamsters, and got out of the car with a lead pipe.

The Teamsters had a karate expert who had been beating up people. When he tried to use that on our picket, the picket broke his arm with the pipe.

We moved immediately, kicked him out of the picket line and told him he couldn't be with us any more. But the Teamsters continued after him.

FROM JACQUES LEVY'S NOTEBOOK

Tuesday (continued)—This evening, Bill Grami talks to the press, issuing another declaration of war. He charges that the UFWOC-Teamster pact has been "flagrantly violated in several aspects."

"It is remarkable to me and unbelievable that an organization like UFWOC could sign an agreement with a tremendous amount of publicity and then turn around and violate it," he says. "This illustrates more than anything else why the growers resist UFWOC so tenaciously. It reflects on its credibility and stability."

While this is going on in public, a highly secret meeting is in progress at the Franciscan retreat, in the library of the main building, a formal, stately room with half a dozen chandeliers hanging from the ceiling. The lights, however, are not on, and the room gets darker as dusk falls.

Only three men are there when I arrive, Cesar, Will Lauer, and John M. Fox, chairman of the board and chief executive officer of United Fruit, who has flown in from the East Coast. The talk is quiet, friendly, three cultured men meeting in a formal library.

Fox is saying that the Teamsters haven't yet rescinded their contract, that the next twenty-four to thirty-six hours will be crucial because, after that, he fears, all sides will harden, and it will become brutal. United Fruit wants to end the whole battle. The company is worried sick. They plan to talk to AFL-CIO President George Meany and others, and hope heat will be put on Western Conference of Teamsters chief Einar Mohn quickly.

CESAR CHAVEZ RECALLS

Fox and Lauer were very worried about the boycott and wanted to see me. But they opened up by saying they were 1,000 percent in accord with what we were doing. They might not agree with the methods, but they were not against the Union.

In their own way they tried to tell me that they had heard I was a very reasonable man. While they didn't say it, they intimated that Dolores wasn't reasonable. I'm sure that was one of the reasons why I came on very strong, letting them know that I was even worse than Dolores.

I opened up by telling them that they couldn't get away with what United Fruit had been doing in Latin America for all these years, which really stung them. They got really defensive. They're very diplomatic, but it showed. It came through the skin.

I told them, "We're going to have a Union whether you like it or not."

Of course, they didn't come in with hostility. I wasn't hostile, either, I just wanted them to know that they were not going to get an easier deal from me than they would from Dolores.

Once that was established, we got down to the boycott. They thought it was unfair.

So I said, "Do you really think it's unfair? You might think it, but you really don't believe it."

After I got them committed to saying it was unfair, I said, "What could be more unfair, us boycotting Chiquita, or you guys signing a sweetheart agreement in the back?"

They were embarrassed and said they had nothing to do with it, which I kind of believe. "We're getting it straightened out," they said.

When we talked about resuming negotiations, they said, "Give us time," but I answered, "No, you've got to do it right now, or we call the boycott."

They were worried that the Teamsters could stop their trucks here, and their bananas there. So I said, "But all that is illegal."

"You know it's illegal, but they still do it," Lauer said. "By the time you go to court and get into a big fight, there would be a lot of blood."

"You don't want to fight with the Teamsters. You want to save your skin at our expense," I said.

"No, no, we're not saying that."

"Well, work it out then," I said and related the Perelli-Minetti struggle and DiGiorgio. "That's how we take care of them. And the best way to get the Teamsters out is to put the heat on you."

When they brought up two negotiating items that worried them —money and making the foreman part of the bargaining unit—I told them I wouldn't talk to them about money and gave them a good education about the foremen. I told them how vicious foremen had been, that with or without the consent of the company, they had done some horrible things against our people. I brought up the use of dope, giving dope to workers to make them work extra hours. And I said, "I catch you guys doing that, and I'll blow the whistle on you."

They listened very attentively. One said, "Well, we have to agree there are a lot of things we don't know."

I told them, in this case, all the students and all of the radicals would be coming out of the woodwork. I said, "You know, I think we've got you guys." And they agreed. We parted friendly, but I warned them, "If we don't get this thing settled, the boycott goes on."

FROM JACQUES LEVY'S NOTEBOOK

After the two executives leave, Cesar drives to San Jose to see Jerry Cohen at the hospital. There we meet Dr. Jerome Lackner who is very worried. He plans to wake Jerry every two hours during the night to check his reflexes, he says, as he has detected weakness affecting the left side of Jerry's body. Only time will reveal how serious is the brain concussion.

When we go in to see Jerry briefly, he seems more concerned for Cesar than for himself. He fears Cesar will be arrested for violating the restraining orders—which now cover thirty growers—and tells him to remember two points: The union's position must be that the injunctions are illegal; that to be legal, the union has to be duly selected by the employees first.

Then he warns Cesar. If he is put in jail, he should not eat the food. Jerry has learned from one of the California Rural Legal Assistance attorneys that a prison guard poisoned an inmate recently.

On the way back to St. Francis's retreat, Cesar is pessimistic. He says the strike cannot be maintained for more than a few days, as some of the workers will leave the area, and others will start scabbing.

CHAPTER 9

"Concentrate on Chiquita!"

FROM JACQUES LEVY'S NOTEBOOK

Wednesday, August 26, 1970—at 3:00 P.M. Cesar calls boycotters across the country. "Concentrate on Chiquita. Hit the buyers today, the brokers tomorrow, and we announce the boycott publicly Friday!" In Boston, one picket is sent to picket United Fruit headquarters.

Later in the afternoon, long distance calls start zipping cross-country—the union to John Fox, Fox to Will Lauer, Lauer to Dolores Huerta in Stockton, where she is negotiating with grape growers, another United Fruit vice-president to LeRoy Chatfield in Los Angeles, who then calls Cesar, Dolores to Cesar.

At the 7:30 P.M. rally in the union headquarters parking lot, before more than a thousand workers, Cesar's talk is unusually strong and firm, unlike his normal lecturelike style. Talking of the injunctions, he says defiantly, "Men who are seeking justice are not going to be stopped by unjust decisions."

Then he announces that the strike is being expanded to include Bud Antle and other grower-shippers not previously struck. The workers feed from his strength and roar their support.

But when he gets back to his office, Cesar winces. "Boy, if I live through today, I'll live to be one hundred!" Rubbing his back, he heads for his hospital bed to continue phoning.

His secret office, about a block from union headquarters, is a small, empty store with a tiny back room. For security reasons, the pane glass front and glass front door have been painted. No one can see in, but the filtered light accentuates the bleakness and dreariness of the surroundings, dingy walls, and a couple of battered wooden desks and chairs. The back room is all but filled by the hospital bed. A heavy metal bar cradled on metal brackets lies across the back door, a substitute for a broken lock.

A call comes from Anna Puharich in New York. Fox has heard about the planned press conference Friday.

Then Cesar calls Bob Antle, whose firm has had that Teamster contract and loan since 1960, to tell him he's going to be struck. As a courtesy he wants to notify him first, he says.

"Why me, Cesar?" Antle asks.

"Well, Bob, your workers want to strike, and we've stopped them up to now."

Antle calls it blackmail. He calls Cesar a gangster.

"You've got the right name, but the wrong union," Cesar answers. "We're not causing you a problem. You caused it . . . No, we're not intimidating your workers. You can't believe that propaganda. You know farm workers don't want Teamsters, but want UFWOC. Why don't you sign with us? Is it because we are Mexicans? You signed quickly enough with the Teamsters . . . No, it's not against the law. The day picketing and striking is illegal in this country, that's the day we better leave . . . Yes, you can stop the strike by sitting down tonight and negotiating a contract."

And so the conversation goes, but Antle does not back down.

About 9:45 P.M. a call comes from Bill Kircher in Washington. Cesar lies on the bed listening most of the time. He argues that United Fruit has been making promises for three weeks now.

"No, we can't postpone the boycott anymore. It's started. They're breaking our strike. Workers won't stand for it."

After he hangs up, I ask if Kircher was arguing for United Fruit.

"Our friends are always trying to negotiate," Cesar answers. "The bishop is mad at me. Kircher is mad at me. They forget the workers. They think they solve the strike, but it's not them, it's the workers striking and boycotting."

Then he adds thoughtfully, "But they help us, and we need them."

At 10:30 Kircher calls again. Cesar asks him, "How long does it take to get here from Stockton? Three hours? No, better have them tomorrow. Well, let me call her before you call."

When Cesar finally locates Dolores in Stockton, they set the talks with Inter Harvest for 1:00 P.M. tomorrow at the lettuce shed.

"There's pickets there," Marshall Ganz breaks in.

"We can't have workers cross the picket line," Cesar agrees and tells Dolores to find another location.

Fred Ross, seemingly tireless, although he has been averaging only four hours sleep every night, arrives for a lengthy report. Cesar lies on the bed, eyes closed, listening.

The growers have stopped allowing workers to eat in the labor camps. Between two and three hundred men are involved, and Fred discusses several alternatives.

They also talk about possible violence at Antle. Fred says Bob Antle warned him, "If you strike us, you're asking for it. The Teamsters will protect their contracts."

Thursday, August 27, 1970—When Cesar gets a message from radio reporter Mark Bragg, who has learned that the growers and Teamsters now know where Cesar is staying, he sends word to get his children out of the house.

At 1:45 P.M., Dolores arrives from Stockton, where she has just signed eleven Lodi tokay grape growers, and takes off for one of the Inter Harvest ranches south of Salinas to resume negotiations with United Fruit in a ranch lunchroom.

Will Lauer opens on a tough tone. He first wants an agreement that the workers will end their strike and go back to work tomorrow morning. On the company side, he promises, "We intend to negotiate until we get a contract."

Dolores calls a caucus. "Impossible," say some. "Huelga!" say others. The workers reject the request. So they return and tell Lauer who sits with his hands cupped over his mouth.

All on the company side look glum. The silence hangs heavy over the room. Lauer must backtrack or the talks collapse.

After a long silence, he retreats gracefully. "The company reserves the right to schedule the work tomorrow morning. We'll reserve judgment on that later."

The afternoon slips by, and the talks continue through the dinner hour.

Meanwhile, outside union headquarters, wind and fog don't dampen the spirit at the big workers' rally. When Cesar appears, the air fills with wild cheers of "Huelga! Huelga!"

UFWOC's foes are hoping that fear and hunger among its members will wear down and eventually break the strike, Cesar warns them from on top the flat-bed truck. "But the strike is getting bigger. The farm workers here, like in Delano, are willing to last as long as it takes to win the strike."

Speaking in Spanish, he tells them that Inter Harvest is back at the negotiating table. "Chiquita is very frightened. I am hopeful that by tomorrow we will have the best news in the valley."

In the unheated lunchroom, the damp air is chilling. Dolores wears her poncho, the workers their sweaters, and Lauer has put on his carcoat over his windbreaker.

The talks drag on into the night, as both sides tackle wage rates for members of lettuce machine crews—cutters, lifters, wrappers, packers, closers, loaders, and water boy—and members of lettuce ground crews, cauliflower crews, celery crews, tractor drivers, and irrigators.

Each time new proposals are made, both sides split up to work out their calculations. In one room the workers scribble on pieces of paper and hand over figures to Dolores.

Slowly the company's offers inch up. By 2:00 A.M. Lauer proposes $1.97 an hour now and $2.02 next year for machine lettuce cutters. The rate is a nickel above the Antle contract.

"I truthfully don't understand where we're going," he says.

"We're going for a better way of life for the farm workers," Dolores answers.

"Not tonight!" Lauer replies.

But the bargaining continues. It's Monsignor Higgins's turn to pace the floor. Those on the sidelines are struggling against sleep, despite the cold.

Dolores, who early this morning was negotiating in Stockton, appears as strong now as she did when she started, yet her day has been the most grueling of all.

Someone has just brought in coffee and food, and everyone revives a little. As they eat, Lauer comments, "We can't blow it now!" He also says that now that he has had dinner with both Cesar and Dolores, "that will raise my credibility."

"With whom?"

"My two sons," Lauer answers. They both support UFWOC.

Again the union caucuses. At 3:27 A.M. Dolores reports the workers still are not satisfied.

"In my own experience, there's only one way to resolve this," Lauer says. "It's by whittling away one by one, piece by piece. It's a tortuous way to do it. But we must work it piece by piece and nail down all of it. We're not that far apart."

"When I think of the pain," Dolores says, "to see those people bent over like angle worms for $1.97 an hour for nine hours, it makes me sick. $2.25 for work with a long-handle hoe is underpaid!"

"Well, are you willing to take it off some other place and put it there? That's the name of the game," Lauer answers.

"Pay less taxes," Dolores snaps.

"Unless we do try, we're not going to make the game." Lauer keeps the talks moving gently but firmly, stepping aside a problem when Dolores digs in her heels. At one point he remarks, "I'm being very agreeable, take advantage." The two clergymen are standing, glaring at both sides. They would prefer to be asleep by now.

At 4:30 in the morning, some of the workers must leave to go picket the company. Lauer ignores their action. The talks continue briefly, but finally adjourn until 10:00 A.M.

Friday, August 28, 1970—More wage proposals are exchanged after the talks resume, and caucus follows caucus.

"I think we may have a deal," Dolores finally says.

Carlos Valencia, one of the workers, announces they have come up with a figure of 40½ cents piece rate for a two-year period. After checking some figures, Lauer agrees. That's 9 cents above the present rate and 7½ cents higher than the Teamsters' contract.

Briefly they discuss celery rates before breaking for lunch, then Dolores goes to see Cesar, who is taking off to talk to strikers in King City.

Can he announce a rally for 1:00 P.M. tomorrow, he asks. "Will you have the contract?"

"Yes," Dolores answers.

Cesar smiles. A victory will help. The bad news is that the court restraining orders now cover fifty growers. "The shackles are being forged," he says.

But when Dolores returns to the negotiations at 2:45, none of the company negotiators are there. After a forty-five-minute wait, Lauer arrives looking disturbed and asks for an hour's recess.

"Something that I feared has happened," he says, declining to say what.

Monsignor Higgins, who knows, says it has nothing to do with UFWOC. Then he corrects himself. "It's nothing you can do anything about."

At 5:00 P.M. Lauer returns and announces that the strawberry firm, Pic 'N Pac, has gotten a court order requiring Inter Harvest to show cause why it should not be permanently enjoined from signing a contract with any other union.

He asks for a suspension of the talks to determine what the legal consequences will be. But Dolores is opposed. The union wants no more delay.

It's Lauer's turn to talk tough. "Well, let me tell you of another development," he says angrily. The newspapers quoted Cesar as saying Chiquita is "running scared" and negotiating out of fear of the boycott.

"If Cesar is quoted accurately, I'm extremely disappointed, and UFWOC has lost friends in United Fruit as a result of it. That news story has damaged the relationship we were building up."

He complains, too, that the company is getting reports from everywhere that retailers are going to stop buying Chiquita products. "UFWOC has set itself back with the only friend you've got."

"I'm very sorry this developed," Lauer says. "I think we had a good thing going." And he ends the talks.

Later that night, when Cesar has returned from rallies in King City and Watsonville, Dolores reports on the afternoon's developments.

At Cesar's suggestion, she gets on the phone and tracks Lauer down in a Monterey restaurant. As Cesar and Marshall Ganz gather around, she talks to him, firm in her insistence that talks must be resumed immediately. But when she doesn't seem to be getting anywhere, Cesar grabs the phone.

"This is Cesar," he says bluntly. "We have no choice but to boycott if talks are not resumed," he warns. "No, this is no threat! A threat is when you say you'll do something and don't. I intend to do it. You haven't seen anything yet!"

His tone is angry.

"We were just giving you a little education." And in answer to something Lauer has said, he retorts, "No, I didn't break my word. The talks had stopped."

"Yes, I ordered the boycott started and told people you were running scared because it's true! You are terrified of the boycott!"

Cesar now is speaking in his angriest voice. The Pic 'N Pac suit shows United Fruit conspired with the other growers to sign a Teamster contract, he says, and Lauer knows the workers want UFWOC.

"Damn right we're singling you out!" he lashes out a short pause later. "The suit says you are responsible, and that makes you something special! I want you to negotiate a contract, or we'll hit you with everything we've got and won't let up until you come to the bargaining table. And you'll be paying a lot more than you would now! Your company has been exploiting our brothers in Latin America for a long time, and we won't let you try the same dirty corrupt politics here!"

Another pause.

"The boycott hasn't started! We were just giving you a little education. I want a contract!"

When Cesar hangs up, Marshall and Dolores burst into cheers. But Cesar shakes his head. In a soft and sad voice devoid of all anger he complains, "I was mean. I hit him a couple of low blows. I hit him below the belt." The distaste shows in his face.

Then he tells them that United Fruit got a release from the Teamsters today because of AFL-CIO pressure. After Einar Mohn signed the rescission agreement, the Teamsters notified Pic 'N Pac which filed the suit.

MONSIGNOR GEORGE HIGGINS RECALLS

John Fox flew out to California, and Einar Mohn didn't make it too easy for them. I recall Fox and Lauer saying it wasn't the most pleasant experience they'd ever been through. Mohn didn't refuse the rescission, but he made them cool their heels, that sort of thing.

Here's the president of the company flying all the way from Boston. They could have given it to him over the phone or sent it in the mail.

So I think the Teamsters were telling United Fruit something. And they certainly were telling the smaller growers something.

CHAPTER 10

Enter the Goons

FROM JACQUES LEVY'S NOTEBOOK

Saturday, August 29, 1970—Before resuming talks, Will Lauer demands that Cesar publicly announce the end of the Chiquita boycott, but Cesar first wants assurances an agreement is near. They agree to meet on neutral ground in my room at the TraveLodge at 2:30.

Cesar is already there when Lauer arrives with Dwight Steele, an Inter Harvest attorney. Dolores, arriving late, takes a seat on the bed, her back against the headboard, her feet stretched in front of her on the covers.

Because the boycott is going full blast, Lauer starts off candidly, he used the Pic 'N Pac suit as an excuse to halt the talks and assess the situation.

"We've had a bad image in labor relations," he admits, and the company has worked hard in the tropics to change that. Cesar's remarks tarnishing Chiquita are very damaging and must be rectified before they can conclude negotiations. The two sides are very close, he stresses.

"Let's put the issues on the table and see if we are close," Cesar answers, "and then I'm prepared to reverse that statement."

"We don't like it to look that the company did it only because of a gun at its head," Lauer explains.

Turning to the points in conflict, they discuss a compromise on the foreman issue and wages.

Lauer estimates the Teamster contract would have cost the company $483,000 a year, but the proposed UFWOC wage rates would cost $1.6 million, not counting fringe benefits.

"One of the damnable positions of this industry is that the workers have been subsidizing the industry," Cesar answers, turning Lauer's argument against him.

Lauer estimates the fringe package at another $1.6 to $1.8 million. Then the talk turns to the hiring hall and the boycott.

"The time on the boycott is critical," Lauer says. "It must be stopped now. Are we close?"

But Cesar won't be hurried. He wants to know about the successor clause and a few other issues. Then he asks to talk to Dolores alone. The two company men step outside and wait on the balcony.

What really troubles Cesar suddenly comes out for the first time. The contract may prove a threat to the union. He turns on Dolores.

"I'm talking about bringing the union to more than a thousand workers," he says. "I'm worried. We don't want them to put in machines, or we'll have war with our members. You have to tell the workers what's in store for them if we accept these rates." Leaning toward Dolores he repeats, "We've got to tell the workers they may knock out workers and put in machines."

Dolores disagrees. Her words come out in a rapid stream. The only way to stop machines is to make it more expensive to use a machine, she says. Besides, these rates won't force the company to use machines.

Cesar doesn't believe her. "I'm afraid this could destroy the ground crew. I'm really frightened about that."

He thinks Dolores has made a serious error and also fears the high rate may mean only Inter Harvest will sign up with UFWOC. All the other growers will be scared away.

But it was the workers who pushed up the rates, Dolores argues.

"The workers don't understand these things. You have to teach them."

For a while their tempers flare as they argue. "I'm posing a problem," Cesar says heatedly. "Don't try to belittle me about it. It may stop the organization of the union. What I'm saying is, let the workers make the decision. We may lose the strike, but it's better than losing the union."

Then he changes the subject. "Are we, or are we not closing the contract?" he asks.

Dolores looks down. "Yes," she answers. The storm has subsided.

When Lauer and Steele return, Cesar asks whether the company plans to use more machines and less ground crews.

Lauer explains that if the company can sell a higher volume, it will use more machines. But the machines are used only for wrapped lettuce, and the sale of wrapped lettuce must be promoted. He assures Cesar that the number of ground crews won't ever be reduced, as there is a large market for naked lettuce for restaurants and institutions.

Cesar presses the point. He wants to make sure the company won't switch to machines.

"It won't happen," Lauer insists. "It simply won't happen fast. If I saw it was in the works, I would tell you."

Finally Cesar agrees to issue a statement saying there is no boycott of Chiquita, the company has been negotiating in good faith.

The negotiations resume at 10:00 P.M. at company headquarters. Time slips by. No one notices 2:00 A.M. go by, nor 3:00 A.M. nor 4:00. But nerves are getting edgy. Lauer needles Dolores mercilessly as the sparring continues.

At 4:20 A.M., Cesar calls to find out the progress.

Efficiency drops, eyes droop, and tempers harden. Finally, as the early morning sun seeps into the room, they agree to break for breakfast. It's 6:30 A.M.

Dolores and I go over to an all-night cafe and thumb through the Sunday papers. She searches for her astrological prediction. When she reads it, she laughs. "All social and business ventures will be succesful beyond expectation," it says.

By 8:45 the talks resume and continue until close to 2:00 P.M. when a short lunch break is called. After lunch, as if by magic, the pieces seem to fall together. As both sides bend over yellow pads, figuring out the advantages, the final compromises are reached.

"Do we have a deal on that basis?" Lauer finally asks.

"Right!" Dolores answers.

"With no reservations," Lauer smiles. "My voice is giving out."

Dolores explains the final compromise to the workers in Spanish. They are exuberant.

"Viva la Causa!" they cheer and shake hands all around.

The agreement includes many of the hard-fought changes sought by the union, including a hiring hall, some control over pesticides, and the inclusion of foremen under the contract.

The basic wage scale, which was $1.75 an hour, jumps to $2.10 now and goes up to $2.15 next year. The Teamster rate is only $1.85, going up to $1.96 next year, and $2.08 the year after.

CESAR CHAVEZ RECALLS

The day the contract was signed, we called a big rally with all the Inter Harvest leadership there. As this was the first contract, people were just elated. Carlos Valencia and Luis Morales, of the negotiating committee, made a presentation on what they'd gotten. When they announced the hourly rates, women hugged each other. And when they announced the piece rate, they just couldn't believe it. They felt the power coming through them.

It was one of the best contracts we have ever gotten in a first contract—so good, it's giving us problems in organizing other workers, a very big problem.

Our plan was to get the biggest lettuce company and have enough lettuce under contract to call a boycott. Then we could do with the growers what we did at the beginning of the success in the grapes, use the same theories, the same approaches.

So then we went after Freshpict, and that was Purex. We didn't put pressure on the Teamsters, because if we went to the top and said, "It's our jurisdiction," they would begin to whittle away, and we would have to give more and more and more.

I knew that if we took care of the grower, that would take care of the Teamsters. That way, we would keep everything we needed. It's harder, but that's the only way.

FROM JACQUES LEVY'S NOTEBOOK

Saturday (continued)—Reports come into headquarters of Teamster goons intimidating strikers with baseball bats and chains and of a picket wounded in the foot by a shotgun blast. The man wielding the gun says it went off when he ducked some rocks thrown by pickets. Growers report windshields were broken in a number of rock-throwing incidents.

The number of Teamster goons staying at the Towne House has climbed to more than forty.

CESAR CHAVEZ RECALLS

The violence was very definitely planned. We began to see the effect on the picket line. Although workers still came out, it did discourage the picket line.

One day, before we signed with Inter Harvest, I got a letter from this woman in Carmel or Monterey just knocking the hell out of me. She said she saw me coming out of an expensive restaurant in my black limousine with all of my goons.

It was so ridiculous I wasn't even going to answer, but I think Jim Drake thought we should. About a week later we got another letter apologizing, saying it was the other side. She confused the name Gonsalves and Chavez. Ted Gonsalves was head of Teamster Local 748 in Modesto.

MONSIGNOR GEORGE HIGGINS RECALLS

Speedy Gonsalves moved into the Towne House with his guards or goons, whatever they were. Their sheer presence was a kind of threat to everybody.

It was the weirdest thing I ever saw, a guy from another local, no relationship to Salinas, coming in with goons. I never counted them, but they were everywhere I looked. I just assumed they had weapons—I don't know what they would be doing there if they didn't have blackjacks or guns. And Speedy would ride around in town in that great big, black limousine, right out of a B movie.

I had only two or three incidents with Speedy, none with his staff.

I'd go into the restaurant alone, start to read the paper, and Speedy would be across the room with his gang. Once or twice after a few drinks, he would shout across the room, "We're going to get the clergy, too. We're sick and tired of the Catholic church. I'll cut off your water."

One day he did it very loud, so I asked the waiter, "Would you ask that gentleman to come over here."

When he came over, I said, "Look, Speedy, we'd better have an understanding. For all I know you've got a gun, and maybe your people have got guns or blackjacks. But in any event, I'm in no position to fight you physically."

I said, "I can't, therefore, throw you out of the restaurant, but if you do that once more, I'll get on the phone immediately and call Fitzsimmons in Washington. And I'll give it to the newspapers, and I'll demand that Fitzsimmons withdraw you and take away your charter and destroy you. You're not going to make a fool out of me in a public restaurant." He was very apologetic.

Then, the night United Fruit settled, everybody was exhausted. I went out to dinner with Will Lauer, kind of a little victory dinner out of town on the edge of Salinas, when who walks in but Speedy and his boys. I think it was just a coincidence.

He paid his respects to me, the usual stuff, "You dumb clergy," and all that. But then he practically threatened Will Lauer. So again I had to go through this act.

I remember saying to Bill Grami, once at least in the course of that period, "This guy's bad news, bad medicine for the Teamsters. You ought to get him out."

"Oh," Grami said, "Gee, I know it. Is he still around? My God, I told him to get out of here." He was washing his hands of it.

Well, I never believed that. He never could have been in that hotel where Grami was living and had his headquarters unless somebody either brought him in, or permitted him to be there. All Grami would have to do is to tell him to get out, and he'd have to get out.

CHAPTER 11

Ambush

CESAR CHAVEZ RECALLS

There was a tremendous reaction against Inter Harvest after they signed. "They're from Boston," local growers said. "It's a conspiracy to put the local grower out of operation. Inter Harvest has no interest in the valley, just in making money."

The opposition formed a "citizens committee," and Teamsters and other pickets started picketing Inter Harvest the day after we reached an agreement. The drivers, of course, refused to leave the yard, and work stopped.

We put heat on Inter Harvest. "Our people want to work. They've been out of work for a long time. If you don't get them to work, they're going to leave," that kind of pressure.

"We'll take care of it, it's just community reaction. It'll go away, and we have to deal with it," they answered.

Interestingly enough, the large growers were not coming to those picket lines. They were getting that element from down county, from King City, the small family farm guys, and the Teamsters and the goons.

Our big problem was with other workers who were now getting frightened because, they said, "If we sign a contract, it means we don't work."

We spent most of our time reassuring them, "No, no, it's just a passing thing."

But Inter Harvest workers weren't as worried. I sent some out to see if Inter Harvest was doing this because they didn't have any pressure on the harvesting end. When word came back that they were losing lettuce, I thought it wouldn't last too long.

There was always the possibility it could be a Teamster's scheme to get some money out of Inter Harvest. When I suggested that to the company, they said, "No, we're not going to pay a damn penny."

On the last day of August, George Meany announced the end of the grape boycott at the convention of the California Labor Federation in San Francisco.

We had to have a clear ending at some point. I didn't want the victory to fizzle out. I wanted to have a very sharp ending.

We also wanted to make it clear in the minds of the Salinas growers that the grape boycott was over, that the message to them was, "Okay, we're now ready to take you on."

The next day I ate grapes for the first time since the boycott started five years before. They were sweet grapes of justice.

On the next day, too, Pic 'N Pac dropped their suit against Inter Harvest, which was a good lead to what was going to come. It suggested that there might be a change of heart in their resistance to the Union.

But before they dropped the suit, Cal Watkins, the personnel manager for Inter Harvest, filed a sworn affidavit which proved what we had said about the grower-Teamster conspiracy.

He testified that he attended a meeting of the Grower-Shipper Vegetable Association negotiating committee on July 23 when it was decided to get powers of attorney from members to "feel out the Teamsters and explore the prospects of negotiating an agreement for agricultural workers."

On the next day, his affidavit said, "the committee reported that the Teamsters were interested and receptive," and twenty-nine firms signed a recognition agreement. On July 25 they started negotiating with the Teamsters. "The union did not claim to represent any agricultural employees at this time," Watkins said.

And, his affidavit concluded, "About a week or ten days later, Harold Bradshaw, then director of harvesting for Inter Harvest, phoned the union to inquire about the status of the employees regarding union membership. He talked to Ralph Kottner, who advised that around 108 of our employees had signed up with the union. We employed in excess of 1,000 employees at that time."

FROM JACQUES LEVY'S NOTEBOOK

Wednesday, September 2, 1970—Members of the Seafarers Union appear on the scene from San Francisco. Their job is the same as in 1966 at DiGiorgio, to make their presence known to

Teamster goons, in the hope of stopping intimidation of pickets.

In Redwood City, Superior Court Judge Melvin E. Cohn issues a temporary restraining order to halt Teamster and grower harassment of UFWOC members.

Today, too, Jerry Cohen is released from the hospital and returns to work.

Thursday, September 3, 1970—In the cold, damp, foggy darkness about 5:30 this morning, big tough men gather in the 300 block of Abbott Street in Salinas where sixty-five Inter Harvest trucks are kept. On the west side of the street are some two hundred growers and their friends milling in front of the produce truck dispatching lot. Some one hundred yards down the street, about fifty Teamsters stand staring at another group of men across the street. There, in front of a Speedee 7-11 market, a dozen members of Local 78A of the Butchers Union stare back. They are cooling plant workers who support UFWOC.

"It could get a little rough before breakfast," one of the meat cutters cracks.

But standing between the growers' group and the drivers in the Inter Harvest lot are eight Salinas officers and three private security guards.

Suddenly, a dozen trucks turn their lights on and start their motors, the deep roar shattering the stillness of the morning and drowning out the low voices of the men on both sides of the street.

A noticeable tension spreads through the men, but just as suddenly as the motors start, they are turned off, and the tension eases.

About ten minutes later, one truck turns on its light, starts its motor and rolls slowly toward the exit.

"Come on, let's block this road," a man shouts.

"Clear the driveway!" an officer hollers through a bullhorn. But the angry men present a solid, sullen mass as they crowd around the big white and green truck's cab and press against the front bumper.

"Get a good look at his face!" a Teamster picket yells.

"It's got the hammer and sickle," another picket answers.

"Boy, you better park that truck!" a third man threatens.

For five minutes the truck squats there, its huge motor idling, seemingly impervious to the threats. Then the gears grind, and the rig slowly starts backing up, returning to its parking place. Cheers, jeers, and more threats fill the air.

"You're going to get your ass whipped for even trying it, you stupid bastard!" someone yells into the darkened lot.

After a while, the cooling plant workers disperse, disappointed that Inter Harvest doesn't resume production.

The tough, angry mood of defiance continues throughout the day in front of the Inter Harvest truck parking lot. Demonstrators carry picket signs with red letters urging, "Don't buy Chiquita Bananas," and distribute a list of boycottable commodities produced by United Brands.

In the afternoon, a caravan from King City of twenty-five trucks loaded with lettuce, celery, and carrots harvested despite the strike roll through downtown Salinas on their way to the vacuum coolers. All are flying the American flag. From the look of those in the caravan, it is obvious they believe they are the true patriots fighting to preserve the "American way of life." And the set of their jaws suggests no one had better stand in their way.

The second anti-UFWOC ad in two days appears in the local paper. "The true purpose of the boycott is control of our food supply," it says quoting Rex T. Westerfield, identified as author of "Sour Grapes," a John Birch Society pamphlet. According to Westerfield, "the object is to unite American agricultural workers in a single union under the control of revolutionary leaders— known Marxists and identified Communists. The goal simply put, is control of America's food supply."

The ad is sponsored by the Adam Smith chapter of the Young Americans for Freedom.

CESAR CHAVEZ RECALLS

After Inter Harvest signed up, we changed our target immediately and began to boycott Purex, the parent company of Freshpict. I told the people not to do it too heavily, just to go out and make a lot of contacts and tell people this is the next boycott.

But we began to find some immediate response. We found out it wasn't hard to take the stuff off the shelves. We were very surprised. And, of course, Purex's President William Tincher began to really react. He was frightened. By Friday, he was ready to recognize us and get a Teamster rescission.

FROM JACQUES LEVY'S NOTEBOOK

Friday, September 4, 1970—When Cesar returns from a noon rally in Guadalupe, 160 miles to the South, his back bothers him so, he goes straight to bed at the office. The news he gets isn't good. There are reports of goons with baseball bats smashing the windshields of cars belonging to pickets, and of someone being beaten. The atmosphere of confrontation and violence is increasing.

Then Bill Kircher arrives. First, as he starts to speak, the AFL-CIO official sits by Cesar's bed. But he is soon pacing the floor, gesticulating, for he hasn't yet gotten over the experience he has just undergone, an experience that started with an innocuous phone call.

WILLIAM KIRCHER RECALLS

About 11:00 A.M., I got a phone call from a guy who introduced himself as Albert Hansen. He had run into a guy from the AFL-CIO who heard I was in town. He said much could be avoided if we could meet, so I suggested my motel room at the TraveLodge at 2:30.

Before going to my room, I walked into the motel office to check something, and the manager said that the room I wanted was all set up right next to mine. He had gotten a call, something about a Junior Chamber of Commerce meeting. So he gave me the key to the room.

The chairs were set up, about twelve to fifteen chairs. I figured it was a mistake and gave the key back. Then Tom Trehern of the Seafarers and I went to my room which was on the second floor. It was a little room with two twin beds.

Tom and I sat on the bed and Hansen and Bryce Barnard, his superintendent, on the only two chairs. I asked about the room next door, but Hansen said he had nothing to do with it.

I had my back to the window, but Tom saw a Teamster walk by on the balcony. Then a few more. He knew something was wrong when he saw Ted Gonsalves go by with his arm in a sling. By this time there seemed to be quite a crowd of Teamster thugs outside and in the rooms on each side of mine.

Then there was pounding on the walls and men yelling, "Don't break any of Kircher's bones. Just give him a soft going over," "Get your guns ready if you need them, but don't hurt Hansen! Be careful!" and these sorts of very ridiculous statements.

Tom says to me, "Goddamn! I think we've been set up!"

Immediately we suggested to Hansen and Barnard that they keep their mouths shut if they wanted to get out in one piece. I went to the phone and told the gal at the desk that the party she expected wasn't what she thought it was.

"Your property may get damaged," I told her. "You better call the police."

Then I called the Downtown Motel where the Seafarers were staying. It's right around the corner from the TraveLodge. Within ten minutes we had ten to fifteen Seafarers up, and we ran Hansen out.

Then I invited Ted Gonsalves in. I figured he was hiding a gun in that sling.

Some of the guys they had were really funny. They had a gentleman who looked like he had attired himself from a page in The Godfather. He had a tight-fitting, pin-stripe suit with broad lapels, a black shirt and white tie and a dark hat. And as God is my judge, he was carrying a violin case.

When they were in the room, I called Einar Mohn at the Burlingame Western Conference Teamster office, but he wasn't there. Instead I got Buddy Graham and told him what was going on. We used to play golf together. He was Einar Mohn's assistant in Washington. Then I told Gonsalves to get on the phone.

"Oh, we're not doing anything. We live here at this hotel," he lied.

I grabbed the phone. "Buddy, call the desk and find out how long they have been here!"

You should have seen Gonsalves's face. He offered to take me out for a drink, and I told him, "I wouldn't have a drink with you. You're nothing but fucking trash."

FROM JACQUES LEVY'S NOTEBOOK

Cesar, Marshall Ganz, and I listen incredulously as Bill Kircher tells his story. After answering a few questions, Kircher says he is considering closing down the ports of San Francisco and Los Angeles and having all the Seafarers come to Salinas to maintain order.

"This is no bluff!" Kircher says. "I mean it."

He has set up a meeting with the mayor of Salinas for tomorrow, he says, when he will ask for a clamp down on the activities of the "citizens committee" and the Teamster goons.

"And if the meeting doesn't go good with him," Kircher says, "I'm going to tell him that we're prepared to help him do the job. Unless they do it, we're going to close the port of San Francisco, close the port of Los Angeles, and get every able-bodied seaman!"

Some of us laugh.

"I'm not kidding," Kircher says sternly. "I've already got clearance! The Seafarers have promised me officially they'll close both ports."

"Wow! Just closing the ports . . ." Cesar starts, but Kircher interrupts to recall a similar plan he had several years earlier. When 140 black hospital workers in Charleston, South Carolina, struck demanding that their union be recognized, Kircher said, Governor Robert McNair called out the national guard.

So Kircher called a press conference and threatened to close the port of Charleston. "You should have seen it," Kircher laughed. "It went up like smoke. And forty-eight hours later we had a settlement."

Before he leaves, Kircher decides he better not stay at the Trave-Lodge that night. He gets a room at the Downtowner, where the Seafarers are staying.

CHAPTER 12

"Clever Tactical Reasons"

FROM JACQUES LEVY'S NOTEBOOK

Saturday, September 5, 1970—7:45 A.M., Jerry Cohen reports more violence. Guns were fired near the Hansen ranch, a shotgun and a hand gun. A picket was struck by a car. Goons used baseball bats on UFWOC pickets yesterday and smashed their car. At the Silacci ranch, a rancher shot his weapon in the air, aimed it at pickets, and threatened to "blow your guts out."

There was a bomb threat called in to union headquarters. Some pickets have been involved in rock-throwing incidents and dropping nails in driveways, and both sides report broken windshields and flat tires.

At 8:40 A.M. LeRoy Chatfield calls, and Cesar tells him there is "a lot of violence." Three times during the conversation he repeats that. It obviously troubles him greatly. Jerry also is worried. He feels Cesar's security is bad, and he wants Cesar to get Mack Lyons back to handle security. But Cesar does not respond. We are all on edge.

The secret office is just not that safe. The place is a firetrap. It would be easy to toss a Molotov cocktail through the front window, Jerry fears, and pick off Cesar if he tried to run out the back through the parking lot.

During the morning, Kircher goes to city hall to meet with Salinas Mayor G. Sid Gadsby, the police chief, and the city manager. After the meeting, Bill Kircher and the mayor hold a press conference, but there is no mention of closing the ports. The mayor says he is convinced Inter Harvest can move its trucks safely Tuesday, the day after Labor Day.

409

When I return to Cesar's office after the press conference, I find him on his bed, obviously not feeling well. At times he keeps his eyes closed as Fred Ross reports that the strikers' morale was hurt badly when deputies started to enforce the no-picketing rule on six ranches.

At 2:00 P.M., Dolores Huerta and I take off for the Highway Center Lodge to meet with Tom Driscoll and several other strawberry ranchers in their upstairs bedroom. For three hours, Dolores answers their questions about union contracts.

As the conversation ends, one of the growers looks out the window into the parking lot. "It looks like a parade is starting," he remarks.

We go over to look. A number of cars and trucks are parked one behind the other. They are flying American flags and have posters pasted on their sides. Directly below is a yellow pickup with a familiar figure standing beside it.

"Look," I say excitedly. "That's the guy that beat up Jerry!" The massive three-hundred-pound Jimmy Plemmens is lighting a cigarette.

As Dolores and I stand at the window watching him, another man runs up carrying part of a metal jack which he tosses into the back seat of a sedan. We notice other hefty men standing around.

"You better call the police," someone suggests.

"And the union," Dolores says.

About twenty minutes later, we look out the window again. Some thirty men are in a football huddle directly below us. When the huddle breaks up, the men head for their vehicles. Only three men at the center of the huddle remain standing in the parking lot.

"Why that's Grami and Gonsalves!" Dolores exclaims. And sure enough it is. Then Bill Grami and Ted Gonsalves head toward a room at the rear of the motel as the caravan starts to pull out.

We decide to follow the caravan and run down the stairs to the car. The third man in the huddle is still standing there and recognizes Dolores. He is a Teamster named Johnny Frank.

"How you doin'?" Frank nods in greeting.

"Winning!" Dolores answers as she speeds by. Then we head out the parking lot and onto the freeway, but the caravan already is out of sight. So we go back to warn Cesar.

"Don't worry, Dolores," Cesar says, "they're not the devil. They'd be crazy to come here."

"They are crazy!" Dolores replies. She suspects the caravan will try to break up the union's nightly rally.

"The people would take care of them if they tried anything," Cesar says, trying to reassure her.

"That's just what they want, Cesar, to start a riot!"

Bill Kircher quickly moves into action. He calls a Teamster friend to let him know what we have seen and to notify Einar Mohn. He also calls the police. Then he gets ahold of the Seafarers and assigns them to be on the lookout in front of union headquarters.

Cesar goes to the rally as if nothing is wrong and gets up on the flat-bed truck to speak to the workers.

As the rally continues, the sky turns pale blue and luminous. A few swirls of clouds above the setting sun turn amber, pink, and orange as the light slowly fades. The crowd is quiet and relaxed, unaware of the tension along the curb.

But the caravan never appears.

Sunday, September 6, 1970—Kircher has a meeting with Western Conference Teamster chief Einar Mohn at 2:30 P.M. and calls in at 4:30. They will meet again Tuesday.

Tonight there is another bomb threat against Cesar and the union. Police call Dolores Huerta who refuses to tell them where Cesar is. They also call Jerry Cohen, who has the headquarters and office cleared, but he, too, refuses to say where Cesar is, despite police insistence that "we have to find him!"

Dolores fears her phone is tapped, so she makes no calls out at all. Jerry, on the other hand, goes to a public phone booth to alert Cesar.

Labor Day, September 7, 1970—Cesar is in his office, where he spends most of the day and evening.

In the morning Jerry argues with him about security, especially because of last night's bomb threat, and wants him to go where it is safe, somewhere away from here.

"I don't want to live in a tomb. It's not worth living that way," Cesar argues from his bed. He suggests moving to the camp set up for the striking workers south of town, but Jerry is against it. "I feel safer among the people than isolated," Cesar says.

Unable to sway him, Jerry changes the subject to tomorrow's meeting with the Teamsters. The two men agree to keep the conversation polite, but to avoid any negotiations. Stick by the pact, Cesar says, and warn them, "We could have pulled the guys out of the canneries, but we haven't. If you want war, we'll get the sheds and canneries."

Seafarer Tom Trehern arrives as sporty as a movie idol with his jaunty corduroy hat, his thin moustache and long, slanting sideburns that sweep from his ear line toward his mouth, and his open shirt that shows off his hairy chest.

Trehern says he plans to send a couple of Seafarers to the growers' rally at Hartnell College where they can tape the proceedings.

Later we learn that Albert Hansen and three other growers have held a press conference to accuse UFWOC of a "reign of terror." They give many examples of rocks thrown, workers being intimidated and threatened.

The main event, though, is the rally sponsored by the Citizens Committee for Agriculture which was started last week as the Citizens Committee for Local Justice.

After it's over, the Seafarers come back to report to Cesar. They estimate there were about twenty-five hundred persons there. A plane pulling an American flag flew over head. There was much talk about union violence and the threat to the local economy. Signs sprinkled through the crowd proclaimed "Reds Lettuce Alone" and "Boycott Chiquita."

While Cesar listens to the tape of the rally, Marshall Ganz is called to the phone. Three pickets have just been hospitalized after being attacked in Hollister by eight strikebreakers with chains.

Late tonight, the Seafarers at the Downtowner Motel have one guard watching the parking lot. He spots Ted Gonsalves—with no arm in a sling—taking down license numbers.

A short time later a Teamster caravan goes by with lots of hooting and hollering, and circles the block. The caravan returns and parks across the street. About seventy-five men pile out, far outnumbering the Seafarers who have come pouring out into the parking lot. Some from the caravan have chains.

Tom Trehern calls his boss in San Francisco and is asked, "Are you safe?"

"Right now, yes."

His boss says he'll clear the port and send more guys down in the morning. But there is no way to help right now.

Then the police arrive in force and order the goons back in their cars.

"It looks like Ted wants us all to know he's still here," Trehern says later.

JERRY COHEN RECALLS

The presence of the goons had Inter Harvest shut down for a nine-day period, and that was important.

The picket line became a citizens committee line every morning at 6:00 or 7:00, but from 3:00 to 5:00 A.M., when they were trying to move their trucks, there were plenty of Teamsters on that goddamn line. They stopped Inter Harvest.

Once there was going to be a battle. The Seafarers came and lined up on the other side of the street. And Cesar said, "You get our guys away from there and send them home. This is not a war!"

Here was a situation where Bill Grami had been outflanked by Einar Mohn. The rescission had been granted, and Grami disclaimed the fact he was involved in this picket line.

I could see a lot of tactical reasons for the Teamsters bringing the goons into the valley.

The threat was, if you sign with UFWOC, you know what's going to happen to you. You're going to get your operation shut down.

So it logjammed other growers who were interested in signing, number one. Number two, they knew that we were about to use the boycott as a tool, and we needed union lettuce. It prevented the flow of union lettuce for over a week. At that point, those were two very critical problems.

So there were two different kinds of activities going on—direct intimidation of growers who indicated a willingness to talk to us, and shutting down the facilities. There was one meeting that I have been told about when the growers met, and Gonsalves and his guys surrounded the growers' meeting. Some growers, like D'Arrigo, were intimidated. They were told, "If you sign, we'll take care of you!"

Now, add to that the whole mess that was going on in the valley in terms of injunctive relief that was pending. I think it was very helpful from the point of view of the growers' legal tactics to prove that there was always violence. No judge wants that going on in the valley. And that was a very important factor.

In addition, I think it had an effect on our organizers. When we get bomb threats called into our office every other day, when people shoot at our office, when organizers are afraid to go to camps at night because there are goons around, it has a practical effect on the people trying to do a job of talking to the workers. There were some camps our organizers were afraid to go into, and rightly so. Who would go into the Hansen camp after their lawyer was put in the hospital by the guys out there? There were a lot of workers at Hansen that they should have talked to, but they never did because they were afraid to go into that camp.

There were a lot of very good reasons, clever tactical reasons, why those guys were useful.

FROM JACQUES LEVY'S NOTEBOOK

Tuesday, September 8, 1970—Police arrive at the Inter Harvest dispatching lot about 4:00 A.M. Ten uniformed officers stand near the lot, several more are stationed on the roofs of nearby buildings, and a reserve force is nearby. A crowd develops of about two hundred, mostly farmers, who boo when police clear the driveway. Besides groups of men standing on both sides of the Inter Harvest driveway and across the street, a moving picket line of cars and pickups sporting American flags are in the area.

But Inter Harvest decides not to move its trucks.

Cesar is like a tiger in a cage today, out of sorts, angry, and restless. When Marshall Ganz reports that thirty-nine pickets have been arrested at the Bruce Church ranch and asks, "What should we do?" Cesar answers. "They should stay in jail. They disobeyed orders." He sharply criticizes Marshall for lack of organization.

In the evening the workers go to the jail for a vigil. It is a peaceful gathering, but noisy, with strike songs and repeated cries of "Huelga!" Suddenly the scene turns ugly when deputies use tear gas to disperse the pickets.

Today, too, Jerry Cohen meets in Palo Alto with the Teamsters.

JERRY COHEN RECALLS

The day after Labor Day, Irwin De Shettler of the AFL-CIO, Bill Carder, and I went to the Palo Alto Cabana. Monsignor George Higgins and Monsignor Roger Mahoney were there for the church. Einar Mohn was sitting at the head of the table like a pompous little king. Bill Grami was at the other end. There also were some other Teamster people, including Pete Andrade.

Mohn was pretending that we'd violated the pact. He was shocked. "You've struck! Explain why you've struck!"

And I remember saying it was very clear we had the right to strike.

The public pact is different from the total agreement, and now Mohn was saying that the no-raid provision of the public pact applied, and we shouldn't have struck—which was not the agreement. We had the pact, we had the confidential memorandum and we had an oral commitment that Grami had made to Monsignor Higgins because, he had said, he couldn't put it in writing for legal and political reasons.

So I gave my version of the agreement, which was the total

agreement—that we had a jurisdictional pact, that the Teamsters were getting out of the lettuce, that they were going to help us with the strike activities, that, as a matter of fact, we gave them a ten-day moratorium. Now that moratorium clearly implied the right to strike.

And it was all very clear.

But Mohn pretended it wasn't, and that we'd struck in violation of the pact.

Grami sat at the other end of the table. I remember him saying, "Well, Einar, Jerry's just a very clever boy, and he's just taking advantage of us."

I thought, you son of a bitch! Of all the lying sons of bitches! So I just had to repeat. And at that time Higgins came down.

Higgins was very straight, playing it right down the middle. Earlier we had the disagreement with him—me in particular—just an honest difference of opinion on whether the ten-day moratorium was automatic or whether it would be six days and then four.

Now he stopped the argument and said, "As the third party that was there, there's nobody who was in that room"—the people that negotiated the pact were Grami, Bill Carder, and me, with Higgins and Mahoney as the witnesses—he said, "There's nobody who was in that room that doesn't know that what Jerry is saying is the truth, that you had the right to strike,"—talking to us, the farm workers—"that the moratorium was just a delay of the right," and he went through the whole outline of the agreement.

And Mohn didn't want to say anything more because he was boxed. He was there like a little judge to find out.

Grami made some typical Grami remark—they're always ambivalent—to the effect that that may have been someone's understanding, but it wasn't his. He stuck to his guns all the way.

Then all I remember is, when we were leaving, Mohn looked at us and said to Carder, "You know," he said, "sons," or "young men," something like that, "You know, drive carefully. The roads are dangerous."

And Carder took that as a threat, and I took it just as a silly-assed thing that Mohn had said. It was ambivalent. It was said with a smile. It was said in a condescending way. But there was an implication there.

CHAPTER 13

Forced to Boycott

Wednesday, September 9, 1970—When I arrive at union headquarters at 5:15 A.M., Marshall Ganz tells me Cesar is planning to go to jail, and mass arrests are planned in a nonviolent picket line.

Jerry Cohen says people will be arrested 15 at a time after the sheriff is notified that they plan to violate the injunction on the grounds that it is unconstitutional. He will tell the sheriff not to panic like last night, not to use tear gas.

Dolores arrives. "Is he in a good mood?" she asks of Cesar who isn't here yet. She says she took a shower. "We're late, but clean."

Then Cesar arrives. "We must talk to the sheriff," he says, "and tell them exactly what we're going to do. There will be no violence, and there will be movie cameras there." He is afraid the police may get rough, and cameras will be a deterrent.

"I plan to be the first one," Cesar says firmly. He looks at Dolores. "Don't you get arrested! We need you outside."

"Aw, shucks! I could have stayed in bed," Dolores jokes.

At 7:45 A.M., at a rally outside headquarters, workers are told what is going to happen, and many volunteers are recruited for the arrests. The first group will be women.

A short time later, Helen Manning, a Salinas Californian reporter, mentions that the Inter Harvest trucks went out this morning. She saw four go out, and reporter Eric Brazil saw eight others leave.

"They had thirty-six or forty police officers there," she says.

"They made five arrests. The law and order guys were saying, 'Communists!' to the cops. 'Send that truck back to Moscow!' The last thing I heard was 'Let's have a tea party in Chualar!' And one of the guys went out to Chualar to find the Inter Harvest crews."

Cesar, thinking about being in jail, asks me to take care of his dog Boycott for him. Then someone brings him breakfast, a half-cantaloupe and some nonfat milk.

There is more talk about jail. Marshall reports conditions there are bad. Thirty guys share sixteen mattresses, and the toilet doesn't work. Conditions are so bad, in fact, the prisoners have decided to fast.

An hour later, at a press conference, a large number of TV cameras focus on Cesar seated at a table with the group of women behind him who have volunteered to be among the first group arrested.

"We feel that freedom is lost when it is not defended," he says. "And we intend to defend our freedom. We feel that a jail with bars is no worse than a jail without bars."

And he issues a challenge. "We believe that if the authorities believe that the court order is legal, they will arrest us. On the other hand, if the authorities feel that the order is illegal, they will permit us to picket."

"It's up to the courts and up to the sheriff, and I think it's up to the conscience of America to decide this one," he says.

A reporter asks if his health will permit him to take a long jail term.

"It will be a vacation," he answers, "because jail could never be as hard as this!"

Shortly after 11:00 A.M., the caravan of UFWOC pickets and press arrive at a ranch in Gonzales, south of Salinas. Big lettuce trucks and trailers loaded with packed lettuce are coming out of the ranch, and others are going in empty, ready for a load.

Fifteen women and Cesar start picketing beside the entrance to the fields, walking back and forth carrying the union flag. A black deputy just watches.

After about twenty-five minutes, Cesar tells a reporter, "I can't stay too long because of my back."

The picketing has been going on about an hour when a pickup drives by. Some of the farm workers notice one of the men in the truck has both a rifle and a hand gun. They holler to warn Cesar, but the truck drives by slowly, and nothing happens.

A short time later, another pickup drives by, goes down the road, then comes back. It repeats the maneuver several times. I warn Jerry Cohen who answers, "I know. I don't think he's got a gun, though."

After about two hours of picketing—and no arrests—Jerry announces, "I had a long discussion with the sheriff this morning about our reasons why we thought this jurisdictional strike injunction was improper and unconstitutional. And it is our feeling that since the sheriff has decided not to enforce it, that he probably agrees with us. So as of now, we're going to begin to picket all over the valley full blast!"

In the afternoon, I go over to Cesar's secret office to wait there for him with Cesar's secretary, Ann Carpenter. We are puzzled by a strange phone call, some crank who asks for Cesar. We wonder how the caller could have learned the unlisted number. When a second stranger calls, we become worried.

On a hunch, Ann calls information and asks for Cesar Chavez.

"Which number do you want?" the operator asks, explaining that there are two, one at union headquarters and the other at— and she gives the address of the secret office.

I call a telephone supervisor to get them to stop giving out the unlisted number and address. She says nothing can be done because this is a holiday, Admission Day.

When Cesar returns, we tell him of the security breach. Then he receives a report of trouble in Chualar where sixteen police cars and twenty-two officers have arrived. It seems that when two officers arrested a captain of the picket line on a charge of throwing tacks on the road, pickets surrounded the two deputies. One of the deputies, a Chicano, pulled his gun, then returned it to his holster, and called for help. Lawmen arrived in force, pulled a pregnant girl out of a pickup and made four or five more arrests.

Cesar asks who was in charge of the picket line. "They're doing a very bad job," he says. He wants strikers disciplined for breaking rules and wants organizers replaced by others who can enforce discipline.

That evening, a group of boycotters from across the country fills the office—the first contingent from the boycott machinery which is being dismantled.

"At the end of the grape boycott, I promised you a party," Cesar tells them with a rueful smile. "Welcome."

He tells them of the troubles on the picket lines and asks the boycotters to go there and "exercise leadership."

"We don't want any more confrontation with police," he tells them. "They'll kill people and break the strike. We expect you to take over if there's violence. I don't want any escape hatch. You're responsible to stop it! The people don't understand how dangerous this is. They're sitting ducks to any stupid cop who pulls out his gun. I expect you to stop violence, and I hold you responsible."

CESAR CHAVEZ RECALLS

One of the last things the boycotters did in New York was to boycott D'Arrigo's wholesale house. That put tremendous pressure on them. So I wasn't surprised—on the same day the Inter Harvest trucks rolled—that negotiations started with both Freshpict and D'Arrigo.

I knew that we were going to get involved in a very long lettuce strike, and the big worry I had with the boycotters was demoralization. How could I ask them not to come back and then say, "Look, you've got to stay on another boycott for a long time."

I decided to bring them back after the strike started, and when they got here, they would get this impact—all these striking workers—then they would get turned on, as we were, and if we didn't win and had to call the strike off, they would be ready for another boycott.

Under two hundred boycotters came back, probably just over one hundred out of about four hundred. Some stayed where they were and quit. They were volunteers. A lot of them just went home.

FROM JACQUES LEVY'S NOTEBOOK

Wednesday evening the jail vigil goes on without incidents. About thirty members of the clergy are present.

Jim Drake tells me the financial situation is critical. The union may run out of funds in a week or two.

"What then?" I ask.

Jim shrugs. "It will be just like 1965. We had no money then."

Friday, September 11, 1970—Cesar sends a telegram to Herbert Fleming, president of the Grower-Shipper Vegetable Association, saying he would like to resolve the situation without an international boycott. "Your cooperation and help is needed. Unless I hear from you, I will be forced to start the boycott shortly."

The State Supreme Court rules that the union challenge to the temporary restraining orders deserves a court hearing. This should stop arrests of pickets until the case is heard.

This evening, the largest artichoke grower, L. H. Delfino of Watsonville, recognizes UFWOC.

Saturday, September 12, 1970—When a message arrives that Herb Fleming is willing to meet with Cesar man to man, with no one else there, a meeting is set up at the Downtowner Motel.

Meanwhile, in the Freshpict and D'Arrigo negotiations, Dolores is finding rough going. The companies make a big fuss about the workers going back to work carrying union flags.

Dolores checks and finds out one worker had a UFWOC flag on his car antenna, and when a supervisor complained, several other workers put up their flags. The supervisor insisted they couldn't work if they had the flag.

"We took away our flags when we agreed to talk to you, so why can't you take away yours?" one of the company negotiators asks Dolores.

"What flag did you take away?" Dolores asks.

"We were flying the American flag."

"Well, that's our flag, too. Why did you take it away?" Dolores snaps back.

The rest of the session remains acrimonious.

After meeting with Fleming from 2:00 to 4:00 P.M., Cesar returns to his office in a buoyant mood. Asked what happened, he paces back and forth, puts his hands in bragging fashion up to his chest, puffs out his chest, and pretends to puff a big cigar. He is sorry the strike is all over, he jokes, now he will have to retire. Jim Drake, Marshall Ganz, and the others laugh.

"That's all I know," he mimics, "striking!"

After some more banter, he turns serious. Nothing has been settled. He says the conversation ranged from the price of lettuce to loyalty to country.

Fleming said he thought Cesar was a very honorable man, an honest man, a good man, but the growers don't like and are frightened of Dolores, Jerry Cohen, Marshall Ganz, Jim Drake, and those others "because they do not have any principles."

Cesar answered that he would not discuss other people on his staff any more than he would criticize members of the staff that Fleming has.

After discussing the hiring hall and other issues, Cesar told Fleming about plans to boycott lettuce, saying he had scheduled a press conference for 10:00 Monday morning in Los Angeles to announce the boycott.

Fleming was surprised. "Why Los Angeles?"

"Because it's the largest produce center in this state."

Fleming asked him if he couldn't postpone the press conference, and Cesar said he couldn't, that he already had his press staff arranging it.

"Well, what if I could arrange a meeting with some growers, is there any chance that you could postpone it then?"

Cesar smiled. "Well, if there *is* a meeting, yes. Yes, I could postpone it for a couple of days."

Fleming said he could try to arrange a meeting with maybe a hundred growers, and he would like to have all the growers he could get, but only Cesar, and no one else, could come with him.

"It wouldn't be negotiations," Fleming explained.

"Yes, I understand that."

"It might not get anywhere."

"I understand that."

"And it might not produce anything. And it might not get any negotiations started."

Each time Cesar said, "Yes, I understand that." So Fleming said he would see what he could do.

Cesar says that he thinks he cleared away many misconceptions Fleming had about the union. He found Fleming very nice, he jokes, but when it comes time for negotiations, "I'll unleash Dolores and tell her, 'Go get him, Dolores! Go get him!' "

Marshall Ganz then reports good news from the fields. Near King City a big tomato rancher by the name of Hill came out to the picket line and said, "I'm tired of fighting. I can't get any labor to work for me. I want to settle with the union. Who do I talk to?"

At another picket line, the pickets were having a very difficult time reaching the workers who were way out in the field. A sheriff's deputy asked them what was the trouble, and they explained they couldn't be heard. So the deputy let them use the loud-speaker on his car to talk to the workers.

"They know which way the wind is blowing now. You can tell!" Marshall says.

Tuesday, September 15, 1970—Bill Grami tells the press that the Teamsters are signing new workers and are considering chartering a state-wide, or even a Far West local for farm workers.

"This has been the idea we had been working toward initially, and it is being considered at this time," he says. "But there has been no decision on the matter—at this time."

During the day, Herb Fleming meets with growers and then calls Cesar to tell him they are not interested in further talks. The lines are stiffening.

But there is one crack. Meyer Tomatoes and Brown and Hill request a preliminary meeting. Meyer is the largest green tomato shipper on the West Coast—some three thousand acres in the state—while Brown and Hill have about one thousand acres. Together they employ about one thousand workers.

The discussion lasts about two hours before Jerry Cohen writes out in longhand a union recognition agreement which both firms sign. Negotiations will start at 9:00 A.M. tomorrow.

Wednesday, September 16, 1970—Superior Court Judge Anthony Brazil grants permanent injunctions against picketing to thirty growers, on the grounds this is a jurisdictional dispute which is illegal in California.

UFWOC Attorney Bill Carder argues that the growers are using the Teamster contract "to insulate them" against another union, since the Teamsters don't represent the workers.

The growers' attorney, E. J. Leach, answers that while Carder's position might be desired, "That's not what the law is." Judge Brazil agrees.

When Cesar gets the news, he calls off all picketing and asks striking workers to come to Sunset Beach near Watsonville for a meeting and barbecue. The union must switch from picketing to a national boycott.

Thursday, September 17, 1970—Both sides call press conferences.

"We are sending people to sixty-four cities in North America, and we're leaving immediately," Cesar tells the press. "The boycott will be on until the last lettuce grower is signed up!"

Grower Herbert Fleming has more to say.

"UFWOC is losing the war that Chavez declared on the Teamster Union and growers," he tells reporters. "He is losing the war because his organization has been unable to recruit support among field workers."

As for the boycott, Fleming predicts it won't work because "it will be trying to boycott produce that is grown, harvested, and shipped by union labor.

"The fact is that the courts have ruled this dispute to be what it is—a jurisdictional dispute, an attack by one union upon another," he says, "and we are sure that when the public, the grocery store owners, and the produce brokers realize these facts, they will not participate in any petty jurisdictional boycott that would penalize the vast majority of our field workers and deprive the housewife of her right to free choice."

"We've beat them in the fields. Everything had gone according to pattern. We knew that he would hit us hard, and he did! It was terrible! It was terrifying out there," Fleming says, rolling his eyes.

"You just can't believe the intimidation, the threats, the—hell! People were taken for rides, you know, and stripped and threatened with castration and made to walk home twenty miles in the dark, things like this. They're experts at this, this is the nonviolent union that is expert at this!"

Before leaving for Delano this afternoon, Cesar meets in his office with Marshall Ganz, Fred Ross, and Dolores Huerta. They discuss what to do with boycotters, and Cesar predicts 75 percent of them will not want to go back on the boycott—and he hasn't talked to them yet.

Marshall puts his hands to his head. "Gee, that will be a disaster! We must do something!" he cries.

Cesar gets upset. "Don't do anything, Marshall! Don't do anything!" And he stresses, "Don't tell them anything, understand?"

He repeats that he has made a commitment to the boycotters that the boycott ended with the grapes, and they must not be shamed or pressured into going back.

Fred agrees. "Any pressure," he says, "and when they go, they'll want to come right back." The union must recruit lettuce and celery workers to go on the boycott.

Friday, September 18, 1970—Pic 'N Pac cracks. The S. S. Pierce Company, which owns the giant strawberry-growing firm, announces it is ready to recognize the union, provided the workers want to be represented by UFWOC.

Monday, September 21, 1970—Talks between UFWOC and Freshpict break down.

A delegation of Salinas Valley growers meets in Sacramento with Assembly Speaker Robert T. Monagan (R-Tracy) to ask for legislation curbing farm labor unions.

Wednesday, September 23, 1970—At midnight, Cesar receives a call from Manuel Chavez in Calexico, who has just learned of a shooting of a Teamster organizer in Santa Maria. The organizer is reported in critical condition, and three UFWOC members have been arrested.

Thursday, September 24, 1970—At an impromptu press conference in the parking lot behind his secret office, Cesar blames himself for the shooting.

"I should have been there," he says. "If I had been there, nothing would have happened.

"It's a difficult thing, and it's a damning thing for us. It's inexcusable. It shouldn't have happened, and it's the first time it's happened in five years. So we feel very badly."

The man accused of the shooting is the same man who was banned from the picket line after breaking the arm of the karate expert with a lead pipe.

That night, Cesar tells the boycotters about the shooting. "If we mean nonviolence," he says, "we have to say, 'Damn it, we mean it, and it's not going to happen. If it happens, then you can have your own strike, and you can't be a part of us.'"

The victim, shot seven times, later recovers from his wounds.

The Salinas Valley harvest is nearing its end, and the tempo of events slows down perceptibly. The union eventually signs contracts with Brown and Hill Tomato Packers, Freshpict, Delfino, Pic 'N Pac, and D'Arrigo.

But the opposition reacts.

Daryl Arnold, Freshpict Northern California division manager, quits the company, soon becomes president of the Free Marketing Council, and starts campaigning across the country against the union.

And on November 4, at 1:30 A.M., a dynamite bomb explodes outside the UFWOC Hollister headquarters shattering the door and windows of the building.

CHAPTER 14

Inside Salinas Jail

CESAR CHAVEZ RECALLS

We started singling out Bud Antle on the boycott, and it began to sting him. We'd made up our minds that we were going to ignore the injunction prohibiting us from boycotting him, and were doing all kinds of legal maneuverings to keep out of court.

Then Antle set a deposition for me in late November in Bakersfield. Antle came with two or three of his attorneys. I came with Jerry Cohen.

We had a lot of fun with them that day. They didn't want to ask me directly if we were boycotting, because they thought I was going to deny it. So they spent hours with all kinds of intricate questions trying to trap me into perjuring myself.

I was taking care of myself, and after a while I was enjoying it. During a break, Jerry and I devised a plan. If they asked us directly, we were going to tell them, "Yes, we're boycotting, and we'll continue the boycott. We're breaking the injunction."

But they never asked. Finally they said, "Well, we haven't got anything else," and they got up and stretched, looked around, and put their coats on.

"Well, if that's it, we're going to leave," we said.

"Wait a minute. I just have one other question. Sit down."

So I sat down, and the attorney asked, "Are you boycotting Antle products?"

"Yes," I said.

"Oh, my God! What did I hear? Are you boycotting?"

"Yes, we are."

"Did you hear that?" And they jumped around and did a little dance.

And I said, "What's wrong? We enjoy boycotting Antle products. We're boycotting the hell out of them."

"That's all we wanted to hear! That's all we want. Make sure you take that down!" Then he said, "You know there's an injunction?"

"Yea."

"Are you willfully and disrespectfully . . ."

"Yes."

For about five minutes they were just ecstatic, just going out of their minds. And Jerry was out there laughing, and I was laughing too.

FROM JACQUES LEVY'S NOTEBOOK

Calls from the Teamsters Union to Antle urge that the court hearing not take place. The thought that Cesar might be jailed, and the publicity that would develop, worries the Teamsters. It also worries AFL-CIO President George Meany, who asks Bill Kircher to contact Cesar in the hopes of working out a compromise.

But Cesar also realizes the value of the contempt of court trial to bring the lettuce boycott to national attention, and Kircher, despite repeated tries, can't reach him.

The day before the contempt hearing, Judge Gordon Campbell denies two UFWOC motions—that he disqualify himself on grounds of prejudice and that this be a jury trial.

Early Friday morning, December 4, delegations of farm workers start arriving at union headquarters in Salinas about 5:00. The air is cold and wet as they come in from Coachella, Delano, Stockton, Santa Paula, and from throughout the Salinas Valley.

In the steamy headquarters, they get refried beans and coffee, then head for the unpaved parking lot behind Cesar's secret office.

In a back room at the headquarters, Cesar is making his final plans. If he is jailed, he wants a statement given to the press, a simple, hard-hitting statement of defiance that can be used by the boycotters—"Boycott Bud Antle! Boycott Dow Chemical! And boycott the hell out of them! Viva!"—the union has discovered financial ties between Antle and Dow Chemical.

If the judge only imposes a fine, he says, the union will start a public appeal to raise the money. And if the union wins its case, then the boycott will be pushed and expanded.

Meanwhile the farm workers start out, some two thousand strong, along Alisal Street, for the mile-long march to the court-house. The procession takes about thirty minutes to pass a single point as the workers march quietly in double-file with their flags and candles.

When they reach the courthouse, they keep their double line and line up from the courtroom on the third floor, down the cor-ridors and the stairs, and out into the courtyard.

They stand silently, sometimes kneeling to pray, waiting for the trial to start, and then waiting while it is in session. And so they stand—men, women, and children—for more than three and a half hours, until the trial ends, so quiet that no one in the courtroom can tell there are two thousand farm workers in and around the building.

Inside Judge Campbell's courtroom, the decor is incongruous, including as it does two eighteenth century tapestries, one showing several carefree ladies washing their feet in a stream while angels watch, tapestries that once might have graced an ornate salon in a duke's palace. One of the tapestries hangs behind the judge's bench, while the other is on the wall behind the jury box.

During the hearing union attorney, Bill Carder, argues that the injunction is deficient, vague, ambiguous, and unconstitutional. Richard Maltzman, Antle's attorney, walks a tightrope. He wants the union fined and its boycott stopped, but he doesn't want Cesar jailed.

"We have no desire to see Mr. Chavez put in jail for jail's sake," he pointedly tells Judge Campbell. At another point he repeats, "I'd like every opportunity be given for him to comply before a jail sentence is imposed."

Finally the judge calls a ten-minute recess to prepare his judg-ment. Stern-faced, the old gentleman strides out of the courtroom.

"He hates us," Cesar comments, predicting he will be jailed. He also mentions that a deputy tried to poison a prisoner at the jail not long ago.

Just as the ten minutes elapse, Judge Campbell reappears, walks briskly to his seat overlooking the courtroom, and shuffles through a sheaf of papers.

Then he begins to read, his voice droning on through the charges, and his views that his orders have been violated. For more than ten minutes he reads the long and complex ruling, making it obvious it could not have been typed during the ten-minute recess.

"If the law is to continue to have any meaning," Judge Camp-bell reads, "it must continue to apply equally to the weak and the strong, to the poor and the rich, favoring neither the one nor the other. No man or organization is above or below the law. If the objective is a noble objective—and many say there is a noble objective here—improper and evil methods cannot be permitted to justify it."

Then he sentences Cesar to jail on each of two contempt of court counts, and orders that Cesar remain in jail until he has notified all UFWOC personnel to stop the boycott against Antle.

Judge Campbell is so angry after imposing sentence that he stomps off the bench. But he has forgotten the fine. He stops in mid-step, faces the courtroom again, imposes a ten thousand dollar fine and turns toward the exit.

UFWOC attorney Carder's mouth drops open. Judge Campbell is halfway out the door as Carder calls him. The ten thousand dollar fine is illegal, the lawyer says. The maximum fine for contempt of court is only five hundred dollars. And he cites the code section.

Judge Campbell turns to face the courtroom again. He pauses, his chin quivering.

"You're right," he finally says. He reduces the fine to one thousand dollars—five hundred dollars for each of two counts—then spins on his heels and disappears.

Nearly as quickly, Cesar is in custody and whisked out of the courtroom, facing a jail sentence that could last years. One thing is certain. He will not order the Antle boycott stopped. Instead the order goes out, "Boycott the hell out of them!"

CESAR CHAVEZ RECALLS

They led me from the courtroom and put me in jail, locking all the prisoners up so they couldn't get to where I was, while they put me in my cell. They told me that I was a civil prisoner, in for civil contempt, not criminal, so they put me in by myself, which I didn't mind at all.

It was a very tiny cell, maybe about five by eight feet. There were about six cells the same size in a litle cellblock. When they opened the door, I could walk back and forth in the corridor, which wasn't too much of an exercise.

When I first got in, there was so much excitement I didn't think about it; but the next day I began to feel very badly about being in jail. I wanted to get out and fight. The second and third day were rough days because I wasn't organized. Then, on the night of the third day, I thought, I've got to do something about this, otherwise I'm going to be in trouble. So I began to plan every minute of my life in jail.

I just made a schedule, almost by the hour, to keep myself occupied. Once I got that down, I was okay. There was a time for meditation, a time for reading, a time for my mail, a time for exercise, a time for planning, and times to wash up and shave and clean up.

Then I found I couldn't keep the schedule according to the hours I had, because I was near the drunk cell. At night there were all kinds of noises, roughly between 10:00 in the evening and about 3:00 in the morning, and sometimes longer, depending on how drunk they were.

So I would read during that period, then I would sleep. They would wake me up at 5:30, I'd eat and go back to sleep until about maybe 9:00. Then I'd get up, say a few prayers, do my exercise, open my mail, and begin to answer all the letters. I had sacks of mail. It took me three or four hours to read it all. I read every single letter, and if it was a very good letter, I would set it aside and reread it.

At night I would do some exercise, walk, then take a shower. At first the light was very bad, and I couldn't read well. Then I became friends with a deputy who gave me a bigger light. He said it was against all regulations, but he put in a big bulb and left the heavy steel mesh open. I could reach in there and turn it off when I wanted to sleep and turn it on when I wanted to read. It meant a lot.

FROM JACQUES LEVY'S NOTEBOOK

It is damp, dark, and foggy when the vigil starts in the parking lot across the street from the jail, the day Cesar is locked up.

Some three dozen votive candles flicker in a makeshift shrine in the back of a rented pickup. The candles throw a soft light on the gold and brown Virgin of Guadalupe, flanked by flowers. The altar is draped with black cloth and decorated with the American, Mexican, and union flags. Tinsel borders the black cloth, and a small banner with Viva Chavez is pinned on it.

Alongside the truck, several dozen farm workers vow the vigil will last as long as Cesar remains in jail. One of them, Modesto Negrete, a tomato picker from King City, pledges to fast for the duration.

The next day, a woman drives up to the shrine and starts talk-

ing to one of the workers. She tells how she was against the Cause because she thought the people were dirty, and she was outraged by the union's red flag and the strike.

But, she says, she was at the courthouse yesterday and saw one of the farm workers put out his cigarette on the floor. Then another worker came up to him and told him it was wrong. So the first worker picked up the butt and put it in his pocket.

The lady says she was deeply moved by that and the workers' behavior, and she wants to give five dollars to the Cause.

The worker thanks her and asks for her name and address; so the union can send her a thank you letter.

No, the lady says. She wants to remain anonymous.

"Why?"

"My son is a grower."

The day after Cesar is jailed, Dr. Jerome Lackner arrives to check Cesar's health. The union wants the doctor to prescribe a special diet; so Cesar won't eat jail food. But the doctor doesn't need the fear of poisoning as an excuse for his prescription. He is shocked at Cesar's condition, reporting that his nails are as thin as tissue paper from lack of protein. He orders that a special diet be given the prisoner.

CESAR CHAVEZ RECALLS

All the people in jail are poor people, every single one that was there that I know of. I didn't go to all the floors, but I had contacts with a lot of them. They were just poor people, poor blacks, poor Chicanos, poor whites. Other people come in for two, three hours, but the moment they're sobered up, they're sprung.

The guys inside were very good. I wasn't eating that much, and bread becomes a big item in there. Because the doctor came in, Nonie Lomax, a union staff member, was cooking vegetarian food for me. She'd make some tremendous soybean enchiladas and other good stuff. Since I could only eat about a third of what she cooked, I would give the rest to the trusties. And then I would give the jail food, meat and eggs, to them, since I'm a vegetarian.

My attorneys were coming two and three times a day to see me, and some other visitors came, too. They let Bishop Patrick Flores come, and Coretta King, the widow of Martin Luther King, Jr. She didn't tell me, but I could see that this reminded her of her husband being in jail. Unlike a lot of the farm worker women who came and cried, she looked at being in jail as part of the struggle. Ethel Kennedy was the same way during her visit.

FROM JACQUES LEVY'S NOTEBOOK

When Senator Robert F. Kennedy's widow arrives in Salinas December 6, all the ingredients are there for disaster. About two thousand farm workers are in the parking lot across from the jail facing a huge flat-bed truck where the mass will be celebrated. Brown Berets line the crowd, and beyond them policemen pace.

Across the street from them, in front of the jail, about two hundred tough-looking and angry men picket and jeer. Their signs set the tone. "Kennedys are jailbirds," "Ethel go home," "Reds Lettuce Alone," "Chappaquidick Now Salinas," And they keep up the chant, "Ethel Go Home."

Night has fallen before Mrs. Kennedy arrives and mounts the flat-bed truck, which is surrounded by a sea of dark faces as mass is celebrated. The lights on the TV cameras make a target of all those on the platform, and the quiet of the service is pierced repeatedly by the angry cries of the men across the street.

After the service, Mrs. Kennedy has no choice but to walk across the street, past the threatening pickets, and down an alley to the jail door. There is no escape.

Grim-faced, she starts out, the ever-present TV cameras keeping the spotlights on her. Police and Brown Berets form a protective corridor, while union members act as a human shield before her. Close by her side is her huge bodyguard, Rafer Johnson, the former Olympic decathlon champion.

Despite all that protection, a picket with a sign in one hand plunges toward her and makes an obscene gesture in her face. Another demonstrator lunges at her and grabs at her hair. Just as quickly, one of the guards' hands comes down hard on the grabbing arm before it can do more than brush her locks. She walks on, unhurt, down the alley and into the jail.

After talking fifteen minutes to Cesar through a glass partition, she is whisked off to the airport. On the way there, she turns to the UAW's Paul Schrade, who invited her to Salinas, and says, "Paul, you throw some weird parties!"

Meanwhile, in front of the jail, a young girl suddenly dashes across the street with a union flag, slips through the hostile pickets, and dashes up the stairs to the building's front door. From her perch, separated from any protection, she starts waving the red banner with the black eagle.

The television cameramen, looking for excitement, just as quickly light up the scene with their portable lights, drawing attention to what is happening.

Shouts of support go up from the farm workers, but the "Vivas!" turn to cries of anger as several demonstrators rush the girl and knock her down the stairs.

A few young farm workers set off to her rescue. For a moment, it looks as if a nonviolent visit may turn into a bloody riot. But the Brown Berets quickly lock arms along the curb and stop everyone from crossing the street.

The girl manages to scramble to her feet, dashes back across the street, and the police prevent anyone from chasing her. Tempers cool as both sides disperse peacefully.

CESAR CHAVEZ RECALLS

My experience, I'm sure, was a lot different than almost all other prisoners there, because I had a lot going for me outside, and a lot going inside.

I was sure I wasn't going to be there that long. I knew something had to give. There was a lot of good work being done with the appeal, and a lot of good boycotting work being done.

I could tell a lot of people were angry throughout the country. A lot of the letters I received almost had tears in them, exclaiming how unfair it was. And the lettuce boycott was beginning to pick up steam. So I rested and began to feel that strength in my body and mind. I began to feel relaxed, very relaxed. Being in jail is what you want to make it. If you want to make it hard, you can make it hard. If you want to make it easy, I think you can make it easy.

FROM JACQUES LEVY'S NOTEBOOK

A week after Cesar is jailed, the State Court of Appeals denies a union petition that the Antle injunction be temporarily set aside. So the union appeals the decision to the California Supreme Court.

On Christmas Eve, twenty days after he is jailed, the Supreme Court orders his release pending its review of the case.

As Cesar leaves the jail, a mass of thanksgiving is held in the parking lot for about four hundred union supporters.

"Jails were made for men who fight for their rights," Cesar tells them. "My spirit was never in jail. They can jail us, but they can never jail the Cause."

Four months later—in a unanimous decision—the California Supreme Court finds Judge Gordon Campbell's injunction unconstitutional. It rules that UFWOC has the right to boycott Bud Antle.

CHAPTER 15

Secret Lettuce Talks

November 18, 1970—Modesto Bee news item: Cannery Workers Union Local 748 members last night accused their secretary-treasurer, Ted Gonsalves, of misusing as much as twenty-four thousand dollars in local union funds for organizing activities in the Salinas Valley last summer.

Gonsalves answered the charge during a packed union meeting by saying he has covered the expenses from his personal funds, and the International Brotherhood of Teamsters will reimburse him.

"I worked for the Teamsters for thirty years and have yet to steal my first nickel from them," Gonsalves said. "I'll show you my expenses anytime. They're a hell of a lot less than any previous secretary."

December 16, 1970—Modesto Bee news item: During a two-and-a-half-hour meeting of Local 748 last night in Modesto, William Grami is asked to investigate the use of twenty-four thousand dollars in local union funds to fight Chavez.

The dispute is so severe, some members risked expulsion by sneaking a Bee reporter into last night's meeting.

Grami said he will be in Modesto about two weeks looking into the charges.

December 31, 1970—Modesto Bee news item: Six Modesto men indicted for federal gun-control law violations were linked yesterday with attempts to foil Cesar Chavez's efforts to organize lettuce pickers in the Salinas Valley.

434

A link also exists between some of the six men and Local 748. The six are accused of conspiring to make, possess, and transfer firearms, including explosives, between October 29 and November 3.

One of the six indicted men said he worked as a picket during August and September in Salinas, was paid by personal check from Ted Gonsalves, and stayed in the Towne House.

Gonsalves, interviewed today, said he was in Salinas at the request of the International Teamsters Union. Off and on, Gonsalves said, he probably had seventy men in Salinas under his command. Most were Local 748 members, and most were from the Modesto area.

January 7, 1971—Modesto Bee *news item:* Voluntary trusteeship was urged upon Local 748's executive board by William Grami.

In an interview yesterday, Grami said that he had concluded the local should be in trusteeship whether the local agreed or not.

At first, Gonsalves told the members he had been ordered into Salinas by the International Teamsters, but later he changed his statement to say he had been "invited."

Grami said that Gonsalves was invited to a number of meetings there at which Teamster activities were explained. He was neither ordered nor invited to bring men to Salinas for the struggle with Chavez, and after Gonsalves brought the men, he was asked to leave, Grami said.

Grami also said he asked Gonsalves to leave Salinas three times. Gonsalves "did us more harm than good. His methods were unorthodox, to say the least."

Grami apparently referred to what one Salinas lawman called Gonsalves's "outlandish pose," which included being driven around in a black, four-ton limousine. Department of Motor Vehicles records show Gonsalves purchased the television-equipped car early in September.

The car was built by the Lehman-Peters Company of Chicago and originally cost eighteen thousand dollars, according to a former Modesto owner. The vehicle came equipped with two air conditioners and reportedly is the same model as used by Governor Ronald Reagan.

January 19, 1971—San Franciso Chronicle *news item:* The Teamsters Union has placed its Modesto cannery workers local under temporary trusteeship while it investigates charges that the secretary-treasurer spent "more than fifty thousand dollars" without authorization.

William Grami has been appointed interim head of Local 748. An audit of its books has been ordered.

JERRY COHEN AT SAN FRANCISCO PRESS CONFERENCE

I think sending Grami out there as trustee is like sending Typhoid Mary out to cure an epidemic of typhoid.

FROM JACQUES LEVY'S NOTEBOOK

Four of the six men indicted on charges of conspiring to make, possess, and transfer firearms pleaded guilty to the charge. The other two were tried and convicted. They were sentenced to San Quentin Prison.

CESAR CHAVEZ RECALLS

There was a meeting in Monterey on May 7, 1971, with growers, the Teamsters, and ourselves. The AFL-CIO sent Joe Keenan, vice-president of its executive board, and Al Woll, its general counsel. There were about thirty or forty growers there, the big and the small, all of them, but most of the contact on our part was with Herb Fleming and attorney Andrew Church. Both Grami and Andrade were there.

Einar Mohn made a statement telling the growers that the Teamsters were out. "We don't want the contracts. We're out."

Then the growers said, "How can we negotiate with the boycott on?" The others began to put pressure on us to call the boycott off and sit down and negotiate.

So we called a moratorium on the lettuce boycott to show the AFL-CIO and everybody else that we were reasonable, and so we could negotiate.

Because the growers wouldn't negotiate unless there was somebody from the AFL-CIO present, the federation assigned Tony Gallo, a retired officer from the Gypsum Workers Union.

FROM JACQUES LEVY'S NOTEBOOK

On May 20, 1971, a second meeting is held at the plush Fairmont Hotel in San Francisco. Present are members of a growers' committee representing growers in the Salinas Valley, the Santa Maria area, the Imperial Valley, and Arizona; AFL-CIO vice-president Joseph Keenan and the Federation attorney J. Albert Woll, Bill Kircher; Cesar, Jerry Cohen, and three other UFWOC members.

The growers want to negotiate a contract that they can then take to those they represent for acceptance or rejection. When the union asks that those negotiating at least pledge to accept the final contract, Herb Fleming insists that all growers must stick together.

Finally, both sides agree to negotiate, but the growers will keep their Teamster contracts until a UFWOC contract is approved. They also agree there will be no publicity about the talks, and both sides will suspend all pending lawsuits.

The first negotiating session takes place on June 2 in the Fleet Room of the Marina Del Rey in Los Angeles. They continue on a weekly basis through the summer and fall.

During July, in other negotiations, the union gets closer to a contract with Heublein Corporation for its workers in California vineyards, when all of a sudden those talks turn sour. So UFWOC starts a quiet boycott of Heublein products and finds itself pressured by the AFL-CIO to stop.

When George Meany comes to San Francisco in August to attend the AFL-CIO Executive Council meeting, he plans to confront Cesar.

Instead, Jerry Cohen calls a press conference in San Francisco to announce the filing of a lawsuit against the liquor conglomorate, basing one charge on the allegation that Meany has been "deceived and defrauded" by Heublein into opposing the farm union's boycott.

Not only does Meany not talk to Cesar—though Cesar does not come to San Francisco for a far more compelling reason—but the Heublein boycott continues without letup. Meany, of course, is not pleased, but Heublein finally resumes negotiations, and a week later signs a contract.

CESAR CHAVEZ RECALLS

After going around and around with those lettuce negotiations for more than five months, we found out they weren't serious. Jerry and I decided the negotiations were going no place, and we'd better halt them and start fighting again.

First, I went to our executive board and suggested that we do something to find out if the growers were sincere. I told the board, "I'm sure these guys won't sign anything. Even if we're willing to give them the Union, they won't take it."

We had some big arguments. Some board members were afraid. But finally I got the board's agreement—reluctantly—that I should propose a very bad contract.

I wanted to show the AFL-CIO that these growers really weren't negotiating. I orchestrated everything. First, we called Andrew Church and Herb Fleming to a special meeting, a very QT meeting with Jerry and me.

"Look, we know that we've been unreasonable on some proposals," I told them, "and we have these problems." So I agreed to give them everything in exchange for recognition, the same wages as the others, the whole thing!

They looked. "We can buy that. That's very good."

"But this is nonnegotiable," I said. "We don't negotiate from this point. This is all you get."

It was a very short meeting. Then we called another in Los Angeles about a week later with all their committee there. I reported what we had done, laid it out, and offered the package "provided we agree that there is no room for negotiations."

Well, they wanted to negotiate even more out of that. So Kircher came in and did the final job, and we broke with them. That was on November 10.

FROM JACQUES LEVY'S NOTEBOOK

Months before the lettuce negotiations collapse in November 1971, major attacks are initiated against the union. In California and other states, legislation is pushed by the Farm Bureau and agribusiness to stop the farm workers, while the federal government plans a frontal assault on UFWOC.

Toward the end of July, the union gets the most chilling news of all from U.S. Treasury agents who have learned there is a twenty-five thousand dollar contract on Cesar's life. As yet they do not know who has put up the money, but they identify the trigger man as Buddy Gene Prochnau, wanted for the ambush-slaying of a Visalia wrecking-yard operator.

The treasury agents give the union a picture of Prochnau, warning that they have no idea of his whereabouts. His chief identifying marks are a notch missing from the right ear and a "Born to Lose" tattoo on the right calf.

Top security precautions are taken immediately. Cesar disappears from sight, his location known only to his closest aides. He can no longer attend the lettuce negotiations, and, of course, he can't see Meany in San Francisco. But the public is told only that he is suffering from a recurrence of his back ailment.

Both Cesar and the union have become targets for destruction.

Book VII

TARGET FOR DESTRUCTION

1971–May 1975

By 1971, the time had come to stamp out the farm workers' union. Its opponents understood, as few others did, La Causa's potential and its power, despite the infinitesimal number of the total agricultural work force covered by union contracts.

The political climate was ugly. In Washington, the most corrupt administration in American history ran the government, an administration that believed in buying power and selling influence. Facing national elections in 1972, the Nixon administration had turned to the Teamsters for its core of power within labor and had dispensed favors to many, including major segments of agribusiness.

It was a climate favorable to the plans of the union's foes, who turned to the federal government, state legislatures, and the Teamsters. A few even thought it would be quicker to assassinate Cesar Chavez.

The ensuing onslaught severely wounded the union, as all but a handful of its contracts were lost. But the UFW could no more be destroyed than a cork could be sunk in a stormy ocean. Too many farm workers had shed the shackles of exploitation and experienced the dignity of equality. In addition, slow and patient organizing had spread the farm workers' struggle beyond the confines of agricultural counties to the cities and suburbs, where La Causa developed the firm support of powerful forces—organized labor, a multitude of faiths, minority groups, and students.

Then in 1975, a new governor took over in California, the son of the governor who in 1966 had avoided the farm workers when they ended their pilgrimage to Sacramento and who later that same year had helped them set up a fair election at DiGiorgio. The new Governor Brown, however, was a different brand of politician than his father. Instead of trying to duck the farm labor issue, he gave it top priority. At last an atmosphere of justice appeared to dawn for farm workers in the state.

And even as the union fought to regain lost contracts, Cesar Chavez was planning how to spread La Causa further by assigning veterans of the movement to donate their expertise to others less fortunate. The poor farm worker who took that giant step in 1962 realized that the techniques developed by La Causa could be successfully applied by the poor in the U.S. and farm workers in other lands.

CHAPTER 1

Assassination Plot

CESAR CHAVEZ RECALLS

My first reaction when I was told of the plot was the hell with the plotters. I didn't want to leave Union headquarters at La Paz. But I did leave in deference to the people, who were very concerned. We spent one month just wandering like gypsies, and by the third day I was just like a caged lion. I thought it was a waste of time. August is a key month.

But it may be that it was a good decision. I'm still alive.

For a long time I didn't believe there was a plot, but Watergate made me feel otherwise. Watergate just forced me to believe. There's a certain amount of jealousy about your country. You don't want to think the worst of it until you're shocked into it. Then you have to realize that it's true.

And it's hard to explain the strange behavior of government agencies who investigated the assassination plot.

FROM JACQUES LEVY'S NOTEBOOK

Despite government attempts at a cover-up and Cesar's unwillingness for more than a year to believe the facts, there is no reason to doubt that there was a plot to kill him and to burn union records.

Much of the evidence is on tape and is reported in a secret U.S. Treasury Department report signed on September 23, 1971, by Treasury agent William J. Vizzard, head of the Bakersfield office

443

of the Treasury Department's Alcohol, Tobacco and Firearms Division.

The plot, as first reported by a police informant named Larry Shears, involved an unknown number of Delano area growers who gave some twenty-five thousand dollars to a Bakersfield man named Richard Pedigo. Pedigo, in turn, was to hire a trigger man to assassinate Cesar, and he asked Shears to burn some union records.

Since ATF couldn't base its case solely on the word of a police informant, it sent in an undercover ATF agent named Lester Robinson whose findings are reported in Vizzard's final report.

According to that report, undercover agent Robinson met with Pedigo, one of the largest drug dealers in the Bakersfield area, on Wednesday, August 18, 1971. Coincidentally, that was two days after trigger man Buddy Gene Prochnau was captured thirty miles from Salinas by the California Highway Patrol. The Robinson-Pedigo meeting was secretly tape-recorded.

Vizzard's report, based on the tape recording, states that Pedigo "discussed the arson of Chavez's records. He said that he had seen the building and that it was wood frame and easily broken into. Pedigo says that the people who want the arson done are farmers in the Delano, Jasmine, McFarland area, and that they have so much money that they are probable not affraid of an inquiry."

Two nights later, at about 10:30 on Friday, August 20, the report states that ATF agent Robinson again met Pedigo alone and secretly recorded their conversation.

"The conversation started with Pedigo explaining that the conspiricy was off because Chavez was no longer putting pressure on the Farmers in the Delano area," Vizzard's report says. "He stated that at one time about two months prior he had been given $25,000 to do the killing and arson. He had, in turn, made arrangements to have it done for $18,500.00 but the person who was to do it 'never got his shit together.'"

But the ATF report also discloses that just before Pedigo told Robinson the plot was called off, Pedigo had learned there was a police informant inside his organization—the thirty-three-year-old Bakersfield heavy-duty mechanic named Larry Shears.

And at 4:00 that same Friday afternoon, a grower's son the ATF knew was a link between Pedigo and the growers was seen by Shears bringing a paper bag into Pedigo's home. After the grower's son left, Pedigo told Shears he now had the money for carrying out the plot.

This proves significant because at 7:00 A.M. the next morning, ATF agents raided Pedigo's home and arrested him on charges of selling amphetamines to agent Robinson the night before. In

Pedigo's safe, agents found $6,830. And in the refrigerator they found $22,000. The $22,000, however, is not mentioned in Vizzard's final report.

Then ATF let it be known that Robinson was an undercover ATF agent and that Larry Shears was an informant, thus destroying the only undercover links to the plotters, whose identity remains unknown.

After Pedigo's arrest, ATF dropped the assassination plot investigation on the grounds it no longer had jurisdiction. Yet that same weekend, both agents Vizzard and Robinson told Shears in separate recorded telephone conversations that they had been "pretty close" to solving the case.

Nearly four months later, when Larry Shears reveals the details of the plot on a Bakersfield TV station, the cover-up starts. Both ATF and Kern County Sheriff Charles Dodge claim the only proof they have of a plot is Shears's word.

The union and the state AFL-CIO, worried about Cesar's safety, ask State Attorney General Evelle Younger to investigate. But after assigning only one agent to the case—agent Robert Manning— Younger's office issues a press release on March 31 stating that there never was a plot. "Lie detector tests have cleared two men Shears claimed were at the action end of the conspiracy," the attorney general's office tells the press, and Shears refused to submit to a polygraph.

But that claim is false, and Shears has the tape recording of his interview with agent Manning to prove it. On tape, Agent Manning even repeats the informant's position, which is that Shears is willing to submit to a polygraph provided it is given by "some institution or university where there were competent people to administer it and interpret it, and if the operators were not part of any law enforcement agency."

When the attorney general's office refuses to have an independent expert administer such a test, I ask Vincent South, a nationally recognized polygraph expert from the Bay Area, to test Shears. Over a two-day period, South gives extensive tests that cover many aspects of Shears's story, then concludes that Shears is telling the truth on the key parts of his story.

Months later, the Fresno deputy district attorney, who is prosecuting Richard Pedigo on an arson charge, calls the attorney general's polygraph test of Pedigo "worthless."

Meanwhile, at the request of Senator Edward M. Kennedy, the Civil Rights Division of the Justice Department conducts its own investigation, mainly going over the material obtained by ATF. Two years later, after finally offering Pedigo immunity if he will

name the growers who provided the twenty-five thousand dollars—
an offer Pedigo declines—the Justice Department drops the case.

A letter signed by Robert Mardian, then assistant attorney general for internal security, also has raised questions of possible interference in the investigation from the highest levels of government. For Mardian was President Richard Nixon's political hatchet man in the Justice Department and is later convicted for conspiracy to obstruct justice in the cover-up of the Nixon Watergate scandal. Mardian also is familiar with UFWOC, since his family owns a vineyard in Arizona which, his brother later claims, was forced into bankruptcy after signing a contract with the union.

Fifteen days before ATF abruptly ended its investigation by arresting Pedigo, Mardian sent a letter to ATF asking to be kept advised "as to the developments at all steps of the investigation."

Rex Davis, director of ATF, says there is nothing in ATF files to indicate Mardian was kept advised, and Davis denies political interference.

ATF agent Robinson says Pedigo's arrest was made to "throttle" the plot. "The safety of the person involved means more to me than arresting those who put up the money," he tells me.

The plot is obviously throttled. Pedigo is sentenced to from two years to ten on the drug charge and to another two years to ten when found guilty of arson in another case involving a Delano grower. Trigger man Buddy Gene Prochnau is sentenced to life when found guilty in the Visalia murder for hire.

But the growers who want Cesar killed in 1971 when peace reigns in the Delano area, are still at large two years later when the grape industry again decides to take on the union.

CESAR CHAVEZ RECALLS

The Kern County district attorney and the sheriff's office are not our friends. So it was very easy for them to do nothing about the plot. They had hardly any pressure on them.

The way Attorney General Younger responded, I'm pretty sure that he, too, was covering something up. At least he was very quick about saying there was no plot, and people believe it.

On the federal level, I think the investigation was stopped by someone high up there, and the Civil Rights Division of the Justice Department just went through the motions.

As for the existence of a plot, I think it shows that nonviolence is working. They wouldn't go as far as trying to kill me unless they were very worried about our success.

CHAPTER 2

The Power of People

CESAR CHAVEZ RECALLS

I think a wholesale agribusiness conspiracy against our Union started in 1970 after we won in Delano. Actually agribusiness is more than growers. It includes all the people who sell and cater to growers. In the rural counties and communities, unfortunately, it also includes part of the church—they have part and we have part. And agribusiness has strong government support—federal, state, county, local, the courts, and the police.

When this agribusiness conspiracy against us started in 1970, the American Farm Bureau Federation, other grower organizations, and extreme right-wing groups started legal attacks and introduced legislation to stop us. The Farm Bureau coordinated the effort and spent a lot of money on it.

The reason all those right-wing groups don't want us to succeed is very simple. They know that once our Movement wins, it's going to have concrete power in terms of workers, in terms of things it can do for people.

And they know it's not going to stop there. They know that in a few years, farm workers will be sitting on city councils, county boards, and the courts. That's where the Movement is going to lead us. That's why the politicians on the right are so worried. Rural areas will no longer be conservative strongholds.

So they introduced legislation in California and other states outlawing boycotts and strikes at harvest time, and setting up election procedures geared to letting a very few people determine whether they wanted a union—in effect, disenfranchising most workers. This meant the company people would be deciding for everybody, and we would lose.

We got involved in all the legislative fights. In California we defeated the Cory Bill and others in 1971. We also defeated bills in all but three states where they were introduced. One in Kansas was passed without our knowing it. Then others passed in Idaho and Arizona. Our big fights were in Oregon, Washington, Arizona, New York, Florida, and California.

FROM JACQUES LEVY'S NOTEBOOK

On June 24, 1971, the California Assembly Labor Committee passes a farm labor bill sponsored by Kenneth Cory, a Democrat from conservative Orange County. The bill is heavily weighted in favor of the growers.

Two weeks later, when the bill is scheduled for a vote before the Ways and Means Committee, some two thousand farm workers rally on the steps of the capitol where Cesar is to speak.

Inside, in one of the halls, Dolores Huerta bumps into Assemblyman Willie Brown, the Chairman of Ways and Means, who suggests she see Cory to ask him to kill the bill.

With a priest, a farm worker, Richard Chavez, and me, she goes to Cory's office, which has numerous pictures of Robert Kennedy and Presidents John Kennedy and Lyndon Johnson prominently displayed.

"We are here about your bill," Dolores tells the tall, lanky assemblyman with shoulder-length hair.

"Yes, what can I do?" Cory asks, leaning like a half-folded jackknife over his desk. He already has been visited by top AFL-CIO leaders in the state lobbying against the bill.

"You know what you can do!" Dolores says, her voice tough, yet hardly louder than a whisper.

Cory remains silent, his head bent over a small piece of paper on which he appears to be writing. Then he looks up.

"I want to help," he says. "I want to be sure that the grain workers have a chance to organize."

Richard tells him they will, but the first task is to organize the great bulk of workers. Then the rest will fall in easily.

Cory again asks what he can do to improve the bill.

Dolores tells him it cannot be improved. It should be killed. Then she excuses herself a minute and leaves the room.

Cory remains silent for a long time, his head down. Then he asks Richard to open up a dialogue. "Promise me you'll talk to me next September or October on the kind of bill you need, and I'll kill this bill," he says.

And Richard, uncomfortable, agrees.

When Dolores returns, Cory tells her tensions are too high to talk now. He is emotionally upset, and she is, too, he says. They should meet again after both have had a chance to cool down.

Dolores starts to speak. "Let me tell you something. Do you know why we loved Robert Kennedy so?"

Cory interrupts her. "Not now, Dolores. We are too emotionally involved."

"Let me finish. It won't take but a second," Dolores breaks in, plowing right ahead, her words spilling out too rapidly to be cut in on. "Do you know why the poor loved those millionaires, John Kennedy and Robert Kennedy? It was their attitude. I think Ted has it, too. Robert didn't come to us and tell us what was good for us. He came to us and asked us two questions. All he said was, 'What do you want? And how can I help?' That's why we loved him."

Cory says nothing. He thanks them, and they walk out.

A short time later, Assemblyman Willie Brown announces the Cory bill is dead.

CESAR CHAVEZ RECALLS

At the same time we were fighting the Cory Bill, the Oregon legislature passed a law sponsored by the Farm Bureau. We were really stretched thin, and I sent Jerry Cohen there. Our supporters, the boycott and labor people helped.

The Oregon story is important because we were trying to keep them from setting a precedent. The only thing was, my heart wasn't in those fights. They slowed us down terribly.

JERRY COHEN RECALLS

That was a weird assignment that Cesar gave me. On a Friday he called and said, "Look, they passed a bill in Oregon, and the governor has a week to veto it. He's going to call a meeting of people interested in farm labor on Monday to talk about it. Why don't you go up and see what you can do about it."

I didn't know what the hell I could do about it, not knowing a hell of a lot about Oregon, but I got up there, and the first thing we did was meet with the boycotters. They knew all kinds of friendly groups and friendly people from labor to the church to the students, you name it. They had done their organizing work.

There were some liberal attorneys that warned, "Don't be too rude," and don't do this and don't do that. Our position was, the governor is a politician. He has to feel pressure.

If you work with Cesar for a while, you get a pretty realistic view of politicians, no matter if they're liberal Republicans or liberal Democrats. If there's an issue they don't feel any pressure on, it's a little hard for them to make a political decision.

There were also some Chicanos that were sort of rough Raza bullshitters. They had had a demonstration in the capital yelling "Viva Juan Corona!" right after Corona had gone and allegedly killed about twenty people. When I asked why are people yelling "Viva Juan Corona?" they said, "Well, he's supposed to have killed so many Anglos."

Now these were not the kind of people we want. These were some people that were on the fringes of things, that saw a chance to exploit their position.

So I took them aside and said, "Just confidentially, between you and me, all those people—if it's true that he killed them—number one, he's a labor contractor, and number two, all those people he killed were secretly carrying union cards." That completely confused them.

On Monday, when we met with Governor Tom McCall, he insisted the meeting be open to the press.

I said, "If you sign this bill, Oregon will become the Mississippi of the Northwest. We're going to put a picket line up around your state and prevent people from coming in"—which, of course, if you think about it, really can't be done. But the press thought it was really impressive. That was the headline.

So the next day we thought, if the governor wants to see how much public pressure we can put on him, we'll show him.

At a press conference, I said I knew the Farm Bureau had sponsored the bill, and the bill was horrible. In addition to the ban on secondary and primary boycotting, the ban on strikes, and the tricky election rules, it specifically banned bargaining about pesticides.

And I said that the reason it banned bargaining about pesticides was because of the Farm Bureau's interest in selling pesticides to farmers. It was a classic conflict of interest—which is true.

But then I went ahead and said that they sell about eighty million dollars' worth of pesticides a year to farmers.

Well, the next day, the Farm Bureau came back and in all their brilliance said that Cohen was lying. "We only sell twenty-five million dollars' worth."

Then I thought, we need something. And what I remembered was seeing the power of people praying in Texas.

The first thing I did in 1967 when I came to the Union was go down to Texas with Cesar. The Texas Rangers had beaten the hell out of 140 strikers, and some of the men wanted to get the Rangers. They wanted to physically get them out of town.

Cesar said, "You give me a chance."

Now this was a classic situation. The Rangers were at the Rangold Hotel, and every day at about 4:00 they left the hotel and walked across the street to the Catfish Inn to drink beer.

So when the Rangers walked out of that hotel one day, there were women, all related to our organizer Magdaleno Dimas—his grandmother, his mother, his sisters—dressed in black, praying for the Rangers' souls.

And there were some people there to cover it from the press, of course.

In twenty-four hours Governor John Connally had gotten the Rangers out of town.

So it was just like second nature. I knew that if some women would only pray on the steps of the capitol, that Governor McCall would feel the power of prayer.

We asked a priest named Jim Conroy to set up an altar on the steps of the capitol. And we had women there for four days.

What's the governor going to do when women are praying on the steps of the capitol that he could become enlightened and compassionate enough to be just to the farm workers? It's like water running down hill. You don't fight that.

Some people say, you put the altar there, isn't that a crass use of religion? I think that's utter bullshit because, number one, there were these weird guys running around using this bill for their own purposes, raising this kind of anti-Anglo feeling, and making a hero out of Corona. So we squelched that.

But there was energy there, and those women really wanted to show McCall how much it meant to them. The Union meant a lot to those people.

I think there's some people that would say that was cynical, but I just think they misunderstand the way poor people view whatever power they have. I knew those women believed in what they were doing, but the women also knew that they were putting pressure on Governor McCall by praying there rather than in church.

So it was a religious act and a political act at the same time. And if there are some purists that don't understand that, then they haven't been around the poor long enough to understand. The farm workers themselves had no qualms about it.

And the priest was talking very straight, clear language about justice, and about how to him religion should relate to justice. And whether you were religious or not, something was going on in Oregon that related to justice. And the power of the people really bubbled up.

On Friday, the governor vetoed the bill.

People that were away from it thought that really was something that was unbelievable, that within a week we were lucky enough to get that kind of pressure. But it wasn't that unbelievable, because in the state there were a lot of people who were moving, and we had boycotters all over the country calling up and telling Oregon lumber that not a stick of lumber was going to come into their state, if the bill was signed.

It was really a perfect example of how the boycott machine and a few really organized people could be mobilized. All the ingredients were there. It was just a question of guiding it a little bit, and not being afraid to raise a little hell.

It showed the strength of the union, and it really showed the power of people—when they move.

CHAPTER 3

La Causa in Florida

FROM JACQUES LEVY'S NOTEBOOK

Changes are occurring within the union. Larry Itliong, vice-director since 1966, resigns in October 1971, craving a greater role outside of Cesar's shadow. He decides to work to help retired Filipinos.

Four months later, a landmark passes almost unnoticed. UFWOC becomes a full-fledged union receiving its charter from the AFL-CIO. Later it will adopt the initials UFW. But the occasion causes hardly a ripple. There are too many battles to fight, too many fronts requiring attention and decisions.

A week later, Manuel Chavez signs up Coca Cola in Florida, after a spirited organizing drive. Coca Cola, deeply injured by an NBC documentary the year before depicting deplorable conditions in its labor camps, is in no mood to take on the union. It wants to avoid a possible Coca Cola boycott, the possibility of turning the country into the unCola generation, as Cesar says jokingly to friends.

On March 21, 1972, H. P. Hood and Sons, Inc., a major northeast dairy firm, also signs a contract with UFW for its Florida Citrus Division.

But the union's success in Florida spurs the opposition's attempts to hamstring it. They introduce a bill in the Florida Legislature, and Eliseo Medina is assigned to defeat it.

ELISEO MEDINA RECALLS

*Florida is a right-to-work state. Right-to-work is one of the holy
cows in the South. Actually, right-to-work is a phrase that was
coined by the employers to undermine the labor movement. It
doesn't give workers the right to a job or a decent wage. It creates
an open shop which makes it possible for the employer to drive a
wedge between workers, keeping them divided along union and
nonunion lines to weaken their potential power.*

*And in 1971, a right-to-work bill was introduced in the state leg-
islature. Then, toward the end of the session, somebody got the
bright idea of including one section, exclusively for farm workers,
that prohibited hiring halls in the state. This would perpetuate the
growers' power over the workers.*

*The reason a hiring hall is important to us is because of the way
people get jobs in agriculture. In Belle Glade, Florida, for instance,
workers get up at 3:00 A.M. to look for a job and go to the loading
ramp where all the labor contractors park their buses.*

*If there are more workers than jobs, the labor contractors hand
pick you just like if you were cattle. "You're too fat, you won't be
able to bend over." Or "You're too old, too skinny, or a known
trouble maker." You never know what you're going to be paid, and
if you complain about the housing or conditions, you get fired on
the spot. The hiring hall changes all this, establishing rules by
which people can get jobs without discrimination. And you can't
be fired just because a foreman doesn't like you. It provides job
protection.*

*The 1971 session ran out without getting the bill through. So
we were forewarned that they would try again.*

*We knew that we didn't have the power that we have in Cali-
fornia to be able to go down in mass to Tallahassee, and that unless we started organizing with enough time, we would be in one
hell of a lot of trouble come the legislative session.*

*So about two or three months before the session began, I assigned
a university professor to start making contacts with legislators so
that when the time came, we could give him backup through our
field offices, our four organizing offices, and our boycott offices.
Then we started meeting in all the field offices—the whole Florida
staff of about twenty-three, some of the key ranch committeemen
and stewards from the Coca Cola company, and some of the workers in the organizing areas.*

*Some people suggested that we have a mass petition campaign,
then a relay of farm workers from Homestead, say, to deliver it to*

Tallahassee, a distance of over five hundred miles. It wouldn't be a small legal-size petition, but a big scroll-type thing that would be signed by thousands of workers, and we'd have the publicity of the farm workers walking to Tallahassee to bring the message to the legislators.

We decided against that primarily because there are a lot of Ku-Klux Klanners and John Birchers in some of the rural areas in Florida, and we felt that unless we had a large group to accompany the relayers, we would have people that would be killed or beaten up.

Finally, the growers unintentionally did us a favor by introducing the bill before the session began. This gave us the time to start organizing against the bill before it could be heard.

The bill outlawed the hiring hall for agricultural workers and had many other things that would affect other unions besides ourselves.

Always when they introduce these antilabor bills, they shield them with the right-to-work label. It's like wrapping the American flag around it. And other unions had to fight it on those terms. So naturally, it's a very difficult fight. But we knew that it should be fought on the grounds that it was an anti-farm-worker bill. We'd been used to not fighting on the growers' level.

It was easy for us to say it was an anti-farm-worker bill since the Florida Citizens for Right-to-Work, sponsors of the bill, has an impressive list of growers on its executive board. The president was also the president of a county Farm Bureau, the secretary was the president of one of the largest sugar mills, and on the board were the president of South Bay Growers and the vice-president of United States Sugar Corporation.

First we talked to labor people who all said, "Look, you're fooling yourself. This bill is going to pass. Instead of wasting your efforts trying to kill it, exercise all your efforts to get Section Six out, which is the one you're against. Compromise and get it out."

We said, "No, once your beginning point is a compromise, then you're going to have to compromise on your compromise." So we said we had to try.

Everybody told us it couldn't be done. Well, I guess we just didn't know any better.

We decided we had to do something to show some muscle. So we discussed a letter-writing campaign. But to whom? Who was the key person? We decided on the chairman of the committee that the bill was assigned to, because if we started writing to five, ten different people, the real impact of it would be lost.

So in the cities like Miami and Jacksonville, we went and organized committees. We went to talk to churches and to students,
and we got people to write letters right there and then and send
them off to Donald Tucker, chairman of the committee.

The Coke people, all the stewards, went around getting people
to sign letters and contribute a dime toward the postage, because
we had no money to finance the campaign.

Then, at night, in the organizing areas, we went to the labor
camps. It was illegal for us to go there. They called it trespassing.
So we went in at night, house to house, sat down, and talked to
the workers, explained to them who we were. A lot of them had
never heard of the Union. After we talked to them for a long time
about the Union, we asked them to sign letters, and most of them
did.

At first we had a major concern. What's going to happen to
these people who sign letters? What if Donald Tucker turns
around and starts giving the letters to the representatives from the
areas where they're coming from, who are all grower-connected,
and they trace them back to the farms. A lot of people raised that,
but they said, "Well, that's a risk we have to take!"

By then the professor had left, and I had gotten a girl, Susan
Stratil, to do the job. She was fantastic, really did a lot of work.
One day she called me to say Donald Tucker was really getting up
tight, and the word was really getting around. She said, "All of a
sudden, I walk in and someone says, 'Oh, yes, Miss Stratil, what
can we do for you?' "

In a period of two months we got, by our count, approximately
twenty thousand letters in to the chairman of the committee. By
the growers' count, thirty-three thousand people wrote letters
against the bill.

Tucker was getting really pissed off. He was getting bags full.
Everywhere he looked there was this pile of letters.

But the significant thing was that out of those twenty-thousand-
odd letters, over half came from the rural areas, from farm workers
themselves becoming involved in trying to save the Union, even
though for most of them, the Union was only a promise for the
future.

Then we made a decision to visit every single senator and representative in the house and in the senate. We took committees of
workers—a Coca Cola worker to tell about the benefits of the
Union, and non-Union workers to tell how they get screwed by
labor contractors. Because, by taking away our hiring hall, they
were basically saying, let's perpetuate the labor contractors system.

The legislators were surprised. Some were just ignorant, and some were plain racist. We had a lot of comments like, "Gee, I'm glad you came. You're really articulate." Like saying because you're a farm worker, I expected you to be dumb.

Out of 120 legislators, we visited about 103. Out of 40 senators, we visited about 32.

Then, while we were doing all this work, something very unfortunate happened. We learned about a typhoid epidemic in Homestead. A couple of people and I went down there. This camp, which was called the best labor camp in the state of Florida, the model labor camp, was run by the city of Homestead. For two years they had known that the water was contaminated, but they had done absolutely nothing about it.

The health department came and checked and just told them to put more chlorine in it. They had actually found feces coming out of the faucets in the samples, and the workers complained about it, but they didn't listen to them.

We decided our role was to help the people and assure that what was happening here was not allowed to happen anywhere else, because the health department was very busy covering it up. But when we went to a meeting of the Dade County delegation of the legislators to talk about this problem, they refused to put us on the agenda.

Tourism is Florida's number one industry, and if it gets out that you've got a typhoid epidemic, what is it going to do to tourism? So they were down-playing it, saying, "It's nothing serious, one or two cases, isolated."

The first two weeks people were going to hospitals and being sent away with an aspirin and a glass of water and being told, "We ain't got no room." They went to private hospitals which wouldn't take them unless they had a hundred dollars. So we started raising a lot of hell about that.

We said we'd be damned if we're going to let them hush this up. We forced them to call a meeting of the full Dade County legislative delegation. The main health department guy was there, and a guy from the Center for Disease Control out of Atlanta, and a guy from the Health and Welfare Department, and they were all explaining why it happened, and why it couldn't be so bad.

By the time they got done, we were given about ten minutes to testify. There just weren't too many people willing to listen to us.

It happened, though, that the mayor of metropolitan Dade County and a few of the metropolitan councilmen were friendly, so we asked them to call a hearing on it. By that time, the number of people sick with typhoid had risen to approximately two hundred.

This time we said we wanted to be the first ones to testify. So I took one of the doctors from an OEO clinic with me who testified how rotten their care had been, and that we were just lucky that people hadn't been dying. The mayor was very interested, and the rest were reclining back listening to what was to them an unfortunate accident.

"Well," the health department director, while defending himself, said, "sure we knew for two years, but, it's a common problem. We also have known that, for the last two months, the water in Miami Beach has been contaminated."

And everybody jumped up. "What! You mean that the water for the last two months has been contaminated here in Miami Beach, and you haven't said anything about it!"

They started grilling that guy. They made him admit that the water was bad. All the TV cameramen, everybody ran out to call their editors, and within half an hour they had that guy on TV, live TV on all stations, telling all the residents to boil their water.

Congressman Claude Pepper got on the phone and in twelve hours had an Air Force plane from Atlanta, Georgia, fly down two more chlorine injectors to install in the water system to purify the water. Within twenty-four hours, two hundred and twenty thousand people in Miami Beach had clean water.

But it had been two years, and two thousand people in a labor camp still didn't have clean water. They still had the same crappy water coming out of those faucets. No politicians or news media had mobilized to help them in all this time.

Then I called Gilbert Padilla, the union's secretary-treasurer who was in charge in Washington, and said "Look, we need to spotlight national attention on this because it's a major problem," and we got a congressional investigation down there.

We forced the state to go in and check all the labor camps, and start closing some down. There are labor camps in the state of Florida that have no chlorine injectors, none whatsoever, just wells there, contaminated water. Camps that are not even registered. They have only registered about one hundred out of about four, five thousand camps.

The epidemic peaked out at about 280 victims. That was early March of 1973.

The bill was due to be heard on March 20 in a subcommittee meeting. So all this, of course, just raised the consciousness and the awareness about farm workers. All of a sudden people were saying, "What are they trying to do to farm workers?"

By then we had the bill supporters backtracking. They were trying to explain to people how, no, it's not an anti-farm-worker bill.

So we went back to our campaign and God, if a short time later, our guys working with somebody else don't find this guy named Joe Brown, a labor contractor, who's keeping twenty-nine farm workers as slaves.

For years you couldn't get most sheriffs or anybody to move on those things, but with this typhoid epidemic, it created a climate where they couldn't hide it. So they came and busted this labor contractor.

When they arrested him, he had a 1973 custom-built, baby-blue Cadillac and forty-five thousand dollars in cash. He would go in this Cadillac as far as Georgia, drop into hangouts where the poor people were, or some drunks, people who were broke. Then he'd say, "I've got a job down in Homestead. I'll pay you good wages, good housing. You can live in the camp, or you can live in town if you want. You get $1.60 an hour."

Then when they got in the car, usually when they were going down the highway at seventy miles per hour, this guy would pull out a gun and say, "From now on you're going to do what I say, and if you don't like it, get out right now, and I'll let you out, but you also got to give me twenty dollars."

These guys are broke. What are they going to do? He'd get them down to the labor camp. He had a little room just long enough for one cot down each of three walls. That's the room they had to sleep in.

The only place they could buy food was from the company store. He gave them little chips to say they were going to be paid. He would take them into town, get food stamps, and take the food stamps away from them, and then go buy food with it and sell the food back to them.

Most of these guys—those that were lucky enough—were making two to five dollars a week. There was a guy there that had been there for two years and never been paid.

And when there was no work, he'd load them all up on the bus. He had another guy working with him. He'd take them and park the bus in front of his house, and the guy would sit there with a shotgun, and if anybody tried to escape, they'd get the hell beaten out of them.

There was guy name of King, an old man, finally escaped, and they caught him, brought him back and beat the shit out of him in front of the other guys.

Of the twenty-nine, about six had very serious psychological problems, most were undernourished, a lot of them had open

sores on their bodies where they were beaten, a couple had tuber-
culosis, a few had diabetes.

That hit the news about a week before the hearing in Tallahassee. During this time we were in Homestead trying to help
these people.

Then we got the idea to try to get some of these guys to go
with me to Tallahassee to testify. But it was a wild idea. You have
twenty-nine people that were destroyed as human beings—I mean
totally destroyed, wouldn't even look you in the eyes when you
talked to them.

But I found one guy, his name was Robert Washington, and another one that had escaped, Theodore Johnson. Theodore was
drinking a lot, and we found him in Belle Glade.

When it came time to go to Tallahassee, the state-wide news
media was really making the labor contractors an issue. It had happened before. In July 1972, there was a labor contractor convicted
in Ruskin for keeping six farm workers as slaves, and there were
cases in Jacksonville and Georgia in 1971.

So I took Johnson with me and went down a couple of days before the hearing, and I had Susan Stratil just schedule us solid with
TV and radio programs. I went on radio and started talking about
what this bill meant, and I said, "I've got this man here who just
escaped from a labor contractor who can tell you what it means to
work for them."

Johnson was scared to death the first time. He wouldn't talk.
But in two days you could see him gaining more and more confidence. And then Washington came in, and they knew each other
because they had been kept together.

By the time we went in there and testified, Tucker had letters
all over the place. The weekend before, we organized a last-minute
push out of Miami.

We organized about thirty people to go into these fancy law offices which friendly lawyers let us use on Saturday and Sunday.
We took our mailing list and called people and said, "Look, we've
got this bill coming up on March 20. We need some support, and
we'd like to send a telegram in your name and charge it to your
number. Do you give us permission?"

When we got their permission, we wrote up the telegrams,
signed their name, phoned it in to Western Union, charged it to
their phone number, and sent it off. That Saturday and Sunday we
got about one thousand telegrams shipped off to the chairman of
the subcommittee.

Then, about one day before the hearing, Mack Lyons and some

of the people came up with workers from Coke and some of the unorganized ranches, and we just went up and down all the offices in the state capitol visiting everybody. Wherever they turned, there were farm workers running around.

Then I had Johnson and Washington testify to the subcommittee. Man, it was so powerful! I believe the subcommittee voted 7 to 2 against the bill. Then their report went to the full committee that afternoon.

By then the AFL-CIO told us, "Look, we'll do whatever you guys want. You tell us because they're only going to allow four, five witnesses against."

So we went before the full committee, and they had the president of the Farm Bureau Federation who was also on the Right-to-Work Committee, talking about how we were trying to smear farmers, how they had nothing to do with these slaves, they had nothing to do with the crew leaders not being registered under state law. We found out that only twenty-seven labor contractors out of about two thousand had registered, and we hit them with this.

We said, "You say you have nothing to do with it, but your members, the growers that belong to your association, are the ones that are hiring these people." Then we came in with Johnson.

The sponsor of this bill was representative Lou Earle from Winter Park near Orlando—John Birch and Ku-Klux Klan territory— a young guy, dentist, very ambitious. He thought the right-to-work was his baby. It was a safe issue on which to build a career.

And when Johnson got up to testify, Earle was sitting there. Johnson started talking about how they kept him, how they were beating him up, and he looked straight at Earle who just sank in his seat. He couldn't respond. The vote, I think, was something like 15 to 7. That killed the whole bill. And that killed their chances for another bill. They tried, but never got anywhere.

Incidentally, that labor contractor, Joe Brown, later was tried and found guilty by a jury. But the judge reversed the verdict on the grounds of insufficient evidence.

A lot of good things came out of that campaign. We had a lot of meetings with the Health Department. We forced them to start really checking and enforcing the labor camp registration law. We forced the state to start enforcing the crew leader registration act. It also gave our people at Coke the best education that you can get in the Union. You can't talk about political education in conferences. You learn about political education by doing. And we also educated a lot of people about the Union.

All this cost the United Farm Workers something like five hundred dollars. Everything else the workers paid for themselves. For instance, when the Coke workers went up to Tallahassee, the other members would subsidize them out of their paychecks; so that the worker that went did not lose his wages for the day. It really developed a close tie for what we were doing.

That was my first experience of that kind. The way I see it, everything is like a big machine with a lot of buttons. You never know which is the one that starts things, so you just have to go out there and push all kinds of buttons. Pretty soon, if you go and start a campaign, and it's not going anywhere, you know that it's not the right approach. So you try something else.

I joined the Union on September 17, 1965, when the Delano strike started. I had been on the fringes of it for a long time, but like a lot of other people, I kept saying, why should I pay dues for nothing? I'll join when I have to.

I was about nineteen then. I was born in Mexico and we came to the United States when I was ten years old; I started working in the fields along with my family. I went to school and worked on weekends, vacations, and whenever it was needed. I started working full time out in the fields when I was fourteen. I've only been working full time for the Union now eight years, come July 1974.

After that legislative hearing was done, a few of us went and got bombed. One of our guys, an organizer named Orrin Baird, a big guy, didn't have no money to buy shoes. So in the grab bag he found this pair of black shoes. He didn't want to bring his old torn-up boots, so he put on this pair of shoes that were about a size too small.

That evening, he was walking on the sides of his feet, because his feet hurt so bad. So on the way back, he took his shoes off, and there we were walking down the middle of Tallahassee with his shoes in his hand and having a good time singing Union songs. We had a good time!

CHAPTER 4

Two Showdowns

In Arizona, when the legislature on May 11, 1972, passes a Farm-Bureau-sponsored bill, the union hopes to persuade Republican Governor Jack Williams to veto it.

But the governor acts with unprecedented haste. As soon as the bill is passed by the senate, he has a member of the highway patrol bring it to him for signature. Normally a bill is checked out by the state attorney general's office to make sure of its legality. But this time the governor signs the bill forty-five minutes after it passes the senate.

Later, when he is asked about the farm workers who want to meet with him, the governor answers, "As far as I'm concerned, these people do not exist."

The same afternoon, Cesar starts a "fast of love." "My concern," he explains, "is the spirit of fear that lies behind such laws in the hearts of growers and legislators across the country. Somehow these powerful men and women must be helped to realize that there is nothing to fear from treating their workers as fellow human beings."

CESAR CHAVEZ RECALLS

Because we were dealing with a national campaign against us, we wanted to have a showdown, and Arizona became the best place, other than California, to have it.

We knew that if we just went and cried about the bill being passed, or tried to get a special bill through the legislature, that was not going to put the pressure on anyone. We wanted to make the governor who signed that bill pay for it.

We also didn't want to keep fighting similar bills in other states. So we thought if we recalled this governor, got him voted out of office, the others would get a little religion.

Arizona is not a big state. Its population is very concentrated, with a very high percentage of Chicanos, Indians, the poor, the working guy, and Democrats.

I asked Jim Drake, Marshall Ganz, and Leroy Chatfield to come to Arizona for a big fight and asked them to think about what we should do there. They got the idea of the governor's recall the same day our slogan "Si Se Puede" was born, about the fifth day of the fast.

We had just come from California where everywhere we went, farm workers were fighting. In Arizona the people were beaten. You could see the difference. Every time we talked about fighting the law, people would say, "No se puede, no se puede—it's not possible. It can't be done."

My brother Richard mentioned that at a staff meeting in the motel at Wickenburg, and when it was Dolores's turn, she said, "From now on, we're not going to say, 'No se puede,' we're going to say, 'Si se puede!'"

I picked up on it immediately. "Okay, that's going to be the battle cry!"

After the first five days of the fast, I moved to the Santa Rita Community Center in the Phoenix barrio. There was a little room there where I could remain in bed, and a hall where we could hold mass and have meetings. I wanted to receive Communion every day, and I also could meet alone in my room with the farm workers who came to see me. It worked out well, much better than the fast in Delano.

FROM JACQUES LEVY'S NOTEBOOK

As happened in Delano, farm workers from throughout the state come to the Santa Rita Center to see Cesar and attend the nightly evening mass which he leaves his bed to attend.

There is a strange chemistry at those masses packed with rugged farm workers and supporters. Sitting hunched in his rocking chair near the makeshift altar is Cesar, obviously physically drained, weak and fragile, a yellow pallor to his face, a sadder look in his eyes, his shoulders hunched in quiet pain. And yet there is a strength of spirit emanating from him that obviously touches those who see him.

When Father Joe Melton blesses the wine for the sacrament, the priest tells the congregation this is no ordinary wine, but wine harvested by men working in dignity under the protection of a union contract. And the hymns are union hymns, sung in Spanish and English.

The meeting follows without a pause. Farm workers with contracts arrive from California to tell how they benefit from the union. Telegrams and letters are read from the great and the small to show the support across the country for the workers' struggle, to show they are not alone, they are not ignored, they, too, have powerful friends, and they, too, have a chance.

The number of signatures on the recall petition and lettuce boycott pledges are announced, growing slowly day by day as seeds grow imperceptibly until the time has come for harvesting.

One week Cesar is bolstered by the visit of Senator George McGovern, who interrupts his campaign for president to visit him and pledge his support. On the nineteenth day of the fast, Coretta King, widow of the Reverend Martin Luther King, Jr., comes to visit and attend mass with him.

Cesar, who has been too weak to attend the past several days, summons strength to attend, but is forced to leave early when weakness overcomes him.

The day after Mrs. King's visit, Dr. Augusto Ortiz orders Cesar taken to the hospital, for fear that in his weakened condition, he could catch a fatal infection. Only the day before, the doctor treated a little girl for a strep throat who had attended the mass. But Cesar still refuses to end the fast.

It is hard for those steeped in the American culture to understand. "The fast is a very personal spiritual thing, and it's not done out of recklessness," Cesar explains. "It's not done out of a desire to destroy myself, but it's done out of a deep conviction that we can communicate to people, either those who are for us or against us, faster and more effectively spiritually than we can in any other way."

The power of the message, however, sometimes is unexpected, as when Cecil Miller, Jr., president of the Arizona Farm Bureau, calls a press conference to counter the publicity generated by the fast.

He wants it known, Miller reads, that the Farm Bureau really cares for the welfare of farm workers. But he can't help interrupting the reading of his prepared text to make an observation.

"I understand Cesar Chavez was taken to the hospital yesterday with stomach cramps," he says. "I sincerely hope it wasn't something that he ate."

Later, when asked for his reaction to the fast, Miller answers, "One of the freedoms we have here in America is the right to do our own thing. I think in terms of fasting, Gandhi conducted many fasts in India to achieve his ends. And as you know, after all those fasts were ended, some seven million people were butchered there."

CESAR CHAVEZ RECALLS

Although the pain during a fast usually lasts about seven days with me, in Arizona it stayed with me from one end to the other. I was miserable. The heat had an impact on me and the Phoenix water. Although I had to drink water, my body rejected it. I began to drink distilled water and other kinds of water and got into trouble. Pretty soon I couldn't drink anything. My uric acid level shot up. That's why I was hospitalized. It went completely out of wack.

I had to take bicarbonate of soda. Gandhi used to take a pinch of that in his water, and I consented to that much.

I also got in trouble with my heart. It was erratic, and there was a lot of concern. But I didn't want to break the fast on a bad note, to get off the fast because I was sick. I was hoping to fast for thirty days, but it was impossible.

I got off the fast on June 4, the twenty-fourth day, at a mass. There were an estimated five thousand people there, but I couldn't tell. I was very nauseated, so I stayed in bed and went at the last moment, sat down, and then rushed right back to bed as soon as it was over. If I hadn't been that sick, I would have been able to enjoy it.

FROM JACQUES LEVY'S NOTEBOOK

Among those who participate in the mass are Senator Robert F. Kennedy's son Joseph and Joan Baez, the folk singer who has done so much for La Causa.

Cesar is too weak to speak, but his statement is read. "The fast was meant as a call to sacrifice for justice, and as a reminder of how. much suffering there is among farm workers," part of it says.

"The greatest tragedy is not to live and die, as we all must. The greatest tragedy is for a person to live and die without knowing the satisfaction of giving life for others."

There are tears in Cesar's eyes as the statement ends, and there are tears in the eyes of many others, including Helen and their children.

CESAR CHAVEZ RECALLS

I had my first juice about 5:00, just strained water in which two or three vegetables were cooked, and then I took carrot juice for two days straight. When I was given tests, everything was normal, the uric tests, my heart, everything. The doctor just couldn't believe it. The third day I went up to the mountains to recuperate and slept that day and the next. On the fifth day we went for about a twelve-mile hike down a canyon. My legs were weak, but I felt great. I was twice the age of the guys with me, but I kept up with them.

After the fast I toured Arizona, visiting Chicanos, Indians, farm workers. And the recall campaign accelerated. It had never happened before in Arizona—or anywhere.

We calculated that on a recall election we couldn't hope for more than 30 or 35 percent of the people voting, just the partisans on both sides. Since a lot of the people who would be voting our way were not registered, we went on a registration drive—the old CSO method. We gathered signatures and registered people the old way, the only way, door to door, at the stores, wherever people congregate.

The effects on Arizona politics were tremendous. Those campaigns tend to wake up the people. You can't lose for winning. While the recall fell apart later because of lack of money and a good candidate, the work was there. We collected more than enough signatures for a recall election, but county clerks took months to count them, and the state attorney general declared more than sixty thousand signatures invalid because they were obtained by deputy registrars.

Eventually we got a ruling in federal court that the signatures were valid, but by that time it was too close to the general election to make a special recall election worthwhile.

FROM JACQUES LEVY'S NOTEBOOK

The fast, the registration drive, and the recall has a profound effect on Arizona politics. The recall drive gathers 168,000 signatures, of which 108,000 eventually are declared valid, five thousand more than needed to force a recall.

Although the recall election is eventually blocked by the state attorney general, the heavy registration of Navajos, Mexican-Americans, and other poor is reflected in the regular 1972 elections. For the first time in Arizona's history, four Mexican-Americans and one Navajo are elected to the state senate and another Navajo to the state house of representatives. A third Navajo becomes a county supervisor and numerous Mexican-Americans are elected to local courts, school boards, and city councils.

A rash of local recalls are also initiated, the most successful being in Coolidge where all five councilmen are thrown out and a Mexican-American is elected mayor.

Two years later, the impact is even greater. Democrat Raul Castro is elected governor by a forty-one-hundred-vote margin. Castro's seven-thousand-vote lead among the newly registered Navajos tips the election in his favor. In addition, the Democrats capture the state senate and name Senator Alfredo Gutierrez majority leader. In the lower house the Democrats gain five seats and elect Eddie Guerrero minority leader.

"We've turned Arizona around," says Bill Soltero, business manager and financial secretary of Construction, Production and Maintenance Laborers Local 383. "Si Se Puede was born with the fast. This is what gave us the strength, and this is the reason we're making Arizona a decent place for all people."

CESAR CHAVEZ RECALLS

While the fight in Arizona was important, we were faced with an even bigger one in California, where an initiative written by the Farm Bureau got on the November ballot. It was known as Proposition 22.

Actually, proponents had a hard time getting enough signatures. They had to lie to get them, and they had to pay money. One thing led to the other. Finally they even went to the extent of committing fraud. It cost them a lot of money.

When we found out it was fraud, we turned the cards on them, and that helped defeat them badly, but first I put LeRoy Chatfield in charge of the drive. That was one of the first campaigns where I didn't get myself involved completely. I just did appearances, helped raise money, and did a lot of work with the media.

We used a lot of the boycott people. In fact, the lettuce boycott ceased to exist. We brought a lot of people back to California and put them in the fight.

We beat Proposition 22 by 58½ percent to 41½—a higher vote than Nixon got in California in his landslide. It gave us a very strong encouragement about our right to exist.

While fighting Proposition 22 did slow our organizing efforts, it settled the issue once and for all—that and the recall of the governor put the lid on, I think.

CHAPTER 5

Dangerous Alliances

FROM JACQUES LEVY'S NOTEBOOK

By 1972, the Nixon administration is ready to destroy the union. Three of the five members of the National Labor Relations Board are Nixon appointees, and the new chairman, Edward B. Miller, already has compiled a strong antilabor record. Of his first sixty-one decisions, he is on the side of management fifty-nine times. Of those fifty-nine, he is with the minority on thirty-nine decisions and the sole dissenter on thirty-eight of the thirty-nine.

Both Jerry Cohen and Cesar are sure the union's use of the boycott soon will be challenged, even though farm workers are specifically exempted from the National Labor Relations Act.

If the union can be proved to represent any workers in a commercial shed, the board technically would have jurisdiction, and the union would be prohibited from secondary boycotting, while its members still would be deprived of all the benefits and protection of the law.

The union, therefore, must tread carefully, making sure that none of the sheds it represents are technically ruled to be "commercial"—which they can be if they handle produce from more than one grower.

CESAR CHAVEZ RECALLS

It was a mistake. Marshall Ganz was in charge of the boycott, and while the moratorium on the lettuce was on because of the negotiations, he insisted that we get into another boycott, and I gave in. We took on nine small wine companies in the Napa Valley right after we signed up Heublein. It was my fault that he convinced me.

Peter Nash, the new general counsel of the National Labor Relations Board, came after us, ruling we were a covered union because we had a few people in one of those wineries in a commercial shed. He was stretching the meaning of the law very far to get us.

The board always had sustained our position that we were not a covered union, but Nash filed a suit on March 9 in Fresno's Federal District Court to stop our secondary boycott activities. If he won, our best nonviolent weapon would be taken from us.

For about four days we held a strategy meeting with the officers and key staff members. I don't know whose idea it was, but we decided to make the Republican party responsible, because Nash's decision was a political decision, not a legal decision as far as we were concerned.

We decided to attack Republicans everywhere we went. We even had bumper stickers, "GOP hates farm workers." Our goal was to put a million letters to the chairman of the Republican party, Senator Robert Dole. Then we picketed Senator Jacob Javitz in New York and Senator Edward Brooke of Massachusetts, because they would respond sooner than the others.

FROM JACQUES LEVY'S NOTEBOOK

On March 16, 1972, union supporters and members picket Republican headquarters in 150 cities across the country. Cesar says the picketing may spread later to the White House itself, and he talks of plans to send twenty-five thousand farm workers to the Republican Convention which is scheduled to be held in San Diego. About two hundred pickets appear in front of what is to be the headquarters hotel there.

As the political pressure increases, Senator Edward Kennedy calls on the General Accounting Office to investigate the NLRB to see if it has expended any funds in its investigation of the union. The Nixon administration, he charges, "has decided to use federal agencies to harass the efforts of the farm worker to organize and acquire for himself decent wages and decent working conditions."

In the House, the thirteen-member congressional Black Caucus, a number of Spanish-speaking congressmen, and other liberals announce they are considering legal intervention in the court action.

CESAR CHAVEZ RECALLS

Eventually we got what we wanted. They negotiated the issue and reversed the decision by another political decision. Nash dropped the charges while we agreed to stop the boycott of these wineries. Our campaign took about eight or nine weeks.

Because of Nixon's background, we weren't surprised he was against us. He'd been harassing farm worker organizations since the late forties when, as a congressman, he took on the DiGiorgio strikers. He had the full power of subpoena and investigation and cross-examined those poor farm workers. He ate them up alive. He's an evil man.

When he ran for president in 1968, he was the only national politician to eat grapes publicly, stuffing himself with grapes before the cameras in Fresno. And that year he got the Teamsters' support. I think that was the only labor group he got, and they developed a very close friendship.

In 1971 Nixon worked out a deal with Frank Fitzsimmons to get Jimmy Hoffa released from prison, but to castrate him so he could not be an officer in the union until 1980. That assured Fitzsimmons the presidency of the Teamsters.

Then the White House set up the meeting between Fitzsimmons and the Farm Bureau at their convention in Los Angeles after Nixon's landslide victory in 1972. That's when the deals were made to destroy us.

MONSIGNOR GEORGE HIGGINS RECALLS

Fitzsimmons was mesmerized by Nixon's courting. I think he enjoyed being the celebrity. He was appointed to the Wage and Price Board. He was invited to all the dinners at the White House, and above all, he had White House Counsel Charles Colson.

Colson was the hatchet guy in the White House who put together the pro-Nixon labor combination that was going to help sweep Nixon in.

In December, when Fitz went to speak to the Farm Bureau, he was naïve enough to think that he was the number one labor leader in the country. I talked to him before he gave that speech. I said, "You're idiotic, Fitz. For a trade union president to go down and talk to the Farm Bureau Federation would be like Dan Tobin speaking to the NAM in 1905." Tobin was the Teamsters' first president.

And Fitz more or less good-naturedly said, "Well, why don't you mind your business, and I'll mind mine."

FROM JACQUES LEVY'S NOTEBOOK

August 15, 1973, news item in the Real Paper, Boston: Two of White House Counsel Charles Colson's memorandums to the Justice and Labor Departments and the NLRB stressed that these agencies were not to intervene in the Teamster-UFW fight unless their actions would be harmful to UFW. Colson noted in the memos that the president had taken a "personal interest" in the case.

Colson's first memo, in May 1971, said, "Only if you can find some way to work against the Chavez union should you take any action."

In his second memo, about a year later, Colson wrote, "We will be criticized if this thing gets out of hand and there is violence, but we must stick to our position. The Teamsters Union is now organizing in the area and will probably sign up most of the grape growers this coming spring and they will need our support against the UFW."

May 31, 1973—Los Angeles Times news item: "So widespread is the evidence of fraud and schemes for looting Teamster pension funds through illicit finders' fees, payoffs, and kickbacks that an investigation is under way on two fronts—federal and local—into at least four Mafia operations, reportedly bankrolled by Teamster money. . . .

"Several law enforcement officials, including Los Angeles County District Attorney Joseph P. Busch, Sheriff Peter J. Pitchess and Orange County District Attorney Cecil Hicks, told the Times that the activity of known Mafia figures had increased markedly in recent months. . . .

"Millions of pension fund dollars have been lent to build Las Vegas casinos and developments like the Teamster-financed La Costa Country Club near Carlsbad in San Diego County, described by a Justice Department attorney as 'the West Coast R & R (rest and recuperation) center for all sorts of hoods from throughout the country.' "

An FBI informant provided investigators with details of Palm Springs meetings and mob–union discussions of kickbacks and payoffs in connection with a proposed health care plan described as "a possible billion-dollar a year business."

"In Palm Springs, according to information developed by the government's Los Angeles-based Organized Crime Strike Force, Fitzsimmons met on Feb. 8 to discuss the plan with Sam (Orlando) Sciortino, 54, of Fountain Valley; Peter J. Milano, 47, of Sherman Oaks; and Joe Lamandri, of San Diego, identified by the FBI as members of the Mafia. . . .

"In the next two days, Fitzsimmons met with Lou (The Tailor) Rosanova, 51, executive director of the Teamster-owned Savannah Inn and Country Club, 'the mob's Southern watering hole.' Rosanova was named by a U.S. Senate crime committee in 1963 as a top chieftain of La Cosa Nostra.

"The Justice Department has put Rosanova on its 'top 300' mobster list in the Chicago area.

"Others seen in discussions with Fitzsimmons at the Mission Hills Country Club and the Ambassador Hotel in Palm Springs were identified as Tony Accardo, aging Chicago Mafia boss; Anthony Spilotro, accused gangland executioner; Marshal Caifano, also known as Johnny Marshal and of Chicago, along with Lloyd J. Pitzer of Los Angeles, Charles B. Greller of Chicago, and Richard Strummer, friends and business associates of Rosanova. . . .

"At 11:30 P.M. on Feb. 12, two days after the Palm Springs meetings, Rosanova met with Fitzsimmons again at the La Costa Country Club.

"The following morning, the Teamsters president drove to San Clemente where about 9:30 A.M. he boarded the presidential jet with Mr. Nixon at El Toro Marine Air Station for the flight to Washington."

CESAR CHAVEZ RECALLS

If the Watergate scandal hadn't been exposed, the White House would have really been on us in 1973, and on a lot of other groups that they were going after.

But all that stopped. The start of impeachment proceedings were a good sign for us. Another good sign was that Colson was indicted and then jailed in 1974 because of his involvement in the Nixon scandals. That really shook up Frank Fitzsimmons who had hired Colson as a Teamster attorney in 1973. And then, of course, Nixon resigned.

But before then, a lot of damage was done.

CHAPTER 6

"Everything Is Going
to Go to the Teamsters"

CESAR CHAVEZ RECALLS

Jimmy Herman of the Longshoremen called during the summer of 1972 to warn me that the Coachella grape growers weren't going to renew their contracts when they expired in April. He told me the message came from Lou Goldblatt, the secretary-treasurer of the ILWU. None of us panicked. We took it as a challenge to go out and renew them.

The first hint that the Teamsters were moving in came from the growers. But it wasn't until December of 1972 that it became very clear, when I met with the workers and started a tour of all the growers trying to talk them into signing an industry-wide contract.

I spent two or three days in Coachella, and every single grower, including those who were really fighting us, would pat my back and say, "Chavez, we're with you, we're with you."

And it got to me a little, why would they be saying they're with me?

Then this little grower invited us to his home one evening. He had a few drinks and told me the Teamsters were going to come in.

I said, "How can they come in? They don't represent the workers."

"They're going to come in. They can come in. They've got transportation. They've got us cold," he insisted.

Finally I got mad and said, "If you guys want them, they'll come in, but if you don't want them, they won't come in. How can they come in? They don't represent the workers."

December 29, 1972—The California Supreme Court rules that the 1970 Salinas lettuce strikes were not jurisdictional strikes since the growers used the Teamsters "as a shield" to protect themselves against a legitimate union.

The court rules invalid the injunctions which broke the strikes.

The court rules it is "uncontradicted" fact that it was the growers who approached the Teamsters, and that it is "undisputed" that the Teamsters "did not represent a majority, or even a substantial number" of the field workers.

Instead, the court says, "It appears clear" that "at least a substantial number, and probably a majority" of the workers favored UFW. And "from a practical point of view," the court says, for the growers to sign contracts with the Teamsters under those circumstances "must be considered the ultimate form of favoritism, completely substituting the employer's choice of unions for his employees' desires."

One month after the state supreme court ruling, grape growers with UFW contracts meet with Teamster representatives at the El Morocco Motel in Indio in the Coachella Valley. The Teamster officials promise to abolish the UFW hiring hall.

January 17, 1973—San Francisco Chronicle news item: The Teamsters Union announced yesterday that it has renegotiated its controversial contracts with 170 major vegetable growers.

William Grami also said the Teamsters are considering an attempt to organize "disgruntled" workers currently under contracts with UFW in both the vegetable and grape industries.

Although the article doesn't say it, renegotiating the contracts can—through a legal technicality—cloud the state Supreme Court ruling that no jurisdictional dispute exists between UFW and the Teamsters.

February 22, 1973—San Francisco Chronicle news item: At a Miami Beach press conference, AFL-CIO President George Meany accuses the Teamsters of "absolutely disgraceful" actions which are "tantamount to strikebreaking" in their renegotiations of contracts with 170 major lettuce growers in California and Arizona.

CESAR CHAVEZ RECALLS

The Teamsters tried to come to the vineyards, and people threw them out. In a few places they were welcomed, but in most they were thrown out. They were always with the supervisors, or the labor contractors, or the growers themselves.

They tried to get people to sign Teamster cards during working hours, and they got that small percentage that's always anti, like the labor contractor, his wife and cousin, but I don't think they went much past that.

Of course, there was intimidation about getting fired if they didn't sign, even though our contracts were still in force.

Giumarra asked us to give him a complete proposal. He was speaking for most of the Delano, Arvin, Lamont growers—well, the whole industry—so we gave them a proposal, but we couldn't get a counterproposal from them until late February.

Then they turned our proposal down and gave us one that was unbelievable. They wanted to take everything back, take away the things we already had, the hiring hall, the guts of the pesticide protection clause, our right to discipline our members, and they even wanted to mess around with our dues.

They rejected our ideas of a joint hiring hall to eliminate their complaints about how the halls were run. I was trying to solve the issue by saying, "Okay, let a third party immediately tell us who's wrong, and we'll abide by it." But the hiring hall was not a real issue.

Actually, the real issue is who is going to control the work force, and a lot of unions have gone through this second fight. The day that the growers agree that we're going to control the work force —no problems. But they're worried that if we control the work force, we're going to be excessive in our demands.

It doesn't work that way, because the Union has natural built-in stabilizers and a lot of forces outside our Union and the growers who can pressure how we negotiate. One is the public. The more stable we become, the more prices are going to go up—it's natural —and the more the public is going to say, "Wait a minute!" The public is going to be negotiating for us in ten years or maybe sooner.

On March 15, during our negotiations, Al Kaplan, the growers' negotiator, said that he received a telegram from the Teamsters claiming that they now represented the workers.

We said it was nonsense and, furthermore, we could prove that they didn't. If the growers didn't believe it, we should have an election.

So Kaplan said, "As far as we are concerned, the Union represents our employees. We're prepared to negotiate a contract if you're prepared to sign our proposal."

Then on March 30, negotiations were expanded to include all the California grape industry, but on April 5, Kaplan and his growers walked out. Since then we have been told that about twenty growers opposed Kaplan walking out. But some of these twenty growers said they followed him out like sheep.

On April 10, before the expiration of the Coachella area contracts, a committee of church leaders, congressmen, and labor leaders went and polled the workers. They went to thirty-one fields, talked to about one thousand workers and found 795 for our Union, 80 for the Teamsters, and 78 for no union.

Five days later, about nine hours after the contracts expired at midnight, and, of course, without consulting their workers, all but two of the Coachella Valley growers signed four-year contracts with the Teamsters for $2.30 an hour, no hiring hall, no pesticide control, no grievance procedures. In effect, that's no union.

Steinberg and Larson signed new one-year contracts with us that included a jointly run hiring hall, improved grievance procedures, a pension plan, unemployment insurance, a $2.40 an hour minimum and a 20 percent salary increase across the board.

Of course, we asked the others, how could they sign with the Teamsters when the Teamsters didn't represent the workers, and we asked for elections.

But the Teamsters said, "It's too late for elections. We have the contracts." And the growers said privately, "We don't want to have elections, because you would win."

We were ready. Before the contracts expired, we took a strike vote at a beautiful rally in Coachella.

The strikes in 1973 were a lot more severe than any other strikes we've had. They were as vicious as any I've read about.

The first Coachella Valley contracts expired April 15, and the next day there were about one thousand farm workers on the picket lines. I estimate about two thousand people were involved. Most of them came out, a good many joined us, and a good many left the area. We stopped the thinning of the grapes.

The growers were frightened and spent a lot of time calling the Teamsters to come save them, calling the goons to go to one picket line and then another. And, of course, they went to the courts for injunctions. Judge Fred Metheny issued the first one for the Tudor ranch the first day of the strike, then more the next day for Tenneco, Melikian Sons, and CID.

Before the harvest was over in the Coachella Valley, there were eighteen injunctions limiting the number of pickets and the use of bullhorns. The worst was the Tenneco injunction which prohibited all picketing. And the day that was issued, Teamster goons appeared at various picket lines armed with grape stakes, clubs, baseball bats, metal pipes, and knives. None were arrested.

We talked to the workers, telling them that the only way we could win was to disobey the injunctions and go to jail, since obeying the injunctions would break the strikes. I was a little worried that they would be afraid, but they were ready to go. They don't look at jail like most people do. Once you're in the struggle, your fear of jail disappears with the strength that comes from the solidarity of so many brothers in the picket lines, the intensity of the struggle, and the commitment. So they were going to jail as fast as deputies could arrest them. In fact, they were volunteering to be arrested.

Thirty of our pickets were arrested on the second day of the strike, 74 the third and 134 the fourth. By Good Friday, there were more than 300 arrests.

FROM JACQUES LEVY'S NOTEBOOK

Maundy Thursday, April 19, 1973—We leave at 4:00 A.M. for the picket line. All remains peaceful as dawn breaks, but the tension hangs heavy with the Teamsters on one side of the road, the pickets on the other, and police in riot gear standing in the middle facing both lines.

At mid-morning the pickets are called around a flat-bed truck at the edge of the vineyard and mass arrests are proposed. Jerry Cohen tells the strikers about their rights and the flaws in the court order. But he leaves the decision up to the workers who vote to violate the worst injunction by picketing Tenneco.

The decision is followed by prayer.

The Reverend Chris Hartmire stands on the battered flat-bed truck facing more than a hundred workers whose scarlet union banners stand out sharply against the unbroken blue of the sunny sky and the lush green of the vines. Men bare their heads, and all eyes focus on the youthful-looking minister dressed in sport shirt and slacks.

"Today is the very day Jesus was betrayed," he says, and a Teamster across the road hollers, "Cut out hiding behind the church."

Hartmire continues. "But Jesus is alive and with you, and all the people who want to be free."

"Leave God out of this. He won't help you," another Teamster yells.

Most of the Teamsters stand and stare at the praying workers. Many sneer. But one, short and large of paunch, takes off his yellow hard hat as the prayer starts. He shifts uncomfortably on his feet, and pretends to brush his hair back. But he keeps his hat off throughout the prayer.

Then the pickets head in a long car caravan for a Tenneco vineyard where they start hollering at the crews thinning the grapes. Police and Teamsters arrive quickly. So does the paddy wagon.

When deputies order the strikers to disperse, they kneel in the sand along the edge of the vineyard while the Reverend Hartmire leads them in prayer. One by one officers start the arrests. Some workers walk to the paddy wagon while others remain limp and are carried or dragged there. After Hartmire is arrested, the Reverend Frank Plaisted, a tall, gaunt, white-haired Episcopalian minister representing the bishop of California, continues the prayer until he, too, is put in a paddy wagon.

While the arrests are going on, I talk to Al Droubie, head of the Teamsters, who invites me to speak to some of the crews working the vines. With Droubie is tough-looking Johnny Macias, known to the picket line as Yellow Gloves, because he always has them on.

I get in Droubie's car with Macias, and we drive inside the ranch to where some workers are sitting under the vines.

Macias volunteers to translate for me when I talk to a large woman with a wide-brimmed straw hat.

"How long have you been working here?"

"Two weeks."

"Are you a union member?"

"Yes."

"Which union?"

She looks at the man next to her who could be her husband. They smile at each other, and there is a long silence. Finally the man looks at me and says, "Chavista."

The answer needs no translation, and Macias is beside himself. "No, no no!" he shouts in Spanish and starts a rapid harangue, explaining why they are now Teamsters.

When I return to the picket line, I learn 134 strikers have been arrested including Jose Perez, his wife, and their three children under five.

April 20, 1973—Riverside Enterprise news item: Sheriff's deputies arrested 135 picketers, including Cesar Chavez's daughter Linda and a nephew, yesterday morning.

That evening, Judge Fred Metheny goes to four crowded tank rooms inside the Indio County jail.

"I'm Judge Metheny," he tells the jailed farm workers. "You're here because you are charged with a violation of this court."

After explaining that they have violated terms of the temporary restraining order, the judge says he will release them if they promise to appear for arraignment in court at 9:00 A.M. April 27.

"After your release, you are not to interfere with pruning, thinning, harvesting, or transportation of grapes. I will not tolerate violence in any form."

The interpreter is repeating in Spanish what the judge has said when Jerry Cohen bursts into the tank-room corridor and shouts, "Your honor, I object to this proceeding. My clients do not promise to appear on April 27!"

Judge Metheny asks the prisoners if they understood what he said, and they shout, "No!" and "Huelga!"

Cohen tells the judge he wants to advise his clients of their rights.

"I'm telling you to be quiet," Metheny answers.

"Are you denying me the right to speak to my clients?" Cohen asks.

"I'm telling you to be quiet."

As the interpreter finishes giving the judge's instructions in Spanish, Cohen angrily paces the hall. He keeps telling the judge he objects to the proceedings.

"If you interfere again," an angry Judge Metheny shouts back, "I'm holding you responsible for any violence, just as I'm holding you responsible for much of the violence that has taken place at the scene of the picketing."

A similiar scene is repeated at each of the four crowded cells.

JERRY COHEN RECALLS

Our position was that people should be released on their own recognizance, and we also didn't want people to sign promises to appear, because the court didn't have proper jurisdiction over them, and we weren't about to confer jurisdiction on the court by having them sign.

Now technically, that's probably not really what they would have done, but we were just upset enough about the whole procedure to really force the issue right then.

I objected to every single thing the judge did. I just kept the heat on, and he was very upset. I remember one time winking at somebody, because the workers were getting a kick out of it.

It was clear that the judge was really affected. So he called me into his chambers right after we got out of the jail.

He told me he was sorry if he'd deprived my clients of their constitutional rights, but he hadn't done it intentionally, and I realized that he really hadn't. Normally he would issue temporary restraining orders in the context of a divorce where First Amendment rights are not an issue, and you don't need prior notice to the other party, and he automatically did it.

I think he felt himself trapped having done something that he really regretted, and he reacted by going down to the jail and telling people what their rights were, which compounded the error, because he was taking away more rights, like the right to a public hearing.

As it turned out, I think that scene affected Metheny a lot, because I think he's somewhere inside a fair man. He's not a scholarly judge. He always says, "Down here we have country justice." Well, he does try to work things out and compromise and be fair.

He eventually gave us unlimited picketing across the street from any fields, and the growers had to go in and get an injunction field by field and give us notice. And we worked out procedures which really were the fairest procedures we've ever worked out with any judge.

But it was unclear that night in the cell whether I was going to get thrown in jail for contempt, or whether we were going to be able to make him see what the problems were.

I think the fact that he really had shot our constitutional rights affected him, and I think really that one of the amazing things was the spirit in that jail.

I mean he saw these people there, here were normal farm workers—women, teen-aged girls, men—all in full fight, full of spirit, really good humor. It was an amazing scene in that jail. It was typical of what happened all across the state all summer long. People's spirits were really high in jail.

But I've never been in a jail scene that was quite that exciting or hilarious. I mean I had a hard time at times keeping a straight face because we had him right by the balls, and the workers knew it, and I knew it, and the judge eventually knew it.

FROM JACQUES LEVY'S NOTEBOOK

April 20, 1973—At a hearing in his courtroom set up to amend the restraining orders, Judge Metheny says he walked into a vineyard to check conditions for himself.

He says he was confronted by a Teamster "carrying a big twig." The judge says he immediately identified himself, and the guard dropped his club.

Judge Metheny then went into the vineyard and asked some workers whether the picket lines harassed them. The workers said no.

After hearing arguments from attorneys from both the growers and the union, Judge Metheny expunges all contempt arrests and rewrites the restraining orders to permit unlimited picketing sixty feet from vineyards where workers are.

At the request of the union, the judge also includes what Jerry Cohen calls a "goon squad" clause.

The clause says, "workers shall be protected when they attempt to leave the fields, and no person shall try to prevent workers or pickets from entering or leaving the fields with the use of guns, knives, clubs, baseball bats, grape stakes, or other dangerous instruments."

April 25, 1973—Steve Roberts of the New York Times, interviewing Cesar, expects to see a beaten man, but is surprised at Cesar's attitude—relaxed, smiling, exuding confidence.

"This means we won't have contracts for a while," Cesar tells Roberts. "But we won't dry up and fly away. The workers aren't going to stand by and let them return to the feudal days of labor contractors."

He discloses and explains his coming tactics. "We have to improvise, and be very creative. We have to let the employers support the people, yet do enough to make their costs soar. And we have to keep in touch with the workers to keep their support. We tell people not to work hard, and to be loyal to the union. That's the only way a strike can last without a strike fund.

"I think the opposition is banking on the public not giving a damn about boycotts anymore. I'm sure they're wrong."

Then he predicts, "Everything is going to go to the Teamsters, but we kicked them out four different times before, and we will again.

"By 1975 or 1976 these guys will be screaming for elections, but we're not going to boycott for three years and then, when they hurt, give them elections."

At the end of the interview he reflects, "This may be a blessing in disguise. This might be the ultimate confrontation. If we win, they'll leave us alone. Systems die a slow death, and the farm worker feudal system will take a long time to die."

That evening, after following a group of strikers who go to talk to workers at the Indio labor camp, I return to Cesar's office and find mass being held around a green metal office table which, during the day, is used by the legal staff.

Three priests, two nuns, and Cesar are around the table which has been cleared of law books and files. On it now are a bottle of wine, a metal chalice, and ceremonial wafers.

The only other person in the room is a girl sitting in the corner by the phones.

CHAPTER 7

A Pattern of Violence

CESAR CHAVEZ RECALLS

In Coachella, police were very worried about the violence. I think that Lieutenant Paul Yoxsimer did a fair job, but there were so many incidents they couldn't keep up with them. The Teamsters had a few trained goons who knew what they were doing and got us every time.

There was no way that we could organize ourselves to get the protection of numbers. People with families, older guys and young guys—it was very hard to organize them to stay together. We had a lot of women in the picket lines who were easy prey for attacks.

The papers reported that the Teamsters were paying their goons $67.50 a day, and Harry Bernstein, the *Los Angeles Times* labor reporter, said there were 350 in Coachella. We suspect the growers paid part of the cost, if things went like Salinas. And since the Teamsters kept the goons for about eighteen weeks, and they stayed in the best motels, it must have cost them around a million dollars.

FROM JACQUES LEVY'S NOTEBOOK

April 25, 1973—Shortly after 6:00 P.M., about ninety-five UFW members go to the CID camp to talk to people about the strike. For about twenty minutes everything is peaceful. Then thirty Teamsters, headed by Al Droubie, charge in, tear up the water-

cooler stands to make clubs and start hurling rocks at the strikers.

A few outnumbered policemen spray everyone with tear gas. Finally police reinforcements arrive, drive off the Teamsters, but make no arrests.

Later, Celia Horton, thirty-four, who was in the union sound truck, tells what happened. "The people couldn't escape because the Teamsters were along the only road out of the camp." She grabbed the mike and started singing "We Shall Overcome," and the strikers joined in as rocks pelted them.

"We knew our lives were at stake," she says. "You have butterflies in your stomach, but you keep on singing."

April 28, 1973—Los Angeles Times news item: Western Conference of Teamsters leader Einar Mohn said farm workers will not be able to take part in Teamsters Union meetings "for about two years," when he expects more "whites" and fewer Mexicans in California fields.

Mohn was quoted in the doctoral dissertation by Jane Yett Kiely, a student at the Graduate Theological Union in Berkeley, who interviewed various industry and union leaders.

"I'm not sure how effective a union can be when it is composed of Mexican-Americans and Mexican nationals with temporary visas," Mohn told Ms. Kiely.

"Maybe as agriculture becomes more sophisticated, more mechanized, with fewer transients, fewer green-carders, and as jobs become more attractive to whites, then we can build a union that can have structure and that can negotiate from strength and have membership participation."

CESAR CHAVEZ RECALLS

I went to the AFL-CIO Executive Board meeting in Washington in May. By that time the Steel Workers had endorsed us, and the president of the American Federation of State, County and Municipal Employees, Jerry Wurf, who was very worried about what was happening to us, wanted something done.

I told the board we needed financial help. I didn't ask for any amount. I said just whatever you can give us. We think we can win if we get the money.

They had some questions and then asked me to leave. The issue that the growers were raising was that they couldn't trust us because we don't keep our word, we're not a Union. So the board asked, "Would you be willing to have the AFL-CIO guarantee your contracts?"

I wouldn't even let them discuss it. I said, "Sure we will, any moment, on the spot!" They all looked up. I said, "What's there to guarantee? We're not covering anything up. We're not playing games. If the contract's there and we're wrong, we're wrong. And if we're right, we're right."

That took them aback, because that's a very internal kind of thing. If you get hung up on how important you are, all those things become issues. But we don't care. Why should we? If the AFL-CIO wants to tell the growers, "Okay, we will guarantee you that the Union is going to act as a union according to the contract," that puts us in a good position. It cuts the water from the growers' argument. The whole lie becomes pretty bare.

So I left and went over to Bill Kircher's office, where I waited about an hour. Then Bill came back, really ecstatic, and said they just approved an assessment of four cents per member for three months. He started figuring it out. "That means about a million and a half dollars," he said. Actually it came to exactly $1,698,283.76.

Afterward, George Meany held a press conference and called the Teamsters' actions "the most vicious strikebreaking, union-busting effort I've seen in my lifetime. We're going to do anything that's necessary to keep that Union alive."

FROM JACQUES LEVY'S NOTEBOOK

May 30, 1973—Wall Street Journal reporter William Wong and Father John Bank, a thirty-three-year-old Ohio priest doing public relations work for UFW, walk into the Trukadero restaurant in Coachella for breakfast, after a few early hours on the picket lines.

A short time later a dozen Teamsters walk in, take tables near the pair, and start taunting Father Bank.

After about five minutes of silence, Father Bank can contain himself no longer. "If they cast a B movie, they couldn't have done a better job," he gibes.

"Oh, you think it's funny!" says a huge man with a bushy beard.

"Yea, I think it's funny," Bank answers.

The man, Mike Falco, stands up, uttering an ugly laugh. "I'm going to stop laughing, and then it's not funny any more," he says, taking his sunglasses off and staring at Father Bank. A few of the other Teamsters close in.

"This is worth going to jail for," Falco says as he stops laughing. Before Father Bank can stand or duck, Falco's fist smashes his nose.

Falco, who police say weighs about three hundred pounds, is later charged with battery, while Father Bank is taken to the Indio Community Hospital.

June 8, 1973—Wall Street Journal news item: "A funny thing happened when the Teamsters Union set out to polish its image through a $1.3 million-a-year public relations campaign. It wound up with an image-polisher whose own image is rather tarnished. . . .

"For the associates and fees of the little-known firm the Teamsters selected are raising questions both within the union and among federal investigators.

"That firm is Hoover-Gorin & Associates, and it wasn't even incorporated until eight days after getting the Teamsters' contract. Its headquarters is a few blocks off the Las Vegas Strip. . . .

"For a public relations firm representing the nation's largest union, Hoover-Gorin seems surprisingly ignorant of labor protocol. The firm's folders and stationery don't bear the all-important 'union bug' that would indicate they have been printed in a union shop. . . .

"Although Hoover-Gorin boasts of branch offices in Los Angeles and Cleveland, it actually relies mostly on a 'consultant' in each city. Each consultant has a criminal record. . . .

"Mr. Hoover, a gaudy dresser (burgundy and white striped suit with burgundy patent leather shoes for a recent interview) who ducks questions about his real first name, is a 34-year-old one-time Los Angeles disc jockey who more recently was host for a movie show on a Nevada television station. He says the Teamster contract has been a boon to his firm. He has also landed the advertising account for Circus-Circus, a local casino heavily in debt to the Teamsters' Central States, Southeast and Southwest Areas Pension Fund. . . .

"The agency's consultant in Los Angeles is Harry Helfgot, who uses the alias 'Harry Haler' in his public-relations work. The 54-year-old Helfgot has a criminal record that includes a fraud conviction, according to Southern California law enforcement authorities.

"The U.S. Attorney in Chicago recently issued a complaint accusing Helfgot of trying to use $175,000 worth of stolen Treasury bonds and notes as collateral to obtain a $100,000 loan at a Chicago bank in April. Helfgot says he's innocent, and he's currently free on $100,000 bail awaiting grand jury consideration of the complaint. . . .

"Hoover-Gorin's consultant in Cleveland is Tony Liberatori, the business manager of Local 860 of the Laborers International Union. Law enforcement officials say Liberatori's local has a 'close working relationship' with a Teamsters local headed by Louis (Babe) Triscaro. Liberatori was paroled in 1958 after serving 20 years in prison in connection with the 1937 murders of two Cleveland detectives."

CESAR CHAVEZ RECALLS

I really spent more time in Coachella than anywhere else. I was mostly a symbol, as they had good leadership there. I would just go out and prep the troops; handle emergencies like getting people to go to jail and not be afraid; and deal with leadership problems, money problems, attorneys, and nonviolence and discipline on the picket lines.

When I went to the picket lines, I figured things for people to do so that they wouldn't get discouraged, and got them to understand how important it is to get the people inside to slow down and do lower quality work if they can't get them to leave, things that will mean money to the employer.

We had some administrative hang-ups, but I could do that and still be involved everywhere, as we had more leadership. I forced the leadership to do a lot of things themselves, forcing them to make their own decisions.

FROM JACQUES LEVY'S NOTEBOOK

June 8, 1973—The Teamsters put on a show for the TV cameras, pulling workers out of the field to wave blue Teamster flags along the edge of the vineyard facing the UFW picket line.

Both sides soon are yelling at each other, exchanging taunts and slurs.

Later, Cesar chews out the picket captains. "For the first time I saw a lot of hate," he tells them. "You've got to go back and work with those people."

The picket lines should not insult the scabs, he says. That just pushes them into the Teamster camp. "If we had elections, we'd lose them today. We would have won them yesterday."

He urges the picket captains to win the workers over if they leave their work to face the UFW lines.

CESAR CHAVEZ RECALLS

On June 19, I got a very indignant call from Jack Henning, head of the California AFL-CIO. "What's this I hear about you guys shot Grami?"

"What!" I said. "Nobody shot Grami." And I made fun of Henning. I said, "You know us better than that."

But the Teamsters had it synchronized. Grami is known for pulling those stunts—like the time he claimed he was "kidnapped" and beaten and left chained to a tree while organizing the apple canneries near Sebastopol. This time Grami said he was shot at 5:00 A.M. at the Indio labor camp where our pickets were. The same morning in Sacramento, the Teamsters' lobbyist told Assembly Speaker Bob Moretti that Grami was shot in the head by our people.

It showed how desperate they were.

FROM JACQUES LEVY'S NOTEBOOK

June 20, 1973—Southern California Teamster news item: "As the Teamster went to press it was learned that Bill Grami was shot in the head at approximately 5 A.M. Tuesday, in the vicinity of a Coachella farm workers' labor camp. . . .

"Grami was struck by the single bullet approximately three inches from his eye."

Riverside Enterprise news item: "Last night, Sheriff Ben Clark reacted angrily to the Teamsters Union method of trying to publicize Grami's injury. A representative of that union called two wire services and newspapers to report that Grami had been shot.

"Clark said that the sheriff's department knew from the outset that no gunshots had been fired."

Bill Grami calls a press conference today and appears with a patch on his forehead.

"The UFW-instigated violence that has occurred during the past two weeks must be stopped," he says. "We don't want to be forced into a position of retaliation."

He says his head wound caused "internal muscle damage" that required four internal stitches and eight external ones.

Riverside Enterprise news item: "A Las Vegas public relations man dispatched to this area as part of a million-dollar effort to 'improve the image' of the Teamsters Union has filed a complaint against a Teamster who he says hit him in the face Monday night and told him to 'get out of town.'"

Murray Westgate had charged in a press release last week that the UFW was bringing in "bruticians . . . to stage intimidation, reprisals, violence, destruction and possibly even worse."

In the same release, Westgate said Teamster guards, who have been called "goons" by Cesar Chavez "aren't goons at all," but rather "our security force here to protect workers."

The man he filed the complaint against with Indio police is reportedly a member of that force.

Westgate claims he was eating dinner Monday night at the El Morocco Motel in Indio, where the Teamsters are staying, when the man came up to his table, told him he was a Teamster, and said he wanted to meet him. Westgate said he stood up to shake the Teamster's hand and was struck in the face.

Westgate said the man then told him, "Get out of town, and if you don't, there are four other guys just like me who'd like to do the same thing to you I just did."

Westgate left for Las Vegas that night, stopping only in Indio to file the complaint.

June 21, 1973—Six Teamsters are arrested on charges of hurling rocks at a three-car caravan in which Cesar is riding from one picket line to another. Deputies say the rocks weighed about twenty pounds each. No one was hurt. The men are released on a thousand dollars bail each.

June 22, 1973—Riverside Enterprise news item: Two Teamsters were arrested yesterday morning by Riverside County Sheriff's deputies on charges of attempting to commit murder and kidnapping.

The victim, Israel Guajardo, twenty-eight, of Mecca, was mistaken for a UFW member by the Teamsters, sheriff's deputies said.

The incident occurred two days after William Grami asked for additional law enforcement officers in the Coachella Valley to supplement county sheriff's deputies.

Guajardo was taken to Indio Community Hospital with ice pick wounds to the back of his shoulder and neck.

June 23, 1973—Francisco Campos, his wife Patricia, and their two-and-a-half-year-old daughter Elisa, all of Brownsville, Texas, nearly died early this morning when their small trailer is destroyed by flames in an open field.

A neighbor, John Leal, seventeen, tore out a window screen to awaken them when he was unable to open their trailer door. Another neighbor saw two cars drive into the field where the trailer is located and heard someone yell, "We're going to burn down your house, Cisco!"

This is the first year in the grapes for the Campos family. Campos joined UFW in February. When the strike started April 15, he walked out of a Richard Glass vineyard and became a picket leader.

Teamsters came to his trailer looking for him a few weeks ago, he says later, and he was threatened several times by them on the picket line.

"We've never been in a union. We're very firm in our belief we're going to win. This is a Cause, not an alley fight," he says, looking at his little girl. "This fight is not with little babies."

And Campos says firmly, "We're not going to get scared because of that. We'll finish the huelga."

The fire destroyed everything they owned.

On the picket line the next morning, 180 Teamsters charge into a UFW picket line with iron pipes, clubs, tire irons, and machetes. The four hundred farm workers and volunteers defend themselves, and the battle rages in an asparagus field beside the vineyard for more than an hour.

Deputies report twenty-five to thirty persons injured, four requiring hospital treatment. Two UFW members are admitted with head wounds. The deputies make eleven arrests—six Teamsters and five UFW members.

June 28, 1973—Riverside Enterprise news item: "Internal dissension exists within the ranks of the Teamsters who are contesting the United Farm Workers Union for the right to represent the grape workers of the Coachella Valley."

Fact-finders sent into Coachella by Teamster President Frank Fitzsimmons say they either have been threatened with violence or subjected to violence at the hands of Ralph Cotner, who now is running the Teamster Coachella operation.

Cotner says, "The statements are too ridiculous to comment on."

Cotner also is accused by Teamster Ray Griego of being "the

man who's responsible for all the violence that's going on out there."

Bill Grami, Cotner's direct superior, said that he has consistently given orders that Teamsters in the Coachella Valley shouldn't initiate violence of any kind.

"I can't understand the confusion in carrying out my orders," Grami said. "Maybe I just don't want to believe that instructions for violence were given contrary to my orders."

The violence that Grami refers to is the activities of the past week, which spokesmen for the Riverside County Sheriff's Department say Teamsters have instigated.

A melee that occurred in an asparagus field—east of Thermal—on Saturday, June 24, was, according to Lieutenant Paul Yoxsimer, field commander for the sheriff's department strike task force, "the most violent eruption of the entire strike."

"The offensive on Saturday," Yoxsimer said, "or the move toward the people, was instigated by the Teamsters."

Captain Cois Byrd, who is in charge of the sheriff's department strike operation, said he personally saw Ralph Cotner at the scene of last Saturday's violence. "It appears to us that those persons (Teamsters) . . . acted in concert at a given signal, the signal being a firecracker going off!"

CESAR CHAVEZ RECALLS

Just as vicious as the Teamster attack in Thermal was the one four days later at the Kovacevich ranch in Arvin. It was planned. They drove up in their trucks, got off, and beat the hell out of people with sticks and pipes and chains while deputies just watched.

We had some women, kids, and men, some older men. There was no way they could resist. Juan Hernandez, who was sixty, had his skull fractured and ribs cracked. Others also were badly injured.

Al Leddy, the Kern County DA, totally disregarded his responsibilities as a law enforcement officer. Although deputies arrested twenty-nine Teamsters, Leddy dropped charges on all but one, and he eventually got off, too. These were the same goons the Teamsters used in the Coachella Valley.

FROM JACQUES LEVY'S NOTEBOOK

July 4, 1973—Cesar tells me he's been worried all week about how to end the Coachella strike, and the people today came up with the answer. They know it's now unproductive to keep the picket line here and suggest they go north to get jobs in Arvin and Delano before the strikebreakers get them.

July 5, 1973—Riverside Enterprise news item: William Grami said yesterday his union "will immediately withdraw all guards from agricultural areas being picketed by the United Farm Workers Union. We are doing this because we believe that local law enforcement agencies have realized the need for increasing their forces to the point where their protection appears adequate."

July 7, 1973—Riverside Enterprise news item: "More than 2,000 UFW pickets demonstrated at orchards and vineyards in five California counties yesterday, but for the second straight day, no incidents were reported.

"Law enforcement authorities in Riverside, Kern, Fresno, Tulare and Monterey counties cited the absence of Teamsters Union guards as the major reason for the lack of confrontation between opposing labor unions."

CESAR CHAVEZ RECALLS

Paul Hall came to see me in Coachella when the violence was at its peak. He was prepared to give unlimited help. I admire Paul. Even though he talks tough, he's got a soft heart for workers, which is very admirable. He is truly concerned about them. But I turned down his offer to bring in the Seafarers.

FROM JACQUES LEVY'S NOTEBOOK

I learn of Paul Hall's offer a year later from Fresno Bee reporter Ronald Taylor, who interviewed the head of the Seafarers International Union at an AFL-CIO convention in Florida. Taylor says Hall told him that his Seafarers were prepared to do what was necessary to get the Teamsters out.

Later, when I tell Cesar that Hall told Taylor he was angry because, "Cesar could have won it right then," if he had given Hall his okay, Cesar says quietly, "Probably so."

CHAPTER 8

Filling the Jails

FROM JACQUES LEVY'S NOTEBOOK

On July 10, 1973, the nation's largest winery, Gallo Brothers, which has had a contract with UFW for six years, signs a four-year Teamster contract.

After signing, the company announces that its workers voted 150 to 1 for the Teamsters, but at the time, all but 27 of its regular workers are on strike.

Earlier, Gallo refused to hold elections, despite UFW requests.

Gallo then tries to evict from its labor camps some seventy families who have been with the company up to fourteen years. The families, with four hundred children, are striking UFW members.

Franzia winery also refuses to renegotiate its UFW contract. So does White River Farms, formerly owned by Schenley. There, after the workers strike, the company has no workers in the field for nine days. But 288 arrests and imported strikebreakers help break the strike.

CESAR CHAVEZ RECALLS

What happened at Gallo was pretty much like the other growers. They had a pattern. They always found one item where they refused to give during negotiations. The only way Gallo would agree to deal with us was if we had agreed not to sign a contract. They wanted us out.

So we lost nearly all our contracts that summer, most of them to the Teamsters, who are head-hunters.

There was no comparison in law enforcement between River-side and the San Joaquin counties. In Riverside they tried to pre-tend that they were fair, but in Kern, Tulare, and Fresno Coun-ties, it was different.

Kern County was just a disaster, turning the power of the police against us to break the strike. The police would not let people get near the pickers, chasing them off after declaring that a street was not a public place. And they called the picket lines illegal assemblies.

They beat people who went into the fields to deliver leaflets, and used their helicopter to scatter our picket lines, flying so low it blew dust and clods into their eyes.

Then they were vicious with arrests. After identifying the lead-ership, they began to arrest them at 2:00, 3:00 in the morning at their homes, going in with two, three squad cars and just con-verging on them. It was out and out harassment.

Tulare County was worse—a bunch of dogs. They had a goon squad, a legal goon squad of twenty-four deputies in riot gear that went around threatening people, macing them, and beating peo-ple up. Tulare just didn't give a damn. They were going to break the strike.

Fresno was probably less vicious, but just as effective in terms of arrests. In four months, the courts in the four counties issued 58 injunctions, and there were 3,589 arrests. Fresno had the largest number, 1,993 people jailed, including 70 priests and nuns who came to Fresno to bear witness. It's hard when we can't picket. That's the only force we have, and they take it away from us.

We counted forty-four people that were beaten up by cops in the valley, where blood was drawn, and where workers were shot at from inside the vineyards.

We had nearly two dozen law students as volunteers who did a fantastic job of documentation, getting affidavits signed on the spot, and getting cases processed. At least one of them, Eduardo Rivera, was beaten by goons in Arvin on June 22. And often police refused to distinguish between them and the pickets, ar-resting them illegally. But they did a lot of work, and we had all the evidence we wanted.

FROM JACQUES LEVY'S NOTEBOOK

July 13, 1973—UPI news item: William Grami was named head of the Teamsters' thirteen-state Western Warehouse, Industrial

Aerospace and Allied Clerical Workers Council. He also will remain active as head of the Teamsters agricultural organizing drive.

July 21, 1973—*Los Angeles Times news item:* The Kern County Sheriff's Department sought to relieve the jail crush two days ago by releasing about 120 pickets who had been arrested for the first time. But in a show of solidarity, the first arrestees refused to sign citations and leave the jail unless all their companions went with them.

Similar tactics were used by UFW members in Fresno County, where deputies arrested 885 persons at Five Points, Parlier, and Reedley.

Sheriff Melvin Willmirth reported that the pickets refused to accept citations, as 452 arrested the day before had done. He said yesterday's arrestees were demanding to be jailed.

CESAR CHAVEZ RECALLS

On July 22, nine workers in the Fresno jail were put in the hole. Some of the other prisoners started a fire, and our guys were blamed for it. Then the deputies formed a gauntlet and forced the workers to run through it while they beat them.

When we told the press, Sheriff Melvin Willmirth called our charges "despicably false and blatantly irresponsible." The whole thing was whitewashed and denied even after the sheriff fired one reserve deputy because of the beatings.

FROM JACQUES LEVY'S NOTEBOOK

The same week as the beatings in the Fresno jail, Kern County deputies charge the picket line one morning on Edison Drive by the Giumarra ranch. They use their billy clubs and mace.

Seventeen-year-old Marta Rodriguez, a small, slender girl, has her arms pinned and twisted behind her and is dragged by deputies across the street into an orchard. Terrified by the brutality all around her, she screams in terror.

Frank Valenzuela, former mayor of Hollister and now an organizer with the American Federation of State, County and Municipal Employees, goes to her aid. He offers to take the hysterical girl to a police car to calm her, but officers converge on him, strike him in the legs, spray mace in his eyes, then hit him in the stomach.

They pin his arms behind him, shove his face into the ground, and arrest him.

Five-foot-tall Harriett Teller, twenty-three, who is on the scene as a legal aide to the union, is pushed with a police club and maced as she tries to take pictures.

Tomas Barrios of Coachella, a picket captain, is jumped on by Teamsters and police rush in. Four deputies grab him, one with a strangle hold, and he is choked until he passes out. Then he is arrested, and the Teamsters are let go.

Other pickets have their hands handcuffed behind them and are beaten. The police helicopter swoops low to scatter the pickets by spraying dirt clods in their midst. In all, 230 pickets are arrested, including three Jesuits.

On July 21, some two thousand union supporters and farm workers march through Delano and hold a rally in the park to impress on Delano growers the strength of the union. Their contracts expire Monday, July 29.

The following week, about two thousand farm workers gather at Forty Acres and vote to strike if the Delano growers don't sign a new contract by midnight Sunday.

Bill Kircher promises them support. "I'm here to tell you the same thing I told you in 1965—that the working people of the AFL-CIO are with you, and we'll stay with you. This is Delano. This is the heart of the union, the core of the farm workers movement, and there isn't a power on earth than can destroy it."

July 29, 1973—At the Ramada Inn in Bakersfield, the negotiations between UFW and the Delano growers recess at 3:30 A.M. Eight hours later, the two dozen farm workers return to the conference room and wait for the growers to appear. Unless the impass is broken in the next few hours, they face another painful strike. They sit silent, serious, and tense.

Suddenly Cesar leaps up on the negotiating table, facing the growers' empty chairs. He arches his left arm upward while stretching out his right—thrust, parry, thrust. In the best swashbuckling style of Errol Flynn, he shadow fences his enemy.

"This is Zorro," he jokes as he goes through his pantomime. The farm workers smile and relax, their tensions eased.

But when Giumarra and the others file in, the talks go nowhere. John Giumarra, Sr., complains of a headache. He didn't sleep an hour, he says, his eyes half-shut. He can't take aspirin. He has an ulcer. "You need guts of steel, and that's not good enough. You need stainless steel," he comments.

They get down to business, but fifteen minutes later the talks collapse. "If you change your position you can call us," says the growers' attorney.

"You have our phone," Cesar counters.

"Huelga!" shout the workers as they file out.

That night, at a rally at Forty Acres, the old NFWA sign is on the back of the flat-bed truck used as a speaking platform. "That's our sign of victory," Cesar tells the mass of several thousand farm workers, reminding them of their history.

"Eight years ago in Delano, the idea that workers should have a union came forth out of some of us here. There were few of us. Eight years ago we were being paid ninety-five cents an hour, and if you lived in the camp, it was seventy-five or eighty-five cents an hour. What the growers are trying to do with the Teamsters is a fraud."

"We shall take out our huelga flags, which are a symbol of freedom and justice, all across the country, and we shall go to the picket lines," he says. "We'll make sure the growers pay double for the price of picking. We'll make sure the quality is disastrous, and that wherever possible the grapes turn to raisins on the vine. We'll make sure the price paid for grapes is below cost!"

He predicts it will take a couple of years to win, but, "I'd be surprised if it takes more than two years. These kinds of things are healthy. Our salvation is in struggle!"

And thinking of the five-year strike, he tells the workers, "Now we're in heaven compared to eight years ago. In those days we were inspected by every department in one week. We had no place to meet, no money, no cars. Now we have a trained staff, a hall. We'll have a thirty times easier time this time!"

July 30, 1973—The Delano table-grape pickers leave the vineyards and set up their picket line. After three peaceful years, the long strike for their own union is resumed.

August 1, 1973—More than forty priests and nuns from throughout the U.S. are among three hundred pickets arrested in southeast Fresno County. The number of pickets in the three San Joaquin counties is estimated by deputies at some three thousand.

In Delano, UFW picket Joe Moncon, eighteen, is shot in the right shoulder while getting into a car near the Tudor ranch vineyards. The shotgun blast is fired from a truck passing the picket line. There are no arrests following the shooting.

CESAR CHAVEZ RECALLS

Dorothy Day has been a good friend from the beginning and has helped us a lot. She's been coming to visit us every summer for a number of years. I heard about her during my CSO days, when she was editor of the *Catholic Worker,* and I met her in 1965 when we started the strike.

She has been campaigning for the working man for a long time, putting them up, giving them food, going on the picket lines, dedicating her entire life, without pay, to the service of other workers, developing a progressive Catholic front so that the church and Christ's teachings were more than just prayer and mass.

In 1973, when she heard that we needed people, she said, "Let's go!"

FROM JACQUES LEVY'S NOTEBOOK

August 2, 1973—Several hundred farm workers are in the city park in Parlier when Cesar arrives at dawn. He tells them of the plans to continue mass arrests, to fill the jails in defiance of the injunctions.

In the background is Dorothy Day, looking frail but determined, her militancy undiminished after seventy-six years. Yesterday she was on the picket lines at the Giumarra ranch in the Arvin-Lamont area hoping to be among those arrested. But there were no arrests. So this morning she has traveled one hundred miles north to Fresno County where the mass arrests are continuing.

When Cesar is through talking, she walks up to him, holding her cane whose handle opens into a seat.

"Say a prayer that this time they'll take me," she asks Cesar.

"I will," Cesar answers.

He, too, decides to be arrested, but first he must call a number of people in the union to alert them. By the time he completes his calls and reaches the picket line, it is gone. All have been arrested. He searches out another line, but again arrives too late. His attempt fails.

Dorothy Day, however, is jailed.

CESAR CHAVEZ RECALLS

The day after Dorothy Day was arrested, I visited the Fresno jail with State Senator George Moscone. It was horrible, like a dungeon, sweltering hot inside.

In one place there was a sewer pipe leaking right into the cell-block. The cops took all the mattresses away from the people, wet the floors, and they had to sleep there. The cops were vicious.

When I got there, the workers weren't that crowded because a lot of people had been moved to the county industrial farm, but before that they were crowded, and their medical needs were ignored. One epileptic farm worker was given no medication for three days. He convulsed three times before he was given treatment, and then only at the insistence of one of our clinic nurses. Another with ulcers was given only two meals a day, fourteen hours apart, with nothing in between.

FROM JACQUES LEVY'S NOTEBOOK

The union sends its doctors and nurses to give the prisoners health checks. They find three workers whose TB check is positive, but Fresno County officials refuse to do anything about it. Two others have high blood pressure and one a bad heart, but the county refuses to release them without bail.

The jailers prohibit the nuns, Jesuits, and other religious representatives from holding daily mass on the grounds they might get drunk on the wine. They also refuse to let the nuns have mosquito repellent on the grounds they might sniff it and get high.

When Cesar visits the county industrial camp, one moving scene follows another. Each time he enters a men's barrack, the imprisoned workers crowd around him, embrace him, and cheer. But the most moving scene is in the women's barracks where Dorothy Day is housed.

"Don't waste your time in jail!" he tells the women, whose spirit seems even more militant than the men's. "You should have classes twice a day."

Addressing Dorothy Day he says, "Tell them the story of the labor movement," and turning to the nuns he says, "Tell them about the life of a nun."

In a lighter vein he comments, "The sisters' network is really humming these days! I'd hate to be a judge!" When the laughter dies down, he says, "You should pray for Judge Pettit. You're in heaven compared to him."

"What's happening here is no different than what happened in Selma," he says. "It's truly a blot on the conscience of America."

Juanita Escarano, a Sanger farm worker, is one of several who express their feeling about being in jail. She steps up on a wooden table that has become a makeshift platform. "It's very evident we're very happy to be here because this is the best way to win the struggle," she tells her fellow prisoners and Cesar. "This kind of spirit can't be jailed."

August 4, 1973—In Tulare County, the sheriff's tac squad tries to incite Juan Cervantes, a nineteen-year-old picket captain, into a fight, but the youth keeps his cool. Back at the Forty Acres he describes to Cesar what happened at the Dispoto ranch.

As he yelled "Huelga!" at the scabs, a deputy snarled, "If you don't keep your mouth shut, we'll take care of you, you four-eyed monkey."

Another officer threatened, "Don't worry. We've got your license plate. We'll kill you."

"Are you threatening me?" Cervantes asked.

"You can call it what you want," the cop answered. And the racial insults and threats continued.

August 7, 1973—About 250 pickets are massed on the north side of the huge Giumarra vineyards in Lamont. Several dash into the vineyards to talk to the strikebreakers who are deep in the vineyard.

Kern County deputies spot them and rush in, but instead of arresting them, they beat them with their clubs.

Anger spreads through the picket line, and the picket captains, to cool things off, call off the pickets and move them to neutral ground on the railroad tracks.

Giumarra's security guards and the deputies soon have them flanked on the north, east, and west. When an officer orders them to leave the track area, a picket captain tells him they have a right to be on the private property unless requested to leave by the railroad.

Again police order them to move, but the pickets instead kneel down to pray. Then the police charge, their clubs flailing, their mace canisters spraying.

As the workers panic and flee toward their cars, they find that police have them surrounded. They must charge through the police lines to escape, ducking both the clubs and the mace.

Among those badly injured is forty-three-year-old Ernestina Ramon who is struck across the eye by a club, and AFL-CIO organizer Joe Lopez from New York.

A number of pickets prevented from getting to their cars by police are forced to walk miles back to union headquarters.

JERRY COHEN RECALLS

The vast majority of the arrest cases were dismissed. Most of them were for violating an injunction or for unlawful assembly. There were a few assorted charges—like people would throw dirt clods, several threw rocks, and there were some in for assorted scuffles.

But when you think that 3,589 people were arrested, I think well over 3,400 of those were clear First Amendment issues and had nothing to do with even alleged disturbing the peace or stuff like that. So it was an amazing performance by the farm workers. They really kept their cool when they were attacked.

And that shows, in the words of that justice in the Massachusetts Supreme Court, how the courts have been acting as a cavalry in the employers' army by issuing those injunctions. Because what happens is the arrests effectively inhibit strike activities.

CHAPTER 9

"Two Men Are Dead"

FROM JACQUES LEVY'S NOTEBOOK

After much pressure from top AFL-CIO executives, the clergy, and others, the Teamsters agree to meet with Cesar in Burlingame on August 9 to work out another jurisdictional pact. AFL-CIO General Counsel Al Woll and Federation Vice-President Joseph Keenan act as mediators.

But on the second day of the talks, word arrives that the twenty-nine Delano growers signed Teamster contracts the night before. It is a clear violation of the agreement Teamster President Frank Fitzsimmons made with AFL-CIO President George Meany, that there would be no more contracts signed until after talks are held to resolve the conflict.

Cesar ends the negotiations, telling the press as he walks out, "We have been stabbed in the back. They are not talking in good faith."

On the way back to the strike scene in the San Joaquin Valley, Cesar decides to stop by the home of Joan Baez who lives near Burlingame and wanted to see him. There, he calls strike head-quarters and learns that two UFW pickets were shot on the picket line near Richgrove at the Missakian ranch. Paul Saludado, six-teen, was shot in the hip and Marcelino Barajas, twenty-four, suf-fered a flesh wound in the head. It is the fourth shooting incident in twenty-four hours, but the first with injuries.

Joan Baez asks if it would help if she came down to the picket line.

"Yes, it would," Cesar says.

"When should I come," the folk singer asks. "Tomorrow, Sunday, or Monday?"

"Come right now."

Joan gulps, but agrees. She packs a few clothes, and we take off, Cesar in the front seat and Joan cramped in the back seat of my small sports car. During the four-hour drive, the two talk about nonviolence, then Cesar, exhausted, falls asleep. Joan starts singing softly.

Later in the day, Fitzsimmons and Einar Mohn repudiate the Delano contracts signed by Jim Smith, the Teamster area supervisor, but John Giumarra, Sr., maintains the contracts are valid.

August 13, 1973—Fresno County officials agree to free all the pickets without their posting bail, and this evening the prisoners are released, including the seventy priests and nuns. As Father Eugene Boyle of San Francisco walks out of jail after nearly two weeks, he says, "We've come out of a tomb. It's like a resurrection."

At a mass and meeting on the lawn in front of the courthouse and jail complex, Father Boyle tells the hundreds of farm workers, "This is the greatest number of religious persons ever jailed in the United States. I hope it says something about our deep and profound belief in your cause. We know you will overcome."

MARSHALL GANZ RECALLS

Because we were toning down the strike in Arvin and building it up in Delano, we had a party in the Arvin park on August 13 after the regular strike meeting.

We got home kind of late that night. So the next morning I got to the office a little late, about 5:30 in the morning instead of 4:00.

Right away I saw Pablo Espinoza, who was in charge in Arvin. Pablo asked me, "Did you hear about Nagi?"

I said, "No, what happened?" Nagi Daifullah was one of our picket captains.

He told me, and I talked to other people who had been there, Frank Quintana and Gregorio Cortez and others.

It seems that shortly after midnight, after the party, they were across the street from the Union office—there are several restaurant-tavern kind of places there—and they were standing talking. A cop came up to them, this guy Gilbert Cooper, and said that they had to disperse.

They asked why, that there was no picket line going on, that they were just standing there talking. And he said if they didn't disperse, he was going to have them all arrested.

The Kern County Sheriff's Department was using this kind of Gestapo technique. Everybody was in violation of the injunctions, everybody, but they wouldn't make any mass arrests. They would get a warrant on the basis of an injunction violation against the picket captains and keep bopping them in jail. We were on a merry-go-round. We would go in and out of jail several times a week.

Like Frank Quintana was busted two or three times at his house at 1:00 in the morning. They'd wait until he was home, in bed asleep, and they'd go bang on the door routine and pick him up and take him.

So Cooper told them they were going to arrest them if they didn't disperse, and this was 12:30 in the morning on a public street, and no picket line or anything.

Well, people got kind of excited, and one thing led to another. I understand that something was thrown by somebody, but nobody knows who. And Nagi took off running and Cooper took off after him.

Then, as he caught him, Deputy Cooper smashed him with his flashlight and knocked him to the ground. Then he dragged him back from where his head hit the pavement to the place right in front of the bar. There was a line of blood there.

So immediately I got ahold of a friend of mine, Said Al-Alas from Aden in Arabia, who was working at the clinic down in Weedpatch. He'd worked for the Union for a while up around the Porterville area.

First, of course, we got a doctor from the clinic down to the General Hospital to find out about Nagi's condition. He hadn't regained consciousness. Then we tried to get a hold of Nagi's family in Yemen. It was a whole complicated thing. Eventually we found out the name of his father and sent cablegrams to Yemen, and we weren't sure of the address.

Then we set to work getting the word out to all the Arab brothers. We went to all the Arab camps and told them what had happened. Of course, some of those that were not on strike joined the strike. In fact, the whole Roberts Farms camp joined the strike at that point. We said there was going to be a vigil in front of the hospital.

That night at the hospital, there must have been about seventy or eighty Arab workers and another one hundred or so mostly Chicano workers. There was a priest, and the Arabs brought a prayer leader.

So it was one of those beautiful things that happened. I mean everybody was there because they cared very much what was going to happen with Nagi.

The Arab brothers formed these prayer lines with the prayer leader in front, and all knelt down facing east.

All the other people gathered around, not in back, but around the sides with an opening out to the east, forming a kind of cathedral of people. It's hard to describe. Then they began their prayers in Arabic, and, of course, nobody knew what they were saying except themselves.

It was this beautiful kind of thing. As they finished the Arab prayers, one of the ladies from Lamont began saying Rosary. Then all the Chicano workers joined in. Then everybody joined in singing "De Colores."

It was terrible what was happening with Nagi, but that was a very beautiful thing because it was a real coming together, a real spiritual kind of binding that took place there.

The next evening Nagi died.

I was in charge of the funeral. We got together a committee of Arab workers to work on it and decided it would be in Delano. We couldn't get ahold of his family in Yemen, so we just tried to do the best we could.

We understood that he had a cousin up around Stockton and got word to him. It turned out the cousin was a foreman for Del Monte Corporation and hated the Union. He came down, and when he heard what was happening about all the Union people involved, he was very upset.

He'd heard that Nagi had been drinking, and he said that he died in dishonor because you're not supposed to drink according to Moslem law. So that was one of Said Al-Alas's special projects, was dealing with the cousin.

Then we asked the Arab brothers what was the best thing to do, whether he should be buried here or sent back to Yemen. Well, they were very impressed with that, because apparently it had never happened in the history of Yemen that a worker who had died outside the country was shipped back. It would be like a great honor. So we felt we should do that.

The day after Nagi died, I was in the Lamont office in the mid-afternoon, and I was about to go to Delano for a meeting on the funeral arrangements, when one of the strikers called me.

All he could say was, "One of the brothers has just been shot." He didn't know who.

I told him that we would call the police and an ambulance, and to go back and just wait right there.

We were on our way out there when somebody else arrived and said that the person who had been shot was Juan de la Cruz, whom I'd known since 1965 when we first started organizing in Arvin. He was sixty years old, one of the original DiGiorgio strikers.

They had taken him to the clinic in Weedpatch, and we got there about one minute after Juan had left in an ambulance for the Kern General Hospital. I talked to the doctor at the clinic who said, "Yes, he'd been shot, but he will be all right. It's amazing, he's a very strong man. He'll be all right."

Well, we just felt tremendously relieved.

We went back to the office and met Cesar and Congressman Don Edwards who had just arrived from the airport. Together we went down to the site where Juan had been shot and saw the blood on the ground; and the bullet holes in the windshields of about five cars. We were told Juan was standing by one of the cars when this scab drove by in a pickup firing a gun. He hit Juan and barely missed Maximina, his wife, who was standing next to him.

About an hour later, on our way to Delano, Pablo and I stopped at Kern General to see Maximina and see how Juan was. Just as we got in the door, there was a man leaving Maximina, and she was just bursting into tears.

We went over and asked what happened.

And she said, "He died! He died!"

FROM JACQUES LEVY'S NOTEBOOK

August 15, 1973—UPI news item: Shots were fired at the son of Cesar Chavez today at the George Lucas ranch near Earlimart during a rock and dirt clod fight between pickets and nonstriking field hands.

Sergeant Richard Morris of the Tulare County Sheriff's Department said Fernando Chavez, twenty-four, took cover behind a parked car. Three bullets lodged in the vehicle, but Chavez was not injured.

Chavez, an intern on the staff of State Assemblyman Richard Alatorre, had joined the pickets as a legislative observer.

When Cesar learns of Nagi Daifullah's death—the day before Juan de la Cruz is killed—he issues a statement calling on all members and supporters to start a three-day fast Monday, August 20, "to honor the life and sacrifice of Nagi Daifullah. . . . It must be a time to think again about violence and nonviolence. We also want to remember to pray for Deputy Sheriff Cooper during this time."

August 17, 1973—About seven thousand farm workers gather silently in Delano Memorial Park for the funeral procession to the Forty Acres. Somberly they gather in groups from their various ranches and towns, many carrying black union flags they have made for the occasion.

A group of Arab workers are at the head of the procession proudly carrying a huge picture of Gamal Abdel Nasser.

As we wait for the procession to start, the workers keep arriving, an endless silent stream of somber men, women, and children, dressed in clean work clothes, a black ribbon around one arm. The sight stirs even the most hardened reporters to comment on the deeply moving impact of their dignity and their numbers and their sorrowful silence. They are like the ghosts of generations of farm workers marching by.

Finally Nagi Daifullah's casket is carried out of the funeral home next to the park by eight slender young Arab pallbearers. Slowly the procession starts its three-and-a-half-mile march past rows of vineyards to the Forty Acres, where both Moslem and Catholic services are held.

It is a strange irony that the first two UFW martyrs are Nagi Daifullah, an Arab moslem, and an eighteen-year-old Jewish girl, Nan Freeman of Wakefield, Massachusetts, who was struck by a truck on the picket line at the Talisman Sugar Company in Belle Glade, Florida, on January 25, 1972.

August 17, 1973—Kern County District Attorney Al Leddy tells the press that Nagi Daifullah, "over whom Chavez is to spend three days praying and fasting," had been working Thursday for the Kovacevich ranch and had informed the ranch that he was a spy for the Teamsters.

MARSHALL GANZ RECALLS

I think all our activity preparing for the funerals was a godsend, because I don't know what would have happened if people had been able to stop and think about what had happened.

Right away everybody went to work making black flags, finding trucks for the park, doing this, doing that. We wanted to use a

small building in the middle of the DiGiorgio Park in Arvin for
the chapel for Juan, and the Board of Supervisors wouldn't let us
have it. So a whole bunch of women went up to the Board's meeting, demanded it, and got it.

But it was just great that there were all of those things to focus
on, because I think if there hadn't been, it would have been very
difficult to keep people nonviolent.

And those things are strange, because you often don't realize at
the time what's happened. We just did what had to be done.

FROM JACQUES LEVY'S NOTEBOOK

August 21, 1973—The second moving funeral is held today, the
procession walking five miles in the hot sun from the Arvin park
to the cemetery. More than five thousand workers attend.

After the burial services, the press is more interested in getting
Cesar to comment on a letter sent to the Delano growers by Teamster President Fitzsimmons which says the Teamsters "have no interest in organizing your employees in the vineyards in and around
Delano. We therefore disclaim and repudiate such purported
agreement as being unauthorized."

Cesar charges the letter means nothing. "They're just trying to
make news to offset what happened here today," he says. "The
fact remains two men are dead, and the Teamsters and the growers
and the police are responsible."

He says the union sent out a scout car today, and it was shot at
from the fields. "Sheriff's deputies don't want to protect our lives
in any way."

August 31, 1973—Los Angeles Times news item: Nagi Daifullah's death was ruled accidental by a coroner's jury in Bakersfield.

Jerry Cohen terms the ruling an outrage. "There's no way they
can call that an accident," he says. "It was death at the hands of
another. It was a bad verdict."

CHAPTER 10

Teamsters Go All Out

FROM JACQUES LEVY'S NOTEBOOK

September 1, 1973—Five hundred farm workers take off for boycott cities across the nation after a dawn rally at Forty Acres. The cars are blessed and divide into caravans for the South, the East, the Midwest, and Canada. Among those leaving are two of Cesar's daughters, Linda and Sylvia, and their children.

As the cars roll out of Forty Acres, they are reminiscent of the westward migrations in the thirties, filled with families whose suitcases are tied to their roofs. But this time the cars are headed east and fly the union flag or have union posters decorating their doors.

For many workers, it is their first adventure to the big cities so foreign to their way of life.

CESAR CHAVEZ RECALLS

There were several factors that made us call the strike off, certainly the deaths and the shootings, but there were others.

The spirit was really high for workers to go on the boycott, and we were out of money. When we stop a strike, we stop spending money, but if the strike has been going on for several weeks, the growers continue to lose money.

We spent more than three million dollars on that strike, the money that the Federation gave us, some loans that we made, and the one dollar a week strike assessment on our members. All of it went. We paid seventy-five dollars a week to thousands of striking workers that summer.

The strike was successful. When the leaves came off the vines because of the frost, we saw lots of grapes still hanging on them in Delano, Fresno, all those areas. And there were still raisins on the ground.

We also know the growers dumped a lot of grapes at night. We found one pile near Richgrove they tried to cover up with dirt. Then we got word Giumarra sent a lot of grapes to Los Angeles for cold storage.

I also think the strike helped us build a Union, even though we didn't get contracts. Unlike the lettuce workers, the fresh grape workers in the Union weren't radical before the strike. They weren't educated to the point that they would go to jail three, four, five, and six times. That hadn't happened in fresh grapes.

We were successful—with the help of the cops—in getting everybody in jail, to expose the workers to an entirely different view of their Union, looking from the inside out through the bars. And they voted to go to jail every time.

We also had some great victories in 1973 in the melons and tomatoes. They're obscure because people think in terms of signed contracts, but if they think in terms of organizing people and getting their response, they're good.

We forced the growers to give the melon workers a very good wage by the strikes Manuel led in Arizona, the Imperial Valley, and the San Joaquin Valley all the way up to Los Banos. Cantaloupe workers are really organized with us, even though they're members of the Teamsters.

Then in Stockton on tomatoes, although we didn't want contracts because we didn't want a long, prolonged fight, we got them seven cents a bucket in four days. And we also got an increase for the lettuce and, more significantly, for the grape, even though we didn't have a contract.

FROM JACQUES LEVY'S NOTEBOOK

September 14, 1973—San Francisco Chronicle news item: Officers of two vegetable packing firms and a former Modesto Teamsters Union official were indicted by a federal grand jury yesterday on charges of conspiring to block Cesar Chavez's organizing drive in the Salinas Valley three years ago.

The executives were accused of paying a total of $12,700 in cash and paying $3,400 in food and bar bills for the Modesto man's squad of "outside" Teamsters.

Indicted were Ted Gonsalves of Teamster Local 748; Thomas Hitchcock, general manager of Let-Us-Pak, a lettuce wholesaler; and James Robert Martin, vice-president of Cel-A-Pak, a cauliflower processing firm. Martin served as head of the Salinas Valley Grower Service Center, an ad hoc group formed in August 1970, to deal with the Chavez challenge.

CESAR CHAVEZ RECALLS

Since we had gotten our charter from the AFL-CIO, we had to hold a constitutional convention and elect a new board and officers. We organized the convention in a very short time under a lot of pressure and held it at the Fresno Convention Center from September 21 through 24. I thought we did a good job putting it together. The workers got an education, and I think it was run very democratically.

We were trying to establish many precedents. We wanted a working convention, not a lot of drinking and parties, and we wanted the delegates to stay together throughout the three days, which they did.

FROM JACQUES LEVY'S NOTEBOOK

The Fresno Convention Center—in the heart of the San Joaquin Valley, the stronghold of California agriculture—is decorated with huge union banners and behind the platform there is a giant mural painted especially for the occasion. The 346 delegates represent 60,069 votes from ranches throughout California, Arizona, and Florida.

Most of the delegates have never been to a convention before, but they sit listening attentively and aren't afraid to speak up when they don't understand a point.

"Who is this Mr. Roberts you are always talking about? Where is he from?" one delegate asks, when Cesar announces that the convention will be run according to Roberts Rules of Order. "Why do we have to follow his rules? They don't sound very democratic."

"When we go out in our cars to drive," Cesar explains, "we follow certain rules. This is so we all will drive in the same direction and not crash into one another. It is the same at a big meeting like this. We use rules so that we go in the same direction."

The explanation continues for some twenty minutes until the

delegate is satisfied. Simultaneous translations in Spanish and English are provided via a closed radio hookup.

Periodically, the business of the convention is interrupted by speeches from special guests such as Leonard Woodcock, president of the United Automobile Workers; Paul Hall, representing AFL-CIO President George Meany; or Senator Edward Kennedy. But the bulk of the time is devoted to the adoption of the 111-page constitution, which is painfully gone over section by section.

Then the officers are elected and the other members of the executive board. Cesar has no opposition, but there is spirited political maneuvering for members of the board.

"I hate this political stuff," Cesar tells me the night before the vote. But he has strong ideas about who will contribute the most to an effective, working board, and he works out a strategy for his slate.

The next day the campaigning goes on while he remains on the podium going through each section of the constitution. Finally, when the vote is taken on the board, the Chavez slate wins.

Gilbert Padilla is elected secretary-treasurer, Dolores Huerta first vice-president; Philip Vera Cruz second vice-president; Pete Velasco third vice-president. Elected board members are Mack Lyons, Eliseo Medina, Richard Chavez, and Marshall Ganz.

When the convention is over, Cesar flies to Washington where the AFL-CIO and the Teamsters are trying again to hammer out a peace agreement.

CESAR CHAVEZ RECALLS

The convention was a big help to me, making many changes. It set rules which are law and have to be obeyed. Before we improvised, and I had to make all the decisions. Now we have a clearly constituted authority to act between conventions. The executive board makes the policy decisions, which I carry out.

We have a very good board, very hard workers. I came out of the first board meeting with more than a hundred items to take care of, and in seven days we'd handled every single thing except one.

I keep comparing how deep the leadership of the Union is now compared to before, and it's a good feeling. The days when the Union was just "una buella de guesto"—just one happy bunch—are over.

A lot of workers participated in the convention, and they feel responsible for what they did there. They still carry the badges, "I'm a delegate"—like being a congressman. They either have it in their pocket, or clipped on their coats. That's very good.

After the convention, we started the task of really dealing with the administrative problems that we've had for a long time. I felt I had to straighten out La Paz, the Union headquarters. I couldn't allow sloppiness and independence as it existed. I was ready to fire everyone if necessary and start from scratch. It had to be done.

I started working from 2:00 or 2:30 in the morning until about 10:00 at night for a couple of months just to learn what was happening in the Union, and to determine who was responsible for what.

Now, for the first time, we have a ninety-day budget, and I know how much money comes in daily and how much money is spent. I can plan now.

I'm not fearful that La Causa will crumble. And it can't crumble if one man leaves it. That's not by accident either. I've worked very hard at it, and I take more pride in that than anything else. We have a very good base, and we have very good second, third, and fourth string leadership. My position is to get it going, and get out and turn it over to them.

I won't stay here forever. They'll get rid of me sooner or later after they no longer need me, when they get to the place where they feel secure. That's the way it should be in a Union and in any movement.

FROM JACQUES LEVY'S NOTEBOOK

September 29, 1973—San Francisco Chronicle news item: The Teamsters Union and the United Farm Workers have made peace. The Teamsters Union will renounce contracts it has signed with California wine and table-grape growers this year as part of its peace pact with the UFW.

The UFW will have the sole right to organize field workers. The Teamsters, in turn, will retain sole jurisdiction over cannery and other processing plant workers.

Official disclosure of the terms won't be made until the pact is fully reviewed by Teamsters Union attorneys.

A spokesman for Teamsters President Frank Fitzsimmons said the review is routine, and he knows of no problem issues.

November 17, 1973—San Francisco Chronicle news item: AFL-CIO President George Meany accused Fitzsimmons yesterday of reneging on their agreement under which the Teamsters would hand over their California farm field contracts to the UFW.

Meany said the settlement worked out in negotiations in Washington in September was "a full and complete agreement and was not subject to further negotiations."

Meany said, "It appears the Teamsters have decided that their interests lie in maintaining the alliance they have created with these employers, rather than in maintaining their integrity as trade unionists."

November 22, 1973—San Francisco Chronicle news item: Frank Fitzsimmons accused Meany yesterday of treating farm workers as "chattels" to be exchanged between unions without asking the workers what they want.

Fitzsimmons said the contracts the Teamsters would honor included thirty with grape growers in the Delano area which he earlier had repudiated.

March 29, 1974—Los Angeles Times news item: The Teamsters have launched a massive hundred thousand dollar a month organizing campaign among farm workers in a vastly stepped-up battle to eliminate the UFW.

April 8, 1974—UPI news item: The AFL-CIO announced that it is throwing its full support behind the lettuce and grape boycotts.

In a letter sent to all AFL-CIO central bodies and affiliates, George Meany wrote, "The Teamsters and the growers are jointly seeking to destroy the farm workers."

CHAPTER 11

The Best Source
of Hope Is the People

CESAR CHAVEZ RECALLS

I've been expecting now for years that public support is going to
dwindle and disappear, and that we're going to one of these days
wake up and find no support there. That's happened to movements. In the last twenty-five years I've seen them come and go
very fast, but our Movement hangs on. I think it's struck deep
roots.

In fact, we've been able to keep this support and increase it because we generate it the hard way. We have organized millions of
people. It keeps growing because we put the time into it.

What people don't understand, they think that support just
springs up. They're used to llamarada de petate—a flash in the
pan—some issue comes, people come to the defense, and then
support drops just as fast.

But we go to the cities and do nothing but organize. Our people
each hold meetings at least four times a week with whoever will
meet with them—church groups, union people, community organizations, political groups, house meetings—just people, house-
wives, consumers, everybody.

Ours is an economic struggle, a genuine struggle, and people
don't give up on those very easily—anymore than on religion. If
we had any other kind of struggle, we'd be dead. It would have
been over. But it's an economic struggle, and it's very difficult to
turn off. With public support, we can go on indefinitely.

RICHARD CHAVEZ RECALLS

The boycott this time is a little harder than the first big one when we could snap our fingers and get a picket line. We have to work very hard to get a picket line now. But the number of people that are willing to boycott grapes, Gallo, or lettuce is greater, I think. It's still a good weapon.

When I was sent to Detroit in February 1973, the boycott there was in bad shape. People were inexperienced. It's not that they weren't working, but they weren't producing.

After I started changing things around, we went from about four picket lines to about fifty or sixty. We organized a lot of committees and recruited people. I was there about eight months, and we got about five major chain stores to stop handling grapes.

After about eight months, Cesar asked me if I wanted to go to New York. I took some people from Detroit with me. By that time, I could do that and still leave good people behind to keep the Detroit boycott going.

From about nine picket lines, we went up to sixty-six in about a month and a half. Then we started doing some of the deep organizing, forming committees, and getting strong volunteer help.

But most of the farm workers that were there started getting sick, and this and that. Of the 150 that we had, we only have 7 left. We started using all volunteer help.

It's hard work. One winter day in Detroit, we picketed two to three hours. There was about two inches of ice on the sidewalks, and it must have been below zero. When we were ready to go home, Cesar's daughter Linda got in the car and turned on the heater, she was so frozen. She got emotional and started crying her heart out. But at the same time she was saying, "Those goddamn growers! They're going to pay for all of this!" That touched everybody.

Then A&P got injunctions against our picketing and there were arrests. The picketers appointed Cesar's granddaughter, Sylvia's four-year-old daughter, picket captain.

When the police came around, they wanted to talk to the picket captain. So the pickets pointed Theresa out.

"Don't be funny. I want to talk to the picket captain," the cop said. He was coming in kind of rough.

"Well, she is the picket captain," they insisted.

So the cop asked her, "Are you the picket captain?"

"Yes."

His attitude changed. "Why are you picketing?"

"I'm picketing against the Teamsters because my grandpa don't like them," she said. And she started telling him. "They took my grandpa's contracts away."

Theresa organized that cop for us. There was no bust on that picket line. We got busted somewhere else.

I don't think we can get victory without the boycott. Obviously we can't do it through a strike alone, because growers bring in illegals and other strikebreakers. But there's not too much that they can do about the boycott.

And there's no doubt the boycott is going to be successful, but it's taking twice as much work. It's twice as hard because we're fighting two enemies. If the Teamsters hadn't become involved, we would win sooner.

FROM JACQUES LEVY'S NOTEBOOK

November 4, 1974—Fresno Bee *news item:* A fierce power struggle has broken out in Teamsters Farmworkers Local 1973. Within the past week at least twenty-nine of the seventy-five local employes and officials have been fired and more firings are pending.

Those who have been let go include Cono Macias, one of the top three leaders of the local, the medical insurance plan administrator, and most of the organizers and business agents in the Indio, Arvin, Delano, Fresno, and Stockton offices.

Taking Bill Grami's place is Ralph Cotner, who worked for a short time in the 1973 farm organizing campaign.

David Castro, appointed secretary-treasurer of Local 1973 by the head of the Western Conference of Teamsters when the local was formed, told the Bee two months ago that the local did not plan to hold elections for at least two years.

"Suppose we had an election and it was stacked and I lost," Castro said. "To be very honest, I have to make sure the local is going to make it."

November 27, 1974—San Francisco Chronicle *news item:* Former Modesto Teamsters Union leader Theodore J. (Ted) Gonsalves has been sentenced to one year in prison for illegally soliciting and accepting payments from growers to combat the UFW's organizing drive in the Salinas Valley four years ago.

Gonsalves had pleaded "no contest" to five charges of violations of federal laws concerning payments from employers to union officials.

Two growers who were indicted with Gonsalves—James Robert Martin and Thomas Hitchcock—were acquitted of most charges by a jury last month. The jury deadlocked on a conspiracy count against Martin, and the charge later is dismissed.

December 1974—Suits filed by the UFW against the Teamsters during the past year ask for damages totaling $700 million, and more suits are expected to be filed in 1975.

The legal burden now facing the Teamsters because of their actions in the fields has become a significant factor in the course of future events.

CESAR CHAVEZ RECALLS

Everyone in the Union has no doubts that we'll get our contracts back. The Teamsters somewhere along the line are going to have to get out. They can't stop the strike. They can't stop us.

We don't say this because of blind faith or hope. We have a pretty good idea of what organizing a community means, and what the boycott is and its impact. We have a good idea, not by statistics, just by feel, feeling the people, feeling what's happening. It's not a hard thing to judge for us.

After we get the contracts back, then there's no stopping. That will legitimize the organization more than ever. The workers are pretty open to our Union throughout the country, I think. They all know about us now.

We've developed a lot more leadership. We can fight on two, three fronts at the same time and take care of ourselves.

Then we'll start winning strikes, too.

We're confident—not overconfident. It's just a matter of doing what we've always done since we started the Movement, working very hard and not giving up and doing the work that must be done to win.

But if we're not careful, we can begin to misunderstand and mismanage the whole idea of the trust that the workers have given us to lead and direct and administer and wrestle with the problems that we've had.

I've learned two very big things that I knew and had forgotten. The same methods that we used to build a Union, very effective in the beginning, still apply today and much more so. We thought because we had contracts that there were other things we could do. But I'm convinced we can't. We've got to do exactly what we did back in 1962, 1963, 1964. We must go back to the origins of the Union and do service-center work. The contracts are no substitute for the basic help we provide workers in all aspects of their lives. In some cases we thought that this work didn't deal with what we consider to be trade union business. But they deal very directly with human problems.

The second thing I know from experience is that whenever a critical situation hits us, the best source of power, the best source of hope, is straight from the people. It's happened to me so often.

There's a Mexican dicho that says there's always a good reason why bad news comes. And I think that in our case probably this will save the Union. I think that we were making a terrible mistake in the direction of the Union. We were isolating ourselves from the workers.

When I'm out with workers, they teach me every single day. It's an amazing thing. Obviously I don't know everything, I just know a little bit. Perhaps because I've made more mistakes than anybody else, I've had a chance to learn more than anybody else. But still, the workers teach me every single day as I teach them.

What happens is that in most unions and most societies—be it the church, politics, or whatever—there is a tremendous pull away from people and into paper work and into direction at the top away from the people.

The power came from the people, but no sooner is that power acquired than the man who got the power begins to isolate himself, insulate himself from people. There is so much competition for his time that the workers lose out, sometimes even with their consent.

And in our present struggle, we must organize not only among farm workers but also among consumers. So we are pulled by two constituencies, and we must remain in contact with both.

CHAPTER 12

A Very Important Lesson

CESAR CHAVEZ RECALLS

In 1974, as the boycott again started taking hold, I began to worry that the same thing would happen as had happened in 1970. After our victory then, we analyzed what had happened and found out the growers had used Europe as a dumping ground for the grapes they couldn't sell in the United States and Canada. Grape sales to Europe went up about 140 percent.

To prevent the same thing from happening again, an organized boycott was needed in Europe. George Meany and Leonard Woodcock sent letters of introduction for me to the top leaders in the European labor movement.

FROM JACQUES LEVY'S NOTEBOOK

As plans for the European trip are put together, Cesar insists he only will go if the trip is not financed by UFW. His friends quickly come to his aid. The World Council of Churches provides his air fare, and European unions guarantee his room and board in their countries. Then Bishop Joseph Donnelly and Monsignor George Higgins initiate plans for a possible audience with Pope Paul VI.

To Cesar, the idea of a papal audience is all but overwhelming. And when Dorothy Day learns of that possibility, she not only insists that Helen must accompany him, but provides the funds to make it possible.

So on September 16, Cesar and Helen fly off to Europe, accom-

panied by their son-in-law Richard Ybarra and myself. No sooner do we land in London at 8:30 P.M. than Cesar is whisked off to the BBC's TV studios for an interview on that night's news show.

The next day the largest British union, the powerful Transport and General Workers Union, sets up a press conference for Cesar and the TGWU executive board. Jack Jones, head of TGWU, endorses the boycott, saying the TGWU has broken relations with the Teamsters because of its intervention with UFW.

"The problem is to get the Teamsters in line with the rest of the trade unions in the world," Jones tells the press. "We've got to boycott all grapes from California. Let them rot! We will do what we can in our various ways. We want your union to succeed and for justice to be done."

Labor's reaction to Cesar's soft-sell approach is sympathetic in London, Oslo, and Stockholm. The Norwegians already are blockading grapes and lettuce, but they warn they cannot continue it for long unless other countries join in. The Swedes, too, urge a coordinated European boycott.

Then on September 24 at 4:30 P.M., Cesar receives an urgent message in Stockholm from Monsignor Higgins in Rome that he must arrive by 10 A.M. the next day for an audience with the pope. The news galvanizes everyone into action, but a quick check at a nearby travel agency reveals there are no flights from Stockholm which will reach Rome on time.

When Cesar gets the news, he remains calm. "We'll make it," he says quietly, uninfluenced by the gloom of those about him. "Don't worry. I know we'll make it."

Even when the American embassy, which relayed Monsignor Higgins's message, calls to confirm there are no flights, Cesar's faith never wavers. He is positive he'll be in Rome—some fifteen hundred miles away, across the Baltic Sea and the breadth of Europe— by morning.

Another try is made at the travel agency. As the minutes slip rapidly by toward the agency's closing time, the clerk pours over airline schedules. Perhaps there are connecting flights to Rome from Paris, Copenhagen, Geneva, London, Hamburg, or Brussels. But a check of each city brings nothing but bad news.

Then another clerk joins the hunt and finds the link. A British plane leaving Stockholm at 6:55 P.M. lands in London forty-five minutes before a Nigerian plane takes off for Rome. But by now it is 5:30 P.M., and the airport is an hour away through rush-hour traffic. Nor is there any way to confirm seats on the Nigerian airline.

Cesar remains calm as we hunt down a taxi, drive to the hotel to pick up Helen and the suitcases, and then make the long dash to the airport. There, while we get the tickets, Cesar arranges for Victor Pestoff, the UFW volunteer in Stockholm, to call UFW friends in London. If the plane from Stockholm is late, he hopes the Transport Workers may delay the flight to Rome until we arrive.

As it turns out, we make London on time, and members of the Transport Workers expedite the transfer of our luggage and take us directly to the Nigerian jet. It's shortly after 1:00 A.M. when we meet Monsignor Higgins at the Rome airport.

Although Cesar expects to be one of thousands attending a general papal audience, he is stunned to learn a private audience has been scheduled for his party, Bishop Donnelly, and Monsignor Higgins.

At the Vatican later that day, the pope is resplendent in his white habit with a gold crucifix hanging from a gold chain around his neck. He greets Cesar and the others warmly, giving each a strong handshake. While Pope Paul appears relaxed, standing in the large reception room, everyone else is tense, awed in the pontiff's presence. Cesar, wearing a white ceremonial Mexican shirt and dark slacks, genuflexes as he kisses the pope's ring.

After a few informal remarks, Pope Paul is handed a statement which he reads in English, standing on an Oriental rug while everyone stands stiffly in a semicircle around him.

Despite his Italian accent, the pope's words are clear as he praises Cesar for his "sustained effort to apply the principles of Christian social teaching," and for working with the American bishops and its Ad Hoc Committee on Farm Labor. The pope prays "that this laudable spirit of cooperation will continue and that through the all-powerful assistance of the Lord, harmony and understanding will be promoted with liberty and justice for all."

"In the spirit of our own predecessors in this See of Peter," Pope Paul continues, "we renew the full measure of our solicitude for the human and Christian condition of labor and for the genuine good of all those who lend support to this lofty vocation."

After the statement is read, Cesar presents a UFW flag to Pope Paul, unfurling it and posing with the pope while the papal photographers flash pictures.

"What does huelga mean?" the pope asks, pointing to the word on the flag above the black eagle.

"It means strike," Cesar answers, and the pope steps back, a little startled, and chuckles.

The next day, the Vatican's support of La Causa is again made clear dramatically. At a meeting of the Pontifical Commission on Justice and Peace, where Cesar is guest speaker, Archbishop Giovanni Benelli, probably the pope's closest aide, makes an unusual appearance.

As the meeting ends, he rises to read another statement in English praising Cesar. "We are all, indeed, grateful to Mr. Chavez for the lesson which he brings to our attention. It is a very important lesson: to know how to be conscious of the terrible responsibility that is incumbent on us who bear the name 'Christian.' His entire life is an illustration of this principle," the archbishop reads.

"What attracts our attention in a particular way is the commitment that is manifested: the commitment to work for the good of one's brothers and sisters, to be of service to them in the name of Christ, and to render this service with the full measure of all the energy one possesses."

Some two hundred leaders representing the major religious orders for men and women are present. Several comment privately that the archbishops' presence and statement are all but unprecedented.

The next day, about seventy American bishops in Assisi are apprised of the audience and Archbishop Benelli's statement when Cesar joins them as their guest. From their reaction, it is obvious that the American Catholic church's support for the boycott will be intensified.

The rest of the European trip is equally productive. In Geneva Cesar gets pledges of active support from Dr. Philip Potter, head of the World Council of Churches. The WCC will help the union locate shipments of boycotted products in Europe. And in Brussels, Cesar wins a preliminary endorsement to coordinate a European boycott by the staff of the International Confederation of Free Trade Unions.

In Brussels, too, Cesar gets word that the Teamsters are sending representatives to Europe to speak to the labor leaders he has met.

CESAR CHAVEZ RECALLS

One of the highlights of my life was the visit to the Pope. It's such a personal experience that I have difficulty expressing its meaning, except that being a Catholic, having a chance to see the Holy Father in person, to have a special audience, is like a small miracle.

Getting his blessing was especially significant to both Helen and me, and more so because he took the time just before the bishops' synod started and even though he was in ill health. It was a tremendous joy, something that I never thought would happen. And what was really significant was the statement that he made about the farm workers and the Mexican-Americans in the United States.

Even though I just went to Europe, I came back with a better insight about building free unions in Latin America, Africa, and Asia and a better understanding of our responsibility and of the fantastic possibilities to help other people once we build our Union.

Our experience in organizing workers is unique, and can be an example to others. We have the same problems in building a union that people have in Latin America, Asia, and Africa. The growers there are very powerful and can destroy unions that only strike and fight the growers on their own ground. The unions must go outside, all over the world, and get a lot of people to help them defeat the growers. That's a very simple strategy, and it works. We have some knowledge of how things can be done, and we'd like to tell them how we do it so they can be more effective. We'd like to show them how to substitute manpower for money.

For us, setting up the boycott in Europe was a great investment in many ways. It helped us immediately, but it was also an investment for the future. Once we help other people learn how to organize a boycott, then the same people can help others. For the boycott is not just grapes and lettuce, the boycott essentially is people, essentially people's concern for people.

CHAPTER 13

Surprise in Sacramento

September 15, 1974—New York Times Magazine feature article, "Is Chavez Beaten?" by Winthrop Griffith, is one of many that appear in magazines, newspapers, and TV features, all suggesting the end of Cesar Chavez and the UFW.

"No one who sympathizes with him," writes Griffith, "wants to admit that he is defeated. Some of his Anglo supporters still pace the sidewalks in front of city supermarkets, imploring customers to boycott the grapes and lettuce inside, but their posture now indicates to the skeptical outsider that they are engaged in a lonely vigil, not a dynamic national movement."

February 22, 1975—The UFW starts a 110-mile march from San Francisco to Modesto, headquarters of the E & J Gallo winery. Other contingents head out from Fresno and Stockton, thus converging on Modesto from the north, south, and west.

One week later, joined by supporters from throughout the state, they march past the boycotted winery's headquarters and end the march at an enthusiastic rally. Police estimate the crowd at fifteen thousand, far greater than the final day of the original march to Sacramento in 1966.

CESAR CHAVEZ RECALLS

The march to Modesto was Fred Ross, Junior's, idea. He had been working for the Union for about five years, part of the second generation which is now in the Movement. At the time, he was in charge of the Northern California boycott operation. I didn't discourage the march, but I wasn't too enthusiastic about it because I didn't think it would be very successful.

On the last day, I was expecting about two or three thousand people, but when I started getting the reports, I began to think that this would be a good shot at legislation.

Before our convention in 1973, I had told the executive board, "It's time that we go on the offensive on legislation, that we talk about a Bill of Rights for farm workers." We gave the project to the legal department, and Jerry Cohen made a list of all the issues as he saw them. Then he met with the board and with me for many sessions. We went over all the issues. I also met with the field office staffs, the people who had been involved in the strikes, the workers, and we just touched every single base we could. There was tremendous input. So Jerry finally drew up an ideal bill.

By the time of the Modesto march, Jerry Brown was governor, and the political climate had improved. Nothing could have been as bad as Governor Reagan. As soon as Brown was in office, he made a lot of appointments, appointing some of the people who worked with us, and some of the very close friends of the Movement. For example, he appointed LeRoy Chatfield as his director of administration, and Dr. Jerome Lackner as director of the Health Department.

I think that Governor Brown is very different than most politicians. He knows that changes have to be made. He is looking for the areas where they should be made, and for ways of bringing about meaningful changes, not just cosmetic ones.

But there had been rumors that the governor had said that he was going to introduce "fair" farm labor legislation that no one was going to like. So I was concerned. And since we had about twenty thousand people at the Modesto rally, I warned them about the legislation.

Then I pointed in the direction of Sacramento and said that we liked Governor Brown, but we liked the farm workers more, and that maybe we would have to go to Sacramento.

The reports I got back were that the governor didn't like that statement. But at that point he became very interested in legislation and started working almost full time on it. Shortly after the march, we had a meeting with him and his staff for one whole day and laid out what we thought had to be covered. When we left his Los Angeles home, I had a good feeling that he was going to come up with a bill that was going to be acceptable.

Well, I think what happened was that he let his assistants draft a bill, and they butchered it. When it was introduced, it was a devastating bill. We let him know immediately that we were against it, and we began to fight with him, not only in California, but throughout the country. We didn't know if we could get him to change it.

LEROY CHATFIELD RECALLS

During my years with the farm workers, my feelings were that legislation probably wouldn't solve the problem. I had so little trust in politicians. It was very difficult for them to really understand the issues. And once "good legislation" was introduced, it would get so whittled down that when the final product came out for our governor to sign, it would be so weak that you'd have the weakest people, namely the farm workers, up here in Sacramento demonstrating against signing a bill that was supposedly in their best interest.

Also I'd never worked with Governor Brown before. I had to go through a period of really convincing myself where his mind was, where his heart was in respect to the farm worker thing in general.

Now, the closer I worked with him, the more I realized that he genuinely wanted to see if he could put this thing together—and for the right reasons—and do the right thing. He knew he was going to piss off people on all sides.

So once I knew that he was on rock bottom, then I felt that if a bill came to his desk that was harmful to the farm worker movement in general, he would veto it. He's a very principled person, and he felt very strongly about this.

But at first I remembered how Cesar and Marshall Ganz talked about what legislation did to the Civil Rights Movement in the South. It seemed to take the wind out of its sails. So whenever the governor or any of his staff would ask my opinion, I would explain that I was opposed to legislation, and I would speak out in favor of what I called a negotiated settlement, using the power of the governor's office to try to bring people together and to hammer out a settlement that all sides would agree to.

The counterargument, and the governor made it on more than one occasion, was that that was very tenuous. There had been agreements in the past. They hadn't worked out. He always said that the idea of going the way of negotiated settlement was like grasping water.

So then he set his people to work drafting legislation. A lot of people had input into it. I certainly did. I was looked to, in an ad hoc and informal way, to represent the farm workers' viewpoint. It was very agonizingly difficult for me. Sometimes the staff or the governor would ask questions right off the wall—What about this? What about that?

I was just straining into my consciousness, anything that I could remember from the past. How should I answer this? I couldn't just pick up the phone and call someone. Sometimes I was very uncomfortable wondering how that would wash, so to speak, with Jerry Cohen, for example, or Cesar, or Dolores, or Marshall Ganz. Am I being unfair to the farm workers? Am I adequately representing their viewpoint? And I wanted to scream sometimes and say, "But look, they should be here! Why should I have to . . ." But that's human nature.

This issue was so important to the governor that he wanted to be in very close contact with those working on it, sometimes it just seemed like hours and hours on end. I mean he literally mastered this question of farm labor legislation. And he personally made known his views to those who were drafting legislation. I was just really amazed at how quickly and vastly he brought himself in tune with what really goes on out there.

Politically, Governor Brown is extremely astute. Later, when he was talking with growers, when he was talking with Teamsters, when he was talking with farm workers, he could sense soft points, weakness, if you will. He could sense strength. Instinctively he began to feel what was giveable, what was not giveable.

GOVERNOR EDMUND G. BROWN, JR., RECALLS

After all the years of struggle, I felt it was time to have a secret-ballot election law and appropriate machinery for handling unfair labor practices. For that reason, I asked Rose Bird, secretary of agriculture, and her staff to start putting a bill together. They invited input from a number of sides, but they wrote it within the agency.

My understanding of the problem is that in order to assure relatively peaceful solution to the disputes, you have to balance economic power, and you need a framework that is predictable so all sides can understand the rules. I felt that if I could write a bill that was in itself a fair and reasonable charter to solve this prob-

lem, I could then convince all sides with very few additions or subtractions.

After the bill was introduced, I invited in the bishops and the religious groups that had supported Chavez, to get support for the bill. I convened a meeting in Los Angeles with supermarket executives, who then communicated with the growers. I even called a New Jersey supermarket president in Hawaii, where he was at a convention, to ask his support for the bill. Then I sent out thousands of letters, too, not only to union officials, but to sheriffs, school board members, city councilmen, county supervisors to enlist the broadest possible support and make the bill that I had introduced the vehicle for compromise.

You can't bring political pressure to bear unless political pressure is already there. I really think truth has its own inherent power, and when it is combined with the historical moment, with maybe a nudge here and there, things happen.

I saw my role as a catalyst. I wanted that bill, and I brought all the forces together and constantly mixed them and made them interact in a way that made things possibly more propitious for solution. I pushed the bill, and then after it was in, I kept working. I suppose if I hadn't done that, the whole issue might have come up later, and then it might not have been possible to solve.

CESAR CHAVEZ RECALLS

The governor began to ask, "What's wrong with this?" And we began to negotiate. Jerry Cohen talked directly with LeRoy who talked directly with the governor. Jerry has a brilliant mind. He's got a really good way of getting the most complicated legal stuff and either complicating it beyond any hope, if that needs to be done, or just really going to the core and explaining it very simply. And he was at his best because it was negotiating over legal language.

There were some very hectic meetings, all night meetings. On Saturday night, May 3, they negotiated all night and all through Sunday and all through Sunday night. By that time it was down to Jerry and the governor and LeRoy and one or two of the governor's assistants. We compromised as much as we could. Finally we said, "This is the minimum we'll accept, and we won't accept changes."

The compromise would set up a five-man board to run secret-ballot elections. It would permit the largest amount of people to vote, requiring that elections be held at peak season employment, so that the migrants could vote. It also was geared so that elections would be held quickly, so that we wouldn't get caught fighting for an election one day, and then waiting two or three months for it, until everybody was gone. It would permit workers to vote on the pre-existing Teamster contracts and set up voting on the basis of all the workers on a ranch, instead of by crafts. It also dealt with unfair labor practices, guaranteeing that a worker could not be fired because he openly declared himself for one union or another. And it prevented the employer from continuing a relationship with the Teamsters, prevented the employer from telling the worker that if he didn't vote for the Teamsters, he was going to get fired. It also permitted strikers to vote.

We gave up some of our rights to boycott, but we kept the right to the primary boycott, and—if we won an election—the right to ask people not to shop at a store if it was selling a product from a grower where we had won an election. That meant that if we won an election, and the grower wouldn't sign a contract, we would have the right to bring economic pressure to him.

On May 5, I was conducting an intensive campaign in Los Angeles County on the campuses to develop support for our position. I went to about six or seven different universities, and we had a lot of press. The next day, we were previewing the film, "Fighting for Our Lives," for the farm workers in Bakersfield. It's a documentary on the 1973 strike.

About 7:00 P.M., a call came in from Jerry. I was already on my way to the rally, so I sent word, asking if it could wait until 9:30. The word came back, "Yes, but we're pushing it. It's extremely important."

The moment the film was over, I rushed out to the phone. I had to go through a lot of people who were very enthusiastic after seeing the film. Many had been involved in the beatings and the jailings that they had just seen. So I had a hard time getting to the phone.

When I did, Jerry told me, "The governor is getting together all of agribusiness here in Sacramento, right now, in his office. They've agreed to the proposal. But they have some preconditions."

I said, "Did we do anything wrong, Jerry?"

So I talked to the governor, and he said, "Look, it's going to be at least a half hour to forty-five minutes, because we don't have everybody here yet. We need a little time."

I said, "Okay, we'll call you." We went over to my daughter's house in Bakersfield. A half hour later I called, and they said, "Well, it's going to be at least an hour, forty-five minutes."

So we drove to La Paz. There I called the governor immediately, and he said, "Well, we're still not quite ready. We're putting some loud-speakers on the telephone."

I found out the growers would agree to accept the compromise provided we did two things—that we agreed that nothing should be changed, not even a period, and that they hear from me personally that we were supporting it.

So I told the governor, "Well, Jerry's there. He's our representative. He's authorized."

"They want to hear you personally."

I thought that it was very ironic that we should have the same precondition, that there be no changes. It showed how much trust we had in each other.

So when they got the phone hooked up to the loud-speaker in the governor's office, Governor Brown got the growers, one after another, to identify themselves and state publicly they were for the bill.

Jerry tells me the growers were all sitting at a table. When the governor asked me if I would support the bill, they all moved out to the edges of their seats, looking at the loud-speaker. And when I answered, "Very, very definitely," they broke into smiles and applause.

ALLAN GRANT, CALIFORNIA FARM BUREAU
PRESIDENT, RECALLS

We were trying for twelve years to get farm labor legislation. I started working on this before Governor Ronald Reagan was elected. Therefore, we were very pleased that Governor Brown saw fit to work so hard on it. He could do some things that the former governor couldn't do, because he is a Democrat, and he had a Democratic legislature.

All the farm organizations supported the governor's bill, with the exception of one or two. The boycott was only a minor reason. It did affect us. It put a lot of small grape growers out of business, and it had some effect in lettuce. But more important was the violence that took place, the property destruction, and the very strong antipathy felt between the two unions.

The growers had gotten along with unions for several years, and they're just the same as any other employer. They could adjust to whatever situation comes along, and costs would have to be passed on to the consumer.

GOVERNOR EDMUND G. BROWN, JR., RECALLS

When the amended bill was heard in committee, there was opposition from the Teamsters, the Building Trades, and the Packinghouse Workers. So it was just a matter of resolving all three in such a way as to keep the growers and Chavez also supporting the bill.

On the day of the next Senate committee hearing, May 19, Jack Henning, head of the state AFL-CIO, called. I invited him in, and he brought in Jimmy Lee of the Building Trades. I saw his amendment. I'd already had Rose Bird draft up some alternate ones.

By this time it was about 1:00 P.M., and we were still trying to get the votes. Three of the Senators wouldn't commit themselves one way or the other; so it was unclear how the vote was going to go unless we could get the support of the Building Trades and the Teamsters. The bill was scheduled to be heard at 1:30 P.M.

We invited the teamsters down, then the growers, then everyone involved. I had Henning and Lee in my office with Rose and my staff. Jerry Cohen was down at the other end of the room. The Teamsters were in another office, the Farm Bureau, and the Agricultural Council in a second office, and the Western Growers in a third. Then negotiations kept going, and we postponed the committee.

We solved the Teamster problem and the Packinghouse Workers problem, but I think it was about 6:30 P.M. before we finally got the language for an amendment satisfactory to both the Building Trades and Cesar Chavez.

We had just gotten notice that the Senate hearing was about to adjourn and postpone the hearing for another week. So Rose Bird, under very trying circumstances, wrote some language that was taken from 8(e) of the National Labor Relations Act. That did it. The bill was endorsed by all parties and passed the committee unanimously that night.

We got what appears to be the solution. I think the bill is a reasonable bill. I think the economic tools that the unions have reasonable in light of American labor history and in light of the principles which we have in this country. In my judgment, this bill sets a model for the whole country as to the manner of resolving farm labor disputes through law.

FROM JACQUES LEVY'S NOTEBOOK

After the committee approves the bill, the governor calls a special session of the legislature to consider it. The move is a technicality which permits the bill to become law within ninety days, after passage. The first elections then can be held in the fall instead of waiting until the 1976 harvests.

While passage of a California Bill of Rights for farm workers would be considered a major landmark, this history of La Causa cannot be ended. It has only begun. Ahead are more human drama, more sacrifice, more victories, and more defeats.

The union's progress will be slow, as each segment of agribusiness attempts to delay the day when its workers are represented by the union of their choice. Legislation setting up secret-ballot elections may ease the question of representation, but an election won doesn't guarantee a contract.

In the future, Cesar Chavez and his followers will repeat the tactics they have used in the past, turning to the public for support to equalize the economic power of those who provide jobs and those who need them.

And the union's opponents will fight back, attempting to discredit La Causa and its leaders; attempting to amend legislation to make it ineffective in providing the majority of agricultural workers the same rights enjoyed by other working people; and attempting to block unionization with the use of local courts and police.

To help counter some of this political power, the union already has plans to organize the poor and the elderly in both rural and urban areas, thus broadening its base and its political effectiveness.

At this juncture, the success of La Causa cannot be measured in terms of numbers of contracts, wage increases, and improved working conditions. Significant advances have been made, but the ground to cover is still great.

Of far greater importance has been La Causa's achievements in showing the way to meaningful social change by using militant nonviolent tactics and by organizing people of various backgrounds, political persuasions, and faiths. In an era of great cynicism, La Causa is showing that individuals can make a difference, can help themselves and others, and can keep their principles, although the task is hard and is never-ending.

CHAPTER 14

Saying Yes to
Man's Dignity

Once we have reached our goal and have farm workers protected by contracts, we must continue to keep our members involved. The only way is to continue struggling. It's just like plateaus. We get a Union, then we want to struggle for something else. The moment we sit down and rest on our laurels, we're in trouble.

Once we get contracts and good wages, we know the tendency will be for the majority to lose interest, unless the Union is threatened or a contract is being renegotiated. The tendency will be for just a few to remain active and involved, while everybody else just holds out until something very big happens. That's true of other unions that we've seen; that's true of other institutions; that's true of our country.

To avoid that, to keep people's attention and continuing interest, we've got to expand and get them involved in other things. The Union must touch them daily.

Our best education, the most lasting, has been out on the picket line. But when the initial membership gets old and dies off, the new people coming in won't have had the same experience of building a Union. So we must get them involved in other necessary struggles.

Poor people are going to be poor for a long time to come, even though we have contracts, and economic action is an exciting thing for them. If they see an alternative, they will follow it. And we've probably got now the best organization of any poor people in all the country. That's why we can go any place in California where there are farm workers and get a whole group of people together and in action. We are hitting at the real core problems.

After we've got contracts, we have to build more clinics and co-ops, and we've got to resolve the whole question of mechanization. That can become a great issue, not fighting the machines, but working out a program ahead of time so the workers benefit.

Then there's the whole question of political action, so much political work to be done taking care of all the grievances that people have, such as the discrimination their kids face in school, and the whole problem of the police. I don't see why we can't exchange those cops who treat us the way they do for good, decent human beings like farm workers. Or why there couldn't be any farm worker judges.

We have to participate in the governing of towns and school boards. We have to make our influence felt everywhere and anywhere. It's a long struggle that we're just beginning, but it can be done because the people want it.

To get it done, there's a lot of construction work needed with our members. Many are not citizens, and others are not registered to vote. We must work toward the day when the majority of them are citizens with a vote.

But political power alone is not enough. Although I've been at it for some twenty years, all the time and the money and effort haven't brought about any significant change whatsoever. Effective political power is never going to come, particularly to minority groups, unless they have economic power. And however poor they are, even the poor people can organize economic power.

Political power by itself, as we've tried to fathom it and to fashion it, is like having a car that doesn't have any motor in it. It's like striking a match that goes out. Economic power is like having a generator to keep that bulb burning all the time. So we have to develop economic power to assure a continuation of political power.

I'm not advocating black capitalism or brown capitalism. At the worst it gets a black to exploit other blacks, or a brown to exploit others. At the best, it only helps the lives of a few. What I'm suggesting is a cooperative movement.

Power can come from credit in a capitalistic society, and credit in a society like ours means people. As soon as you're born, you're worth so much—not in money, but in the privilege to get in debt.

And I think that's a powerful weapon. If you have a lot of people, then you have a lot of credit. The idea is to organize that power and transfer it into something real.

I don't have the answers yet. I'm at the point where I was in 1955 about organizing a farm workers' union. Then I was just talking about ideas and what could be done. A lot of people thought I was crazy. But this is how I learn, by talking and expounding and getting arguments back. That's why we're starting a three-year program to study all of these things. I still know very little about economic theory, but I'm going to learn because the whole fight, if you're poor, and if you're a minority group, is economic power.

As a continuation of our struggle, I think that we can develop economic power and put it into the hands of the people so they can have more control of their own lives, and then begin to change the system. We want radical change. Nothing short of radical change is going to have any impact on our lives or our problems. We want sufficient power to control our own destinies. This is our struggle. It's a lifetime job. The work for social change and against social injustice is never ended.

I know we're not going to see the change, but if we can get an idea and put legs under it, that's all we want. Let it go. Let it start, like the Union.

I guess I have an ideology, but it probably cannot be described in terms of any political or economic system.

Once I was giving a talk in Monterey about the Christian doctrine. When I got through, one man came back and said, "It's very radical, very socialistic."

I didn't say anything, but I was convinced it was very Christian. That's my interpretation. I didn't think it was so much political or economic.

Actually, I can't see where the poor have fared that well under any political or economic system. But I think some power has to come to them so they can manage their lives. I don't care what system it is, it's not going to work if they don't have the power.

That's why if we make democracy work, I'm convinced that's by far the best system. And it will work if people want it to. But to make it work for the poor, we have to work at it full time. And we have to be willing to just give up everything and risk it all.

In the last twenty years, the farm workers' outlook has radically changed, just like day and night. Twenty years ago, to get one person to talk to me about the Union was an effort. They were afraid. Now, we've overcome that.

And the idea of serving without pay—they had never heard about that. Right now we need a good education program, a meaningful education, not just about the Union, but about the whole idea of the Cause, the whole idea of sacrificing for other people.

Fighting for social justice, it seems to me, is one of the profoundest ways in which man can say yes to man's dignity, and that really means sacrifice. There is no way on this earth in which you can say yes to man's dignity and know that you're going to be spared some sacrifice.

Index